Edwin Norris

ASSYRIAN DICTIONARY

Intended to further the study of the cuneiform inscriptions of Assyria and Babylonia

Edwin Norris

ASSYRIAN DICTIONARY

Intended to further the study of the cuneiform inscriptions of Assyria and Babylonia

ISBN/EAN: 9783741173288

Manufactured in Europe, USA, Canada, Australia, Japa

Cover: Foto ©ninafisch / pixelio.de

Manufactured and distributed by brebook publishing software
(www.brebook.com)

Edwin Norris

ASSYRIAN DICTIONARY

ASSYRIAN DICTIONARY;

INTENDED TO FURTHER THE

STUDY OF THE CUNEIFORM INSCRIPTIONS OF ASSYRIA AND BABYLONIA.

BY EDWIN NORRIS, HON. PH.D. BONN,

HONORARY SECRETARY OF THE ROYAL ASIATIC SOCIETY OF GREAT BRITAIN AND IRELAND, &c., &c., &c.

PART II.

Verborum quorundam veritas non nisi ex plurium conjecturis inter se comparatis elici solet

C. MICHAELIS.

WILLIAMS AND NORGATE,
14, HENRIETTA STREET, COVENT GARDEN, LONDON,
AND 20, SOUTH FREDERICK STREET, EDINBURGH.

MDCCCLXX.

A Second Part of my task is done, and I have little to add to what was said on the appearance of the first. I have the same excuses to make for errors and incompleteness, and I find myself not much improved in the knowledge of the language, except, perhaps, in some conjunctional particles and in the structure of the sentences generally. The accumulation of subjects of comparison has made me still more conscious of occasional vacillation, and of having often rendered the same passages differently in different places. Now and then I have rejected a version in favour of another reading, which new evidence has subsequently led me to abandon. All this, however, I anticipated before I began to print, and I can safely say that knowingly I have never essentially altered my view of a passage once printed without acknowledging it on the first opportunity; though, of course, in such a long continued work a good deal must escape the most retentive memory. I may expect at best, and am ready to receive, an application of Martial's well-known line "sunt bona, sunt quaedam mediocria, sunt mala plura," but I hope the *mala* may not prove to be predominant. For the many words in regard to which I have confessed total ignorance, or what may be worse, have made a bold guess without authority, I have little excuse to offer; I will only submit that most of these words are more numerous in the dictionary than in the language, being usually such as occur only once; even in Hebrew, which has been studied so long and so earnestly, agreement among translators in such cases is extremely rare; Castell notices one such case with the observation "sic Interpretes nostri omnes; quod in ἅπαξ λεγομένοις rarissimum." (See Col. 1831.)

Some friends have suggested that I have often quoted a larger number of examples in illustration of a word than was necessary to prove its value; but I have not thought these numerous quotations superfluous. In the scarcity of books they will afford exercise to learners, they generally exhibit varying syntax and orthography, and they sometimes contain difficulties which I could not fully explain. My aim has been to furnish enquirers with means of judging for themselves rather than to pronounce sentence myself ex cathedra, and to supply materials for a future Dictionary worthy of the name. I have preferred a mistake on the side of exuberance to the fault of meagreness, and had it not been for the fear of making too large a book I should frequently have added to my quotations and made them a good deal longer.

I have continued to use the names of gods and kings as they were read when I began my compilation: I write, therefore, Pul and Sardanapalus, and Shamas-Phul and Nuha, and Yav and others; and even Divanubar, though for this last name I have often dropped into Shalmaneser. Translators still differ considerably in all this doubtful nomenclature; in some cases half a dozen names have been successively brought forward and rejected; and lastly, it would have taken much time and trouble to make the proper changes, and would have been very liable to error, particularly in making references to the Inscriptions, where errors are especially annoying. In defence of the continued employment of these proper names I add here a quotation from a letter of Sir Henry Rawlinson, printed in the Athenæum of May 18, 1867, page 661: "I may here repeat the warning that I "have often before given to those interested in Assyrian research, "that the reading of proper names, which are rarely or never pho-"netically expressed, is the most difficult branch of the entire subject, "and must always be received with caution, unless verified by a cor-"responding orthography in Hebrew, Greek, or Persian authorities."

E. N.

BRIGHTON, *November*, 18[illegible].

Addition to the Notes headed "Transliteration" in the Introduction to the First Part of the Dictionary.

Many of the characters pronounced with final m, as *tam*, *lam*, *lim*, *nam*, are arranged alphabetically as if the m were not present, and transliterated *ta*, *la*, *li*, and *na*; but where the m is radical it is considered a letter, as in *ṣalam*, an "image." Most of these letters might be used as u-syllables, especially when finals in the syllabaries; as *tamtu*, "the sea," 5 II. 48; *gabla*, "battle," Syl. 87; *irṣitu*, "earth," Syl. 182.

The small letters occasionally accompanying the capitals which guide the eye in looking for words in the Dictionary, imply inherent unwritten vowels; thus BaL, BiL, BuL, BLa, all representing words which would regularly be headed BL only, as *bal*, *bil*, *bul*, *bilu*, serve to subdivide the number of such words, and lead at once to the page containing the one wanted; *ka*, would be headed Ka, *kua*, KA. In a very few cases a cuneiform character is added at the top of the page, when such character commences a large number of groups; for example, BT represents groups which have for their initial; they precede all other words beginning with BT.

I did not know the distinction between and until I was preparing for press page 428, where I have inserted a note to this effect. In all preceding pages I had written .

Additional Abbreviations used in referring to Inscriptions.

Cyp. .. ... Inscription of Sargon, found at Citium, in Cyprus, now in the Berlin Museum. Unpublished.

2 Esar. .. .. Broken Cylinder of Esar Haddon, in the British Museum, I. I. 54-38.

Hamm. .. Inscription of Hammurabi, published with a translation by M. Joachim Ménant, Paris, 1863.

New Syl. .. Fragments of Syllabaries found since the publication of Part I. Unpublished.

Synchr. .. Synchronous History, printed in R. I., Vol. 2, Sh. 65.

Corrections of the Table of Characters.

The Table of Characters at the head of the Dictionary was prepared in haste; it was confessedly incomplete, and the necessity of corrections was anticipated. The following long list of alterations and additions, divided and numbered in accordance with the plan in the First Part, will doubtless be an improvement, but I cannot flatter myself that it will not require further amendment. It is the besetting defect of all syllabaries that they are continually receiving additions; the very moderate Japanese syllabary, the universally employed Hirakana, which nominally should consist of

50 characters, has grown to something between eight and nine hundred; and types had to be cut to that amount by the Austrian Government, some twenty-four years ago, when it was desirous of printing Japanese books; all these characters were inserted in the great Sprachenhalle, published at Vienna in 1847. But the Assyrian additions were made on a much more reasonable scale. Sargon, in several of his inscriptions, mixed up irregularly a few of the so-called hieratic forms with the ordinary characters, and these are inserted here [marked Sarg.] with the others; a student acquainted with the usual forms only could hardly get on without knowing them. I do not think Sargon's example was followed by succeeding monarchs. In addition to the former subdivisions, the verbal monograms employed in the work will be inserted at the end of the table. In all cases I have endeavoured to supply some evidence of the value attributed to the characters.

ORDINARY ALPHABET.

17 [cuneiform], *add gab to the values.* See [cuneiform] [cuneiform] [cuneiform] [cuneiform], var. [cuneiform] [cuneiform] [cuneiform], Sard. ii. 43, p. 316.

30 [cuneiform], *add* Sarg. [cuneiform].

41 [cuneiform], *add* Sarg. [cuneiform].

44 [cuneiform], *add* tas. See Sard. ii. 101, 102, p. 511.

53 [cuneiform]. I think this Babylonian form is real *nis*, not *ul*.

54 [cuneiform], *add* Sarg. [cuneiform].

57 [cuneiform], *add* Sarg. [cuneiform] and [cuneiform].

70 [cuneiform] equated to [cuneiform]. New Syl.

75 [cuneiform], *add mir.* See Syl. 270, p. 576.

I think [cuneiform] is merely another form of [cuneiform]

82 [cuneiform], *add* Sarg. [cuneiform].

83 [cuneiform], *add* Sarg. [cuneiform] and [cuneiform].

92 [cuneiform], *add* Sarg. [cuneiform].

94 [cuneiform], *add* [cuneiform].

98 [cuneiform], as, dil, ru.

Ina, Assur, Adan, are values of [cuneiform] as an ideogram. See [cuneiform] [cuneiform] [cuneiform], Esar Haddon [Assur-ah-iddina], B. I., Sh. 48, Nos. 4, 5, 6.

103 [cuneiform], *lik, lu.* [cuneiform] is "animal," No. 48 in Ideograms; see note in p. 486.

COMPOUND SYLLABLES.

3 [illegible], *add* before han, ail. See Syl. 301.

6a [illegible] sih. See p. 365, and Syl. 306.

11 [illegible], *add* rab. Var. Sard. i. 21, confounded with [illegible], No. 13 in Ideograms.

15 [illegible], [illegible], [illegible]. Bab. [illegible].

16 [illegible], *add* Sarg. [illegible].

24 [illegible], *add* kal.

30 [illegible]. I have sometimes arranged this under DB.

31 [illegible], lib(?). See Assurb.p. iv. 57. [illegible] var. [illegible], libit.

The following received from Mr. G. Smith: [illegible] v. [illegible] on a slab, and [illegible] is usually translated by the Assyrian verb [illegible], libut, on a bilingual tablet.

38 [illegible], sig.

[illegible] and [illegible] of No. 60 are probably identical. I believe that these, as well as the variant forms [illegible], [illegible], [illegible], and even [illegible] and [illegible], are occasionally confounded; but generally forms with [illegible] are pronounced sig, and those with [illegible] [illegible]. See pp. 162, 316, 376.

41a [illegible], mas. See p. 374.

45 [illegible], [illegible], [illegible]. dir.

46a [illegible], [illegible]. See Syl. 262, p. 303.

50 *For* [illegible] *read* [illegible].

55, 56 [illegible] is not unfrequently put for [illegible]; never, I think, the reverse.

57 [illegible], rather "man" than "ma." See var. Tig. i. 45.

57a [illegible], [illegible]. See Syl. 234 and 43 II. 29 b. See also p. 810.

60 [illegible]. See No. 38 above.

61 [illegible], *add* Sarg. [illegible]. See Botta 145, 11 = 83.

61a [illegible], [illegible]. dar. Syl. 375.

65 [illegible], *add* da. See Sard. i. 85, p. 363; and [illegible]. Kaldai, in Sen. T. iii. 45 (33 is an error); v. 8, 41, p. 349. Cf. [illegible], Bil-kudari, in Canon No. 1, col. iv. l. 33, with [illegible], in Canon No. 2, col. v. l. 18.

70 *For* [illegible] *read* [illegible]

80 [illegible], *add* Sarg. [illegible].

80a [illegible] or [illegible], ma.

83 [illegible], [illegible]. See p. 162.

88 [illegible], *add* sir. See Syl. 387 and 38 [l. 51 c. Var. [illegible], Assur b.p. vi. 106.

[illegible] *sub*, [illegible] *lul* and [illegible], a form of *tar*, are sometimes confounded.

88a [illegible] lul. See Tig. iii. 48.

89 [illegible] *used for sin as well as sun*; see p. 889.

89a [illegible], [illegible], [illegible], sub, tir. Forms of No. 103.

93 [illegible], *add* [illegible], [illegible].

94a [illegible] min. See Syl. 138 and p. 504.

95a [illegible] gub. See Syl. 798, &c., and pp. 108, 314, and xiii.

101 [illegible], *for* sir *read* su. See note at foot of p. 302.

103 [illegible], *add* [illegible], [illegible], Bab. [illegible], sub, tir. See 89a.

105a [illegible] [illegible] din. See [illegible] No. 132.

I was not aware until very recently of the entire equivalence of the Babylonian and Persian [illegible] and [illegible] with the Assyrian [illegible], which reads phonetically din, and as an ideograph signifies "life." (See Syl. 152 and p. 87, l. 4, 9 from bottom.) The sound din or tin is proved by the word [illegible] [illegible], *tin*, "one," which occurs repeated in No. 15, D. 4, 5, and No. 13, E. 4, and also by [illegible] [illegible] [illegible], *iddina*, "he gave," or "he created," in every Achaemenian Inscription. So lately as p. 869, l. 6 from bottom, I printed [illegible], "land," instead of [illegible], "life," in a passage from a document of Nabonidus; while a line from another cylinder of the same king, containing the same words, having "life" written phonetically *balatu*, was printed just four lines higher. I cannot account for my blindness. One of the forms of the name of Babylon, [illegible] [illegible] [illegible], is written on the Behistun rock with the first character [illegible] and [illegible] indiscriminately, though printed throughout [illegible]. See Beh. lines 5, 31, 33, 85, &c.*

---

* The six concluding lines of the note on Babylon, printed in p. 78, are full of blunders, owing to my ignorance of the value of [illegible]; I would cancel them, and write the following instead:—

"At a later period Babylon was denoted by the symbols [illegible] [illegible] [illegible] or [illegible] [illegible] [illegible], as seen on the paper cast of the Behistun rock inscription, taken by Sir H. Rawlinson, though all printed [illegible]. See lines 5, 31, 33, 85, &c. It would seem, however, that [illegible] or [illegible] was not an essential part of the name, for we have it made by [illegible] [illegible] in lines 87 and 89; and [illegible] [illegible] [illegible] [illegible] [illegible], read probably *Babili*, denotes "a Babylonian man" in l. 91; the city or the country is made by the same group without [illegible] [illegible] in E.I.H. iv. 70; viii. 44, &c. Once only (15 RM 67) I find the name in the form [illegible] [illegible] [illegible] [illegible], with [illegible] instead of [illegible]; and singularly enough it is written in the same line with both these characters, [illegible] [illegible] [illegible] [illegible] [illegible].

106a sirari, narara, or nsir.

This character has been pronounced variously, but some recently found variants of the Canon, which I have not seen, show that one reading was nisir; it occurs only in some proper names. King , or , whose name I write Pul and Dr. Oppert Hamlikhaas [Nalcabus], has been recently called Bel-Asir by Sir Henry Rawlinson; see Athenæum, May 16, 1857, p. 661.

111 , *add* kis.

111a ras, kas. See 6 II. 30, 31*b*.

116 , , . See Sen. B. iv. 38, and 42 BM 16.

124 , , , dun, sul.

These forms should be carefully distinguished from those in 89*a* and 168, but they are, nevertheless, sometimes confounded.

125a var. ZB.

130 , , *add* zir. See var. in Sard. ii. 18.

131a , , mars. See 17 II. 45, 50*a*.

129 *For* *read* .

137 , , mub. See p. 485.

137a , , tam. Syl. 258, in p. 71.

137b kir. See Sard. ii. 105.

IDEOGRAMS.

4a , *sharp*. See sikip, p. 341.

5 , , , *city*.

5a , , *ranks (of army)*, Syl. 398; see p. 188.

8a , *greatness, exploits*(?).

He heard the renown of my exploits.—Assur b.p. iv. 76.

11 , , , *month*.

18 , add *6th month*. See p. 50.

12a , *a half*; suer, or sever. See p. 116. See also Hebrew .

14a , *dream, vision*.

14b full; *cattle*. See pp. 221, 368.

On the Great Altar, 61 BM 22, we have , the last letter having a var. , meant for . The phonetically written , bul, is printed in page 91, and a variant, , bul, should have been printed with the passage communicated by Sir H. Rawlinson, in p. 221; , bili, Monol. 62, occurs in p. 380.

15a , , , *left hand.* See pp. 509–10, 516.

32a , *a cubit.* See p. 580.

Appears to be a title in , a *Shari*, the ruler(?) of Egypt, Sarg. 18.

34a turnula; *number.* See Syl. 371 and Sard. i. 88; p. 217.

39 paleg; *select.* See p. 312, and Additions, p. xii.

41 , add *health of body*(?). See Neb. Yus. 93; Esar vi. 42.

42a , *seen.* See p. 656.

We find not unfrequently used in this sense; see Darius 13; but we may say generally that when two forms are used with like value, the more complete form is correct, the shorter being merely used as an abbreviation. See and , *hi*; and , *dup*; and , *bit*, &c.

48 , , *beast of burden.*

See my note to p. 475, which is incorrect as regards the Median sense, where we have, not as in Babylonian and Persian, but , *gamlu*; the sir is expressed in a complex hieratic character.

50 *For* *read* .

51 *or* . I think is incorrect. See p. 376, and the note to No. 88 of Compound Syllables.

55 , . See p. 349.

May also denote "tabernacles of the gods;" see p. 367.

56 . See p. 685.

56a , probably *wool.* See pp. 129 and 552.

62 *For* *read* .

64a gusur; *large timber for houses.* See p. 200.

64b remu; *pardon*

Occurs as a variant reading of on an unpublished fragment of Assurbanipal.

64c , *a month.* See No. 11.

65 , *shade.* See p. 548. Var. in St. 13.

69 [not], *image, statue.*

I have no doubt the above is correct; a bit of syllabary recently found gives the value , Hebrew [illegible]. I believe this value has been for some time adopted, though I was myself ignorant of it.

69a , *right* [*dexter*]. See p. 509–10.

74 , add *wall.* See p. 232.

76 , add *a weight.* Cyp. ii. 6. Dr. Hincks in Journ. R.A.S., Vol. 16, p. 218.

76a bilat; *lady.* See p. 56.

78 bala; *ear.* See p. 274.

78a , *determinative of carnivorous animals.* See , p. 511.

83a , *a weapon.* See p. 630.

91a , *remote, far.* Sen. Gr. 48. 28 BM 13.

91b , , , *life.* See the note on No. 105 in Compound Syllables.

93a , *a weight,* about 130 grains. See p. 212.

97 , add *multitude.* See p. 393.

101a bam.
[illegible] in p. 423, and read for in l. 10.

102a , , eli; *upon.* See p. 485.

105a , , *the 7th month,* see p. 50; *a mound, heap;* Tig. ii. 78; v. 4, 98, 100.
Frequently forms part of the name of a city or province; see ,
Tel-Assuri, Sanr ii. 23.

105b damiq, damaq, &c.; *fortunate, propitious;* 35 II. 71 d. See p. 241.

105c , *the same, ditto.* See 3 II. 40–70 b.
In rare cases put instead of "and." See Menol. iii, 41; p. 281.

105d , *life.* See No. 91 b.

114 , *beast of burden.* See No. 48.

115 , , , *Babylon.* See note to No. 105a in Compound Syllables.

SOME VERBAL MONOGRAMS

1 naqa; *to sacrifice.* Cf. Menol. 106, and Sanl. iii. 133.
See pp. 89, 694.
,, palkat; *to pass by, neglect.* See pp. 90, 93.

2 nakas; *to cut off.* v. , *I cut off.* Sard. ii. 71.

3 gab; *to say.* Cf. 17 BM 8, and .
iqabbu-su, *they call it.* Tig. jun. 10.

4 erib; *to pass.* v. , *I passed.* Sard. ii. 41.

5 halak; *to go.* alako; p. 207. ittikusi. Sard. i. 100; p. 248.

6 tar; *to restore, return; cause to be.* v. *I reduced.* Sard. ii. 60. v. *I returned.* Sard. ii. 75.

7 bana, epis; *to build.* abni; *I built.* Sard. ii. 132; p. 108. var. epus; *I made.* Tig. vi. 86; p. 109.

8 qara; *to call upon.* v. *I invoked.* 42 BM 40 = Sen. B. iv. 41.

9 satar; *to write.* v. *I wrote.* Sard. i. 99; p. 703.

10 nadan; *to give.* See 12 II. 26–28a; 1 Mich. i. 17; p. 323.

11 dabak; *to leave.* v. *I left behind.* Sard. ii. 62.

12 rabu; *to increase.* Sen. T. B. 26, ... ; in the name of Sennacherib.

13 sabat; *to take.* v. *I took them.* 2 Beltis 5.

14 sabat; *to seize, take.* v. *they took.* Sard. i. 67. v. *I seized.* Sard. ii. 106.

" etiq; *to pass.* v. *I passed.* Sard. i. 66.

15 sakan; *to settle, &c.* v. *I placed.* Sard. ii. 7.

16 la; *to have.* Cf. Sard. i. 13, and ... lu lab, *they had not*; ii. 127; p. 217.

17 kasad; *to approach, capture.* v. aktasad, Sard. ii. 39; aksud, *I captured,* Obel. 26.

18 *to favour, protect.* See p. 274.

19 usa, ela; *to go out or up.* See pp. 292, 323.

20 kabad; *to honour.* v. *I am honoured.* Sard. i. 32; p. 580.

21 sarap; *to burn.* v. *I burned.* Sard. ii. 43.

22 rabaç; *to lie down.* v. *they shall lie down.* See p. 221.

ZMB [cuneiform]. Zamba.—Sard. iii. 109.

A province in the high lands north of Assyria, near the Tigris.

¶ [cuneiform]. Ismi-Bel.—Sen. T. iii. 23.

A king of Gaza, to whom Sennacherib gave several towns which he had taken from Hezekiah, king of Judah.

ZMD [cuneiform]. zamid; *Yoked.* Heb. צמד.

[cuneiform] . . . . [cuneiform]. kurra rakub zamid-su asâti . . . . . adabala; *his horse and yoked chariot strong . . . . . I made ready.*—Assur b.p. i. 33.

¶ [cuneiform]. masada sa rakabi; *pole of a chariot.*—27 II. 24 a.

ZMH [cuneiform]. is-mahri.—Sard. iii. 91.

Name of a tree brought from Mount Amanus; it was cut in a province called [cuneiform], probably from the name of the tree, and carried to Nineveh.

¶ [cuneiform]. is-mahhi.—40 BM 38 = Sen. B. iv. 10.

Name of trees cut in Mount Taurus. The meaning would be "large trees;" but from its position in the sentence it appears to be a specific name.

ZMK [cuneiform]. asmaku.—Sard. iii. 90.

I do not know if this be a word, or a part only. It occurs in a passage where Sardanapalus mentions trees cut in Mount Amanus for several temples; we find [cuneiform]. I had read this ana *bit-yasmaku, bit-hidati*, understanding two separate houses; but I find Dr. Oppert translates "ma maison asmaku *bit-hidati*," probably reading ana *bit-ya asmaku bit-hidati*. As the preposition ana is put before all the other temples, and *bit-hidati* would signify "pleasure-house," he is probably right. I should be inclined to say "my pleasure-house called Bit-asmaku," though I fear the interpolation of ya in this case would be exceptional.

ZMM [cuneiform]. sumami.—E.I.H. ix. 23.

See p. 296, under [illegible], for a version of [illegible]. I am now rather inclined to compare two or three Hebrew roots, implying "dangerous," "bad," or "thirsty," ([illegible]), and to translate the whole passage "difficult roads, marked (or arid) paths I widened," or possibly "I approached."

27.2.66 2 Z

ZMN zamâni; *Evil schemes.* Heb. זמם.

musapriqu zamâni; *subverter of evil designs.*—Sen. Gr. 4. Sen. T. i. 9.

¶ Zamani, g. *Zamana.*

Name of the father of *Ammebaal* of *Nairi*, in Sard. i. 12, and of the father of *Bura*, chief of *Izmdamnaua*, in Sard. iii. 105. In Obel. 148 we have a Bit-Zamâni, which appears to be in Armenia.

¶ —39 II. 10a.

ZMS umpikanna.—Black St. iv. 13. Porter's transcript of E.I.H. iii. 41.

umpikkanna.—E.I.H. ii. 31, &c. Birs i. 21. Neb. Bab. i. 25.

mispikhanna.—Botta 62, 74, &c. Sen. Bis. iv. 3. 39 BM 21. 42 BM 46, 47. See 46 II. 6b, 48c.

umpikkani, *g.*—Sen. T. i. 54. Sen. Gr. 16, 57. Tig. jun. 24. Botta 152, 11 = 158; 152, 17 – 161.

This often-mentioned tree, which Dr. Oppert renders *lentiscus*, is variously spelled, but the pronunciation in all the forms is nearly the same. It can hardly be accidental that wherever the word occurs in the genitive case, then, and then only, the second character is made . I think of the Gold. Tab. 13 and of Neb. Gr. ii. 22 must be errors of the writers or copyists. I have registered , musuppuna, but have lost the reference.

ZMR zamri; *Fruits.* Heb. זִמְרָה.

Gula bilat rabit hirat shamsi irtu pinanu lumu ina zamri-su liskun; *Gula, the great lady, wife of the Southern Sun, noxious vapour upon his fruits may she bring.*—1 Mich. iv. 6.

We have nearly the same words in 2 Mich. iv. 15, as far as I can read the peculiar hieratic forms; I am not quite sure of lumu and zamri, but the rest is clear; the of 1 Mich. is written in full letters in 2 Mich. Zamri occurs at l. 54, 55, and ii. 60 of Bab. II, 162 (?), partially translated by Mr. Talbot, and is rendered by him "the earth." See also 18 II. 43a (?).

ZMR [cuneiform], Zamra, s. Zamri, g.

Name of a city in Zamua [Sard. ii. 61] destroyed by Sardanapalus (l. 62). The Simara of Pliny, lib. 5, c. 25, and of Spruner's Atlas, Armenia Minor.

¶ [cuneiform]; see [cuneiform] in p. 332.

¶ [cuneiform], iznir; *A crown.* Accadian.

The value is shown in the extract [cuneiform] in the bilingual lists 25 II. 234 and 44 II. 31 r; and without the determinative in Slab K. 162, where we have the following lines:—

[cuneiform], mir rabû sa qaqqadu, l. 16, 17.

And in the corresponding line, II. 45:—

[cuneiform], agû rabû . . . .

¶ [cuneiform], isvaro; *Prized.* Heb. יקר.

[cuneiform], 1000 sâ is-kababi al isvaro ina libbi-sunu aqpur ana umâgila panu-sun; *one thousand shield-bearers not prized [volunteers] among them I sent away and entrusted to him.*—Botta 151, 9 (17) - 117.

Dr. Oppert reads "lanceurs," influenced by the uncertain is-susvra of II.R. 22. but see p. 332; moreover he ignores the negative.

¶ [cuneiform], is-marbudal; *Carpets.*—Sard. i. 86. Heb. מַרְבַד.

Carried off from from Ahiabab of Sur (Tyre?) with a large quantity of other plunder.

¶ [cuneiform], is-dapranl (Opp.); *Cypress.* Syriac [Syriac] p.

This tree is so written in Botta 152, 15 - 150; Sen. B. iv. 24 - 41 BM 35; with [cuneiform] instead of [cuneiform]. I have no doubt that Dr. Oppert is right in his reading. The more regular orthography is [cuneiform], St. 18. 21.

ZMS [cuneiform], [cuneiform], [cuneiform], azmis; *Strongly.* Heb. עָצַם.

[cuneiform], bit azmis udannin; *a house strongly I fortified.*—R.I.H. iii. 62. In Porter's transcript [cuneiform].

ZMN [cuneiform], bit-su ina Barsipa-ki azmis abni; *his house in Borsippa strongly I built.*—E.I.H. iv. 60.

[cuneiform], malik azmis ina kipa kali rabi saplana.—Neb. Yun. 82.

I am unable to translate this; it appears to relate to the arrangement of statues around the walls of a palace.

ZMT [cuneiform], [cuneiform], samat.—Esar iv. 10, 26. Birs i. 25. E.I.H. ii. 49, iii. 16, 68.

An ornamental stone frequently mentioned. Sir H. Rawlinson renders it *lapis lazuli*. Dr. Oppert generally *copper*, but the frequent epithet *ellati* must point to something more valuable.

[cuneiform], [cuneiform], ibba; *White, pure.*—24 II. 47 a.

[cuneiform], [cuneiform].—40 II. 46 a.

The collation of ellu here, with the value which represents certainly "copper" in Syl. 112, may have led Dr. Oppert to his rendering of samat.

¶ [cuneiform], azmuti, *pl.* *Firm, hard.* Heb. עצם.

[cuneiform], sir irsiti enditte la azmuti haraliki sibatti rakobi-ya ina dame-sunu gabsuti ilallu; *upon the grounds slippery, not firm, the horses yoked to my chariots in their copious blood trampled.*—Sen. T. v. 80.

We have [cuneiform], *azmats*, in Neb. Yun. 51, but the passage is mutilated.

Z(I)N [cuneiform], zin, sir; *Desert, waste, hunting-ground; plains.*

Zin appears to have been the Accadian and *sir* the Assyrian sound of this character; see the following extracts from bilingual tablets:—

[cuneiform], [cuneiform].—17 II. 8 a.

[cuneiform], [cuneiform].—59 II. 43 b.

[cuneiform], [cuneiform].—6 II. 27 b.

In the first and second extract the Accadian appears under the form of zinna, see p. 266, under Cedibbi; the first and third show that sera was the Assyrian equivalent. In the following lines the sound was probably zi, implying the nasal, though I believe very slightly sounded, if at all:—

Suzubu .... su ..... utirra ina tahazi alikta-su (dui) askun; *Suzub ... who .. returned to the fight, his defeat I effected.*—Sen. T. iv. 37.

usatmeh silli-a ina tahazi; *he hath strengthened my feet in war.*—Neb. Yun. 6.

In most cases I assume that zu was the pronunciation. Sir H. Rawlinson adduces the analogy of the Arabic [illegible], which is doubtless correct. I shall however, put the character under ZN, in conformity with the principle of keeping each in the same place, however sounded; and the following line is evidence that the Assyrians sometimes pronounced zinnu:—

ta sinnai; *the beasts of the chase.*—Br. Obel. l. 24.

ragmat qurudi-sunu ina ṣeri bamat sadi va libit alani-sunu kima sudvane l'amqit; *the ranks of their warriors on the wastes, on the mountain tops, and the walls of their cities, like chaff I crushed.*—Tig. iv. 92.

ragmat qurudi-sunu ṣera rapsu umalli; *the ranks of their soldiers the broad waste filled.*—New Div. l. 47.

Suti sabi ṣeri ina ligulti usanqit; *the Suti, men of the desert, to servitude I reduced.*—Botta 151, 4 = 136.

asar usum ṣeri la iblaçu va iççuri [bu] shame la iskkanu qinu; *a place where the beasts of the wilderness had not been, and a bird of heaven had not put a nest.*—Assur h.p. viii. 05.

ZaN [cuneiform]. itti-su amtahhis abikta [sisi] -su askun pagri quradi-su sera rapsu umalli; *with him I fought, his defeat I effected, the bodies of his soldiers the broad plain filled.*—Obel. 146.

[cuneiform]. pull Akkad-ki pargunis ina ṣeri irabbiṣ; *the cattle of Babylonia securely in the plains shall lie down.*

The above is from an unpublished astrological tablet, which Sir H. Rawlinson recently communicated to me. See also Obel. 146. Sard. i. 112.

In relation to the value of this character Sir Henry Rawlinson considers [cuneiform] to be "the god of hunting," and equivalent to Nergal; the name of the grand-daughter of Assurbanipal, written [cuneiform], he reads "Nergal-asaini." See Athenaeum, Aug. 22, 1863, p. 243.

¶ [cuneiform], ṣeri or arki; *To, upon, after; against.*

I have only seen this value of [cuneiform] in the inscriptions of Assurbanipal; the meaning is proved by the variants ṣeri and arki.

[cuneiform]. adki ummani-ya ṣeri Ummanaldas sar Nammanki ustesera harrana; *I assembled my soldiers, after Ummanaldas, king of Susiana, I directed my course.*—Assur b.p. v. 119.

[cuneiform]. aqi-ya sa sulme asabir ṣere-sun; *my messenger of peace I dispatched to him.*—Assur b.p. iii. 78.

[cuneiform]. ṣer (v. arki) Uaiteh sar Arubi . . . illiko; *to (after) Uaiteh, king of Arabia, he went.*—As. b.p. viii. 81.

See also Assur b.p. v. 41, [illegible]; vi. 17; viii. 51, [illegible].

[cuneiform]. Assur u Istar umaizu-inni ṣer gari-ya; *Assur and Istar strengthened me against my enemies.*—Assur b.p. vi. 46.

[cuneiform]. ur-mah izzu sa ṣera-su la uzni-su [pi] arkus; *a strong lion, which after it [in pursuit of which] by his ears I seized.*—R.I. Sh. 7, B. l. 2.

Z(U)N [cuneiform], ur-mah sa pura-su aškun ašbat; *a lion upon which I ran and seized.*—Ibid. D. 2.

[cuneiform] has been made "a tail" in the two last cases, but I think "upon" or "after" may do, though I admit it is an awkward construction, and the last line I cannot construe. But with "tail" we should find the same difficulty; the first line would be read "a lion whose tail by his ears he seized;" in the second, the word [illegible], "I established," "excited," would require a forced construction in any case.

[cuneiform]—17 II. 15*c*.

This extract would give the pronunciation zibbu; the sense of "walls" I do not understand.

¶ [cuneiform], elat uznâ; *over the ear.*—30 II. 6*b*

[cuneiform], " " " 7*b*

[cuneiform], elat inâ; *over the eye.* " 8*b*.

These extracts show that zuna or zunura, as well as elat, would signify "over" in Accadian; the Assyrians have borrowed and frequently used [cuneiform], but I do not remember any instance of their using zuna or zunura.

¶ [cuneiform]; zizi, zinâti; *Arms.* Chal. [illegible].

[cuneiform], mazi bab zini-sa la ikapir; *the openings of its gate of arms shall not be broken.*—Monol. 53.

[cuneiform], ili-sunu zinâti istari-sunu sappâti usib; *their gods armed, their goddesses attired, were reposing.*—Assur b.p. v. 23.

This may be connected with [illegible], "food," and the translation would be "the provision-gate" in the Monolith, and "the well-fed gods and well-dressed goddesses" in the last extract.

Z(U)N [cuneiform], zuni; *Plenty (of food).* See [illegible] Gen. xiv. 23.

[cuneiform], zunî dahdate zanat šalam va barre ana pal-ya lisruku; *plenty, rejoicings, years, prosperity, and fatness, to my time may they grant.*—Tig. viii. 37.

I have twice rendered this differently, in pp. 174 and 290. This time I believe I have given a better version than either, though still doubtfully: it agrees in the main with that of Sir H. Rawlinson in the quadruple version of 1857. The three other versions were entirely distinct.

(c)ZN . azni; *Ears.* See *Uzun*, p. 287.

. parid azni; *who opens his ears.*—43 BM 3. Epithet of Sardanapalus.

, ina azni nigiki sa mušallim rubû Nisroch ina aitaki ramani-ya ana epis suri ramu rabis amtallik; *by the opened [ready] ears which the lord Nisroch has given me for the guidance of myself, on the doing of this work much I deliberated.*—Sen. B. iv. 31 – 41 BM 23.

Both inscriptions are damaged, but the meaning is consistent with the context. Compare Neb. Yon. 77.

, sa Nabu Tasmetû azni rapasta isruku-su; *whose ears Nebo and Tasmit have made wide.*—21 IL 67 a.

A slab marked K. 214, containing a parallel inscription, has , proving the equivalence of , which is also shown in 30 IL 74. See p. 23. I should infer from the singular adjective with the plural noun that had come to be considered as a monogram without reference to the addition of ; though similar instances of false concord are by no means uncommon. For Tasmit see Dr. Oppert's Exp. Més. Vol. 2, p. 355.

ZNG . Bit-Azmik (or Isnuik).

. Bit-Azmik sa Ur-ki ana Sin bil sarum sarruti-ya ussis epus; *Bit-Aranik of Ur to Sin, the lord elevator of my royalty I founded, I made.*—Neb. Gr. ii. 44.

.... zigguratu sunu.... ana Sin .... bil Bit-Isnuik sa kirib Ur-ki bil-ya ussis ma epus; *these towers .... to Sin .... lord of Bit-Isnuik which is in Ur, my lord, I founded and made.*—Nabon. i. 30.

Both names must have appertained to the same temple, notwithstanding the assumption of Nabonidus; but possibly the edifice of Nebuchadnezzar may have been demolished in the interval between the reigns. In three of the Mugheir cylinders we find , *is bitat rabtu*, "the great goddess," instead of Isnuik.

ZNN [cuneiform], [cuneiform], [cuneiform], zanin, c. zaninu, m. *Restorer protector, embellisher.*

Zanin is the participial form of a verb signifying to "protect," "restore," or "embellish," cognate with the hypothetical Hebrew root of צִנָּה, a "shield;" Psalm v. 12. Dr. Hincks believed that the primary meaning was "to cleanse;" Grammar, p. 511(?).

[cuneiform] zanin Bit-Saggatu va Bit-Zida; *protector of Bit-Saggatu and Bit-Zida.*—Neb. Gr. i. 6. Birs i. 6. Neb. Senk. i. 4. See pp. 135, 136.

[cuneiform] anaku lu sar zanin mutib libbi-ka lu sakkanakku libim zanina kala mahazi-ka; *I, whether king provider* (?) *rejoicer of thy heart, or high-priest* (?) *constituted, defending all thy fortresses.*—E.I.H. ix. 65.

[cuneiform] zanin pat Istari ana ili rabi.—Sard. i. 23.

Dr. Oppert renders this "O restitua le culte des déesses, avec celui des grands dieux." The character [cuneiform] being used as a variant of [cuneiform] (see Sard. i. 8) would seem to countenance this reading, but I have always supposed that [cuneiform], "a worshipper," should be read *palih*. Cf. the Hebrew פלח. I cannot, however, suggest anything better.

[cuneiform]. Nabiukuddurusur lu sarru zaninu l'sanbia lam pi-ka; *Nebuchadnezzar, the king the restorer, may he be sustained by thy countenance.*—Birs ii. 30.

I suppose *zaninu* here to be the same as *zanin* in the preceding extract, both really nominatives notwithstanding the accusative termination; the final *u* was probably very lightly sounded, like the final *e* in the so-called mimmation.

A comparison of the following parallel phrases, epithets of Sargina, may help to show our value of *zanin*:—

[cuneiform]. zanin Sippara Nipur Babel; *embellishing Sippara, Nipur, and Babylon.*—Botta 107, 3; 10, 5.

[cuneiform]. sakin sataro Sippara Nipur Babel; *establisher of the beauty of Sippara, Nipur, and Babylon.*—Sarg. 4.

ZNN , zananu; *to restore.* (Infinitive?)

, anaku ana Marduk bili-ya kalmak la badlak Bit-Saggatu va Bit-Zida zananu ustetesser urrdi; *I, to Marduk my lord, steadfast and unfailing, Bit-Saggatu and Bit-Zida to restore, directed my course.*—Nerig. i. 19.

¶ , zinatu, *pl. obl. Embellishment.*

, sa ana zinati Bit-Saggatu va Bit-Zida yumusi anani kunnu; *who for the decorations of Bit-Saggatu and Bit-Zida appointed days hath set aside.*—B.I.H. i. 13. Neb. Bab. i. 7.

See also E.I.H. ii. 42. Nerig. ii. 12.

¶ , zaninut; *Restorations.*

, zaninut-su ebisu usahir-anni; *his restorations to make he hath urged me.*—Birs i. 12.

¶ , zanû, zanni; *Rain.* Ethiop. , "zanama."

, zanû va rîdu usappû libitto-sa; *the rain and tempest loosened its bricks.*—Birs ii. 1.

, ana Yav mesaznin zanû nuhsu ina mati-ya bit-su ina Barsipa-ki azmis abnû; *for Yav, raining rain, the benefit of my country, his house in Borsippa strongly I built.*—E.I.H. iv. 58.

ZNN [illegible] nisi-su mie siqi la idâ ana zunni tik shame tarraṣa ini-sun asqu; *its people, waters drinkable knowing not, and to the rains from heaven directing their eyes, I watered* [*supplied with water*].—Bavian 8.

The verb zanan is used in the sense of pouring down anything, naturally or metaphorically; see Sarg. i. 27, as limut ra ... imnun ... "which upon evil-doers and enemies pour down fear of death," quoted at foot of p. 279.

ZNM [illegible], iz-palmattu, n. -ti, *pl.* *Images?* Heb. צלם.

[illegible] iz-pasur iz-su iz-palmattu hal ḫurasi ..... amḫur; *articles of wood, images, horns*(?) *gilded ..... I received.*—Sard. ii. 123. For *iz-pasur*, see p. 388.

[illegible] rukub ibbitu iz-palmatti ḫuraṣ sa ulite ṣimat sarruti-su amḫur; *a fair chariot, images, gold of weight*(?) *the treasures of his kingdom, I received.*—Sard. iii. 66.

[illegible] ..... [illegible] iz-palmatti la-kal sa ulite .... madatu-su amḫur; *images, ornaments of weight*(?) .... *his tribute I received.*—Sard. iii. 74.

Dr. Oppert translates "parasols," probably reading tsilli; he merely transliterates most of the other articles of tribute; ulite is, I think, always preceded by sa, following some articles of value, in several cases gold; so that the word may be connected with [illegible] "weighty;" or perhaps "in heaps;" see p. 226. We cannot speak with much confidence of any of these objects of plunder.

ZNQ [illegible], zanqi; *Chains.* Heb. זקים.

[illegible] nibiss-su ina ana zanqi lirti sa .....; *his rebels*(?) *he carried to chains and bonds* .....—Synch. Hist. ii. 3 = 65 ll. 3&.

Uncertain; line broken and detached from context.

ZNR is-siri: *Yoke.* See p. 328.

I believe that siri means "feet," and is-siri "yoke," i.e. "wooden feet," though the distinction is not always observed. See the following phrases:—

kurrai ṣimdat is-siri-su; *horses joined to his yoke.*—Sard. ii. 121.

madatú kurrai ṣimdat is-siri eli-su askun; *a tribute of horses tamed to the yoke upon him I imposed.*—Obel. 171.

(v.) is tayarti-ya sa salimaté ...... Ini pan is-siri-ya utirra ana Assur-ki; *on my return, when prosperity and lands(?) under my yoke I had restored to Assyria.*—Assur b.p. v. 101.

rukubi-ya ṣimdat siri; *my chariots joined to the yoke.*—Tig. vii. 20.

Hazaqiahu Yahudai sa la iknusu ana siri-ya; *Hezekiah the Jew, who did not submit to my yoke.*—Sen. T. iii. 12.

We very frequently find and in the sense of "foot" and "feet," but I do not remember, though there are some cases where we should render the ideogram as "yoke" rather than "feet;" but this is not to be assumed necessarily, inasmuch as "taking the feet" might be a form of homage. See the following:—

ana Tarzi alik siri-ya isbatu, *to the city of Tarzu I went, they received my yoke [they took my feet?].*—Obel. 138.

unassiqu siri-ya; *they kissed my feet.*—Assur b.p. ii. 68, 110, 127.

katpai u siri birit̄u sa-bar addi-su; *hands and feet, fetters of iron I put on him.*—Assur b.p. v. 70.

ZNB [cuneiform], in biriti an-bar kasati an-bar utammeha kappai u siri; *in bonds of iron and stocks of iron they kept hands and feet.*—Assur b.p. ii. 91.

¶ [cuneiform], iz-zirhamte; *Weapons, or Snares, traps.*

[cuneiform], armahi in zirhamte usanqit; *lions with clubs* [or *in troops*] *he destroyed.*—Brok. Obel. l. 12.

The weapon might have been a powerful mace, or club. See the Heb. [illegible], "crashing noise," "thunder." Or possibly we have a Niphal form of the verb [illegible], "to raise," indicating the lion-traps with raised gates, sculptured on the bas-reliefs in the British Museum. A space is left in the inscription for the number of lions killed.

ZNT [cuneiform], zinûte. See p. 339.

ZS [cuneiform], lapi; *Strength.* Heb. [illegible].

[cuneiform], Urimizda lapi damno; *Ormazd gave help* . . . . .—Beh. 35, 37.

In both cases we have the same reading in the three languages:—in the Persian it is *Auramazda-maiy upastâm abara*, "Ormazd to me assistance brought;" and in the Scythic, *Auramazda pikti du-sa*, "Ormazd a helper to me was." The Babylonian must naturally have the same general meaning, but grammar and spelling seem very irregular. Possibly it was read *lapi idanna*, Ormazd "strength gave."

ZSQ [cuneiform], igsiqta; *Submission.* Heb. [illegible].

[cuneiform], rabi u nisi mati-ya kali-sunu in tagalte u kireti in igsiqta dildil kirib-sa usasib; *the great and the people all of them, in homage and humility, in obedience peaceful, within it I established.*—Esar vi. 39.

The change of dildil throws a doubt on the meaning, though it suits the context. The sound of the otherwise unknown character is shown in the following syllabary:—

[cuneiform].—Syl. 290.

ZṢN is-ṣindá; *Indian-wood(?).*

hekali .... is-ṣindá ana mutab biluti-ya abni; *palaces of .... (and) Indian-wood for the seat of my royalty I built.*—Sen. B. iv. 3.

The name is a mere guess, from the similarity of sound; the blank is filled up by nearly twenty names of valuable building materials.

ZṢR is-pirdu; *Willows(?).* See [illegible], Talmudic, *Pîra.*

ina taim anum kirib kiari kulû gimir palug is-pirdu va sim unda marab kumpa; *by my command in plantations they planted all select willow-trees and ..... greatly flourished.*—42 BM 43 = Sen. B. iv. 37.

All very uncertain. The printed text is faulty, and the several copies differ considerably.

ZER zairi, zairut; *Enemies.* Heb. צר. See pp. 320 and 338.

mati aipputo va malki zairi-ya ana sipri-ya luskaisu; *countries turbulent and kings my enemies to my feet may they subdue.*—Tig. viii. 82.

litai gurdi-ya irninte tamhari-ya patnus sibi zairut Asur sa Anu va Yav ana sipati lusakû-ni ina nari-ya va timmeni-ya alṭur; *the records(?) of my victories, the triumph of my wars, the subjugation of enemies hostile to Asur, which Anu and Yav to fullness have bestowed on me, on my tablets and my platforms I have written.*—Tig. viii. 41.

See note on *Asur*, p. 370

ZRR [cuneiform], zirâte, *pl. fem.* *Hostile.*

[cuneiform], ana šarrani sireti-su zirâti Assur-ki ispur; *to the kings of his vicinity hostile to Assyria he sent.*—Botta 149, 8 = 92.

"Kings" must imply "countries," and would thus take a feminine adjective.

ZP [cuneiform], zapi, var. [cuneiform], zabi; *the river Zab.*—Tig. vi. 40.

There are variation in the spelling of the name of this river. See other variations in p. [illegible].

¶ [cuneiform], azpi; *Ornamental; sightly.* Heb. [illegible] or [illegible].

[cuneiform], lu ḫuri azpi ḫurași rusi rukkut-su [rukkupa] sitti-sun; *with the handsome ornaments of beaten gold, and anklets (?) of their feet.*—Sen. T. v. 73.

[cuneiform], șimmi unakkis qati-sun ḫuri azpi ḫurași kiris (?) šibbi sa sizi-sunu amḫar; *valuable ornaments I cut off from their hands, the handsome ornaments of gold, the ivory footstools (?) of their feet I received.*—Sen. T. vi. 2.

¶ [cuneiform], is-pa, is-sa-pa; *Sceptre.*

The word is Accadian, meaning "rod of power," in analogy with *Ù-pa*, "god of power," the most usual name of Nebo. This explanation of the Accad word, given by Dr. Hincks, is corroborated by the *is-sa-pa* of the Babylonian monuments, in which the "of" is, I think, always expressed. The Assyrian value is shown in the following extract from a bilingual fragment:—

[cuneiform], ḫarûte.—28 II. 60 *d.*

[cuneiform], tamiḫ ḫaruți (is-pa); *holder of the sceptre.*—Tig. vi. 51.

[cuneiform], nadin ḫaruți va age; *giver of sceptres and crowns.*—Tig. i. 9.

[cuneiform], ḫarațe va kuppa (is-gaza) likim-su; *sceptre and throne may they take from him.*—Sen. T. vi. 73.

ZP [cuneiform], ana ribûtû mat va nisi ullâ risi-ya iddina ḫarat išarti; *for the governing of land and people he hath raised my head, (and) hath given the sceptre of justice.*—38 BM 5.

[cuneiform] ḫarat (is-ma-pa) išarti umalmiḫ qata-a; *the sceptre of justice he hath made my hand hold.*—E.I.H. I. 45. See Nerig. I. 10.

[cuneiform], ša idinaš ḫarat (is-ma-pa) išarti ana paqadû kal dadmi; who *giveth the sceptre of justice to preside over all men.*—E.I.H. iv. 19.

ZPN [cuneiform], is-pan: *the Face, presence.*

[cuneiform], ša ina is-pan galli-ya iḫḫarmidu; who *before the face of my servants fled.*—Tig. ii. 2.

Used in this one instance instead of *pan* only; I am inclined to think it a mistake. The phrase occurs a dozen times before (l. 85) without *is*.

ZPR [cuneiform]. Isparirra.—Bavian 10.

One of eighteen places whence Sennacherib dug canals to supply Nineveh with drinkable water. See p. 163.

ZPS [cuneiform], is-pasar.

Is-pasar is found in Sard. ii. 67 as a variant reading of [cuneiform]; this word occurs in Sard. i. 84; ii. 67, 123; and iii. 61, 67, 73; denoting some sort of wood or material taken as tribute or plunder. It has the plural sign in the two last-mentioned lines, and [cuneiform] is omitted in iii. 67, I think by mistake; in iii. 61 and 67 [cuneiform] and [cuneiform], take the place of [cuneiform]; in ii. 123 there is a trifling variant, [cuneiform] for [cuneiform]. I have always translated [cuneiform], *pasar*, "explanation," from the Hebrew פשר; we have [cuneiform] explained by [cuneiform], *pasara*, in 44 II. 12 *d*; and in a dozen succeeding lines; in l. 43 (putting X. for the word in question) we have "X. [cuneiform], *ruler*;" in l. 44, "X. [cuneiform], *silver*;" in l. 45, "X. [cuneiform], *copper*," &c. &c., which I cannot but read "the explanation of [cuneiform] is *prince*;" "the explanation of [cuneiform] is *sandy*;" "the explanation of [cuneiform] is *bond*," &c. &c. In l. 46 we have "X. [cuneiform]," which I read "the explanation of

ZPN [cuneiform] is the explanation of [cuneiform]." It seems clear that [cuneiform] with its variations is one inseparable character, like [cuneiform], [cuneiform], [cuneiform], and many others; and that, with the apparently superfluous [cuneiform], it should be pronounced *pasar*, meaning both "explanation" and a word so called. I hesitate to decide nevertheless, notwithstanding the corroboration afforded by the first column of Sb. 25 in the same volume, where *pasar* occurs sixteen times as the equivalent of sixteen different words. All these words can hardly have the same meaning, and I can only conjecture that the writer absurdly put the word "explanation" instead of the explanation itself.

In the following extracts, where [cuneiform] and [cuneiform] (as nearly as I can represent Grotefend's copy) are followed by names of deities, I would understand "explanation" in the sense of the doctrines of these deities:—

. . . . [cuneiform] . . . . . kima mie nahri la nibi ina pasar Marduk va Zirpanitâ bile-a lu adamû; [*seven countries named*] *as with waters of rivers unnumbered, with the doctrines of Marduk and Zirbanit, my lords, I gladdened.*—Neb. Gr. i. 27.

[cuneiform], pasar Nabiû va Nanâ bile-a eli sa panû udahhid; *the doctrine of Nebo and Nana, my lords, above what was before, I encouraged.*—Neb. Gr. ii. 34.

In 7 ii. 34*d* I find [cuneiform], *dibru*, as a gloss on [cuneiform], which may be the variant of iii. 67. The Assyrian is *dambar*, [cuneiform], and [cuneiform], *dambar*, in 1. 65.

ZZ [cuneiform], usqi; *Rapid motion.* Heb. [illegible]

[cuneiform], ummani nakiri ina usqi umhanili amhas; *the rebellious soldiers with the swing of maces I struck down.*—Sen. T. v. 67.

[cuneiform], kispâte hinnate va usqi alataka usata tahazi.—Sen. T. vi. 37.

I cannot translate this; the latter part may imply throwing of implements of war.

ZZZ [cuneiform]. iṣiṣi; *Great force.* See p. 331.

[cuneiform], in iṣiṣi leqati an-bar birili an-bar ulammeḳa qati u siri; *with great force the stocks of iron and bands of iron held their hands and feet.*—Assur b.p. iii. 113.

A similar phrase in i. 91 has siri without the determinative.

ZZM [cuneiform], iṣumbi, -bati; *Wagons, cars.*

[cuneiform] horral iṣumbi; *horses and wagons.*—Sen. T. i. 24.

[cuneiform], rukubi iṣumbi; *chariots and cars.*—Sen. T. v. 22.

[cuneiform], rukubi iṣumbati iṣmarai sarruti-suna eqim-sunuti; *the chariots and cars, defences of their royalty, I took from them.*—Neb. Yun. 45.

Some sort of carriage certainly (see the Hebrew [Hebrew] "to roll," in xxii. 18). Mr. Talbot reads "wagons;" Dr. Oppert transliterates ṣ-umbi in his Sargoniden, p. 41. I had read the word as an adjective, but I find it preceding rukubi in Neb. Yun. 88.

ZZR [cuneiform], iṣṣuru, iṣṣuri; *Bird.* Monog. [cuneiform].

See [cuneiform] and [cuneiform] in p. 833.

[cuneiform], nunē iṣṣura sammanu pilā ṣimat appariu; *fishes and birds I placed copiously, ornaments of the lake.*—Neb. Gr. i. 10.

See p. 97 for parallel passages in ii. 29 and iii. 13, with some variants, among others [cuneiform] in both extracts.

[cuneiform], kima iṣṣuri ultu kirib sadi abarsu ma akkisa qaqqad-su [qaqqadsu]; *like a bird from within a mountain I flew, and cut off his head.*—Esar i. 45.

The equivalents of [cuneiform] and iṣṣuru is shown in 40 ii. 16, 17 d. The monogram is very much more in use than the phonetic word; for one example among a thousand, are the following:—

ZZR [illegible], ana gimilat sadi saqûti kima iṣṣuri ibbarsu; *to the summits of rugged mountains like birds they flew.*—Tig. ii. 42.

[illegible], *iṣṣur musi*, "bird of night," occurs in trilingual tablets 27 II. 64d, and 46 II. 79c, but the equivalent words are not complete.

¶ [illegible], iṣṣuris; *Bird-like.*

[illegible], ana er Nagite-raqqi sa qabal tamti iṣṣuris ipparis; *to the city of Nagite-raqqi, which is in the midst of the sea, like a bird he flew.*—Sen. T. iii. 57.

[illegible]. Ullusunu Vannai ipsit etippusu kirib sadi marṣi ismo sa iṣṣuris ipparsid sa isbat sêri-ya; *Ullusun of Van the deeds of prowess in his rugged mountains had heard, and like a bird he flew and took my yoke.*—Botta 146, 14 50.

I take the reading *etippusu* from Dr. Oppert, who makes it the Infinitive, or verbal noun, of his *Iphteal* conjugation of the verb *epes*. This form of *epes* seems to be especially used for narrating martial deeds; see *enuppu* in Sard. ii. 6, and New Div. ii 63; and *etubus* in Obel. 73.

Dr. Oppert here and in l. 146 translates *ipsit etippusu* "deeds of glory" and "deeds of fame." I have preferred "deeds of prowess," as implying "doing," which seems more suitable to a root meaning "to do."

¶ [illegible], iṣṣurate, aṣṣurate; *Defences (?).*

[illegible], sa ipsit qati-ya unakkaru sa lamassi-ya nambhû iṣṣurate ṣiru umasqaku sa ṣimmate-ya upassatu; *he who the work of my hands shall destroy, and my statues shall throw down, the lofty defences shall weaken (?) and my treasures shall despoil.*—Farg. 66.

Iṣṣurate should have here the value of *aṣṣurate* in p. 331; we have *aṣṣurate ṣiru* [illegible] in the otherwise identical passage of Botta 78, 94. Dr. Oppert renders the words which I have marked as doubtful "qui enlève les vases qui contiennent mes richesses;" he must have had a different copy, as I have remarked before when speaking of this inscription. See p. 183, under Gimmu. The long final u in *nambhû* appears to have the force of the conditive one; I think Dr. Hincks has made this remark somewhere.

ZQ izqi: *Power, sway.* Chald. עִזְקָא "a signet ring."

sanati kibrat arbai la izqi-su l'umtilme; *the four countries to his sway may they entrust.*—Monol. 32.

ZQB zaqap; *Planting.* Heb. זקף

ana ... ... va takhlishtu hare nahr zaqap sippati uzun-su al ipsi va al usibil karas-su; *for regulating .... and cultivation, digging canals, (and) planting trees, his ear was not [ready] and he brought not out his edict.*—Sen. Gr. 41.

I think this is rather better than the translation hazarded in p. 257. The possessive pronoun was omitted there after uzun. See in the same page a few lines lower another passage, from Bars I. 8, where the verb substantive after "ear" implies readiness to hear. See also a passage containing zaqap sippati, printed in p. 312, from Sen. Gr. 50.

nisman .... sumb-su al ilmadu u hire nahr-su zaqab sippati-su al ishur; *any one .... its settlement not understood, and the digging its canal (and) planting its trees not laboured at.*—Botta 37, 44.

The above is the passage referred to in p. 4, differing by the addition of zaqap sippati from the passage in Sarg. 34, printed there.

In Captain Jones's large map, No. 3 of the "Vestiges of Assyria," printed by the Hon. East India Company in 1855, the River Khosr, which falls into the Tigris near the remains of Nineveh, is designated "[cuneiform] Zakaphirate of the Inscriptions." Is this a misreading of one of the preceding extracts?

ZQD zaqut: *Ladles.* Heb. יָצַק "to pour."

Vessels of gold sent as tribute to Shalmaneser by Jehu, king of Israel.—Obelisk, Epigraph 2.

ZQP ziqipe: *Stakes.* See *Isziqibi* and *Ziqip*, pp. 333, 341.

sitale la ziqipi azqip; *the common people on stakes I impaled.*—New Div. ii. 54.

ZQP ziqipis; *like a stake, or stick.*

abubis ispunu ma ziqipis imnû; *like chaff he sweeps away, like sticks he accounts them.*—Tig. jun. i. 8.

Epithets of Tiglath-pileser; *kis*, one of the values of [cuneiform], which usually represents *kis*, is omitted in the list of characters.

ZQL Iskalluna; *City of Ascalon.*—Sen. T. ii. 58; Sen. B. i. 20, 21.

Asqaluna; *Country of the Ascalonites.*—Tig. jun. 61.

ZQR Zaqiru.—Tig. jun. 19.

Son of Ba'alla, of Bit-Ba'alli; a country named with Bit-Bilani and Bit-Amukkani, laid waste by Tiglath-pileser.

¶ is-qiras; *Deal; pine, fir.* Heb. קֶרֶשׁ "a plank."

is-gusuri is-qiras piruti usatrisa eli-sa; *beams and long planks I arranged upon it.*—Esar v. 36.

See also Esar v. 15, 48; vi. 1. Sar. Cr. 47. Botta 152, 11–158. We have [cuneiform] in Botta 152, 16–160, a passage parallel to [cuneiform] in Botta 16–161, showing that "pine" is meant; the equivalence is shown also in a bilingual list. This is precisely analogous to our own use of the word "deal," which simply means "plank," for pine and fir.

ZR zir; *Race, family; seed.* Heb. זֶרַע

hirat-su [dam] bari-su tar-mali-su abl-su zir bit abi-su [ad] assuha; *his wife, his sons, his daughters, his brothers, the family of his father's house, I removed.*—Sen. T. ii. 60.

250 zir sarruti-su ina qati usabbit; *two hundred and fifty of his royal race in my hands I captured.*—Botta 148, 6 = 42.

ZR [illegible] sum-su [ma] pir-su ina matti Yuhalliq; *his name, his race, in the land may he destroy.*—Tig. viii. 88.

[illegible] anaku sar piri sa Uvakuistar; *I am a king of the race of Cyaxares.*—Beh. 61.

See also Sen. T. iii. 57. Botta 145. 13–21.

[illegible] bukur Bel tiglati [kull] ili suru-su; *eldest-born of Bel, in service of the gods his lineage.*—Sh. Ph. I. 16. Epithet of Ninib. Doubtful.

I find [illegible], zere ili, "race of the gods," beginning a sentence of which I can make nothing.—Botta 158, 3–171.

¶ [illegible].—ib 11. 37 *d.*

¶ [illegible], *a Brother*; also [illegible] or [illegible].

[illegible] Kambusiya agu-sa ah-su Barziya istin ab-suna is um-sunu; *of Cambyses this, his brother (was) Bardes, one their father, one their mother.*—Beh. 12.

The reading *istin* for "one" is shown by the occurrence of [illegible] in the Persian Tablets No. 13 F. and No. 15 D., where No. 5 D. and No. 1 F. have the more common numeral [illegible]. The same word is found in the phrase [illegible], *ki istin*, "every one," in Botta 151, 10–176 and 152, 7–134; an adverbial form [illegible], *istinis*, "severally," occurs in Botta 151, 10–110. I have no doubt that this word is connected with the curious Hebrew [illegible], "one," as part of the number eleven; it is not uncommon in the Bible; see Ezek. ix. 49, and Zech. i. 7; but it seems to be unknown to other Semitic languages.

[illegible] lu matima ina arki yumi ina ahi tari mari-a zikari u sinnisati; *if henceforth in after days, of brothers, sons of my family, males or females.*—I Mich. ii. 8.

Both characters signify "brother," *ah* in Assyrian, Hebrew [illegible]. Phonetically the first appears to be *sis*, and the second *sis*; these being probably Accadian words: see [illegible], *Bel-sar-usur*, "Belshazzar," Nab. i. 21:

ZR Neb. Br. Cyl. ii. 26; and "Nebuchadnezzar," [cuneiform]. B.M., Vol. I, Sh. 52, No. 7. 17. [cuneiform], Hosea 171. 11, with parallel [cuneiform] in Sarg. 88. See also [cuneiform] in Syl. 276.

¶ Either of these characters prefixed to [cuneiform] or [cuneiform] (*Erech, Warka*) forms with it a compound ideogram meaning *Ur* of the Chaldees, now *Mugheir*; [cuneiform] is found on the bricks from Mugheir (see Sheets 1, 2, 3, in Vol. I. B. Inscrip. and Neb. Gr. ii. 44). [cuneiform] occurs in Botta 142. 4–166, and is equated to *Ur* ([cuneiform] and [cuneiform]) in 46 II. 5 h, 35 c. In these slabs we have the forms [cuneiform] and [cuneiform], the former probably an error of copy. The town of Sinkrieh is made by [cuneiform] instead of [cuneiform] ([cuneiform], Botta 157, 5–137; and see note in p. 277), and Zerghul by [cuneiform] (Botta 157, 4–136); see *Zerghul*, in p. 379. I believe the names attributed to these ideograms have been determined by the places where inscribed bricks have been found in situ. See [cuneiform] on bricks found at Warka (B.M., Sh. 3, No. VIII. 1 and 2).

¶ [cuneiform], airi; *Lofty, exalted.*

[cuneiform], isakku airi; *high-priest exalted.*—Neb. Gr. iii. 1.

This is an epithet of Nebuchadnezzar: [cuneiform] is, doubtless, an error for [cuneiform], which is found elsewhere. See Cyl. Bab. i. 4 and Birs i. 3.

¶ [cuneiform], [cuneiform]. izru, n. izri, obl. *Helper.* Heb. עזר.

[cuneiform]. Anu izru; *Anu the helper.*—Monol. 2a.

[cuneiform]. Yav izru . . . ; *Yav the helper.*—Monol. 6a.

I do not understand the final character; see [cuneiform] in p. 67, where I have hazarded a guess on the meaning, which will hardly hold here.

[cuneiform], ana Ninib izri dandanni; *to Ninib the powerful helper.*—Sard. i. 1.

Sir Henry Rawlinson reads this *gisra*, "daring;" *gis* is a well-known value of [cuneiform], and his reading is corroborated by the epithet [cuneiform] given to Ninib in Sh. Ph. i. 1. We find [cuneiform], "powerful," in Sard. i. 32, interchanging with *izru*. In col. ii. l. 23 of Shal. K. 162, partly translated by Mr. Talbot, we have [cuneiform]. *izru rabu*, but I cannot read the passage.

ZRB [cuneiform], kussu; *Throne.*—46 II. 50a.

See p. 211, where the value of *kussu* is clearly shown. The Accadian [cuneiform] will be the "great piece of furniture."

ZRB —Syl. 383.

¶ Zirubaniti.—Tig. jun. 12. 17 BM 15.

Zirapanita.—Neb. Gr. i. 27, 32. Botta 152, 11 = 143. 48 II. 37 c (p. 199); 38 II. 32, 36, 46, b [a fragmentary inscription of Assurbanipal].

The Goddess Zirbanit. It is probably the same who is described as "the Great Mother" in the following passage of Nebuchadnezzar's slab:—

bit mah .... ana ilu-mah ana baniti-ya ina Babel-ki epus; *a great house .... to the great divine mother who bore me, in Babylon I made.*—E.I.H. iv. 16.

¶ şirpir; *Molten figures.* Heb. [illegible]

am-am eri ekdutâ va şirpir semruti ina şippi-sina usziz; *bulls of hard metal and solid molten figures, on their platforms I erected.*—E.I.H. vi. 17.

am-am eri ekduti va şirpir semruti usziz; *bulls of hard metal and solid molten figures I erected.*—Neb. Gr. i. 45.

rimu eri ekdûti va şirpir-şirpir semrûti ina bab-rab bab-rab-sa usziz; *bulls of hard metal and solid molten figures in its great gates I erected.*—Neb. Bab. ii. 9.

8 şirpir eri semruti sa limnû va aibi lumnu imat muti şiri kuppi ebbi usalbis; *eight molten figures of hard metal, which upon evil-doers and enemies pour down fear of death, I covered with rasi of white silver.*—Nerig. i. 26.

ZRB ... an-am ra ṣirpir band garbu-an mahlu usepis; *which bulls and molten figures tall within it skilfully I caused make* (i.e. within which).—E.I.H. vi. 5.

... ṣirpis ori sa lam kipu bab-bab Bit-Saggatu .... la usziza sar mahri .... epsik; *molten figures of metal, such as in the panels (?) of the gates of Bit-Saggatu .... a former king had not erected, ... I formed.*—Nerig. i. 21.

There is much guess-work in all the above examples; I have given as many in the desire to furnish future students with means for arriving at greater certainty.

¶ ... sirbardu; *Epithet of Sardanapalus.*

... sirbardu kirib umh.—Sard. i. 8.

Dr. Oppert renders this "qui fait la division entre les flots." I do not know his authority; we have פרץ in the sense of forcible action, and פרד of dividing. I would suggest "a bold leader on the waters."

¶ ... ṣirbu; *Burning, ardour.* Heb. צרב

... ṣir gimir ummandti mahiri simati ṣirbu yomnale ahzi kima Yav lagum; *upon the whole of the soldiers, rebels and enemies, ardent as the day I rushed, as Yav roars.*—Sen. T. v. 62.

See p. 116; I do not know that this version is better than the one given there; the exact meaning is still uncertain.

¶ ... is-urbate; *Willow; wicker-work.* Heb. ערב. Ps. cxxxvii. 2.

... in elappi is-urbate ana tamti (addi) ittapku; *in ships of willow to the sea they proceeded.*—New Div. ii. 77.

See Layard's "Nineveh and its Remains," 5th edition, Vol. 2, p. 93, where he describes rafts made of beams bound "with willow twigs." The same Hebrew word occurs in *Levit.* xxiii. 40, rendered in our version "the wood," in obvious allusion to interweaving.

ZRD [cuneiform], *lurat*; *Engravings(?)*. Syriac [Syriac]. Arabic [Arabic].

Timmeinnu dura dure's ulti sa ahulla histi sitir barumme lurat-sa lurit ma subû zindu-su; *a foundation, durable its duration for the future, which of old with writing ..... its engraving was engraved and its strength established.*—Sen. Gr. 36.

I have printed this twice before (pp. 123 & 260). The present version, though still uncertain, cannot be very far from the meaning: it is the second clause of a long account of Nineveh, which city, as Sennacherib informs us half a dozen lines farther on, he had improved and augmented. The *timmin* I believe to have been originally the foundation or basement of a building, which had frequently inscriptions upon it; the word has been translated by "engraved cylinders," and when, as in the second column of the broken cylinder of Nabonidus, we find it "sought for to the right and the left, before and behind," it can hardly be the foundation of a palace; but it may be, and I think must be in similar passages, the inscription on the foundation-stone; and probably it might be any inscription whatever placed on the foundation of a building, whether engraved on barrel, slab, prism, or cylinder. I do not know how to render *barumme*. We have the Chaldee גָּרַם, *vertu, etiam, sed, dumtaxat*; and in Syriac the same root signifies "rotten" or "eaten by worms." The Arabic *zyrt* is a "borer," or "auger:" possibly a tool for engraving.

¶ [cuneiform], *lurid*; *Seal*; *divining rod.*

[cuneiform].—44 II. 27 *c.*

[cuneiform].—44 II. 28 *g.*

[cuneiform].—Syl. 874.

ZRH [cuneiform], Zir'ahi; *Land of Israel, or Jarred.*

Occurs in New Div. II. 22. For p. 25. where the word is erroneously printed [cuneiform]; the two characters are not unfrequently confounded, as observed under No. 167 of the list of Compound Syllables. The character [cuneiform], numbered 167, has been inadvertently placed there, though its sound is *ar*; it is found properly inserted at No. 63 of the Ordinary Alphabet.

ZRZ [cuneiform]. Zarzakka.—Botta 146, 12 = 46.

A city of Van, [cuneiform], captured and plundered by Sargon.

ZRḤ [cuneiform], *sirḫu*; *Crisis, moanus*. Heb. צְרַח. Zeph. 1. 14.

[cuneiform], nisi asib libbi-sa umeda siphitu va sirḫu; *(to) the people dwelling within it I gave occasion for lamentation and wailing.*—Botta 148, 6 = 78.

ZRK Mushi; *the land of the Moschi.*

mandatu sa Kummuhi Muski . . . . amhur; *tribute of Commaha and Moscha . . . . I received.*—Sard. i. 74.

¶ izraku; *I am great.*—Sard. i. 32.

This is made a verb by Dr. Hincks, but the grammatical relation is unsettled, though the meaning can hardly be doubtful. There is a variant , zarpiku.

¶ isri kanul.—E.I.H. iii. 49.

Some ornamental work put up by Nebuchadnezzar, in connection with the Bit-Zida of Borsippa: some water-work probably. See under kanul, in line 71.

¶ urkarina, or likkarina.—Tig. vii. 17.

Some unknown tree enumerated among others brought from foreign lands to be planted in Assyria.

ZRL , kulli, kullat; *All.* See under letter K.

¶ , Zirlabaki; *Zerghul.*—Botta 36, 6.

The ruins of this town (Oppert reads Zari) are still remaining, eastward of Hys on the Euphrates. It is identified with , because of its place in the enumeration of towns which is found on the inscriptions of Sargon: Botta 149, 5–157. Dr. Oppert assumes *Zari* as the ancient name.

ZRM ; see *Kullat*; All.—Sard. i. 15; iii. 128. Esar vi. 46.

ZRN , is-erul.—Sen. T. vi. 42, 47. Neb. Yun. 64. Sen. B. iv. 5.

, is-eri.—Botta 152, 16, 19: 160, 163.

, is erina, u.—Sard. i. 87.

, is-erini.—E.I.H. ix. 10. N. Gr. ii. 16, 22; iii. 26.

, is erini.—Obel. 30, 140.

, is-erina.—Tig. vii. 17.

.—E.I.H. iii. 21, 27; vi. 8, &c.

I believe all these forms denote the same tree, which is "pine" or "cedar." It was brought for building purposes by the Assyrian monarchs from Mount

ZRN Amanus [Sen. T. vi. 47; Sard. iii. 89], and by the Babylonian kings from Lebanon (Neb. Gr. iii. 28). In duplicate copies of the same inscription *eri* is found varying with *eri—ol.* Botta 33, 61, and 46, 63; also 38, 67, and 49, 76. The monogram is found in the same collocation as *erini* and *eri*, and the tree it represents is likewise brought from Lebanon (K.1,18, iii. 21). The analogous roots in Hebrew, [illegible] and [illegible], are usually translated "ash" and "pine," but according to Fürst both are used for any tall slender tree.

¶ [cuneiform], Zarange: *Province of Zarangia.*—No. 6, N.R. 13.

The Sarangæ of Herodotus [iii. 93; vii. 67] and Zarangæ of Pliny and Arrian. The Persian inscription has *Zaraka*, the Scythic *Sarranka*. Probably the present Seistan, between Persia and Affghanistan. See Wilson's Ariana Antiqua, p. 152 *sqq.*

ZRP [cuneiform], masqali; *the Bottom.* Heb. [illegible].

[cuneiform] tel labiru [lu] usakir adi ri mie [ai] lu usbil 120 tigpi ana masqali l'atabi; *the old mound I threw down, to the water I brought it, one hundred and twenty layers on the bottom I made good.*—Sard. ii. 132; iii. 136.

This is not quite clear. I think the following quotation from the octagon of Tiglath-pileser, vii. 71-84, will illustrate it, and shew that the old mound was thrown down for the purpose of making an enlarged foundation. The king says "the gods ordered me to build a temple for them; I made bricks, prepared the ground, took its dimensions, laid its foundation upon a mass of hard rock, piled up bricks as a basis over the whole site;" and then [cuneiform], 50 tikhi ana sapali utibi; "*fifty courses to the bottom I made good.*" After this the building of the edifice follows, "from the foundation to the roof." See also St. 17.

¶ [cuneiform] Zirupanith; see *Zirubanit*, p. 378.

ZRQ [cuneiform]. *Name of a City.*—Sard. iii. 6, 9, 134.

This city, which was near the Euphrates, is written with [cuneiform] and [cuneiform] in l. 6, and [cuneiform] in l. 134. The true sound will be, therefore, *Sirqu.*

¶ [cuneiform], sirqi; *Dust.* Heb. [illegible]. (See Job ii. 12.)

[cuneiform], ummanate-suna kima sirqi usikia; *their soldiers like dust I crushed.*—Tig. iii. 98; see also vi. 6.

ZRR . sirrû.—Bavian 38. Heb. צר.

. sirrû.—Botta 152, 10 = 142.

sirru.—38 II. 39b.

In these three extracts sirru forms a part of lists of choice stones and other valuable materials collected from divers sources for use in Assyria. In the Bavian Inscription the object of making the collection is indistinct, owing to the mutilation of the monuments, but it is certainly connected with the digging of canals and erection of buildings; in the inscription of Sargon the list is very miscellaneous, containing gold, silver, and steel, fine woods and rich coloured cloths, but no object is mentioned; in the third, which is a fragmentary inscription of Assurnasirpal, the word has no determinative, and I think it is merely an epithet of a stone named gabu (see p. 232). The Hebrew term points to a hard flint.

¶ . Zurru, Zurrai, Zurri; *Country and city of Tyre.* Heb. צר.

madatu sa Zurrai Zidunai Gubalai amhur; *tribute of the Tyrians, Sidonians, (and) people of Byblus, I received.*—Obel. 103.

ultu [tu] eli nahr Purrat Hatti Aharri ana sibarti-sa Zurru Zidunu Humri Udumu Palastu adi eli tamti rabti sa dima shamsi ana sipi-ya usaksis; *from upon the river Euphrates, the Hittites, Phoenicia the whole of it, Tyre, Sidon, Samaria [Omri], Edom, Palestine, to (the land) on the great sea of the setting sun, to my feet I subdued.*—I Pal. 12.

See Sard. iii. 88, and (with var.) 43 R III 16.

sa . . . . insapihu Quu va ir Zurri; *who . . . . hath destroyed the Qui and the city of Tyre.*—Sarg. 21.

The Qui, written also Gui, are probably "the Gentiles" of the Hebrews, the Goyim. The word was originally used for a nation generally (see goi gadol, "great nation," in Gen. xii. 2), but subsequently the Jews appear to have restricted the name to their heathen neighbours. See p. 130.

ZRR [cuneiform], ṣariri; *Statues, figures.* Heb. צִירִים Is. xlv. 16.

[cuneiform], kitre ṣariri reme kappi ibbi sirs matlati tamarta habitta rabis ussambir-sunuti; *homage of figures carved, silver white, bracelets many, a copious donation, largely I presented to them* [*made them receive*].—Botta 152, 93 - 167.

[cuneiform], slap Kua ṣariri va abni usalu; *the tabernacle of Marduk with statues and stones I adorned.*—E.I.H. iii. 10.

See 61 II. 41 *c* for "the tabernacle of Marduk."

[cuneiform], ishab sahe ṣariri umma.—E.I.H. iii. 50.

I cannot understand this line.

See a quotation from Assur b.p. vi. 79, in p. [illegible]. I would suggest that ṣarira salu in that passage should be read "a figure of marble."

¶ [cuneiform]: see *Iz-pasar*, p. 368.

¶ [cuneiform], ṣirruti; *Hostility.* Heb. צרה

[cuneiform], ṣirruti idbub-sunuti ma isa.... ubdi marṣi pagar Asâ pal bil-sunu iddû; *to hostility he incited them, and on the heights of rugged mountains the body of Asa, the son of their lord, they cast out.*—Botta 146, 2 - 26. See p. 51, for the word which I have not been able to transliterate.

¶ [cuneiform], ṣirrit; *Enmity.* Heb. צְרָר

[cuneiform]. ul ṣirrit shame rapasti l'ibtin-su; *may not the enmity of the broad heavens destroy him.*—38 II. 50 *c*.

ZRR [cuneiform] ([cuneiform]), ṣirreti, ṣiriti, ṣirrat: *Treasures.* Heb. צרור "purse."

[cuneiform] ḫammami ša arba' iddû ṣirrete [v. ṣirretû].—Sarg. 9.

[cuneiform] ḫammami ša arba' iddû ṣirrati [v. ṣirreta].—Botta 167, 14. [Revers des Plaques.]

The same passage in Botta 163, 9–14 with [cuneiform], addû for iddû. Dr. Oppert has translated the passage in Sarg. 9 "J'ai exigé d'elles (des terres) les symboles de soumission dans les quatre éléments;" and the other passage with addû, in nearly the same terms. Mr. Ménant's version is "J'ai fait voir les symboles de ma domination dans les quatre régions." Both translators give the same interlinear version in Latin—in circumeunte quas quatuor dispertivi symbola dominationis." Some confusion has arisen from the change of person: iddû, "he scattered," and addû, "I scattered;" the fact being that the king in one inscription says "I scattered," in the others that he is the king who "has scattered." I would propose "I have (or who has) scattered treasures in the four regions;" i.e. everywhere.

[cuneiform], ṣiriti kala nisi qatâ-a umallâ; *treasures of all people my hand have filled.*—Nab. Br. Cyl. iii. 26.

[cuneiform], ṣirrat-sina [ṣirragina] ana gati-ya umallû; *their treasures to my hand they have filled.*—Hammurabi i. 14.

¶ [cuneiform], zirritu; *Seed, lineage.* Heb. זרע.

[cuneiform], simat bilutti-su ana kimati va zirritti-su ana manzaz Bit-ḫarris mat-sitra ana daris liqqara; *the stability of his power to his legions and his lineage, for the exaltation of Bit-ḫarris of the eastern land, for ever may they proclaim.*—Tig. i. 21.

[cuneiform], ana ṣâbi va zirati-ya kiribu tabta likrubuni; *to my children and lineage gracious union may they unite.*—Tig. viii. 84.

ZRS [cuneiform]. *Zarisu*.—Sh. Phal. iii. 16, 17.

Names of two petty kings of the Nairi.

¶ [cuneiform], is-erui. See under *Is-erui*, in p. 379.

ZRT [cuneiform], mustabri; *sharp-clawed, or fierce, or beautiful.*

This word, used as an epithet of birds, has a variant [cuneiform] in the long Khorsabad Inscription, showing the sound to be mustabri; as the root may be either [Hebrew], "a claw," [Hebrew], "to tear," or [Hebrew], "beauty;" there is a choice of three values, either of which will be an epithet suitable to "the birds of heaven;" [cuneiform] occurs without a variant in Tig. vi. 53, and Br. Obel. i. 81, always as an epithet of birds.

[cuneiform], sadu kima siqip rû asbar sequddi u iççuri [ša] shame mustapri-su kirib-su la ibara; *the mountain like a sharp stake of iron stood up(?), and its fierce birds of heaven to it had not reached.*—Sard. i. 40.

¶ [cuneiform], parati; *Dignity, elevation*. See [cuneiform], ṣiri.

See under *Is-karu*, in p. 343.

¶ [cuneiform], marati; *Cornice, top*. Heb. [Hebrew]

[cuneiform], marati kibri sa dur dali sa kima ... la utturu la kupri va agurri usepis; *the strong cornices of the high wall which like ...., I did not neglect, with cement and brick I caused make.*—Neb. Gr. i. 40. Uncertain.

Sarati is made [cuneiform] in Bellino's fac-simile, but the mistake is obvious. For the expression rendered by "cement and brick," see p. 60.

¶ [cuneiform], is-rati; *Throne*.

[cuneiform] (v. [cuneiform]), nari-a epus tamsil is-rati-ya ina libbi altur; *my tablets I made; the laws of my throne upon them I wrote.*—Sard. i. 99.

ZRT I translate "thrones," comparing ú-ruti with [cuneiform] = [cuneiform], u-ruti, a variant of [cuneiform] in Sard. I. 44; see 4311.43 a. I would also compare the following line, from Tig. vii. 111, where ruti without the determinative must surely have the same meaning:—

[cuneiform] [v. [cuneiform]] [cuneiform], ina ruti-sunu pirte usesib-sunuti; *in their lofty thrones I seated them.*

¶ [cuneiform], pirti, pirtu; *Lofty, high, tall.*

[cuneiform], ina rukub-tahazi-ya pirti sapinat sahiri ina uggum libbi-ya artakub; *in my lofty chariot of war, the sweeper of enemies, in the vengeance of my heart, I drove.*—Sen. T. v. 56.

[cuneiform], is-bunsul ina kibiti-sunu pirti ana musab sarruti-ya absi; *statues in their high dignity at the seat of my royalty I made.*—Botta 33, 56.

[cuneiform], bilut-ka pirti surikam-sunu bahalti iluti-ka subsi ina libbi-ya surkh; *may thy great power be exalted; in the worship of thy divinity may it subsist* [*be caused to be*]; *in my heart may it continue.*—E.I.H. i. 69.

Surikam-sunu is an irregular form.

[cuneiform] [v. [cuneiform]] [cuneiform], Ninib va Sidu galli-sunu [lakni] laruts va bunni-sunu(?) pirte ana kiri bilati-ya iraku; *Ninib and Sinu their valiant servants and their tall bows(?)* (see p. 331) *for the defence of my dominion have granted.*—Tig. vi. 39.

See also Tig. vii. 111. Botta 37, 35. E.I.H. i. 53; ii. 8.

ZRT ... —2 R. 11. 25 d.

¶ ..., zirqat; *Insignia.* Syriac ... "brilliant."

... ni zirqat sarruti-su lerab hurasi kussu hurasi .... kirib bitat-su ezib; *he, the insignia of his royalty, the parasol of gold, throne of gold .... in his tents he left.*—Botta 151, 23(11) = 131.

... ina biris nahri kima issuri kumi zirqat sarruti-su lukun; *among the rivers, like birds the insignia of his royalty he accumulated.*—Botta 151, 21(9) = 129.

These readings are mainly from Dr. Oppert; in the last he hesitatingly reads *kumi iskun*, "I fit together," where I have *kumi iskun*, "I accumulated." I take *kumi* from the Arab. كام (كوم), but admit the uncertainty of the translation.

ZS ..., ..., is-su.

I have long considered is-su to be the name of some sort of wood of which chariots, among other objects, were manufactured; but after collating several passages I find I am unable to do more than set down a few and leave them for future students:—

..., ina is-su sadadi rada sarruti-ya arbai-pasati.—3 Beltis, 5.

Sadadi has a variant ..., meaning "long." The whole passage refers to the heads of two Susian chiefs cut off in battle, and perhaps carried about in honour of the goddess.

..., rukubi is-su sadadi is-su zilli.—Assur b.p. iv. 126.

..., &c., kai is-sai kai is-rati kai kaspi, &c.—Sard. III. 61.

"Horns(?) of *is-su*, horns of thrones, horns of silver;" some projecting ornament shaped like a horn, as in "horns of the altar."

..., rukubi is-su sadadi ippussi.—Assur b.p. vi. 68.

Printed, with some additions, in p. 388.

28 ia-su: *West; setting sun.*

erib sa samsi; *setting of the sun; lit. passing of the sun.*—38 II. 16d.

ZSG elep; *Ship; tabernacle of a god.* See p. 349.

multabta kirib elippi usarkib; *the remainder in ships he carried.*—Sen. T. iv. 31.

ina elippi Arvadāya irkab nahira in hahba rabte iduk; *in ships of Arvad he sailed, dolphins (?) in the great sea he killed.*—Broh. Obel. l. 1.

The fish is uncertain; Dr. Oppert reads "vorax marina." The value "tabernacle" ["sanctuaire mystique" of Dr. Oppert] is shown in 63 II. 33-44c, where *elep* is repeated twenty-three times before the name of a god: the Assyrian equivalent is lost; see … in 62 II. 41a, and example from E.I.H. iii. 14, in p. 362. I have incorrectly printed *elippi* instead of *eleppi*, in p. 349-350.

¶ sahri, sahrat; *Cedars.*—Opp.

ana Hamani eli is-gusuri is-sahri akis; *to Mount Amanus I went up, beams of cedar I cut.*—Obel. 97.

is-hu is-sahrat is-sarvan kala rikki biblat Hamani .... ultu ris sarruti-ya adi sanat [mu] III kan uqall kisiti; *ebony, cedars, cypress, all smooth, within Mount Amanus .... from the beginning of my reign to the third year, I collected stores.*—Botta 152, 11 - 153.

The actual trees cut are not identified. I have adopted the sense given with hesitation by Dr. Oppert. The version of Dr. Hincks, printed in 1857 in the Dublin University Magazine, was "beams and pillars."

¶ isqiqtu; *Submission.* See p. 385.

ZSH is-mhi ; *Docks, or pits(?).*

ana mbas elappi kirib is-mhi isi rabbi ukira ina naphar mali-sunu ; *for making ships in the docks(?) great trees they felled in the extent of their lands.*—38 BM 10 = Sen. B. iii. 24.

The Heb. שׁוּחָה, "a pit," or שָׂחָה, "to swim," would suggest the meaning given, and the passage quoted would fully justify such meaning; but I cannot apply it to the following lines, which I do not understand:—

is-mhi-su sa pirim matal adub sa abisu-su asmad sa umallá garbáti gimir umani-su abbal aggur in isati [huv] asrup.—Tig. Jun. 24.

ZSP is-sa-pa ; *Sceptre.* See … p. 387.

ZSR is-ar ; *Plantation.*

isi sutunu sa ina sarrani abi-ya [ad-ya] mahruti mamma la izqupa lu alqa ma ina is-ari mati-ya lu azqup va sum is-ar aqra sa ina mati-ya la assu alqá is-sari mat Assur lu ussib ; *those trees, which among the kings my fathers before me none had ever planted, I collected, and in the plantations of my country I planted, and the name I called is-ar ; what in my country I had not raised I collected ; plantations in Assyria I established.*—Tig. vii. 19—27.

I am not sure that I have divided the clauses correctly, and I have some hesitation about "the name I called is-ar," but I think I have given the general meaning. See also New Div. ii. 60 ; Sard. iii. 109, 135 ; Sh. Ph. iv. 17 ; 42 BM 44, 16 ; Sen. B. iv. 57.

Z88 [cuneiform] *isar mahhu tamsil Ḫamani gimir ḫibisti Ḫatti pulug nadi kali-sunu kirib su ḫerram sa aldani itaza'u*; *a large plantation like those of Mount Amanus, the whole desirable, the choice of Syria, the hills all of them in it were cultivated, and I built its walls.*—Botta 37, 39.

A little hazardous here and there, but compare Sen. Gr. 40 and the following passage from Esar Haddon:—

[cuneiform], *is-sar rab tamsil Ḫamanû sa kala sim-mada u is-mada ḫerram itd-sa emid*; *a large plantation like those of Mount Amanus* (in) *which all plants and trees* (were) *cultivated, its walls I raised.*—Esar vi. 14.

¶ [cuneiform], *surman*, sing. *surmini*, plur. *Cedars, cypress, fir.*

Castelli gives as "abies, cupressus, cedrus" as equivalents of the Chaldee [illegible], *sarbin*, which is sufficiently near in sound to *surman*. The plural form *surmini* shows the pronunciation; it occurs in E I. H. (c. 8, 10, where we find the statement that it was employed in building Nebuchadnezzar's palace, "which was completed in fifteen days"* (see viii. 64). The singular occurs very frequently; see Sen. Gr. 47; Esar v. 15, 28; Botta 152, 14–166, &c. In Esar v. 19 it is said to be brought from Taurus and Lebanon. I think I have generally made it box-wood, *from Schaaf*, Leyden, 1686.

¶ [cuneiform], *gursilli*.—Botta 131, 34 = 132.

Dr. Oppert doubtfully suggests some ornament; it is followed by "golden," and I have not found it elsewhere.

Z88 [cuneiform], [cuneiform], *Throne.*—48 II. 51 a.

These two words are equated in the extract cited, and by implication with [cuneiform] and [cuneiform], *kussu*, all signify "throne."

---

* This very curious statement coincides with a passage from Berosus, quoted by Josephus in his first treatise against Apion, i. § 19. I quote Whiston's translation:—"However, as prodigiously large and magnificent as it was, it was finished in fifteen days."

ZT [cuneiform], [cuneiform], zâti, zâte. See *Zaâ*, p. 334.

ZTB [cuneiform], is-tappi; *Planks; fir(?).* Chal. [Hebrew]

[cuneiform], is-tappi kulab babi-sun esnid; *of fir the posts of their gates I built.*—Botta 152, 20(?)-164.

Parallel passages without [cuneiform] occur in Botta 28, 54, and 16 ... 116; and are another in Eme vi. 9 with [cuneiform], *shining*, probably "fir," instead of *is-tappi* (see p. 10).

¶ [cuneiform], is-dapran; *Cypress.* Syriac [Syriac].

A tree used for building.—SL 19, 21; Bard. iii. 89. See p. 555.

ZTM [cuneiform], is-timmo; *Figures of wood.*

The long extract which follows here is collated from several inscriptions out of Botta's Volumes:—152, 18–162; 46, 73; 42, 53; 39, 67; and 16 ... 16 ...: I have included the extract under STT, p. 146, which, partly owing to my having had but one copy, and partly to some oversight, was very incorrectly printed. The subject is the ornamentation of palaces building by Sargon in Khorsabad. Dr. Oppert makes *is-timme* a species of tree, but we have clearly a metal as well as a wooden *timme* in the inscriptions. Some ornamental work seems to be understood, though not necessarily figures:—

[cuneiform]

8 armahi tamme sapar .... saqal 6 susi 50-ta bau bilati maltaqil eri namri sa ina sipar Nin id(?) rabti ibbadqu ma malû namriri sa is-timme is-erni sutahuti sa 64-ta bau kubur-sun bibint Hamani eli sirgale (v. armahhe) ukin; *eight lions pairs, beautiful, weighing six score and fifty* [410] *talents altogether, of shining metal, which for the decoration of Nin, the great power(?), were wrought, and were full of brilliancy, to which wooden figures of cedar were added(?), which, amounting to sixty-four, (cut) in Mount Amanus, over the lions I placed.*

ZTM [cuneiform] timme eri mahhi adi is-timme is-erni rabi biblat Hamanû massat eri aṣabbiṭ ana ṣir nirgale ulziz; *large figures of metal, together with great figures of cedar in Mount Amanus beside (?) the metal, I cut down and over the lions I erected.*—Sen. B. iv. 28 = 1 BM 31.

[cuneiform] ...... [cuneiform] .... [cuneiform] is-gusuri rabi is-timme mahhi .... ultu kirib Ṣirara Libnanu .... usaldidû-ni; *great beams and large wooden figures .... from within Ṣirara and Lebanon .... they conveyed to me.*—Esar v. 14.

The blank is filled by a very large number of wood, stone, and metal objects, sent to Esar Haddon by vanquished kings of Syria and Cyprus. Dr. Oppert translates the words in the first line by "de grandes poutres du bois de *timmi*."

ZTR [cuneiform].—Esar i. 51. See p. 305.

¶ [cuneiform], zakut; *Decrees.* See p. 345.

¶ [cuneiform]. See p. 108, and the note in page v.

¶ [cuneiform], is-tarpi'; *Sort of wood.* Heb. [illegible].

[cuneiform] bekal is-ku bekal is-butni bekal is-tarpi' in er ya Assur-ki epus; *a temple of ivory (?), a temple of pistachio (?), a temple of carving-wood (?), in my city of Assur I made.*—Br. Obel. ii. 15.

Perhaps a word used for carving, analogous to is-daldi, which I have conjectured to be derived from [illegible]. See p. 187. Mere guesses in both cases.

I give here some words which I cannot place in alphabetical order, together with a few additions:—

¶ [cuneiform], is-sitarate.—Sen. T. vi. 56.

Follows "chariots" in a list of warlike stores, for the custody of which a place was provided. Mr. Talbot suggests "baggage-wagons." I propose as a guess "harness," see the Hebrew [Hebrew].

¶ [cuneiform] appears as the name of some bird in Botta 154, l. 160.

¶ [cuneiform], *Buildings.*

[cuneiform] (v. [cuneiform]), ... lim naphar Asur gabbi l'umahiq; *buildings in the extent of all Assyria, I caused construct.*—Tig. vi. 101.

[cuneiform] without the determinative appears to denote the foundation only. See the following extracts:—

[cuneiform], bekal sunta alta usse-sa adi gablubi-sa arpip; *that palace from its foundation to its roof I built.*—Esar vi. 22.

[cuneiform], ta usse-sa adi gablubi-sa arpip.—Sard. iii. 136.

[cuneiform], alta usse-sa adi gablubi-sa.—Bavian 52.

I transliterate by usse ([cuneiform], Heb. [Hebrew]) because the phrase is very frequently used, and almost always with [cuneiform] instead of [cuneiform]. See Tig. vii. 65, &c. The first of the following extracts from the syllabary shows that [cuneiform] signified the "digging" rather than "building" of the foundation; dupur and [illegible], Heb. [Hebrew]. I do not understand the others:—

[cuneiform] . [cuneiform] . [cuneiform].—Syl. 287.

[cuneiform] . [cuneiform] . [cuneiform] ([cuneiform]).—Syl. 288.

[cuneiform] . [cuneiform] . [cuneiform].—Syl. 289.

¶ The eighth month was denoted by [cuneiform]. See the list of months in p. 56.

¶ [cuneiform], rakub; *a Chariot.* Heb. רֶכֶב.

[cuneiform], ekil [alib] tab ina rakub-ya va marga ina aqqellat eri ju abpi; *the good country in my chariot, and the rugged in rollers of iron, I treated.*—Sen. T. iv. 66.

See p. 174.

See also Tig. i. 71; iii. 4, iv. 54. Sen. T. i. 68; v. 29. Sard. i. 86; ii. 62, &c.

We have the word sometimes written phonetically: [illegible], rakuba, in E.I.H. iii. 78; [illegible], rakubi, in Bots iv. 61 and same [illegible], rakupi, in Sen. T. v. 10.

¶ [illegible].

Occurs in Sen. T. iii. 33, as plunder taken from Hezekiah; and in Bel. 151, 23–131, as plunder from Merodach-baladan; whatever it may be, it is made of the same valuable material as the throne which immediately follows it;—"Gold" in Botta's inscription, in Sennacherib's possibly "ivory." Dr. Oppert and Mr. Talbot are both inclined to look upon this as some royal seat. I rather think it may be the crown, which is not otherwise mentioned among the royal insignia carried away. An hieratic character in Lord Aberdeen's Black Stone, l. 29, which appears equivalent to the one in question, is translated "crown" by Mr. Talbot in his amended copy.

¶ [illegible], is-tir; *Babylon-wood.*

[illegible], is erni-ya sa ista Labnanū is-Babel illūti ubla; *my pine trees, which from Lebanon, Babylon-wood excellent, I brought.*—E.I.H. iii. 25.

Dr. Oppert renders this "les plus grands des arbres que j'ai fait transporter des sommets du mont Liban." This is a paraphrase, but nearly of the same import as my reading. I suppose Babylon-trees may have denoted the finest trees, as an Englishman or Frenchman might call the finest work London work and Paris work.

[illegible]; see p. 383.

[illegible]; see p. 385.

[illegible]; see pp. 60 and 200.

[illegible]; see p. 364.

[illegible]; see p. 379.

[illegible]; see p. 311.

[cuneiform] ח

Characters arranged under letter Ḥ.

[cuneiform]. ḫa.

[cuneiform]. ḫi, sometimes ṭi.

[cuneiform]. [cuneiform]. ḫu.

[cuneiform]. aḫ, iḫ. uḫ.

[cuneiform]. uḫ. Not found in the more ancient monuments.

[cuneiform], ḫal.

[cuneiform]. ḫul.

[cuneiform], ḫar, sometimes mur.

[cuneiform]. ḫuḫ.

[cuneiform], aḫ, "an enemy;" or "side." See pp. 24 and 296–7–8.

[cuneiform] [cuneiform] [cuneiform] } aḫ, "a brother." When used phonetically [cuneiform] is pronounced aḫa and [cuneiform] sasar; I have not found [cuneiform] used phonetically.

Ḫ [cuneiform]. ḫa; *Fish*, Accad. In Assyrian *Nun*. Arabic نون.

[cuneiform], nuni [ḫa] u iṣṣuri [ḫu]; *fishes and birds.*— Botta 154, 1 = 169.

[cuneiform], [cuneiform], ḫa = nuna.—7 II. 25 d.

It appears from the following line out of a trilingual list that some sort of stone was named from a fish:—

[cuneiform]—40 II. 15 c.

The first word is clearly Accadian, and the second Assyrian. I think this is usual in the trilingual lists. I have no opinion about the third.

[cuneiform] [cuneiform]. bi; *Knee*, Accad. In Assyrian *Birku*. See p. 181.

The following is from a list of Accadian and Assyrian phrases:—

[cuneiform] . [cuneiform]—16 II. 20 b.

The Accad reads *bi-ea mis dada ma*, word for word "knee my up make-go I." The Assyrian *ullala birkaya*, "I make-move my knees." *Birka* is the dual.

[cuneiform]

ana Istar bilat Ninâ birka-y'amba; *to Istar, lady of Nineveh, (on) my [knees] I sat (I knelt)*.—Sard. iii. 98.

[cuneiform], 2 susi ar-mahi ..... ina rakubi-su pattote ina siri-su ina [haruti] (is-pa) ina birk' iduk; *one hundred and twenty lions ..... in his open (?) chariot, on his feet, with sceptre, kneeling, he killed*.—Brok. Obel. l. 11.

[cuneiform] [cuneiform]. *Many, multitudes.*

In a very few cases we have [cuneiform] in royal titles, where we so frequently find [cuneiform] or *kissati* following the monogram [cuneiform] or [cuneiform]; see [cuneiform]. 1 Pal. 1, [cuneiform] or [cuneiform] in Sarg. 8, and sometimes [cuneiform], in Botta 38, 1; usually translated "king of many," or "king of nations." A small barrel of Assurbanipal in the hieratic character, an impression of which was communicated to me by Sir Henry Rawlinson, had [cuneiform] in lines 1, 4, and 7, and I find the same on the signet-seal of [Tiurri]-gaina, given in the index to Vol. I of Rawlinson's Inscriptions, under Pl. 4. I believe this to be an abridged form of [cuneiform], found sometimes as a variant of [cuneiform]; see [Khors.] vi. 15. "Army" is often rendered by [cuneiform], "warriors many;" see [Khors.] iii. 9, and Obel. 24, 45, &c.; and this group in the inscription of [Shalmaneser] [cuneiform] is always abridged to [cuneiform]; see ii. 15 (incorrectly rendered in the cursive copy), iv. 37 and 42. [cuneiform] is considered a separate word, and it is sometimes found at the beginning of a line, as in Sard. i. 48. See more in p. 858.

[cuneiform] [cuneiform]. ḫu, Accad; *Bird*. In Assyrian ipparu. See p. 370.

[cuneiform]

ana-sunu [Turamsra] ana gimilat sadi saqûti kima iççuri [ḫu] la ipparsu; *their place they abandoned, to the tops of rugged mountains like birds they fled*.—Tig. iii. 60.

[cuneiform] [cuneiform], ṣabī-ya kima ṣu eli-sunu iṣa'; *my soldiers, like birds, upon them came down.*—Sard. i. 63; with [cuneiform], iṣṣuri, in iii. 105.

See also Botta 151, 21(B) = 159. Tig. vi. 82. Br. Obel. i. 61.

The following lines from a trilingual list points to a bird-stone; like the fish-stone, under [cuneiform], at the foot of page 294:—

[cuneiform]—40 II. 17*c*.

[cuneiform]—Syl. 677.
[cuneiform] " 678.
[cuneiform] " 679.
[cuneiform] " 680.

I do not understand these extracts.

¶ [cuneiform] is sometimes confounded with [cuneiform], the horizontal line being removed from the left side to the bottom. See a line from Sard. i. 88, printed in p. 217.

(A) [cuneiform] [cuneiform], ab: *Enemy, rebel; Side.*

This word is Accadian, and when it signifies "enemies" or "rebels" it is read in Assyrian by aibi or aibut. We have sometimes a determinative, [cuneiform] or [cuneiform], and sometimes a phonetic complement, which decides the pronunciation. See p. 74.

[cuneiform], nir aibi ina mat-ya apras; *the yoke of enemies in my country I broke through.*—Tig. vi. 53.

[cuneiform], mutnus aibi sarrut Asur; *subduing rebels hostile to Asur.*—Tig. viii. 40.

[cuneiform] …… [cuneiform]

[cuneiform], sar sa …. matati [illegible] malki aibi-su kima gidbi [illegible]; *king, who* …. *countries turbulent and kings his enemies, like grass hath cut off.*—Sard. i. 42.

(A)[cuneiform] [cuneiform] .... [cuneiform], a .... arki nikrut Asur pagimri-snan ittallaku; *who after the enemies of Assur, all of them, hath pursued.*—Tig. vii. 30.

[cuneiform] ..... [cuneiform]. Sandusarri .... aibu aqqu la palah bilutí-ya sa ili uvassuru; *Sandusarri, ... an enemy, I cut off, not a respecter of my power, who the gods had forsaken.*—Esar i. 37.

[cuneiform] .... [cuneiform], sa ..... malki aibi-su kullat mati-sunu ana siri-su uskniss nikrut Asur saqu u kita istanamu; *who .... the kings his enemies (and) all their countries to his feet hath subdued, (and) the rebels against Assur, high and low, hath opposed.*—Sard. iii. 129.

See Tig. i. 9, 52; vi 55, &c. Sen. T. i. 26; v. 52, 64. I do not understand Tig. vi. 69

[cuneiform], ana mati nakerto sutanu; *to countries hostile he hath opposed.*—Tig. i. 44.

For the second low see the following:—

[cuneiform].—Syl. 564.

¶ A Side:—

[cuneiform]. imna ah humela uszbita; *the right side of the portico (?) I caused occupy.*—Sen. T. vi. 53.

I do not remember to have found [cuneiform] used as "brother," but it appears in 2 R 17. 63 as equivalent to [cuneiform], as also in the name of Sennacherib, as printed in B.I. Vol. 1, Pl. 6, No. vii A. and B. — In Sen. T. iii. 16, I would propose to read [cuneiform], ahrub kimmata, "desolation of families," but doubtfully. — I think [cuneiform], in Esar ii. 22, must have been printed instead of [cuneiform] "rebel;" and the equivalent in the text was probably [cuneiform], nabrut.

¶ [cuneiform] or perhaps [cuneiform], was used in summing up a total; see Tig. iv 93; Sh. Ph. i. 58; 2 Mich. i. 17

(A) II [cuneiform] ahe shamse addu sa sar mahri ushahru ma la ibnû pukki-sa ahe ushahri ana ina kupri va agurri abnâ pukki-sa; *the eastern side [side of sun rising] which a former king had caused dig, and not had built its coverings, (that) side I caused dig, and with cement and brick I built its coverings.*—Nerig. ii. 5, 8.

This relates to a water-course, but the preceding lines are incomplete.

¶ [cuneiform]. *Brother.*

In addition to what has been printed in pp. 73 and 374, the following extracts from the syllabary may be useful:—

[cuneiform].—Syl. 235–9.

[cuneiform].—Syl. 276.

[cuneiform].—Syl. 277.

¶ [cuneiform]. *City of Ur, now Mugheir.* See p. 375.

HA [cuneiform]. *Many.*

I have arranged this under HA, though I believe it is one letter, like [cuneiform] and some others; but one whose pronunciation is unknown to me. It is usually read ma'da, or some form of the word, which is occasionally denoted by a phonetic complement. Now and then it varies with [cuneiform], as in Esar vi. 15; and not uncommonly it may be looked upon as merely a sign of the plural.

[cuneiform] usatkhu aṣâ-sunu ma libitta libnatu; *submission I made them bear, and they made bricks [or bricks many].*—Esar v. 3.

[cuneiform] bit ma'dut ilani sa ali-ya Asur anhûte epus usaklil; *houses many of the gods of my city of Assur, (which were) decayed, I made (and) completed.*—Tig. vi. 88.

HA erani ša Gilḫi ša ina birit sadu-ṣu Aran Aratli mati dannute saknu-ni akšud dikti-šunu ma'di aduk; *the cities of Gilkhi which, among its mountains of Aran in Armenia, strong countries, were situate, I attacked; their fighting-men many I slew.*—Sard. i. 61.

I read saknu-ni without hesitation, from a collation of this passage with the following of similar import in Sard. iii. 98:—*Erani dannute ša ina birit Adani saknu-ni akšud*, "the strong cities which in Adani were situate I attacked;" where saknu-ni is written in all letters. occurs very frequently in this inscription, as in i. 40, 68, 71; ii. 49, and elsewhere, always following the relative ša; see the note in p. 322.

In the following passage appears to signify "much":—

..... 1604 biltat 20 mana kaspu ibbu eri ma'du .... ugali; *sixteen hundred and four talents and twenty manehs of white silver, metal much, ... I collected.*—Botta 152, 9 = 141.

In Sard. ii. 84, varies with, which would be pronounced probably ma'di; in some copies of Sard. i. 71 we have instead of, which would seem to show that is not a single letter, but I have never seen such a division elsewhere.

¶ sabi-ma'di, "warriors many," is used for "army," and generally read without its complement; in Tig. iv. 10 it varies with [illegible].

Aḫuni adi ili-šu rakubi-šu kurmi-šu turi-šu tur-sali-šu ummani-šu aspaḫ-šu; *Aḫuni with his gods, his chariots, his horses, his sons, his daughters, his soldiers, I removed him.*—Obel. 40.

See more in p. 385.

ḪAA Ḫaisappal.—Tig. jun. 52.

Name of a city mentioned with Temal, Ṣab'ai, and Badanai, in an unconnected line, broken at both ends.

¶ Ḫaina.—New Div. i. 53.

Name of a chief of *Samu'ai*, apparently the same with *Ḫani of Sam'alai*, mentioned in i. 42, defeated by Shalmaneser, with several other petty princes, near the Euphrates.

ḤAA haire; *a Husband.*

From the information of Sir H. Rawlinson, who has found the word connected with *hira*, in a vocabulary.

ḤB —Syl. 542.

I only learn from this that may be pronounced *hab*. In the inscriptions of Bavian, l. 2[?] or 19, there is a stage named or , with several others, relating to some water-works erected near a river; but the inscription is too much mutilated to allow of accurate translation.

¶ —Syl. 725.

I understand from Sir H. Rawlinson that he finds *habe* meaning the "left hand;" *kit*, would be , "the hand." *Kit* is repeated seven times in the Syllabarium, from No. 722 to 728, and one of the equivalents (No. 724) is , *imnu*, "the right hand;" the Accadian equivalents are all gone. Our own "left," and the Italian *manca* for the "left hand," both point to "defect;" and the Heb. חָבָא, "to hide," and חוֹב, "debt," contain a like notion. See the following:—

kepâni sa kirib Musur upahhis abu banû-a ana dâki habâte; *rulers whom in Egypt the father begetting me had appointed for the punishment of defaulters.*—Assur b.p. l. 58.

¶ ḫib. See under .

¶ ḫibi; *Something deficient.* Heb. חָבָא or חוֹב.

Often found on the bilingual slabs where something is omitted. This occurs half-a-dozen times in some sheets. See Sh 16 in R.C., Vol. II.

—Syl. 340.

ḤBD ḫi-bit: *Temple, or shrine.* [*Kneel* and *house*, Accad.]

ḫi-bit Bilat Sin u Gulanu Hea-nannu Yav tig rabu shamee irṣiti ih addi; *a temple for Beltis, Sin, and Gulanu, ... Yav, great ruler of heaven and earth, I founded.*—Sard. ii. 135.

HBD ḥabat; *Devastation, injury; spoil.* Heb. חָבַט.

ula ili rabi la iplaḥ va iḥtanabbata ḥabat misir mat-ya; *the will of the great gods he reverenced not, and wasted wasting the border of my country.*—Assur b.p. viii. 49.

nisi Aribi itti-su usabkir va iḥtanabbata ḥabat nisi sa Assur; *the people of Arabs with him he made rebel, and harassed harassing the people of Assur.*—Assur b.p. vii. 113.

In these examples we have a mode of expression common in Hebrew, by which an infinitive or participle follows a verb to denote continued action, as עָלוֹ עָלֹה, "they ascended ascending." 2 Sam. xv. 30, and הָלְכוּ הָלוֹךְ, "they went going." 1 Sam. vi. 12. In the following passage the meaning of ḥabat is not so clear:—

nisi ḥabat istani-ya sa sadi va tamti sit shamsi la libbi u-seib; *men, the spoil of my arrows, of the mountains and sea of the rising sun, in it I settled.*—Esar i. 31.

I have adopted the version of Dr. Oppert, "les hommes que mon arc a domptés."

ḤBL ḥabal; *Corruption, injury.* Heb. חָבַל.

sulum la libi la ḥabal; *to rule, not violence, not corruption [without violence, without corruption].*—Sarg. 40.

¶ ḥibilti, *pl.* ḥibilta, *ac. Injury, grievance.*

musallimu ḥibilti-sun; *repairer of their injuries.*—Sarg. 6.

ḥibilta-sunu akal; *I terminated their grievances.*—Botta 144, 7–7.

HBL [cuneiform], ḥabalu, ḥabalî; *Valley*, const. Heb. חבל

[cuneiform].—12 II. 35 a.

[cuneiform].—12 II. 39 a.

[cuneiform]—40 II. 49 d.

I have not found these words in any text, but they are good Semitic (see Zeph. ii. 5, 6). The forms [cuneiform], given in Sb. 17 as Accadian, are used frequently in all inscriptions, from Tiglath-pileser downwards; and they have, I think, a Semitic root. The word in Sb. 19 denotes some stone, probably named from the locality of its origin.

HBL [cuneiform], Ḥibiltiel.—Sard. iii. 30.

Name of a chief or governor of a city in the country of Laqe ([cuneiform]) on the upper part of the Euphrates. Dr. Oppert reads the name *Khabil-el.*

HBN [cuneiform], Ḥabini.—Sard. iii. 55, 65; Obel. 67. [cuneiform], Hapini.—New Div. i. 35.

Ḥabinu, a petty king of the city of Tel-Abnai, near Arbela (see p. 16), who was compelled to pay tribute by Tiglath-pileser and by Sardanapalus. As the dates of the respective notices differ by nearly twenty-five years, the tributaries were probably father and son. The name of Ḥabinu on the obelisk is damaged.

HBR [cuneiform], Habur; *the River Khabour.*—Tig. vi. 71. Sard. i. 77; iii. 3, 31.

There were more rivers than one of the same name, but the river mentioned by Sardanapalus must have been that one which falls into the Euphrates at Carchemish.

¶ [cuneiform], Tel-ḥibiri.

[cuneiform] ina eli Tel-ḥibiri sa ar Ḥuzaut iqabbu-ni-sini ar epus ar Kar-Assur sum-su (su-su) abbi; *upon Tel-ḥibiri which they call it Ḥuzaut, a city I built, (and) Kar-Assur its name I called.*—Tig. jun. 10.

It would appear from this line that the lengthening of the u in an indirect or subjunctive clause (p. 373) might be transferred from the verb to the enclitic pronoun. I do not remember to have seen any other instance of this; it is in fact superfluous, the suffix ni sufficiently indicating the indirect state of the verb. See [illegible], in Sard. i. 103, and [illegible], in Sard. iii. 128. The usage was somewhat lax generally.

HBS —Obel. 101, 102. Habushkâ.

—Obel. 148, 18 = 54. New Div. I. 20; II. 64. Habushkia.

—Obel. 44. 13 B.M. 8. Sard. II. 80.

The first two of three forms obviously denote the same place, and a comparison of the passages, so far at least as relates to the obelisk and bulls, renders it highly probable that the third form is equivalent to the others. We have *Habushai* in Sh. Ph. II. 27, and instead of in Obel. 177 and Sard. I. 57. The place must be on the north-east of Nineveh, among the mountains near the lake Urmia. It might be rash perhaps to suggest any resemblance between *Habushai* and the Kaduruk of the Modern Armenians, but some phonic manipulation [r—s] might be allowable, and the places certainly approximate.

¶ . Habusna.

Teuspâ Gimirrai zab manda sa asar-su ruqu ina irṣiti [kiti] Habusna adi gimir ummani-su ura(s)sibu ina tigulti [laku]; *Teuspâ, a Cimmerian, a soldier fugitive, whose place was far off in the land of Khabusna, with all his followers I brought into servitude.*—Esar ii, 8.

¶ , , hipisti; *Select; trodden down, layers* (?). Heb. Arabic خشش, *(con)culcavit*, Golius.

. hurag kaspi eri minkhi abni hipisti Hamani pil-su umtrim; *gold, silver, metal precious, stones selected from Mount Amanus (its excellent) I arranged.*—Botta 38, 51.

Pil is again used for *pili* in line 69. *Pilsu*, "its excellent," which comes in so awkwardly here, points to the excellent selected stone from Mount Amanus. I am inclined to believe that when a writer by inadvertance had left out a word, he inserted it as soon as he discovered his error. See under *Hatti*, p. 410.

. hipisti epiri [lal] danu-sun adil; *their large layers of earth I laid down.*—Botta 158, 16 · 160.

Somewhat doubtful. See p. 753.

ḪSS [cuneiform], kiru maḫḫu tamsil Ḫamani gimir ḫipiati; *a large plantation like (those of) Mount Amanus, the whole selected.*—Botta 37, 38. See pp. 368, 369.

ḪBT [cuneiform], ḫubti; *Satisfaction, pleasure.* Heb. [Hebrew]

[cuneiform], itti ḫubti mahdi sallati kabitti salmis atura ana Nineveh-ki; *with great pleasure and much plunder safely I returned to Nineveh.*—Assur b.p. l. 121.

ḪG [cuneiform], *Good.*

This is without doubt a single character; but the Accadian form, with the Accadian adjectival termination *ga* (see p. 156) has induced some students to suppose that we have here an Accadian compound, originally signifying "devout" or "pious," from [cuneiform], "to kneel," like *ma-ga*, "glorious," and *dan-ga* or *kal-ga*, "powerful." This is probable, but the word was used for any sort of goodness, such as a good road. See [cuneiform], Tig. vi. 64, and [cuneiform], Tig. vi. 52, in passages exactly parallel, pronounced *ship tabu*, or perhaps *sell tabu*, "easy country." I shall, therefore, arrange [cuneiform] under *t*. See the list of Compound Syllables, No. 116.

ḪGL [cuneiform], ḫigala; phonetic rendering of [cuneiform].—Sir H. Rawlinson.

¶ [cuneiform], Ḫirimmu, Ḫirimme.

[cuneiform], tabulati or Ḫirimme aibi akṣi; *the people of Hirimmu, rebels, I cut off.*—Sen. B. l. 8.

Occurs also in Sen. T. i. 26, Sen. Gr. 12, and elsewhere; we have the form *Ḫirimmu* in Neb. Yun. 16. I find no positive indication of the locality, but think it was in the mountainous country north of Nineveh.

ḪGR [cuneiform], Ḫagurana.—Sen. T. i. 45. Tig. jun. 8.

A tribe mentioned with about forty more, subdued during seventeen years of the reign of the biblical Tiglath-pileser; and again, with near twenty others, plundered by Sennacherib in his first year. All of these appear to have been Aramæans.

ḪD ḫud, *sing.* ḫudut, ḫidate, *pl.* *Joy, rejoicing.* Heb. חֶדְוָה.

in biṭut Assur sar ili u ili Assur-ki kali-sunu lu ṭub siri ḫud libbi numḫar kabtu ... hittate kirib-sa daris l'urme; *in honour of Assur king of gods, and of the gods of Assyria all of them, in vigour of health* (*and*) *joy of heart, tribute much, plenty hoarded* (?), *within it for ever may it arise.*—East vi. 42.

Not very explicit perhaps; it is simply a prayer that in honour of the gods health and prosperity with wealth and profit may accrue in a palace mentioned previously. Compare Neb. Yun. 92. where a parallel passage occurs: much damaged but with valuable variants: liban, "may it come," for l'urme, "may it arise," and dur dar, for daris. See *Dara daris*, p. 269.

lu-niqut ana ilani-ya sabat nakdan ḫudut sakun; *victims for my gods I obtained* (?), *spectacles for rejoicing I instituted.*—Obel. 70.

This is uncertain, but probable; the passage is an account of the preliminaries to putting up a statue of the monarch, and writing upon it a narrative of his conquests. Dr. Hincks translated, in 1853, "I *offered sacrifices* to my gods, I made (a new temple)." The italics show doubt; the brackets were intended to denote a mere makeshift. Dr. Oppert, in 1865, reads "je vouai des sacrifices à mes dieux, [illegible]." The parallel passage on the bull 15 BM 27 might have helped us, but it is hopelessly damaged.

hekal musab sarruti-ya markas nisi rabati sabat risâti va ḫidûti asar kaiṣuti ukinnu-su; *a palace, seat of my royalty, assemblage of great men, abode of supremacy and gladness, place of pillars* [*capitals*] *I established it.*—Neb. Gr. iii. 30.

..... bit elat atmana qumta sabat ḫidate-sunu musab tanitti-sunu ..... akbud; *a lofty house, an ornamented temple, the abode of their enjoyments, the seat of their authority .... I wrought.*—Tig. vii. 91.

HD . bit hidate; *Pleasure-house.*—Sard. iii. 80.

See *Arunda*, p. 2?.

. —43 II. 81 a.

. —43 II. 82 a.

. —43 II. 21 a.

HDB . Hadabiti.—Bavian 11.

One of eighteen towns from which Sennacherib dug canals to supply Nineveh with drinkable water.

HDD hadat; *Rejoicings.* See *Hud*, p. 105.

¶ hadedá.

amera (aqi) baṣṣurat hadedá etra ikbd.—Asurbanipal's Egyptian Campaign, l. 24.

I cannot read this line, which is incomplete. For the value amera see Syl. 77?.

¶ . Hadada.—Tig. jun. 6.

One of a long enumeration of tribes conquered by Tiglath-pileser.

¶ . hitti, g. *Rebellion.* Heb. חטא

Varies with and in parallel passages; the word must, therefore, be *hitti*, or *hti*. According to Buxtorf, Kimchi considered hen to be equivalent to rebellion. (see Buxtorf's small Lexicon, London, 1646.)

sabi bil-hitti sa itti-su la tigulti asaqqit; *the men rebellious who were with him to servitude I subdued.*—Obel. 81.

The identical passage in 15 BM 73 has .

.... Urbi Aramu .... adi turi sa bil-hitti asaph; *the Arabs (?) and Arameans, ... together with the men of the city* (*who were*) *rebels, I carried off.*—Sen. T. i. 38.

ḪDD [cuneiform], sa ṣariṣi sa ṣariṣ sarrani kil-ḫiṭṭi aḫri-sunu abattiq; *of the officers of the kings' officer, rebels, their limbs I cut off.*—Sard. i. 92. Uncertain.

See also Sard. i. 92, 93. Obel. 155. Botta 145, 23–25.

¶ [cuneiform], ḫiṭṭu; *Evil, sin.*

[cuneiform], makkamshu rabut sa ḫiṭṭu ambaṭu aduk; *the priests(?) (and) the chiefs who evil had done [caused to be] I slew.*—Sen. T. iii. 2.

[cuneiform], ṣitsta-sunu sa ḫiṭṭu va qalluta la isu kabtu nir bilut-ya emid-sunuti; *the common people of them, who sin and wickedness had not in a great degree, the yoke of my power I placed upon them.*—Esar ii. 10.

I am not sure that we should not punctuate differently, and translate the last clause "heavy the yoke of my power I placed upon them."

¶ [cuneiform], ḫiṭati; *Sins.*

[cuneiform], iššu nir-ya ḫiṭati-su la mina abuq sa aviamu mat-su; *he received my yoke, his sins unnumbered I excused, and I left his country.*—Botta 146, 15–31.

Aviamu is an unusual form, but it appears to be admissible. I think the last clause may be understood "I left him in possession of his country."

¶ [cuneiform], ḫiṭiti; *Sinners.*

[cuneiform], ṣitsta-sunu la bel ḫiṭiti va qalluti sa aru ..... la ibsu usur-sun akbi; *their common people not being sinners or revilers, who occurred(?) were not, I declared their rectitude.*—Sen. T. iii. 6.

ḤDD [cuneiform], [cuneiform], biṭṭatâ, biṭṭâti; *Diggings.* Ch. [illegible]. Syriac [illegible].

[cuneiform], ana babi teṭalum anâti Illta asrasti [mui] ina biṭṭatâ sa Nabokudurauzur sar Dintir-ki abṭut; *for the search of that cylinder three years in the diggings of Nebuchadnezzar, king of Babylon, I dug.*—Nab. Br. Cyl. ii. 53. See also i. 54.

([cuneiform]) [cuneiform], biṭṭâti anâta amur; *to those diggings I looked.*—Nab. Br. Cyl. iii. 21. [A broken bit.]

ḤDT [cuneiform]. Hiṭṭu. See p. 407.

ḤDL [cuneiform], biṭlapa; *Varied, diversified.* Heb. [illegible].

[cuneiform], 22 salhat-anâti sa kusba va alpu biṭlapa palte labâ hummura pira-sun ki ṭaim anna sihpi diddi abul; *twenty-two varied figures, which as to form and attitude were varied, their excellence and lustre united (?), over them, according to my will, large store-house I built.*—Sen. B. iv. 23 = 45 BM 27. [Doubtful.]

[cuneiform], ka anqi sa ille rana sa akitmage alita-sun palte kusbu biṭlapa labe anâtâ ina babâ-sin abnid.—80 BM 26 = Sen. B. iv. 7.

In Sen. B. [cuneiform] varies with [cuneiform], and [cuneiform] with [cuneiform]. The first variant, and the unknown and perhaps incorrect ideogram, preclude my hazarding a translation of this passage, which may roughly mean that the writer erected in the gates of a palace some ornamental works of valuable materials, uniting excellence with beauty. But I am not satisfied with this passage or with the preceding. I believe that *biṭlapa* and *hummura* (perhaps *furrera*, "surrounded," from [illegible]) are "permansives."

ḤDL [cuneiform], ḫidali'at.

[cuneiform], sa kima shamme talime sa hippat shame va irşitu mitḫaris in ḫidali'at Anunnaki.

I am now of opinion that *ḫidali'at* is made up of two words; but I retain it here merely to complete the unfinished line from I Bellis 3, printed in p. 149.

ḤDM [cuneiform], ḫitmudis; *Eagerly.* Heb. חָמַד.

[cuneiform], ana er Marqasi ḫitmudis allik; *to the city of Marqas eagerly I went.*—Botta 142, 9 = 66.

[cuneiform], ana Babel-ki sa ana kasadi amaaaru-su ḫitmudis allik; *to Babylon, on the capture of which I had triumphed, eagerly I went.*—Bavian 44.

ḤDN [cuneiform], Hudan.—Sard. ii. 56.

[cuneiform], Hudanai.—Sard. ii. 80.

A city in the hill country north-east of the Tigris. The city was captured by Sardanapalus, and the people made tributary.

¶ [cuneiform]; see under ḤRB.

ḤDS [cuneiform], ḫadis; *Joyfully, beautifully.* Heb. חָדָה.

[cuneiform], ana hekal-su sa kirib Babel-ki ḫadis eram [erub]; *to his palace, which is in Babylon, joyfully I passed.*—Sen. Gr. 9 · Sen. T. i. 26.

[cuneiform], ana Babel-ki suhazi Bel saqal ili ina elis libbi nambar pani ḫadis erum; *to Babylon, the fortress of Bel, who weighs [judges] the gods, in exultation of heart, and tenacity of face, joyfully I passed.*—Botta 150, 9 = 141. *Erum* for *erub*, because of *sa* following.

HDS ana bit senti ḫadis ina eribi-ka .... Tisinkin subȧn-kha; *to that house happily with thy favour ...., may thy sceptre be held fast.*—Nab. ii. 8.

ana Bit-Ura subat bilut-ka ina ḫidûti va risâti libit gati-ya damgâti ḫadis naplis; *to Bit-Ura, the seat of thy power, in rejoicing and pre-eminence, the work of my hand, with blessings, bountifully do thou grant favour.*—Senh. Cyl. ii. 17.

See also Birs ii. 16; Neb. Bab. ii. 25. *Ḫidûti* and *risati* occur also in E.I.H. iv. 8, and Neb. Gr. i. 46, ii. 24, iii. 72. The abridged form appears to have been abandoned in Babylonia.

HDT ḫattâ, ḫattû; *Fear.* Heb. חתת.

isme ma kisitti erani-su Kudur Nahunda Elamû imqut-su ḫattâ; [2]*heard* [4]*and* [3]*the capture of his cities* [1]*Kudur-Nahunda the Elamite* [5]*overwhelmed him fear.*—Sen. T. iv. 71.

sar Nuvaki kasad erani-su isme ma imqut-su ḫattâ (patâ); *the king of Elam the capture of his cities heard, and overwhelmed him fear.*—Neb. Yun. 39.

A comparison of these passages, which record the same story in almost the same words, will show a much more dislocated sentence in Sen. T. than the one which I have noticed under *Ḫalluḫ*, in p. 442. To understand this we must cut the clause into five bits and read them in the order indicated by the little figures inserted above:—"Kudur-Nahunda the Elamite heard the capture of his cities, and fear overwhelmed him." Guided by such an example we may safely venture to correct similar passages.

pulḫi melamme sarruti-ya ishupu-su ma ittabik-su ḫattû; *reverence of the approach of my majesty covered him, and fear pursued him.*—Botta 151, 8(13) = 111.

HDT [cuneiform], Ḫatti, Ḫatte; *Land of the Hittites; Syria.*

[cuneiform], Kashiya Uramiya ṣabi Ḫatte lâ magiri; *Kashai and Uramai, warriors of the Hittites, not obedient.*—Tig. ii. 101.

[cuneiform], Ḫatte dabib sulapti bilut-su izira; *the Hittites, plotting revolt, his power disowned.*—Botta 149, 11 = 93.

This ancient people appears to have spread over the whole of Syria. The name is very frequently written [cuneiform]. In Botta 67, 28, and 41, 45, we have [cuneiform] and [cuneiform] in a duplicate passage. See the following extract:—

[cuneiform], ina elippi Ḫatti tamtâ lu ebir; *in ships of Syria the sea [river?] I passed.*—Sen. T. iv. 26.

See also Obel. 54, 60, 66, &c. 1 Pal. 11. Esar i. 17; v. 11.

¶ [cuneiform].—Syl. 660.

¶ [cuneiform]. Ḫattabi.—Tig. ii. 44.

King of Urukbikana, capital of Pasar, a province of Kummukha, conquered by Tiglath-pileser.

¶ [cuneiform], ḫidata, ḫiditi. See pp. 403, 407, 408.

ḪUD [cuneiform], aḫut; *Brotherhood.*

[cuneiform] (v. [cuneiform]) [cuneiform], Istardar sar Urardi sa sarri abi-su ana abi-ya isanaḫḫarûni aḫut onlumu; *Istar-dar, king of Armenia, who, though the kings his fathers to my fathers had been allied, the brotherhood had neglected.*—Assur b.p. x. 93. Not quite certain.

ḤZ ḫim; *the Breast (of animals).* Heb. [illegible].

nikbê-su ellati eli ša panâ umaîr sa yom istin alpu mahe marî alpu sal ḫim zalabe damgati; *his large offerings, above what was before, I have restored; of one day [daily] a large ox fatted and a bullock, the breast and ribs excellent.*—Neb. Gr. i. 17.

See *Zalabe*, p. 317; I now render this word by "ribs," comparing the Heb. [illegible], the ẓ being sometimes interchanged with ץ.

¶ (…), Hazû.

20 hazba Ilazû sadi abu sagrilmut ana arki-ya uramir; *twenty hazba's, the country of Hazu, mountains of sagrilmut (?) stone, behind me I left.*—Essr iii. 31.

See *Hazu*, p. 79, and a note in Journ. R.A.S., Vol. 1, new series, 1864, pp. 238-9, by Sir H. Rawlinson, who believes *Hazu* to be the [illegible] of the Book of Job.

¶ ahzu, s. ahzi *obl. pl.*—Assur b.p. vi. 70. Sard. i. 85; ii. 67.

Some articles of value, taken as plunder. From its position in Assurbanipal's inscription, it seems to have been some part of a chariot; see under *Zabab*, p. 330. The root is perhaps אחז, "to hold."

ḤZB ḫiphi, *obl.* ḫipuh, *c.* ḫapalati, ḫaplati, *pl.* *Clay.* Chal. [illegible].

Bel mukin isdi er-ya Nin muḫimat ḫispi zikri babi rabi Bel va Nin sa sit iss-ḫildi ambi; *Bel establishing the foundation of my city, and Nin treading the clay, the names of the great gates of Bel and Nin of the north side I announced.*—Sarg. 58. See p. 321.

Dr. Oppert has rendered this word by "la pierre avec laquel on se taint en bleu," Vol. 2, F.M. p. 341; occasionally by "stone" simply. From the [illegible] of Nabuchadnezzar, I have sometimes thought that "amber" was meant; but this is inadmissible here.

1128 hisiti sadi hispi tamdi ibsi kabitti igisā sumuhu ana er ya Babel-ki ana mahri-su userib; *works of the mountain, clay of the sea, beautiful things many, a combination of pleasure, to my city of Babylon, into his presence I have introduced [made pass].*—E.I.H. ii. 34.

Works of the mountain, perhaps "works of the mines." Dr. Oppert reads "minérals." I have read igisā as for *igisā*, but very doubtfully. I think all the rest probable. See p. 181. Compare the following:—

bisit sadi hisap tamdi kirba-su amhur; *works of the mine, clay of the sea, within it I have received.*—Neb. Gr. iii. 22.

(v. ...) mati kali-sina kima hasbatti aduqqiqu; *the countries all of them like clay I trod down.*—Botta 167, 13. [Revers des Plaques, Menant.]

Bit-Silani ana sihirti-su kima hasbatti adaqqiq; *Bit-Silani, the whole of it, like clay I trod down.*—17 BM 8.

ḪZZ Hamas, Hamdi.—New Div. ii. 11. Sard. iii. 71. 43 BM 29.

A city of Syria. Dr. Oppert renders it Gaza.

ḪZN Hazael; *Hazael, king of Syria.* Heb. חֲזָאֵל

nahr Parrat ebir Hazael sa Syria(?) ana tahazi illiká; *the river Euphrates I crossed, Hazael of Syria to battle came.*—Obel. 97. (Qy. Dam-ṣu = Damascus.)

HZN [cuneiform] arka Ḥazael simtu ubil-su; *afterwards Hazael fate took him.*—Rass. iii. 19.

See also Obel. 97; Assur b.p. viii. 9.

¶ [cuneiform], [cuneiform], ḫazanu, ḫazanni.—2 Mich. i. 18; 3 Mich. iii. 10.

Inserted in enumerations of classes of persons, some of whom are officials, as [cuneiform] and [cuneiform], while others seem to be distinguished by physical qualities, as able and unable [see p. 176]; in Assur b.p. vi. 116, we have the *kipani* and the *ḫazanuti* "of cities," both with the determinative [cuneiform].

¶ [cuneiform], ḫuṣanni; *Arms (brachia).* Heb. חֹצֶן Arab. حضن.

[cuneiform], ina alnapari kabtuti ḫuṣanni-sunu uparrih; *with heavy bands their arms I broke.*—Sen. T. vi. 4.

Not very sure; the Hebrew means rather the bosom than the arm; the Arabic rather the upper part of the body. I think we might read "with heavy bands their hearts, courage, or spirits, I broke."

ḤZS [cuneiform], ḫiṣṣat; *Scrutiny, search; attention.* Ethiop. ኀሠሠ, haśaś, *to investigate.*

[cuneiform], ina mikri ini-ya [si-ya] palki va ḫiṣṣat uzni-ya [pi-ya] palkâti sa Hea Bilat ili eli sarrani abi-ya umaira [illegible]; *with the perception of my open eyes, and the scrutiny of my open ears, which Hea(?) and the Lady of the Gods upon the kings my fathers have caused to turn back with attention.*—Botta 187, 20. [Revers des Plaques, Mérant.]

This passage, taken with those which follow in the inscription, informs us that Sargon, "with eyes and ears which the gods had directed towards his royal ancestors," had resolved to build a city and call it Dur-Sargina. The following extract, from a longer document, says precisely the same thing, but at much greater length. The additions made in this last extract are mostly unintelligible to me; I have very recently examined the original cylinder, and made some changes in a

ḤZR few lesters, but the characters are so very indistinct that I have little confidence in the reading which I give here, though I believe it is rather better than the lithographed copy:—

. Ina miri int-ya palki sa ina kibit el sar apsu bil nimeqi ta bis ta sumsunû sa malû niklâti va ḥisṣat uzni-ya palkâte sa eli sarrani abi-ya Nin sannu suba sa ili usatera ḥaqiqi; *with the perception of my open eyes, which in honour of the god, king of waters, lord of mysteries .... and the scrutiny of my open ears, which upon the kings my fathers Sin mother ..... of the gods, have ceased to turn back with attention.*—Sarg. 28.

ḤZQ . Ḥamqiahu; *Hezekiah.* Heb. חִזְקִיָּה

. sá Ḥamqiahu pulḫi melamme bêluti-ya iḫsupu-su; *him Hezekiah, the fears of the approach of my power overwhelmed him.*—Sen. T. iii. 29.

. ana Ḥamqiyahu Yahudai iddinu-su; *to Hezekiah the Jew they gave him up.*—Sen. T. ii. 71.

See also Sen. T. iii. 11. Neb. Yun. 15.

ḤZR . Ḥazur.—Bavian 11.

The river of Nineveh, still known by the same name.

¶ . Ḥuzirina.—Sard. iii. 94–6. Sh. Ph. I. 48.

A city of Mesopotamia.

¶ . Ḥazitu, Ḥazataï; *Gaza and the Gazites.* Heb. עַזָּה, עַזָּתִי

Mentioned with Ashdod and Ekron, showing it to be the city of the Philistines. See Sarg. 19. Botta 145. 15, 14 = 75. 20; 36, 70. Sen. T. iii. 36. Tig.-jun. 67.

HH ḥiḥi; *Rebels, offenders.* See *Hitti*, p. 406.

¶ Aḥḥa.—Tig. iii. 37, 47; iv. 12.

A people called by Sir H. Rawlinson, doubtfully, *Akhi*, and *Akhi*. Dr. Oppert, in his Sargonides, calls them *Kourkhi*. They are mentioned as inhabiting a large territory in the land of the Khirikhi (Cilicia?). Dr. Hincks and Mr. Talbot thought the word signified "strangers," or "enemies," rather than any gentile name.

¶ aḥḥati; *to Brothers* (*dative case*).

—33 ll. 64.

Aḥḥati-su, "to his brothers," must be plural here, though the Accad equivalent has no plural sign. See *Aḥi-šu*, p. 49, and *Aḥu*, p. 13.

¶ aḥḥuzate, aḥḥuzate; *Possessions, effects.* Heb. אחזת.

aḥḥuzate nisirti hekal-su; *valuable effects of his palace.*—Sard. ii. 122.

aḥḥuzate.—Sard. iii. 71. Monol. 40.

In all three cases the word is included among articles of tribute or plunder. It is accompanied by the adjective in the first extract only.

HHR ḥaḥur; *Sort of Bird.*

—37 ll. 34.

Printed in p. 47, where I made the first letter instead of .

¶ Haḥarga.—Sard. iii. 70.

A country passed by the monarch in a march from Carchemish towards Lebanon. Dr. Oppert reads it "Khamarga."

¶ ḥaḥaris; *Like Flour, or dust.* Syriac [illegible], "a cake."

Kaldu ana gibarti-su ḥaḥaris askup; *Chaldea, to the whole of it, like dust I swept away.*—Tig. Jun. 15.

Madai dirri ana patgimri-sunu ḥaḥaris aktum; *Median .... the whole of them like dust I covered.*—Tig. Jun. 32.

For the value *aktum* see No. 1[illegible] of the Syllabary.

ḤT — ḫitu; *Covering, shelter; mantle.* Heb. [illegible]

— ina ḫitu Ilut-ka rabiti suṣib-anni; *with the mantle of thy great divinity do thou preserve me.*—Nab. ii. 20.

¶ —36 II. 8a. See further 9a, 10a.

ḤID — Ḥaydala.—Sen. T. iv. 73. Neb. Yun. 41.

A city of Susiana.

ḤIN — Ḥayanu, -ai.

A chief of Hindan, near the Euphrates, son of Gabbar.—Sard. i. 96. Now Div. ii. 24, 69.

ḤIP — Ḥayapâda.—Sarg. 20.

Name of a tribe in the neighbourhood of Samaria.

ḤKM

— kima sibbir ḫikuma ina gimlat sadi pasqâte paltis etatik.—Tig. ii. 76.

Sir H. Rawlinson left the first words of this passage blank, translating "like ...... on the peaks of the rugged mountains I marched victoriously." Mr. Talbot doubtfully read "like a nimble mountain goat." Drs. Hincks and Oppert passed over the passage altogether, but the latter has since translated it "[illegible] dans les ravins des montagnes tortueuses." I would suggest, comparing the Chaldee and Hebrew [illegible] and [illegible], "thoughtfully and skilfully over the tops of the mountains royally I passed;" but the irregular construction makes the reading doubtful.

ḤL

—Syl. 757.

" 758.

" 576.

One sound of [illegible] is shown to be *ḫal* by No. 758; and it would appear from No. 757 that one meaning would be "reverence," but I have not met with it; there is a little [illegible] over the [illegible] on the slab. See also the following line:—

—7 II. 10d.

ḪL [cuneiform], *Twenty(?).*

We have certainly a number here, the double of [cuneiform], whatever that may be, and in form at least the half of [cuneiform], which is admitted to be "four;" [cuneiform] occurs in 2 Mich. i. 1. See p. 189.

[cuneiform] ..... [cuneiform], 20(?) bilat kaspi 20(?) bilat hurasi .... amhur; *twenty(?) talents of silver, twenty(?) talents of gold, ... I levied.*—Sard. ii. 121.

[cuneiform] ..... [cuneiform]. 60 mana hurasi 10(?) bilat kaspi 20(?) bilat sahum . . .. amtahar; *sixty manehs of gold, ten(?) talents of silver, twenty(?) talents of sahum .... I levied.*—N. Div. ii. 28.

After all I do not think it likely that the numbers I have set down here can be admitted; we should hardly have [cuneiform] and [cuneiform] in the same line, as we find in New Div. ii. 28, if [cuneiform] and [cuneiform] were equivalent. Possibly some fractional quantity is intended.

¶ [cuneiform] is sometimes used as a plural sign instead of [cuneiform]; see [cuneiform] varying with [cuneiform] in Sard. i. 71; ii. 10, and elsewhere; I think we have [cuneiform] in N. Div. i. 29, but the word is in a damaged corner of the monolith. I do not remember to have seen [cuneiform] as the plural sign after any other word than city, unless it may be so read in the following line:—

[cuneiform] [v. [cuneiform]] [cuneiform]. Bil-baladan olai alik pan ummani-sunu ishi-sunu ina kappi [su] aşbita; *Bil-baladan (and) the men going before their soldiers, with them in hands I captured.*—Sard. iii. 20.

Dr. Oppert makes this "Bel-bal-adan, le guerrier qui marchait à la tête de leurs armées, tombèrent entre mes mains." I think "their soldiers" would not suit his translation as well as that which I give.

¶ [cuneiform] is occasionally written instead of [cuneiform]; see [cuneiform] in 2 II. 50 d, which is shown to require the separation of [cuneiform] and [cuneiform] by the duplicate [cuneiform], above, in 2 II. 51a. Such words will be entered under letter R.

¶ [cuneiform], qallala.—2 II. 32 *d.*

Qu. "Crowd of people." Arab. قُلَّة, قُلَل pl.

[cuneiform]—Syl. 660.

ḪL [cuneiform]. Accadian; *Evil, hostile.*

This word occurs frequently in the bilingual slabs, and is rendered in Assyrian by [cuneiform]. See the following extracts, taken from many of the same kind:—

[cuneiform] . [cuneiform].—17 II. 1 a. *Hostile gods.*

[cuneiform] . [cuneiform].—17 II. 4 a. *Hostile genies.*

[cuneiform] . [cuneiform].—18 II. 42 c. *Evil spirits.*

In the same slab we have [cuneiform] as an adjective, with words denoting parts of the body:—

[cuneiform] . [cuneiform], pan limouti; *bad face.*—17 II. 31 a.

[cuneiform] . [cuneiform], ina limuttû; *bad eye.*—17 II. 31 a.

[cuneiform] . [cuneiform], pû limnu; *sore mouth.*—17 II. 32 a.

[cuneiform] . [cuneiform]. lisan limuttû; *sore tongue.*—17 II. 32 a.

I do not know why the Assyrian word varies; the reason for the plural termination does not seem very clear. *Lim* being one of the sounds of [cuneiform], the word [cuneiform] is pronounced *limnu* rather than *ninu*, in order to retain the analogy with the forms in which the pronunciation is unmistakeably *limnu*. The Hebrew [Hebrew] would otherwise be a good authority for *ninu*.

I may remark here that the Accadian *ḫul* appears to be connected etymologically with the Semitic [Hebrew] more nearly than the corresponding Assyrian *limnu* with any other Semitic root known to me. And this is not the only instance, the Accadian [cuneiform] (*er*), "a city," is exactly the Hebrew עִיר, while the *alu*, which always represents it in the Assyrian column of the bilingual tablets, has no Semitic analogous root known to me. See p. 51.

¶ [cuneiform], ḫul; *Armies, troops.* Heb. חַיִל.

[cuneiform], lipara šil ḫuli alḫi asib libbi Sunana; *were broken down the bands, the troops, and the people, dwelling within Sunana* [*Babylon*].—Bl. St. l. 10.

I consider *lipara* a passive of *par*, Heb. פרר. Sunana appears to have been the same as Imgur-bel; see the following extract:—

[cuneiform], [cuneiform]. Imgur-bel = Dûru Sunana-ki.—50 II. 25 a.

ḪL [cuneiform], ḫula, ḫull; *Sand.* Heb. חול.

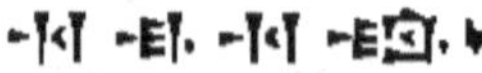

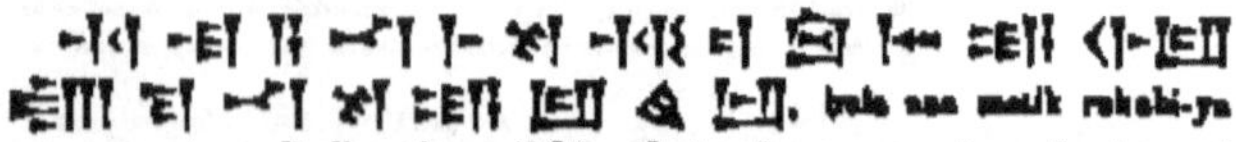

[cuneiform], ḫula ana mašik rukubi-ya va ummanate-ya lutib; *the sand [desert] for the passage of my chariots and my troops I made good.*—Tig. ii. 9.

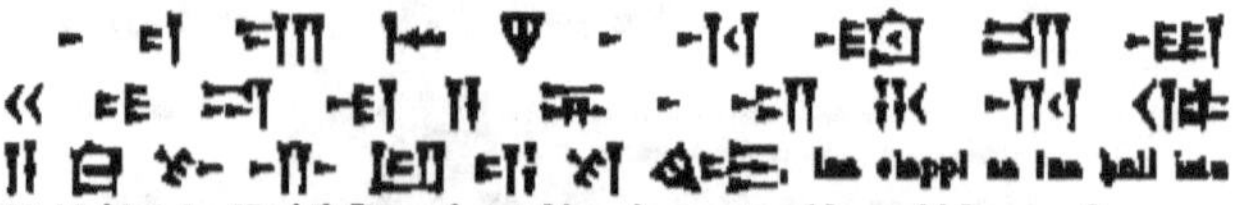

[cuneiform], ina elippi sa ina ḫull istu 20 iddidui ina Ḫaridi Purat lu etebir; *in twenty ships, which were drawn up on the sand in Kharidi, I crossed the Euphrates.*—Sard. iii. 34.

This is another example of a dislocated sentence; see pp. 409 and 410. Word for word this would read "in ships which in the sand from twenty were drawn up, I passed the Euphrates." We might, perhaps, understand "from twenty" as meaning "about twenty," and then there would be no necessity for having recourse to the somewhat objectionable supposition of a dislocation; but I have not found *ist-u* so used. I suppose *iddidui* to be put for *ittadadu*, the Niphal 3rd pers. pl. fem., with the suffix *ui* required by the relative.

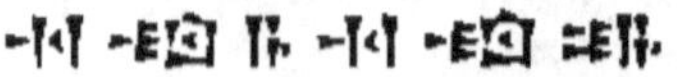

¶ [cuneiform], ḫulis, ḫuliya.

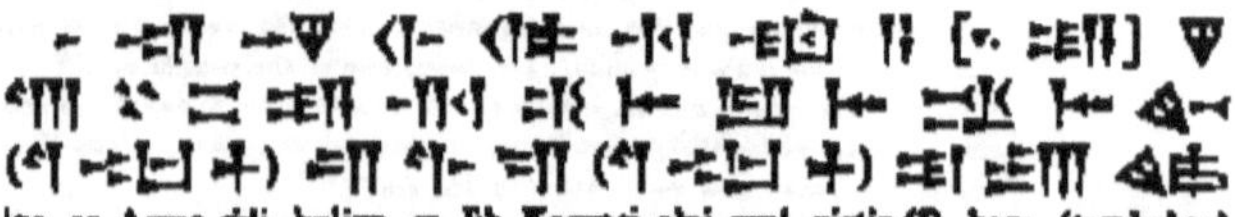

[cuneiform], ina er Asmar siddi ḫuliya sa lib Kasyari alpi seni gimlu(?) ḫam (tamkabar) gurpisi (tamkabar) attaḫar; *in the city of Asmar ..... which is in Kasyari, cattle, sheep, goats(?), and articles of copper I received.*—Sard. ii. 96.

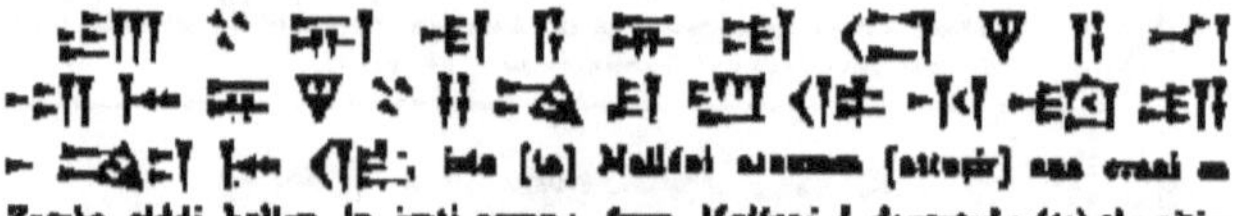

[cuneiform], istu [ta] Mallani atumus [attupir] ana erani sa Zamba siddi ḫuliya ina isati asrup; *from Mallani I departed;* (to) *the cities of Zamba .... in fire I burned.*—Sard. iii. 102.

If *siddi-ḫulia* mean "the neighbourhood of the sand," or desert, as I think likely, we can make sense of the first extract by a transposition. The version might be "in my city of Asmar on the sandy side, which is in Kasyari," &c. I do not see how the second extract can be understood unless by omitting *sa* and *siddi-ḫuliya*. *Atumus*, which is translated "I departed," is a curious variation from the regular [cuneiform] or [cuneiform]. In the long inscription of Sardanapalus *attumir* is very frequently used, but in a few cases we have instead of it *atumus*, as above; *atumus* in l. ii. 7 and 8; *attumis* in i. 58 and several times in col. iii.; besides other forms less different from the usual *attumir*. I do not understand these variations, nor do I remember seeing them in other inscriptions.

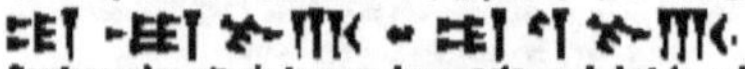

HLA [cuneiform] alm.—Sard. i. 80.

A city of Gilhhi, occupied by Sardanapalus in the first year of his reign.

¶ [cuneiform] Ḫulai.—Sard. i. 102, 107, 108, 110.

A rebel chief of a province in Armenia, captured and flayed by Sardanapalus, in his chief city Kinabu.

HLB [cuneiform] ḫalip; *Protector.*

[cuneiform] ḫalip naḫarrati; *protector of the timid.*—Sarg. 7. Botta 36, 9. 23 BM 3.

Doubtful; in all cases it is an epithet of Sargon. *Ḫalip* is the participle of a verb, signifying "to cover," as shown by varying with *kātim*. I have not found it in another Semitic language. *Naḫarrat* certainly means "fear" sometimes, but it varies with *namurrat* (Sard. ii. 119).

¶ [cuneiform]—29 II. 58 d.

[cuneiform]—18 II. 35 d.

¶ [cuneiform].—Bab-ḫilliba.—Neb. Gr. i. 31. E.I.H. ii. 31.

Name of one of the gates of Babylon; the last letter is ambiguous in both monuments, but I think it most like [cuneiform].

¶ [cuneiform] Ḫalbuda.—Sen. T. iii. 67.

A city in the mountains of *Nipur*, attacked and plundered in Sennacherib's fifth expedition. This *Nipur* is clearly not the place now called *Niffer*.

¶ [cuneiform] Ḫilbunā.—Neb. Gr. i. 22.

A province mentioned with half-a-dozen others, all unknown to me; perhaps Helbon חֶלְבּוֹן of Ezek. xxvii. 18, now Aleppo.

HLD [cuneiform] Ḫaldia.—Botta 146, 4, 5 = 76, 77.

An Armenian god, mentioned in connection with [cuneiform], which might be read *Bagmaśtu*, very much like the Zend *Bag-mash-dis*. Ḫaldia occurs frequently on the Van inscriptions of Schulz.

HLZ [cuneiform] ḫalṣani. See under HLZ.

ḤLH , ——, *the River Tigris.*—Obel. 93. Sard. ii. 104. St. 2.

Both inscriptions of Sardanapalus have the variant , proving the value. See p. 128, and the following extract from II. 11 a:—

——, ḥalḥal - garara sa mee; "*rumbling of the waters.*"

I do not understand the following:—

—— , .—18 II. 46 a.

¶ , , —— .—Syl. 390.

¶ , ḥalḥallat; *Longing, desire.* Heb. [illegible].

....

pir tâlo sâtu ḥalḥallat libbi-ya bekal [bit-rab] abu pili .... usepis; *upon that mound, the desire of my heart a palace of fine stone .... I caused make.*—Bro. T. vi. 41. I think is put for here.

ḤLK , . Ḥilukai.—New Div. i. 64.

This may be Cilicia, but the passage is unfinished.

ḤLL , ——, ḥallû; *Common.* Heb. חֹל. 1 Sam. xxi. 4.

, lû abu lu ḥallû mamma sakuû; *whether a head man or a common man ever he might be.*—Monol. 77. See p. ?.

¶ , ——, Bit-ḥallu. See p. 136.

I think I mentioned in that page all I knew about this word. I will only add here that whatever the warlike implements might have been, they were numerous in the Assyrian armies; in Obel. 89 four hundred and seventy were present, against eleven hundred and twenty-one chariots; whereas they are set down in Sh. Ph. iv. 46 at two hundred, being double the number of chariots; in New Div. ii. 90 the army of Benhadad of Damascus is said to have been accompanied by twelve hundred of each.

¶ . Ḥalli.—Botta 158, 18 30.

Father of Ambris, king of Tubal.

HLL ḫallû; *Profaned.* Heb. חלל

asar [ki] ḫallû usabsi nisi asib libbi-su usarsa sipitta va zirḫa; *the place profaned I caused to be, (to) the people dwelling in it I assigned mourning and wailing.*—Botta 148, 6 – 7.

¶ Ḫalule.—Sen. T. v. 47. Bavian 35.

A city on the Tigris, where Sennacherib gained a battle against the Elamites and Babylonians. The city is named *K'halulina* in l. 47 of the Nebi Yunus inscription.

¶ ḫallupti; *Coverings.*

ḫallupti kurrai ḫallupti sabi; *coverings of horses, coverings of men.*—Sard. i. 80. See also ii. 120; iii. 22.

¶ ḫalliq, ḫalluq, ḫalluqu.

These three words are put here because they may be from the same root, which is used in the sense of dividing and distributing, and sometimes, I think, of carrying away. I cannot understand the clauses in which they occur.

usaḫas iḫappitu iḫappiru ka-sa ana barti(?) asteimû ana ḫalliq salam-ya annie.—Monol. 73.

The three verbs at the commencement, "shall divide, shall carve, shall scrape," may refer to the statues of the king, which I would read "for the separation (breaking up?) of these my statues." See my first attempt in p. 129.

nasu adis ḫalliq.—Monol. 78.

This follows the sentence under ḫalls, in p. 422.

mata ḫalluqa nisi.—Bl. 84. i. 21.

Something about land and people, but the whole sentence is unintelligible to me.

ḤLM , Ḥilmu.—Sen. T. iv. 27. Neb. Yun. 20.

A province on the borders of Elam.

. Ḥilimmu.—Botta 145, 6-20. Tig. jun. 13.

This city, mentioned among places on the borders of Elam, is probably the same as Ḥilmu, notwithstanding the change of the determinative.

¶ , ḫblami, -ut; *Strong men.* Heb. [illegible]

ana lib ḫblami-ya Aramya nikrut Asur bil-ya la allik; *in the midst of my strong men, (against) the Aramæans, enemies of Assur my lord, I went.*—Tig. v. 46.

Uncertain.

¶ . Ḥalman.

ina sitribi sa Simeçi la ris sad Ḥalman urida; *by the pass of Simeçi on the top of Mount Ḥalman, I descended.*—Obel 190.

The above is Dr. Hincks's version, nearly the same as the following of Dr. Oppert:—"Je descendis vers les districts de Simisi vers la naissance du Mont Halvan." Simesi has the determinative in l. 24. This is the close of the Nimrud Obelisk, and the descent is from the country of the Nairi. I have left the determinative in the heading because I think it not unlikely that, not a mountain, but a province or city was intended; perhaps the same as the following city, near the upper course of the Euphrates, named in the more recently found monolith of Shalmaneser:—

¶ . Ḥalman.—New Div. ii. 67.

ḤLN . Ḥulun.—Sard. i. 59.

A city in the country of Dirhi.

¶ . Bit-ḫilâni, -ḫilmuni. Heb. "a jewel."

Bit-appati tamsil hekal Hatti sa ina lisan Marta Bit-ḫilâni isaqqa-su usepis; *Bit-appati, like a Syrian temple, which in the language of the west [Phœnicia], Bit-ḫilâni they call it, I caused build.*—Botta 16bis 107. See more in p. 115.

ḤLP [cuneiform]. Bit-halupe.—Sard. i. 75, 76; iii. 5, 7, 8, 20.

Name of a province and city, near *Dura* on the Euphrates; it would appear that *Dura* was included in the province. There is no determinative in the first column, but in the third column [cuneiform] is put in l. 6, and [cuneiform] in l. 7, both *before* [cuneiform], and this is done with the object of distinguishing the city from the province; in l. 8 the copies vary between [cuneiform] and [cuneiform]; in l. 20 we have the further variant [cuneiform] *Bit or Upalupe.*

¶ [cuneiform], halpu; *Variable, changing.* Heb. חָלַף.

[cuneiform], ina ummat kaṣil halpe suripi ina ummat niphi mul kan-sidi; *in the days of variable storms and heat, in the days of the rising of the star* . . . . .—Br. Obel i. 14.

The "star" which I have transliterated *kan-sidi* occurs among the "twelve stars of Accad," 4931.16; and again in i. 13dy and lastly in i. 48r, among the "stars of Elam."

ḤLZ [cuneiform], halzi, halzani; *Castle, garrison.* Heb. חָלַץ.

[cuneiform], lišt irṣi ana kildnu halzi rabiti ina kupri va agurri abni; *the walls of the citadel(?) for the strengthening of the great castle in brick and cement I built.*—Neb. Bab. ii. 16.

[cuneiform], 27 mahazi adi halzani-sunu sa istu [ta] Salmanaris sar kiprat arbati abi-ya ikkiruni . . . . ina niri-ya uskniš; *twenty-seven fortresses with their garrisons, which from Shalmaneser, king of the four countries, my father, had revolted . . . . to my yoke I subdued.*—Sh. Ph. i. 50.

[cuneiform] comes after [cuneiform], making, as it were, a compound word. I understand the meaning to be "a garrison-town."—

[cuneiform], 11 er-halzani-su marsúti akšud ina išati akru; *eleven of his difficult garrison-towns I took, and in fire I burned.*—Botta 149, 6 - 12.

ḪLZ [cuneiform], er-ḫalzani ali-su urakkis ina ape bab-rab er-su ubira; *his garrison-towns over him I seized, and the posts of the great gate of his city I carried off.*—Sen. T. iii. 21.

ḪLS [cuneiform], ḫilisar.

[cuneiform], maziq ḫilisar asappiḫa eli-sunu; *disaster .... I poured upon them.*—Assur b.p. vi. 112.

I cannot find any satisfactory etymology for *ḫilisar*; but I suppose it may be an adjective qualifying *maziq*, which I doubtfully render "disaster." Heb. נזק

ḪLT [cuneiform], ḫalta; *a sort of Stone.*

[cuneiform] .... [cuneiform], ina yumsuni sa ana abni ka abni ḫalta va abni kagina ina sadini sa Nairi .... assa; *at that time the stones ka, and ḫalta, and kagina, in the mountains of Nairi .... I took.*—Tig. viii. 11.

¶ [cuneiform], [cuneiform].* ḫalti, ḫaltu; *Sickness, evil, injury.* Heb. חלה

[cuneiform], Yav ina ziqir(?) ḫulte mat-su libyu; *Yav with the pouring out of pestilence his land may he lay waste.*—Tig. viii. 84.

---

* I have hitherto made no distinction between [cuneiform] (the determinative of beasts of burden and the name of some such beast, probably "the ass") and [cuneiform], ser or ṣu, which I transliterate by ṣi. Two years ago my attention was called to this by a letter from Dr. Oppert, but having at that time no idea that any distinction existed, I thought he was referring to a typographical peculiarity only. Very recently Mr. G. Smith suggested to me that the two forms were essentially distinct, and I have since then carefully examined several inscriptions with the object of getting at the truth. The result proves, with three or four exceptions, probably errors of the copyist, that Dr. Oppert was right; and I have found incidentally, to my surprise, that his list printed in the Expédition en Mésopotamie, in 1859, contains the two characters clearly discriminated. I think [cuneiform] was sounded *pas*; it is written [cuneiform] several times on the stones which I call 2 Michaux and 3 Michaux, and on the Behistun Inscription in lines 36, 59, and 75. Dr. Oppert also gives [cuneiform] as the Babylonian form. See Syl. 150.

HLT [cuneiform], ana sarrani liveti-su zirati Assur-ki ispur assu hulti ebusu eli nisi liveti-su bilut-su (bilutsu) usakkar; *to the kings of his vicinity disaffected to Assyria he sent; for the evil (which) he did, over the people of his neighbourhood his power I set aside.*—Bells 1 iv, 8 = 92. See p. 367.

I think the relative might always be omitted when the verb following has the augment; see p. 272.

[cuneiform]. enuma Assurdaninpal in tarsi Shalmaneser abi-su eiruma eruti piha ...... amat hulti uselu ma mat usbalkit; *now Sardanapalus in opposition to Shalmaneser his father had made hostilities and commotions ...., he raised a party of evil and caused the land to revolt.*—Sh. Ph. i. 40.

[cuneiform] amat hulte la isimmu; *(he who) a party of evil shall not listen to.*—Monol. 43.

The same without the negative in I. 81.

Hulte must be an adverb; like *birta*, *kibs*, *cant*, *ivira*, &c. The following extract is an example:—

[cuneiform]. ili rabi mala ina nari anni sum-sunu zakru arrat la napsuri hulte l'ruru-su; *the great gods, whoever in this tablet their names are recorded, (with) curses untold grievously may they curse him.*—1 Mich. iv. 21.

I am not quite sure that I have done right in rendering [cuneiform] by "name."

¶ [cuneiform]. Hulain.—Sen. T. v. 36.

One of several tribes who joined Suzub and Umman-menan, king of Elam, in an unsuccessful attack upon Babylon.

HM [cuneiform], *issue*; *Command, decree.* See [cuneiform], &c., in p. 102.

A comparison of the following examples will show that [cuneiform] is but an orthographical variation of [cuneiform]; it will, therefore, have the various meanings of the Heb. [Hebrew]

[cuneiform], ki ina Kummuhi ushakuni temu utteru-ni umá er Suru sa Bit-halupe ittapalkit; *while in Comukha I was stationed, notice they brought me that the city Sur in Bit-khalupe had revolted* [*crossed over*]—Sard. i. 75. See i. 101; ii. 23, 60; iii. 27.

In all these we have umá, which seems to signify the conjunction "that," but I have never seen it anywhere else; compare the following:—

[cuneiform], ki ina er Kalhi ushakuni temu uttera-ni nisu Pattinai Lubarni bil-sunu iduku; *whilst in the city of Calah I was staying, notice they brought me (that) the men Patinai Lubarni their lord had killed.*—Obel. 147.

¶ [cuneiform], Himo.—Tig. iv. 10.

A province of Urkhi, subdued by Tiglath-pileser; one of the Abbr. See p. 116.

¶ [cuneiform].—30 II. 53 d.

[cuneiform] „ 55 d.

[cuneiform] „ 56 d.

[cuneiform] „ 57 d.

These extracts from a bilingual tablet contain the word [cuneiform] equated in lines 56 and 57 with *namru*, "the beginning." They form the foundation of a very learned but rather hypothetical paper by Dr. Hincks, finished a few weeks before his death, and printed in the Monatsbericht of the Berlin Academy, Oct. 1866, pp. 647-651. Dr. Hincks considered *ḫimo* to be etymologically connected with the Hebrew [Hebrew], "to live or recover," and therefore to signify "to emerge" after an eclipse. He translated the first of the four lines quoted "The moon emerged from the shadow while the sun was rising." I would doubtfully suggest "The eclipse (or darkness) was at its height commencing with the day."

ḤMA [cuneiform], Ḥumua.—Tig. iv. 77.

A province of Nairi, one of twenty-three conquered by Tiglath-pileser after crossing the Upper Euphrates.

ḤMB [cuneiform], Bit-ḥamban.—Sarg. 13. Tig. jun. 29, 34.

A province included by both monarchs among several others subdued and rendered tributary. The enumerations are indiscriminate; but the place in question appears, in the smaller list of Sargon, to be in the mountainous country north of Assyria.

¶ [cuneiform], Ḥumbanigas.—Botta 65, 5.

[cuneiform], idem. Botta 151, 15 = 153.

A king of Elam, who joined Merodach-baladan in his war against Sargon. The name is usually written with the non-phonetic form [cuneiform] for ḥumba, the sound of which is known by comparing the names given in the parallel passages pointed out above. See also Botta 145, 11 = 13, and 22 BM 7. Ḥumba or Ḥumban appears to be the name of an Elamite god, and Dr. Oppert, with great probability, suggests that the name Ḥumbanigas denotes "protection of Ḥumba," alleging the Scythic [cuneiform], nigas, "to protect." See Journ. R.A.S. Vol. 15, p. 102.

We have [cuneiform], Ḥumban-undasa, an "officer of the king of Elam," in Sen. T. v. 69.

ḤMD [cuneiform], Ḥimdiel.—Sard. iii. 46.

A chief of Laqa, imprisoned by Sardanapalus, and compelled to an increase of tribute.

ḤMṬ [cuneiform], ḥamṭu: *Powerful.* Chal. [Hebrew] Arab. [Arabic].

[cuneiform], sapin ḥamṭu ṣiru; *the subverter powerful and lofty.*—Tig. v. 42. Epithet of the monarch.

ḤML [cuneiform]. ḥamiluḫḫi: *Stores, collections.* Syr. [Syriac]

[cuneiform]. ḥamiluḫḫi va tala kalla-su enaḫu-ma ultu uššê-su adi gabdibbi-su epuš; *the stores and all its mass had decayed, and from its foundation to its roof I (re)built it.*—Brok. Obel. ii. 2.

This is a rare form; I have sometimes found a triliteral root augmented by repeating one of the radicals at the end, as ṭiddiḫ from ṭ(ḫ)l.; I understand by "stores and tiles" the body of the building and its appurtenances; see p. 255.

ḤMM [cuneiform].—Syl. 268. *Light or heat*, perhaps both.

¶ [cuneiform], ḥammu'i; *Heat*. Heb. חמם.

[cuneiform], malik sarus Amatti sa mašak Ilubi'di ḥammu'i iṣruba sabupis; *the extirpator of the root of Hamath, who the skin of Ilubi'di with heat had burned entirely*.—Sarg. 23.

It is stated in Botta 145, 23–35 that Ilubi'di of Hamath (called there Iaubi'di) was flayed (mašaš-su akus, "his skin I cut off"). This will justify the drift of my translation, but I cannot vouch for its entire accuracy; iṣruba sabupis occurs in a passage of Botta 151, 24–138, where the reading is "the waters of his rivers with the corpses of his soldiers iṣruba sabupis;" iṣruba is here the direct plural, and not the indirect singular, as in Sarg. 23. Dr. Hincks (Armen. p. 46) renders the verb "redden"—"they reddened the waters." This would do for "reddening the skin" also. We have in Tig. iv. 20 pagri quradi-suna [illegible] iṣrub, where this might do, by supplying a preposition before pagri, but better by reading eṣrub, "I strewed," Heb. זרב; and the same in Sard. ii. 16, 56, 115, and in N. Div. ii. 78. To [illegible] I have rendered "entirely." Dr. Hincks has suggested "like a slaughter house," and Dr. Oppert "comme un tronc d'arbre;" but these are not everywhere applicable, and Dr. Oppert himself writes "comme des feuilles," in Tig. iv. 20. Castell gives us "shake out (a cloth)" for the Chaldee [illegible], which would point to something like what I have written.

¶ [cuneiform], ḥammami, ḥammami. Arab. [illegible]

[cuneiform], ḥammami sa arba'.—Sarg. 9.

[cuneiform], ḥammami sa arba'.—Botta 167, 14.

The meaning is clearly the four regions. Castell renders the Arabic word "circuitus regionis," but I do not find this in Golius. See a note in p. 504.

¶ [cuneiform], Ḥammurabi.—B.I. Pl. 4, No. XV. l. 6; ii. 1. Hamm. l. 1, 17.

A king of the ancient Assyrian dynasty, whose reign may be placed in the 16th century B.C. The earliest inscription in the Assyrian language yet found is one of this monarch. I have no doubt that the name [illegible] is Ḥammurabi, as read by Mr. Talbot.

HMM Ḥammath, -ti, -tal.—Cyprus St. i. 62. Tig. jun. 58. Heb. חֲמָת.

The land of *Hamath*. See p. 39, where I have entered some forms of this name commencing with . The country seems to have been something more than the Cœle-Syria of the classical writers, which must have derived its name of *Hamath* from that of a city on the Orontes, either Emesa or Epiphania, called in modern maps *Hems* and *Hamah*.

ḤMN Ḥamanu, -nû, -ni, -na.

Amanus, a mountain chain dividing Syria from Cilicia; may be considered a part of Mount Taurus. New Sen. T. vi. 17? ... Sard. iii. 89. Cyprus St. i. 16. Eme vi. 14, &c.

ḤMR (v.), Bit-ḥamri.—Tig. viii. 1, 15.

A temple built for the god Yav by Shamsi-Yav, one of the ancient sovereigns of Assyria, who reigned about 2450 years B.C., and restored by Tiglath-pileser I. The name may have signified the "red temple." Heb. חָמַר. Ps. lxxv. 8.

¶ Ḥumri; *Omri, king of Israel*. Heb. עָמְרִי.

The name of the king of Israel who built *Samaria* (1 Kings xvi. 24). It appears that this monarch was sufficiently celebrated to give his name to his country and his descendants.

.... madata sa Yahua tur Ḥumri ... amḫar-su; *tribute of Jehu, son of Omri .... I received it*.—Epig. 2 of Obelisk.

¶ Ḥumri; *Land of Israel*.

Bit-Ḥumria; *idem*.

Zurra Zidunu Ḥumri Udumu Palastu; *Tyre, Sidon, Samaria, Edom, Palestine*.—1 Pul. 12.

The territories are certainly denoted here, rather than cities.

sapin Samerina kala Bit-Ḥumria; *sweeping Samaria (and) all Bit-Omri [Israel]*.—Botta 36, 19.

murip Bit-Ḥumria rapsi; *partitioner of the broad land of Israel*.—Sarg. 10.

ḤMR [cuneiform]. Ḥamrana.—Bellino 15, 9, 18. Sen. Gr. 16. Sen. T. i. 45.

[cuneiform]. Ḥamranai.—Tig. jun. 5.

Dr. Oppert translates this by Hamran, which is a probable meaning. We have a city Ḥamranu in Sen. T. iv. 59.

¶ [cuneiform]. Ḥuvarizma.—Beh. 6.

[cuneiform]. Ḥuvarizma'.—No. 6, N.R. 12.

Persian [cuneiform], Uvârazmiya, at Behistun:

[cuneiform], Uvârazmish, at Nakhsh-i-Rustam.

The province of Khwarizm.

ḤMS [cuneiform]. ḥamisserat; *Fifteen.* Heb. חמש עשרה

I have placed this word here, thinking it likely that it was intended to be [cuneiform]. See Syl. 139. The following extracts from bilingual lists contain direct evidence of the numerical value of some words connected with "five:"—

[cuneiform]. ḥansâ; *Fifty.*—62 II. 45*d*. Heb. חמשים

[cuneiform]. ḥamisserat; *Fifteen.*—62 II. 49*d*.

[cuneiform]. ḥamisti; *Five.*—62 II. 51*d*. Heb. חמשה

In almost all cases the numeral was expressed by figures instead of words, as in the following extracts; the sound *ḥamisi* is conjectural:—

[cuneiform]. ina ḥamisi pal-ya; *in my fifth year.*—Obel. 52.

[cuneiform]. ina ḥamisi garri-ya; *in my fifth expedition.*—Assur b.p. Ht. 63.

ḤMT [cuneiform]. Ḥamatai; *Hamath.*—Sard. i. 75. See *Ḥammania*, p. 430.

¶ [cuneiform]. Ḥamut.—Tig. jun. 10. 17 BM 8.

Name of a place where Tiglath-pileser built a city, which he called Kar-Assur. See *Tel-ḥiburi*, p. 467, where I have quoted from Tig. jun. 10 the passage referring to *Ḥamut*. In the bull (17 BM 8) we have [cuneiform], *ḥupaenni*, printed instead of [cuneiform], *ḥpikkisu-ni*. It is just possible that this may be some Accadian form unknown to me; but I am rather inclined to believe it an error of the copyist: the other part of the clause is correct. In the city which I have called *Tel-ḥiburi*, [cuneiform], is written [cuneiform], *ḥuri*, on the bull, which occurs as a variant of *Ḥaurri*, under *Dil-ḥauri*, p. 431.

ḪMT ḫimetl, or ḫiḫilti.—Neb. Gr. i. 20; ii. 33.

In the inscription here cited there is a sentence three times repeated, which is printed in p. 92, signifying that Nebuchadnezzar had placed many fishes and birds in a lake or pond, in honour of the god Marduk. This is followed in two cases by passages which are evidently of liturgical meaning, but they contain so many unknown words that I can make nothing of them. I copy them here as usual, adding in this case a comparative transliteration so arranged as to facilitate a collation of the passages for future students.

dispâ ḫimeti sisbâ dumuk-sa asmû karanû daspâ sikar ṣatû karanû ellu.—Neb. Gr. i. 20.

daspâ ṣira ina karanû sikar ṣatû karanû ellû dispa ḫimeti sisbâ bul-sa asmû.—Neb. Gr. ii. 33.

On examination, these two lines will be found to contain each three clusters, arranged in inverse order; I place them here in juxta-position, reversing the second line to preserve the parallelism:—

Col. i.—Dispâ ḫimeti sisbâ dumuk-sa asmû | karanû daspâ | sikar ṣatû karanû ellu.
Col. ii.—Dispa ḫimeti sisbâ bul-sa asmû | daspâ ṣira ina karanû | sikar ṣatû karanû ellû.

On the third repetition we have only the following short line:—

tibik ṣira ina la sebû mamla karanû.—Neb. Gr. iii. 15.

ḪN Ḫâna.—Br. Obel. i. 17.

One of several provinces where the monarch carried on his hunting expeditions; the only name among them known to me is *Kasiyara*, which was in or near Commagene.

¶ Ḫânu, n. Ḫâni, g.—New Div. i. 42.

Name of a chief of the city *Lutibu*, in the province of Sam'la, not far from Carchemish.

ḪNB Ḫanban.—Obel. 95.

Name of the father of *Yanzu*, who was made king of Nairi by Shalmaneser.

ḤND ḫandi; *Excellent, wished-for.*—Heb. חֶמְדָּה.

mûtu limnu amruk-sunuti ina rum(?) antar ḫandi mimiḫ imas-su akul; *a bad death I inflicted on them; with a sword of excellent iron and the laying on of fire I consumed him.*—Assur b.p. iv. 56. Doubtful.

¶ ḫandiv; *to my wish, willingly, eagerly.*

.... kima anaku .... ḫandiu usaklilu; *as I ...... to my wish completed (it).*—Tig. viii. 81.

ḫandiu laban danauti sa Assur usatlima ina kappi-ya asbat; *eagerly the powerful bow which Assur had entrusted to my hand, I seized.*—Sen. T. v. 38.

¶ Hindanu, -ai.

A city near Suru, on the Euphrates. See Sard. i. 80; iii. 12. 13. 27, 35. Sh. Ph. i. 60.

¶ Hindaru.—Botta 145, 7 = 19; 151, 10 = 177; 16bis 76. Sen. T. i. 44; v. 30.

One of many tribes of South Chaldæa, usually lumped together; written *Hindiru*, in Tig. jun. 8.

¶ Handurai.—Sh. Ph. iii. 47.

Mentioned with many other places belonging to Nairi, all tributary to Shamas Phul.

ḤNT ḫantu; *Circuitous.* Chal. [illegible]

ana misir Assur ki utirru allaku ḫantu ana kirib Nineveh illika-mma usannâ; *to the border of Assyria they returned, a circuitous way to the midst of Nineveh he went, and repeated.*—Assur b.p. i. 62.

ḪNN (). ḫin, ḫinnu; a *Cabin*. Heb. חנות Jerem. xxxvii. 16.

. () ḫinnu elippi; *cabin of a ship*.—62 II. 58*d*.

¶ () () , Ḫanunu.

Name of a king of Gaza (Ḫaziti). See Botta 88, 70; 40, 29; 145, 18–25. Sarg. 19. Tig. jun. 62.

ḪNṢ . , Ḫanuṣu.—Tig. v. 88.

Capital of the country of the Comani.

ḪNQ , ḫinqi; *Narrow parts*. Heb. חנק

, ana ris Puratte azbat adi ḫinqi sa Puratte attarid; *to the head of the Euphrates I took* (*my way*), *to the narrows of the Euphrates I went down*.—Sard. iii. 30.

, ina ḫinqi sa Puratte attigil ina giri-ya sa aquḫru Aziel; *in the narrows of the Euphrates I turned aside in my course, and circumvented Aziel*.—Sard. iii. 44.

ḪNR . , Ḫanirabi.—Tig. v. 34. Sard. ii. 92.

This province would appear to belong to Nairi, as it was subdued in the course of an expedition to that country. Dr. Oppert calls it Khanigalbat. The capital was named Milidia. The name occurs also on the much damaged side of the Broken Obelisk.

¶ , ḫiniraṣ.—Botta 132, 8–141.

Appears to be an epithet of "gold." It is not unlikely that may be a single letter; if this be the case, the word under consideration will be equivalent to of Assur b.p. vi. 62. See p. 387.

ḪNS . ḫansa; *Fifty*. See *Ḫamisserut*, p. 439.

ḪNT , Ḫintiel. See *Ḫibiltiel*, p. 402.

HSD . ḥisad; *Piety.* Heb. חֶסֶד.

. . . , salam Ninib ensiâ sa ina pan la išû ina ḥisad libbi-ya lamassu iluti-su rabitu ina damak abnu sadu va ḥurasi ruse la aksuni; *the image of Ninib, that which before he had not, in the piety of my heart a sacred figure to his great godship in the best of marble and of pure gold I made.*—Sard. ii. 133.

I cannot clearly see through the grammatical order of this passage, but the meaning seems plain enough.

HSM . Ḥaṣanu. See *Diḥunu*, p. 230.

. . . , ista [ta] er Nineveh attusir nahr Tigris etebir Ḥaṣanu va Diḥunu attapalkit; *from Nineveh I departed, the Tigris I crossed, Ḥaṣanu and Diḥunu I traversed.*—New Div. i. 20; ii. 14, 31. (The three passages cited are identical.)

HSZ , ḥasus; *Attentive, investigating.* See p. 414. Arab. حسّ.

. . . , ina la (birit) umi la ḥasas amati ana sarri biṣḥil-anna kisal lakora nalbas pani abira kirib mati-sun.—40 RM 17 = Sen. R. iv. 20.

This is the close of a long passage in which Sennacherib tells us what he had done for the embellishment of Nineveh, in the erection of beautiful statues "brilliant as the rising sun," made from materials obtained by his ancestors, who had employed his soldiers largely in collecting them. I cannot translate this bit, but I am just able to see that it mentions the attention paid to the wants of the men engaged, and to the provision made for their well being. In Sen. R. iv. the word *birit* is omitted.

ḪSS ḫasisu, ḫasisâ, ḫasisâti; *Investigator; attention.*

Assur-ṭsir-pal iŝ-su mudû ḫasisu parid uzni ṣimeqi; *Sardanapalus the mighty spoiler, the investigator, opener of ears to mysteries.*—43 B.M 3.

Hea sar apsi bil malqi ḫasisu; *Hea, king (?) of waters, lord of kings, the investigator.*—Mosul 4.

takhira tamirta'a uzna rapasta ḫasisa palkâ simi simata'a; *do thou favour his approach, O wide ear investigating; amply establish his position.*—Dr. Oppert's Prière de Sargon, l. 5. Exp. Més. p. 339.

This translation is doubtful; Dr. Oppert's is "élevée les yeux (du roi), aimanotée son oreille, à dire qui [illegible] les eaux. [illegible] en voix [voix de l'époque]." I believe the nearest cognate forms are those in Ethiopic, p. 411, and Arabic. Of the Arabic word Golius gives the following meanings among others, "to eradicate, destroy; to listen favourably, to pity; sympathise, love; to see, find out, perceive; to investigate." The variety is a source of difficulty; some bits in pp. 87, 99, 267, 416, may help a future student. Two passages containing and will be found in pp. 414, 415.

ḪSR Ḫuṣur; *the River of Nineveh.* Arab. خوسر.

1½ kasbu qaqqaru ultu kirib nahr Ḫuṣur mâmê daruti asar-sa usardâ kirib ṣippâti satim usabbilu pattis; *one kasbu and half, the earth in the river Khusur of perennial waters, its place I deepened, (and) in those depths I maintained water-works.*—Sen. Gr. 61 = 42 B.M 43 = Sen. Bit. iv. 35.

I understand this to mean that the bed of the river was deepened for one kasbu and a half of its course, and some machinery established there to supply Nineveh with water. Although the meaning seems plain enough, the construction is hardly quite sure. I have twice before hazarded partial translations—under dara in p. 267, and under ṣippu, in pp. 811-12; the last is not the best, though I am not quite certain that asar-sa, "its place," is better than asru, "I removed." The name of the river still remains at Mosul: see Capt. Jones's maps.

ḤE ..., aḫe; *Side.* See pp. 24 and 397–8.

ḤP ..., ..., ḫipi, ḫipe: *Overthrow.* Arabic [illegible].

... rîdu sa mie [ša] zunnu [a lli] ibšnâ ma ḫipi iškun; *the descent of waters (and) rain had taken place, and had thrown it down.*—Nab. Br. Cyl. ii. 37.

... Urṣâ sar Urardi ḫipe er Muṣaṣir salal Ḫaldia ili-su išme; *Ursa the king of Armenia, the overthrow of the city Muṣaṣir and the capture of his god Haldia heard.*—Botta 148, 3 = 77.

ḤPN ..., Ḫapini; see *Habini*, p. 402.

ḤPP ..., Ḫupapanu.—Neb. Yun. 60. Sen. T. iv. 85. Sen. B. ii. 30; iii. 14.

The name of a province of Elam.

ḤPR ..., ḫaparih.

...—Sen. T. v. 80.

This line comes between the account of preparations for a battle and the battle itself. Dr. Oppert translates "J'assemblai autour de moi les……qui éloignent la vie," reading the last words *asbi šarru-a*. Mr. Talbot admits that he does not understand the line; I can neither understand nor read it; the first word may be *ašarîa* or *išpâte*, the second may be *šebriš*. Dr. Oppert's version very probably expresses the drift of the passage, "the gathering of the warriors."

ḤR ..., ḫar; *Bracelet; ankle-ring.* Chal. [illegible], "to perforate."

... ḫari aspi ḫuraṣi kiriṣ ibbi sa sitti-sunu amḫur; *handsome bracelets of gold, white foot stools (?) of their feet I received.*—Sen. T. vi. 3. See p. 367. See also Sen. T. v. 78.

ḪR [cuneiform], ḫari ḫuraṣ; *bracelets of gold.*—Sard. iii, 62, 65.

[cuneiform] ḫari kappi-ša u širi-ša ...... ḫari kappi-ya u širi-ya; *rings of her hands and her feet, ... rings of my hands and my feet.*—Talbot's Slab, K 162, l. 31, 32.

In the parallel line ii. 40 we have [cuneiform], *samir*, instead of [cuneiform], the Hebrew שָׁמִיר, rendered "diamond" in Jeremiah xvii. 1, and "adamant" in Zech. vii. 12. Perhaps "jewels" might be the best translation.

¶ [cuneiform], ḫara, ḫiru; *Digging.* From *ḫara*, "to dig."

[cuneiform] ana sutesur kuter va takkiribati ḫare nahr saqap sippati usnu-su ul ibsi ana ul ustabil haras-su; *for the management of enclosure and cultivation, excavating the canal, and planting trees, his ear was not (given), and his decree was not brought out.*—Bra. Gr. 41. See p. 387, and correct an error there.

[cuneiform], alumma .... sasab-su ul iltanadu u ḫire nahr-su saqap sippati-su ul lakur; *any one .... its settlement not cared for, and the digging its canal (and) planting its trees not laboured at.*—Botta 37, 43. See p. 4.

¶ [cuneiform], tiri; *Castles, habitations.* Heb. טִירָה

[cuneiform], hekal .... in er-ya Assur-ki epus ana tiri 4 burhisi 4 uraski sa abne sdmu, &c., abul ana bu babi-sunu usziz; *a palace .... in my city of Assur I built, for the castles(?) four burhisi (and) four lions of adamant, &c., I made, and in their gates I set up.*—Br. Obel. ii. 15.

ḤR [cuneiform], ḥari (pagri); *Dead bodies.*

[cuneiform], pagri-sun ina gaschi alip; *their bodies in the dust I rolled.*—Sen. T. i. 58.

[cuneiform], pagri-sunu ana kiddâte arrip; *their corpses to heaps I built.*—Sard. i. 109.

[cuneiform], ana napsh napshate-sunu [si-suna] pagri ummanate-sunu adaisu; *for the saving of their lives, the bodies of their soldiers they trampled on.*—Sen. T. vi. 18.

We have here a variant [cuneiform] (which is, I believe, [cuneiform]), the same in ll. 41, where we have also [cuneiform]; in Sard. i. 59 [cuneiform], pagar, the Heb. [Hebrew]; in ii. 55, a doubtful [cuneiform], and ii. 114, an equally dubious [cuneiform]. I do not remember seeing either of these two elsewhere. It is probable that pag may have been one value of [cuneiform].

¶ [cuneiform], ḥiri; *Tempest; violence.* Heb. [Hebrew].

The Hebrew equivalent, usually translated "heat," signifies always the heat of anger, or earnest application. I would avoid the term in speaking of the month of December with its snow.

[cuneiform], arhu yoma ḥiri bilte andanna urnku-sunu ingabtû madtû amcaltu surnu-su [a ili] sunnu va salgu nabli nadlpa sadû adura; *a month and day of tempest greatly aggravated came on, and a copious storm poured forth its rain; [there was] rain and snow, torrents were raging; the mountains I avoided.*—Sen. T. iv. 75.

I have ventured in this passage more, perhaps, than I can fully justify; but I insert here an extract from the Nebi Yunus Inscription, l. 42, narrating the same occurrence in more moderate words, which will show that I have given the meaning:—

[cuneiform], ina arhi X kuppu dannu ḥsunda-sunu ingabtû la shtû illik ma salgu nahlili nadlpa sadû adura; *in the month of Thebet [December] a violent storm approached, and a rain incessant went on, and snow and torrents raged, the mountains I avoided.*

ḤRA Ḥaria.—Tig. iii. 36, 58.

Described as a very far country abounding in mountains and forests; perhaps Aria, if that province should not be thought too remote for the arms of Assyria at that early period. Some of its districts are mentioned:—Aya, Suira, Idni, Sēru, Seiga, Arnasibia, Urupa, and Anisḫa. The more recent form of Aria at Nakhsh-Rustam, and apparently at Behistun, was *Areva*; see p. 67

¶ ḥarinate.—Sard. i. 84; iii. 66.

Some articles of plunder, made of copper.

ḤRB —Syl. 364.

¶ ḥarbasu; *Vehemence.*

ḥarbasu taḫazi-ya eli-su imqut ma iṣruku libba-su; *the vehemence of my fighting burst upon him, and his courage failed.*—Sen. T. iii. 47.

sar Babel-ki va sar Numma-ki ḥarbasu taḫazi-ya isḫub-sunuti; *the king of Babel and the king of Elam, the vehemence of my fight overwhelmed them.*—Neb. Yun. 53.

sû Umman-menanu sar Numma-ki adi sarri Babel-ki Nasikhani sa Kaldi allikut idi-su ḥarbasu taḫazi-ya kima lilan sabar-sun iḫatur; *he, Umman-menan, king of Elam, with the kings of Babel, Nasikhani(?) of Chaldea, accompanying his forces, the vehemence of my fight like . . . . .*—Sen. T. vi. 16. See pp. 33, 337.

Harbasu looks like a noun with the possessive "his," and Dr. Oppert has so translated it in Sen. T. iii. 47, "ma gloire était la bataille avec moi;" but it must be a quadriliteral. The only analogous word I remember in another similar tongue is the Arabic verb خربش, "harbash," given by Castell as "vitiavit;" but this will hardly help us to an exact translation, though the meaning seems plain enough. We have in Assyrian another such root with second radical *r* in barsud, "to flee." This superfluous *r* is not unknown in Hebrew; we find כרסם in Ps. lxxx. 16; שרבט in Esther viii. 4; דרמשק in Chron. xviii. 5, 6, in the name of Damascus.

HRB . ḥigalla; *Fertility.* Arab. بَقْل.

. sabṣa dabda va ḥigalla ina mati-su l'akinnu; *prosperity, gladness and fertility in his land may they establish.*—Monol. 58.

See *Higala*, p. 404, the equivalent of "canal;" we might perhaps understand "irrigation," but the Arabic *baql* is rendered "herbis abundans" in the lexicons.

¶ . ḥaribtu, s. ḥaribta, *obl.* *The Desert.* Heb. חֹרֵב.

. ista Kalḥi atabâr nahr Ḥalḥal etebir ḥaribtu aṣabta ana Ṣûri .... aktirib; *from Calah I departed, the river Tigris I crossed, the desert I took, to Ṣur .... I approached.*—Sard. iii. 28.

Ḥaribu occurs in i. 78, a difficult passage which has not been satisfactorily read. See p. 250, and under *Ḥatoni*, p. 420.

.... . 4 bahal ami dannute saturute ina ḥaribte .... ina isḥum-ya dannate sukut anbar va mulmulli-ya habtute napista-sunu ubalti; *four full-grown powerful very large rimus in the desert .... with my strong arrows, pointed with iron, and my heavy maces, their life I extinguished.*—Tig. vi. 63.

¶ . ḥaripa, *adv.* *In defiance.* Heb. חָרַף "to defy."

. 2 susi rukubi-sunu ḥaripa ina kirib tâḥazi l'utamiḥ; *two sosse [120] of their chariots in defiance in the midst of the battle I held.*—Tig. iv. 93.

ḪRG [cuneiform] (v. [cuneiform]), Ḫargai, Ḫargaya.—Sard. i. 55.

A province named with Gilzani, Nizani, Nimme, Ubumnia, Adavas and Ḫarmasal.

¶ [cuneiform], Ḫargaai.—New Div. l. 17.

This is without doubt the same with *Ḫargai*, being mentioned in connection with the same countries, and situated in the high lands north of Assyria.

ḪRD [cuneiform], Hirit; *Ditch*. See *Ḫiriṣ*, p. 448.

¶ [cuneiform].—Bavian 11.

All the copies have [cuneiform], but I am inclined to think the word should have been [cuneiform], ḫiriṣ; and nahr ḫiriṣ would be "a canal." See p. 448.

¶ [cuneiform], Ḫaridu, n. Ḫaridi, *obl.*

Name of a city near Anatha, [cuneiform], on the Euphrates; written also Ḫaradu.—Sard. iii. 14, 15, 64, 67.

¶ [cuneiform], Ḫilakku, n. -ki, *obl.* *Cilicia.*

See Botta 40, 29; 117, 8. Neb. Yun. 17. East ii. 18.

¶ [cuneiform], Ḫardispi.—Sen. T. i. 70; ii. 2. Sen. B. i. 10.

A city named in connection with *Bit-kilamzah* and *Birtu*. See *Birtuti*, p. 170.

¶ [cuneiform].—Syl. 150.

Proves the sound of *ḫar* appertaining to [cuneiform]. See foot-note, p. 426.

ḪRZ [cuneiform], ḫiriṣ, ḫiriṣa; *Ditch*. See *Ḫiriṣ*, p. 448.

¶ [cuneiform], ḫiriṣte; *Determined, resolute.* Heb. חָרַץ

[cuneiform], Marduk-bal-adanna pal Yagin sar Kaldi zibirti ḫiriṣte lam Umani [sabi] la paliḫu zikar bil bili eli marrati gabas edi ittagil; *Merodach-baladan, son of Yagin, king of Chaldæa, with a multitude resolute in evil, not revering the name of the lord of lords, to the sea (and) the force of his hosts he trusted.*—Botta 151, 14 = 128. See p. 313.

HRZ Harzunu.—Sen. T. v. 32.

One of many tribes which advanced with Umman-Menan, King of Elam, to support Suzub, the Chaldean usurper, in the unsuccessful revolt of Babylonia against Assyria.

HRB Hiriba, -i.—Tig. iv. 13, 20.

A mountainous country, apparently in the north-east. Qy. Cilicia. See Addr, p. 486.

¶ Harhar, Harhâra.

Name of a city and province of Armenia, "somewhere near Holwan," according to Dr. Hincks (Alphabet, p. 350), but placed at Van by Sir H. Rawlinson. It is generally used with the determinative of city, but in Obel. 121 and I Pul. 6 it has [cuneiform]; in Sarg. 30 it has no determinative, only the suffix ki. Sargon (Bot. 147, 8–43) gave it the name of Kar-Sargina. Harhar frequently occurs in the Armenian inscriptions of Schulz, but Dr. Hincks believed that it meant only a chief city or citadel, and was never a proper name. See Sen. T. ii. 29; Obel. 125, where it is [cuneiform]; Botta 147, 1–61, &c.

¶ harhari.—Sen. B. iv. 21 = 43 BM 38.

Some articles of ornament, made of copper; perhaps a plural of *har*, p. 439-9.

HRT harittu; *Sceptre.* See [cuneiform], p. 367.

HRL Harila.—Botta 16bis 72; 145, 6–18. Tig. jun. 5.

Name of a tribe mentioned in an enumeration of countries and people under the rule of Assyria, from Media to Cyprus, from the mountains bordering on the Caspian to the confines of Egypt. From its place in the list, Harila should be in the desert region east of the Jordan.

HRM Hirimu.—Sard. ii. 130; iii. 124. St. 16.

A city in the south country. (In iii. 94 [cuneiform] is printed instead of [cuneiform].) It may have been the Hirimmu of p. 411, which I have there doubtfully assigned to the north.

¶ Harmasai.—Sard. i. 55. New Div. i. 17.

Mentioned with *Sargai* or *Sargani*, in p. 443.

¶ Harmeu-andai.—Sh. Ph. iii. 46.

Name of a city of Nairi.

HRN . — ., ḫaranâ, -nu; *Road, path.* See *Ḫarrana*, p. 451.

. ḫarrana kaittâ tašqqid-su; *the path of justice thou hast prescribed to him.*—E.I.H. i. 69.

. ḫaranâ nasrum uruḫ nummi ertedde; *roads impracticable, paths of the desert, I made passable.*—E.I.H. i. 21.

I have hazarded two translations, in pp. 296 and 353; the present is, I think, better than either; I deduce *ertedde* from a root *radad*, "to tread," like the Heb. רדד with the iteratitive *t*, "to make trodden."

¶ . . Hirina.—Sard. iii. 87.

Name of a strong city of Adani, a province of Nairi. I do not know whether the *Hirana* of Tig. jun. 5 with the determinative is the same, but I rather think it is not.

¶ () (v.). Ḫarsiski, Ḫarsisup; *War-horse.*

(v.). ḫarsiski rabi abnu nuzat ṭib [bib] ussi-su ana Ninevehki er bilati-ya ussu-ma-nuss unnasiqu niri-ya; *steeds large (and) lapis lazuli, valuables of their [his] country, to Nineveh, the city of my power, they brought, and kissed my feet.*—Esar iv. 26.

. ana ḫarsiski-ya patrate ana niri va paqada sallat nakiri kabitta . . . . ; *as to my war-horses trained to the yoke, and the drome, the abundant plunder of enemies* . . . . —Neb. Yun 66.

See also Sen. T. v. 89; vi. 55. Esar vi. 46. In all these cases *ḫarsiski* occurs without the determinative; in fact, I do not remember the determinative anywhere but in Esar iv. 26; the reason may have been that it indicated a beast of burden, and that it would usually be considered inappropriate to a war-horse.

HRS ḫiriṣu. See *Ḫiriṣ*, p. 448.

¶ Ḫaruṣa; *a City of Muṣur.*

ana kasad Muṣri Asur bilu usamhira-ni ana biriti Elamuni Tala va Ḫaruṣa lu aṣbat; *to the capture of Muṣur Assur the lord urged me, and into Elamun, Tala, and Haruṣa I took (my way).*—Tig. v. 69.

The Muṣur of this passage is obviously not Egypt, but a country towards the north or north-east. In l. 73 the Qumani come to the assistance of Muṣur. In l. 91 Ḫaruṣa is again mentioned as being opposite Muṣur.

¶ ḫarsanis, ḫarsanis; *Skilfully, thoroughly, like a workman.* Heb. חָרָשׁ.

kibir-sa in kupri va aguri usakhir ḫarsanis; *its length in cement and brick I completed.*—Neb. Gr. ii. 9.

kisâti dur Babel-ki gan tahazi-su usaqqi ana erbi Babel-ki udanin ḫarsanis; *the buttresses of the wall of Babylon, its defence of war, I raised, and the citadel (?) of Babylon I strengthened thoroughly.*—E.I.H. iv. 44.

See also E.I.H. viii. 2, 63, and do. i, No. 6. l. 5. The explanation appears certain, though the difference of the sibilants would seem to make it doubtful; but such distinctions were less strictly observed in recent monuments. The following quotation from the more ancient inscription of Sennacherib, in Vol. i of B.I., Pl. 7, F, l. 17, has the correct form:—

dur va salḫû naklis usepis ana usaklil ḫarsanis; *wall and outwork artistically I caused to be made and completed thoroughly.*

HRZ [cuneiform] ḫariṣu, n. -ṣi, g. -ṣa, ac. [cuneiform] ḫiriṣ, ḫiriṣi, ḫirit; *Ditch.* Heb. חָרִיץ.

¶ Ḫariṣ:—

[cuneiform] aslata han lapan dur-su rabi usiṣṣi ma 200 ina [cuneiform] ammat sakki ḫariṣi iskun ma 1½ gar ušabbil; *three [cubits?] from his great wall he paved, and two hundred cubits broad of ditch he excavated, and one gar and a half [depth of earth] he took away.*—Botta 151, 7(10)=127. See p. 280.

This is chiefly from Dr. Hincks (Assr. Tablet, p. 40). Dr. Oppert's translation is "Il explora et calcula l'étendue du terrain en avant du grand mur. Il construisit un fossé large de 100 ..... et profond d'un terme."

[cuneiform] 100 ina [cuneiform] ammat rabti ḫariṣa'a usrappis; *one hundred .... great cubits, its ditch I extended.*—B.I., Vol. 2, Pl. 7 F, l. 17.

The last word is printed uncertain with [cuneiform] instead of [cuneiform]; the character is damaged on the monument, but I think [cuneiform] is correct used phonetically, and the form with *rap* occurs frequently; see Sen. T. vi. 60; Sen. B. iv. 8; Botta 153, 10=20.

[cuneiform] ḫariṣu sa er-ya Assur-ki sa 'abtu ma epiri [lu] imlû ista babi rabi ...... adi babi Vastiggar aḫraṣ; *the ditch of my city Assur, which had been destroyed, and which the earth had filled up, from the great gate ..... to the gate of the Tigris I dug.*—Br. Obel. ii. 6.

¶ Ḫiriṣ:—

[cuneiform] mutaḫḫiṣi-sunu ina iskut ammaṣi kima Yav rû-sunu rihiltu usaznin ina ḫiriṣi atbuk-sunuti; *their fighting men with weapons I overthrew, as if Yav upon them tempest had poured; into the ditch I drove them.*—N. Div. i. 46.

ḪRZ [cuneiform]

ḫiriṣ-ṣu aḫre ma kibir-su ina kupri va agurri akṣur; *its ditch I dug, and its length with cement and brick I lined [surrounded].*—E.I.H. vi. 30.

We have [cuneiform] in Neb. Gr. i. 46, and [cuneiform] in E.I.H. v. 3 and vi. 64; in the last-mentioned case Porter's transcript makes it [cuneiform].

[cuneiform]

alta pâdi Kiṣiri adi Nineveh-ki nahr ḫiriṣ ušrid; *from the vicinity of Kisir to Nineveh a canal [river dug] I brought.*—Bavian 11.

See Sen. Gr. 43; Sen. B. iv. 34; 43 RM 12. In p. 450, where we have nearly the same passage, with Harru instead of Hiriṣ.

¶ [cuneiform] ḫuraṣu; *Gold.* Heb. חָרוּץ.

[cuneiform] ibis kaspa ḫuraṣu va takluput tamkahar .... esma babi-su irtetie; *plates of silver (and) gold, and sheets of copper .... combined, were laid over its gates.*—E.I.H. ix. 12.

[cuneiform] sanabit ... sallaru-su ḫuraṣu ruṣṣa .... bit ... ; *I made conspicuous with branches its walls, gold beaten ..... the house I covered.*—E.I.H. ii. 47. This is a mere guess.

In almost every case "gold" is represented by the Accadian [cuneiform], which occurs in 2 R 12. 86 b, explained by [cuneiform] in l. 474. See the following extract:—

[cuneiform] ili-sunu ḫuraṣi va kaspi damak nisimatri-sunu asuḫ; *their gods, gold and silver, the choice of their valuables, I took.*—Tig. ii. 31.

HRR [cuneiform], [cuneiform]. ḫarru, c. ḫarri, pl. *Hollows*. Heb. חר.

[cuneiform] (v. [cuneiform]). pitnte-suun ḫarru nadbaku sa sade lu akul; *their common people (in) the tangled (?) hollows of the mountains I consumed.*—Sard. ii. 16; in l. 87 without variant.

The same line occurs in Sard. i. 53, with the variants [cuneiform] and [cuneiform]; we have thus [cuneiform], [cuneiform], [cuneiform] and [cuneiform], all having the same meaning, which cannot but be read akul, "I consumed." See Sir Henry Rawlinson's note to Journ. R.A.S., 1864, p. 213.

[cuneiform] (v. [cuneiform]). pagri-sunu ḫarru nadabaku sa sade umali (v. umalli); (with) *their bodies the tangled (?) hollows of the mountains I filled.*—Sard. ii. 114.

On the recently-found monolith of Sardanapalus, ii. 42, we have this line repeated with [cuneiform], *ḫarrat.*

[cuneiform]. pagri quradi-sunu ḫarri va bamate sa sadi l'usardi; *the bodies of their soldiers (in) the hollows and tops of the hills I threw down.*—Tig. iii. 55. See also Tig. i. 59; iii. 26, &c.

The omission of prepositions may seem strange, but it is common in Hebrew: see in Genesis only, "I have gotten a man (from) the Lord," iv. 1; "the woman was taken (into) Pharaoh's house," xii. 15; "I will give money (for) the field," xxiii. 13; born (in the) house and bought (with) money, xvii. 13; &c., &c.

[cuneiform]. ḫarri nabalti natba sadi nahr marṣuti ina lugum astandiḫ asar ana lugum rasuqu ina siri-ya astaḫḫit; *hollows, streams, crags of mountains, fierce torrents, in a palanquin I passed over; a place for the palanquin impracticable, on my feet I overcame.*—Sen. T. iii. 75.

lugum (lugum), usually translated "throne," is here certainly the *lugum sardi*, or "palanquin," which is written in full at l. 26, and again in iv. 8; for this I am indebted to Mr. Talbot. See p. 310.

ḤRR [cuneiform].—Syl. 182.

[cuneiform].—1 R II. 35 e.

[illegible], the Hebrew חבל would imply "region, coast" (see Deut. iii. 4; Zeph. ii. 5, 6, 7).

[cuneiform].—4 R II. 49 d.

¶ In the following passage ḫarru is clearly identical with ḫiris (see [illegible] ii, p. 448):—

[cuneiform], ultu pâdi ev Kipiri adi tamirti Ninâ mati-a ina aggullati antar [illegible] ma [illegible] mahr ḫarra; *from the border of Kisir to the vicinity of Nineveh my country, in pipes(?) of iron I brought and confined the canal* [*dog-river*].—42 BM 49 = Sen. B. iv. 34. See also Sen. Gr. 60, and p. 174.

¶ [cuneiform]. aḫralik.

[cuneiform], salâ šarruti-ya epuš ma liti Aššur bili-ya [ki-ni] eli-šu ašṭur ina Išrti er šarruti-šu ukinid aḫralik; *an image of my majesty I made, and the laws(?) of Aššur my lord upon it I wrote, in Išrtu his royal city I set it up, for the future.*—Botta 146, 17 = 53.

[cuneiform], 100 in [cuneiform] ammat rabti ḫariṣa'u uruppiš aḫrališ yoml; *one hundred . . . . great cubits its digging I widened for after days.*—R.I., Vol. 1, Sh. 7, F, l. 18.

We have again aḫralik yoml in Sarg. 64, but the passage is utterly unintelligible to me. I have been inclined to translate aḫralik "hereafter," and when followed by yoml, "for after days;" the meaning in any case being "for future use or ornament." Dr. Oppert proposes "en plusieurs exemplaires," but that version appears hardly admissible with yoml.

ḤRRḌ [cuneiform]. Ḥarriṭ.—Sard. iii. 2.

Name of a river in Mesopotamia. Dr. Oppert calls it Khorsum. I am not sure that the meaning is not a dog river, i.e. "a canal." See Ḫarris, p. 449.

ḤRRK ḥarrakate; *window* (?). Chald. חרכא.

I should like to read "the Arachosians" here; the determinative clearly indicates a gentile name, and we have a notice of conquests in the remote east at the beginning of col. iv.; I think, too, the names in l. 18 are Persian. We should have to translate "the glory which he had acquired over the Arachosians."

damqa Assur bil-ya sa ina mati nakrûte ilbusu ina sis(?) ḥarrakate episa kirib-sa; *the glory of Assur my lord, which in hostile lands he had put on (acquired), on the windows (?) I sculptured in it.*—Esar vi. 13.

ḤRRN ḥarran, c. ḥarranu, n. -na, ac. -ni, -ani, pl. *Road, path, &c.*

I find no analogous root in any other Semitic language, but the following extracts prove the value:—

—38 II. 22b.

„ 23b.

„ 24b. *Urḫu*, "path."

„ 25b. *Durragu*, "road."

„ 26b. *Matagu*, "passage."

ana aḫ-amaś nebira sa nabalkita ḥarran Assur-ki; *to the other side I made cross over, and take the road to Assyria.*—Sen. T. iv. 32.

ḥarrani mat-su upappiḫ ma uparrir buḫar-su; *the roads of his land I laid open, and I broke up his plans.*—Sen. T. iv. 12.

atir ma ana Assur-ki aṣbata ḥarrana; *I turned back, and to Assyria I took the road.*—Neb. Yun. 44.

ḪRRn ṣir Maniye sar Ukki mat Dahe la kanse aṣṣabat ḫarrane; *against Maniya, king of Ukku of the land of the Dahe, I took the road.*—Sen. T. iv. 3. See also ii. 6; iii. 50; iv. 74, &c.

ana kirib Assur-ki ḫarrani iṣṣabat [ruma]; *to the interior of Assyria the roads he took.*—Botta 151, 6(16) = 112.

Ruma must surely be put instead of the verb here. Dr. Oppert, in his Commentary [p. 158], says there are many passages in which this occurs, but I cannot remember to have seen any beside this, though I do not doubt his accuracy.

.... sib ḫarranat sibi mudâte sa ana litute-ya la qirba .... arki-sunu la attarid.—Tig. vi. 40.

All the translations given of this passage are admittedly uncertain. Sir Henry Rawlinson suggested "I have omitted many hunting expeditions which were not connected with my warlike achievements(?). In pursuing after the game," &c.

Mr. Talbot, "Then I went against a foreign (or hostile) city, which had not paid its tribute according to my laws."

Dr. Hincks, "When the governments of foreign countries made default as to the tributes, which were not ready for me to receive, I went after them."

These versions were made in 1857. Dr. Oppert printed the following in 1863:—

"Ajoute à cela les expéditions nombreuses contre des rebelles qui ne fournissaient pas leurs prestations à ma liste des tributs."

Guided by these examples, I venture to propose the following uncertain version:— "Disregarding the advance of enemies (and) the tribute which to my requisitions appertained not (or, which did not approach my stipulations), I went after them."

¶ Ḫarrana, -ni.—Sarg. 6. Botta 36, 8; 16, 10; 144, 10 = 10.

Ḫarranai.—Obel. 161.

Ḫarranai.—Tig. vi. 71.

The name appears to appertain both to a province and a city; probably the Haran of Gen. xii. 5, and elsewhere; Carrhæ of the classical writers.

ḪRRn ḫarrari.—New Sard. 33. See *Ḫarru*, p. 440.

HRRs harris. See *Bit-harris*, p. 137.

—50 II. 51 b. *The east.*

¶ Harris-asma.—Sen. T. i. 58. 17 BM 16. Sen. Gr. 13.

A city of Southern Chaldæa. Dr. Oppert translates it by Chalameh.

¶ Harriaslake.—Sen. T. iv. 57.

One of thirty-four strong Elamite cities destroyed by Sennacherib. See *Bele*, p. 67.

¶ harrisai. See Heb. חָרֶס "the Sun."

bit Nin-harrisai libba Babel-hi ana El-mah ana baulti-ya ina Babel-hi epus; *the house of Nin-harrisai the centre of Babylon, to the great goddess, the mother creating me, in Babylon I built.*—E.I.H. iv. 14.

HRRr Hararati, Hararti.—Sen. T. i. 53. Sen. B. i. 8. Sen. Gr. 17.

A city which sent tribute to Sennacherib in his first campaign.

HRS harsinu, n. harsani, g. *Forests.*

harsâna asqata opis ba'ri-sunu ikbi-sul-su ina imeani huqqi halpe suripi .... ipuda .... arme turâhi a'li yaeli ina qadirate eremmib; (when) *the dense forests called him to chase their game, in days of variable storms and heat .... he hunted, ... the roams, ibexes, wild cattle, and goats in chases he retained.*—Br. Obel. l. 13. See pp. 79, 425. [Doubtful: the names of animals especially.]

ḪRS [cuneiform]. ana ziqqat ḫuršâni zaqûte va gisallat šadî pašqûte ša ana kibis amîl lâ natû arki-šunu lu eli; *to the defiles of deep forests and summits of bare mountains, which to the tread of man were not fitted, after them I went up.*—Tig. iii. 18.

[cuneiform]. ali ša ina kirib ḫuršâni danni iššaknu [šunu] abbul agur ina išati asrup; *the cities which within the dense forests were situated I threw down, demolished, in fire I burned.*—Sard. i. 66.

[cuneiform]. ḫuršâni-ša tamerâti-ša ša ina la mumê šupšuḫa ašbata ša ana tâkultu(?) va niši-ša mê šiqi la idû; *its forests (and) its plains, which with want of water were distressed and constrained, and whose ....? .... and people water drinkable knew not.*—Bavian 6.

ḪRT [cuneiform], ḫirat, c. ḫirta, a. ḫirâti, pl. *Wife.*

[cuneiform]. Gula biltu rabîtu ḫirat Shamas erlu şimma ḫasa ina maḫri-šu lišakna; *Gula, great lady, wife of the Southern Sun, ruptures noxious before him may she bring.*—1 Mich. iv. 6.

The damaged words *şimma* and *maḫri* I restore from 2 Mich. ii. 20 and 2 Mich. iv. 16, where they are well preserved.

[cuneiform], Nin-kit ḫirti Bel um ili rabi; *Ninkit(?) wife of Bel(?), mother of the great gods.*—Monol. 7 a = Obel. 12.

HRT ... makhar Ninkit ummi ili rabi hirtu naramat Asur; *before Ninkit, mother of the great gods, chosen wife of Asur.*—Assur b.p. x. 11. See also Tig. iv. 35.

... Hea Sin Shamas Nabu Yav Ninib va hirati-sunu rabati; *Hea, Moon-god, Sun-god, &c., and their great wives.*—Botta 153, 12 = 156.

...—38 II. 43b.

¶ ..., ahrat: *After, future.* Heb. אחר

..., sipti ina makhar Asur va ilati-sunu rabiti ana ahrat yumi kima sadi kinis l'asaridu; *my feet in the presence of Asur and their great godships, to future days, like a mountain, steadfastly may they establish.*—Tig. viii. 37.

¶ ..., hiritu; *a Ditch.*

..., Itai kar hiriti-su 2 kari dalûti in kupri va agurri abni; *buttresses for the embankment, of its ditch (and) two long embankments, in cement and brick I built.*—E.I.H. v. 27.

..., kari hiriti-su ina kupri va agurri sadanis abni; *the embankments of its ditch in cement and brick, like a mountain, I built.*—Neb. Bab. ii. 5.

This is uncertain. Dr. Oppert translates "en dehors des *bar* de son fossé." I have been inclined to read *kar-hiriti* as a compound word, signifying an embankment made by digging, and *itai* as a plural substantive implying some sort of guard or defence; but I am not quite satisfied. See Syl. 734, which explains *itu* by *nuṣru* and *imnu*, "a guard" and "a right hand."

HRT . Harutu.—Sard. ii. 130; iii. 124. St. 10.

Name of a city in the south; I think it always accompanies Ḫirimu.

.—35 II. 41 b. Heb. [illegible] "brook."

¶ ḫartadû c. ḫartadû, n. *Terror* (?). Heb. חֲרָדָה.

ḫartadû halli mati; *the terror of all nations.*—Obel. 16 = New Div. i. 8. Epithet of Shalmaneser.

.... sa Shamas .... ḫarad [lapu] ḫarte'ad niši ana qati-ya [su-ya] umalmu; *when the Sun-god .... the sceptre, the awe of men, to my hands had entrusted,* .....—Sard. i. 45.

The derivation is not quite satisfactory, but the meaning appears clear.

¶ . Ḫartimi.—Sard. ii. 60.

A city among the hills north-east of Nineveh.

ḪS

.—Syl. 197.

.—Syl. 278.

See 17 II. 23, 55a, where appears to be equivalent to the Accad. I do not understand the phrase explained.

¶ ḫusu; *Combined, mixed.* Ethiop. [illegible], "[illegible]."

busui kaspi ḫurasi ḫusi (ibalmari) ana la mani aslula; *wealth of silver, gold, and copper mixed, not to be counted, I plundered.*—Sh. Ph. iii. 17.

ina ḫipud libbi-ya lamassu iluti-su rabite ina dumuk abni sadi va ḫurasi ḫusi lu abanni; *in the piety of my heart, a sacred bull to his great godship, with choice of mountain stone and gold combined I formed.*—Sard. ii. 133. See p. 211.

HSB [cuneiform], hiṣab; *Clay*. See *Hiṣbi*, pp. 412, 413.

HSD [cuneiform], Ḥamaritti.—Beh. 43, 92; Det. Ins. B.

Xathritas, a name assumed by the Median rebel Phraortes; in the Persian copy we have [cuneiform], *Khshathrita*.

HSH [cuneiform], ḥusaḥḥu; *Want (famine)*. Chal. חסר.

[cuneiform] .... [cuneiform], Yav .... ṣunqu bubuta ḥusaḥḥu pagri ana mâti-su l'addi; *may the god Yav ..... privation of food (and) want (and) dead bodies scatter over his lands*.—Tig. viii. 85.

This is much better than the version in p. 77. I had overlooked the god Yav in l. 83.

[cuneiform] .... [cuneiform] (?) [cuneiform], Assur bil rabu .... ṣunqu bubuta va nibbal va ḥusaḥḥu ana mâti-su l'idd; *may Assur the great lord ..... privation of food and destruction and want scatter over his lands*.—Monol. 95.

¶ [cuneiform], ḥisiḥti; *Wants, requisitions, deficiencies*.

[cuneiform] ..... [cuneiform], sa .... sha kirib ḥursani asar nabnit-sunu ana ḥisiḥti hekal-ya marsis pasqis ana Nineveh-ki usaldidû-ni; *who (marbles) from within the forests, place of their production, for the requisition of my palace, through rugged and desolate paths, to Nineveh (they) brought me*.—Esar v. 24.

[cuneiform], sa ana ḥisiḥti hekali-ya sa Nineveh-ki abtiqu; *which for the wants of my palaces of Nineveh I had fashioned*.—Neb. Yun. 76. See also 41 BM 48.

HSU ḫisibti Bit-Saggatu asnun va anuda sarpâ axrurû-su; *the deficiencies of Bit-Saggatu I restored, and anew I exalted its royalty.*—Neb. Bab. i. 29.

¶ Ḫasḫar.—Obel. 111.

A province east of the Tigris, on the way to the country of the Nimri.

ḪSL ḫasal; *Crushing, destroying.* Chal. חֲסַל.

(v.), ḫasal tâqumate; *destroyer of opponents.*—Sard. i. 2. Epithet of the king.

¶ —Syl. 338.

ḪSM Ḫasmar.

istu Ḫasmar adi Zimaspatti [Zibarpatti?] Madai ruqûti sa ṣit Shamsi ..... ikamu rabtû qat-su [ikšud]; *from Hasmar to Zimaspatti of far Media of the rising sun .... his hands greatly captured.*—Sarg. 14.

ḪSR (), Aḫsuri, n. Aḫsura, acc.

A king of Mannai (Armenia), deposed by Assurbanipal in favour of his son Ualli.—Assur b.p. iii. 44, 55. 65. See p. 279.

¶ See *Ḫamisurrui*, p. 432.

ḪSS ḫasisu. See p. 437.

¶ —36 ll. 18a.

HSS [cuneiform], ḥasusi; *Some official rank.*

[cuneiform], sa eli gimir matâ-sunu sakrisi-su ana ḥasusi istakkanu; *who over all their lands his officers for .... established.*—Botta 36, 17.

I do not know what official is implied by this; in the parallel Botta 68, 14, it is written [cuneiform]. We may, perhaps, read [cuneiform] and [cuneiform] here, meaning "the office of a [cuneiform];" in the same way we find [cuneiform] in Botta 15, 18, denoting the office of a [cuneiform]. It is frequently difficult to distinguish [cuneiform] from [cuneiform].

ḤST [cuneiform]. Ḥastarae.—Tig. iv. 62.

One of sixteen provinces overrun by Tiglath-pileser; all their names are unknown to me.

ḤT [cuneiform]. Ḥuta; *a city of Gilḫi.*—Sard. i. 59.

¶ [cuneiform]. Ḥatâ.—Bavian 9.

One of eighteen towns from which Sennacherib conveyed drinkable water in canals to Nineveh.

ḤTN [cuneiform]. ḥatnu; *Alliances.* Heb. [illegible].

[cuneiform]. Assur-bani-pal sar sa tanata-su dandan hayamana-su ana ḥaribta taramu panu-su ana sitabru-su ḥatnu-su ipsa lib-su; *Sardanapalus the king whose mighty deeds are ...., whose face is resolute to defy, and who has raised his heart to conquests and alliances.*—Sard. iii. 26.

This is an inscription which Sardanapalus informs us he placed upon a statue of himself, erected by him in the city of Sur. It is a very difficult passage, and a satisfactory version of it has not yet been given; I offer the above as approximate only, several words being doubtful. See pp. [illegible] and [illegible].

ḤTR [cuneiform]. Ḥatara; *a City of Gilḫi.*—Sard. i. 59.

ḤTR ..., ḫutartû, *sing.* ḫutarâte, *pl.* *A Rod.* Heb. חֹטֶר.

From the first and second epigraphs on the Nimrud Obelisk; followed by ..., *ina ...*. I would suggest "sceptres from the king's hand."

ḤTT ..., &c. See pp. 410, 411.

WORDS WHICH MAY NOT BE READILY FOUND.

Ṭ ט

Characters arranged under letter Ṭ.

[cuneiform], ṭu; recent forms, [cuneiform], [cuneiform], [cuneiform].

[cuneiform], ṭab.

These two seem to have been the only characters exclusively employed for sounds involving the Hebrew ט or Arabic ط, and for the syllables ṭa and ṭi they used [cuneiform] da, and [cuneiform] ṭi. If ṭa had the sound of our tha in the pronoun "that," da was not a bad substitute; the same cannot be said of the use of ḍi for ṭi; but if the Assyrians pronounced their ṭi like our thi in "thin" (and a comparison of θῆτα with טֵית would lead us to infer that the Hebrews did so), they could hardly find a better representative for it than the hissing ṭi, inasmuch as they were unwilling or unable to invent a new letter for themselves. Inversely our tourists in Wales substitute th for the hissing sound which accompanies the Welsh ll, pronouncing *Langothlen* for the well-known *Llangollen*. In any case beyond the characters mentioned, syllables containing a dental represented t, ṭ, and d indifferently.

Ṭ [cuneiform], ṭu; *Name of a Weight.*

[cuneiform] .... &c., [cuneiform]

154 bilat 26 mana 10 ṭu ḫuraṣi ḫimir-sa ...., &c., aqali kiṣdi; *one hundred and fifty-four talents, twenty-six manehs, and ten ṭu of gold .... I collected the whole.*—Botta 152, 9 = 141.

Dr. Hincks considered the weight of the ṭu to be 189 grains, the 60th part of a maneh; another weight, the [cuneiform], he valued at 1-20th of the ṭu. See Journ. R.A.S. for 1856, Vol. 16, p. 219.

The following extracts from a bilingual tablet, 2 R. 10-21 a, appear to refer to the comparative values of the maneh, the ṭu, and the ṡi (or ṡiw?); I am unable to deduce anything from them:—

Accadian: [cuneiform]
Assyrian: [cuneiform]

Accadian: [cuneiform]
Assyrian: [cuneiform]

Accadian: [cuneiform]
Assyrian: [cuneiform]

TB tub, *subst.* *Goodness, beneficence.* Heb. טוב.

taba, *sing.* tabbat, *pl. adj.* *Good, easy.*

tabbis, tabis, *adv.* *Well.*

tib; *s.* *Good*, in the sense of chattels. See Heb. טוב, "the goods of his master," Gen. xxiv. 10.

The Assyrian verb is used in the sense of rejoicing, pleasing, beautifying, improving, &c., &c.

¶ Tub; *Goodness.*

(v.) (v.) Anu va Yav ili rabi ina tub libbi va kasad irnite tabis l'itarru-su; *Anu and Yav, the great gods, in goodness of heart and acquisition of triumph beneficently may they maintain* [*keep*] *him.*—Tig. viii. 61.

(v.), ina kibid Assur sar ili u ili Assur-ki kali-sunu la tub siri hud libbi nemalar kabidi sebe lattate kirib-su daris l'arme; *in honour of Assur, king of gods, and the gods of Assyria all of them, in goodness of health (and) joy of heart, may tribute much (and) plenty stored, in it for ever accumulate.*—Esar vi. 42. See p. 405, and compare Neb. Yun. 92.

I find , *tub gabi sa be'uri garbu*, in Sharg. 44, but the whole passage is unintelligible to me.

¶ Tab, *s.* tabbat, *pl. adj.* *Good, easy, &c.*

, eklu [alib] taba ina narkabti-ya va marsa ina siri-ya arki-sunu la attarid; *the good* [*easy*] *country in my chariots and the rough on my feet, after them I went down.*—Tig. vi. 51.

ṬB ... sadi dannuti u ekli (eḳlit) namraṣi ṭabu ina rukubi-ya (va) marṣu ina sepi-ya lu etetiḳ; *the mountains (were) steep and the plains rugged; the good in my chariots and the rough on my feet I passed.*—Tig. ii. 71. See also iv. 66.

... kisall ṭabbat is-erini [v. -ni] kasi (?) ṭabbat kipiti is-erini; *handsome altars of cedar, ... handsome, cups of cedar.*—Sard. i. 67.

¶ Ṭabbis, *adv.* *Well.*

... patta assura-man usaḥbiha ṭabbis; *a water-course I led through and covered it up well.*—Esar vi. 21.

> ... and ..., ṭabis, are both found in the first extract from the inscription of Tiglath-pileser, p. 462.

¶ Ṭib; *Goods*, in the sense of chattels.

... kuraini rabûti abnu samdi ṭib mati-su ana Ninevah-ki ir biluti-ya issuû; *large war-horses (and) lapis lazuli, the goods of his country, to Nineveh, the city of my power, they brought.*—Esar iv. 26.

> I do not think ṭib is always taken in this sense. If I read properly the following extract, of which I am in some doubt, ṭib must be synonymous with ṭub:—

... irsi ṭib libbi ultu kirib Nammaki innabta-amma iṣbata siri sarruti-ya; *he petitioned the goodness of my heart; from within Elam he fled, and accepted the yoke of my kingdom.*—Assur b.p. vii. 73.

> See pp. 212, 214, where I have given a number of extracts containing words of this root written with ... &c.

TBS Tabaşi.—Sard. ii. 13, 98, 102; iii. 110.

Name of the father of Labtur (or Caltur) of Nirbus.

TG —40 II. 40 a.

„ 40 a.

TD tuda, *f. s.* tudi, tuddi, tudat, *pl.* *Mountains or morasses.* Arab. [illegible], or Heb. [illegible].

Translators have rendered this word by "hills," "vallies," "deserts," &c. The Arabic would imply "mountains," the Hebrew "marshes" or "swamps." At all events the word means places difficult to pass.

tuda la iptu ana la ašasu tabanu; *the mountain they did not open (pass), they did not make way.*—Bavian 42.

urhi la pituti tudi pasqati sa la pan sadi marçuti altaqi-a kirib-sun mamman la illiku sarrani pani mahruti; *paths not opened, extensive swamps, which in front of the rugged mountains before me, within them never had gone the former ancient kings.*—Sen. T. iv. 4.

This accumulative passage appears to be intended to enhance the difficulties of the royal progress.

tuddi marçute va nirihtu pasqâte sa lib mahra ma-ya amma libba-suna la idû; *the morasses were difficult, and the hills (?) were impracticable, which of old time our kings their interior had never known.*—Tig. iv. 53.

I am not prepared to urge the opinion as to passes expressed in pp. 128-40; but I am still in doubt.

TD [cuneiform], tadat la'ari pasqâti sa asar-sina ladluddu rabis atatiqa; *morasses barren and extended, the place of which is isolated exceedingly, I passed through.*—Botta 145, 3 - 15; and see Sarg. 11.

See at foot of p. 147; the present reading and rendering is an improvement on what was attempted there.

[cuneiform], mupattû tudati sa elit va saplit; *opener of mountains of above and below.*—New Dir. i. 8.

Epithet of Shalmaneser. Also in 12BM24, with [cuneiform].

TH [cuneiform], tuhi; *some sort of Covering (?)*. Heb. [Hebrew] [Qy. sakhl.]

[cuneiform], tuhi samas sai tuhi samal dir; *cover of dark lapis lazuli, cover of blue lapis lazuli.*—Sard. iii. 68.

Variants [cuneiform] for [cuneiform] in both cases. We have [cuneiform] in Sard. i. 68, and [cuneiform] in i. 97; also [cuneiform] in New Dir. ii. 23, 28, 29. See [cuneiform], "dark," or "black," in p. 211, and [cuneiform], "blue," in pp. 254, 266. From all this I would infer that [cuneiform] may be a mistake, and that [cuneiform], [cuneiform], and [cuneiform] are graphic variations. In every case the article in question is an object of private \or plunder—"an image" or "picture;" see Heb. [Hebrew] in Is. ii. 16.

TM [cuneiform], tamakan.

I can make nothing of this, but would suggest that we might substitute [cuneiform] for [cuneiform], and read [cuneiform], comparing the Heb. [Hebrew] "uncleanness;" in an inscription so difficult to read, in which so many mistakes have been made, the change is not much. I give the passage with the alteration:—

[cuneiform], la-niqa akki baqa arruk ma attasi saluh tamei; *a victim I sacrificed, a libation I sprinkled, I carried outside the offal [impurities].*—Sarg. 50.

We might, perhaps, read salahu mei, "the pouring of water." See Arab. [Arabic], "to pour."

TTB [cuneiform].—30 ii. 45a.

I י

Characters arranged under letter I.

[illegible], I, sometimes nit, or better nahid; more recent forms [illegible], [illegible].
[illegible], ya; more recent forms [illegible], [illegible].

I [illegible], nahid; *August, glorious.* Arab. [illegible].

Compare the name of *Nabonahid*, "Nabonidus," which is variously written [illegible] and [illegible], in the several bricks of that king copied in Rawlinson's Inscriptions, Vol. I, Pl. 68; also in Nabonid. ii. 15, in the same sheet. The form [illegible], Nebu-imduk (Nabonid. i. 1), is Armenian [illegible] glory, [illegible] having; corresponding with the Assyrian nahid, "glorious." The [illegible], which Dr. Oppert reads nadi, nadati, and nahid, in lines 34, 194, and 141 of his copy of the inscription of Sargon, I am inclined to consider as merely the genitive case-ending of the adjectives rabbi and [illegible].

¶ .... [illegible], -ya; *My.*

[illegible] .... [illegible], tanali Assur bili-a alqaqat gurdi-ya .... ina garbi-su astur; *the deeds(?) of Assur my lord and the narrative of my victories .... upon it I wrote.*—Obel. 72.

See the same tale told in N. Div. ii. 60, where we have [illegible]. See p. 8.

¶ [illegible], El-Ya; *the God Ya.*

[illegible] .... [illegible], sual gir tambabar epos kisiti mali sa ina El-Ya bili-ya aksuda .... ina eli altur; *a tablet(?) of copper I made, engraved from the countries which, through the god Ya my lord, I had taken; .... upon it I wrote.*—Tig. vi. 16.

The translators of 1857 all made El-Ya a proper name. I have been inclined to render it "my god," as Dr. Oppert has done in his "Chaldée et Assyrie," Versailles, 1865.

IAB , yâbat.—Sard. i. 25. A variant of , aibat, *Enemies.*

IAM , yâme; *the Sea.* Heb.

. —43 II. 38a.

. „ 59a.

Found also in 43 II. 64, 65a, with instead of .

These extracts show that *yam* is an Accad name for the sea; this is not the only instance of the coincidence of Hebrew with Accadian: see also , "city," Heb. I would suggest the reading [illegible], "people of the sea," but for the Assyrian equivalents. See Syl. 376 in p. 366.

IAN , yânu; *There was not.* Heb.

, manama yânu; *any one there was not.*—Beh. 19.

The Persian has nipa aha, "not there was." I do not remember to have seen this elsewhere.

IAS , yâsi; *Persons, people.* Heb.

(v.) , ana yâsi va pirrital-ya kiripta tabita l'iqrabu-ni; *to my people and lineage, good union may they grant me.*—Tig. viii. 34. [Literally "nearness may they make near."] See p. 383.

(v.) (v.) , ina tigulti luzuto sa Assur bile ireuka [v. ipsu] ana yâsi ikhut ummani-a athi; *by the powerful service which Assur the lord granted to my people, my servants and soldiers I collected.*—Sard. ii. 26.

There is some difficulty about , which is rendered "servants" as well as "weapons." I think the word signifies aid of any sort; this passage can hardly be understood otherwise.

IAT , Yati; *I; as for me.*

Yati is an introductory particle used chiefly in the later documents. I am inclined to follow Mr. Talbot, who always translates the word by "as for me," or some similar expression; I think it is usually followed by the name of the writer of the inscription. Sometimes it would seem to have no more meaning than "now," in "now it came to pass" or "now [name illegible] was a soldier."

IAT [cuneiform] ..... [cuneiform], yâti Asurbanipal sar sit(?) rîa reeu mudaiaaû bitnia kappi Asur uvassir-anni ma ana Abiyateh ..... ispur; *as for me, Asurbanipal, king, prince noble, chief mighty, the produce of the hands of Asur, he forsook me, and to Abiyateh .... he sent.*—Asur b.p. vii. 100.

[cuneiform], yati Nabunahid sar Babel-ki ina hitu ilûti-ka rabiti naplih-anni; *as for me, Nabonidus, king of Babylon, under the mantle of thy great divinity preserve me.*—Nabon. ii. 19.

A similar clause in Nab. Brok. Cyl. i. 24, but damaged.

[cuneiform] ..... [cuneiform], yâti Nabonahid (im-duk) sar Babel-ki .... ina palo-a kini ina bulnhil sa Istar Agane-ki bilat-ya biri apte: *now I, Nabonidus, king of Babylon, ... in my time fixed, in reverence of Istar of Agane, my lady, pits I opened.*—Nab. Br. Cyl. ii. 15.

[cuneiform] ...... [cuneiform], ana palo sarri mahri ..... yati asar-sa labiri ustebe ma malak mie-sa kima labirimma ana itê Bit-Saggatu ustetesir; *in the times of the former king ...., I restored its old place, and the course of its waters, as of old, to the margin of Bit-Saggatu I directed.*—Nerig. ii. 3.

The bit omitted is mutilated; the word *ustetesir* is anomalous in its repetition of the servile *t*, but this occurs also in i. 19: in other inscriptions I find ustesir

IAT [cuneiform], yati asru sahtu palaha ili mudû epših; *now, a place of sacrifice and worship of the gods, large, I built.*—Nerig. i. 25.

[cuneiform], yati pal-su restû murasu lib-su Imgur Bel va Nimitti-Bel dur rab-rab su Babel-ki usaklil; *now I, his eldest son, exalting his heart, Imgur-Bel and Nimitti-Bel, the great walls of Babylon, have completed.*—E.I.H. v. 21.

Since writing the above I learn from Mr. G. Smith that he has found iḳbi yati, "he told me," on a slab. The following word, *yatima*, is in favour of Mr. Talbot's rendering.

¶ [cuneiform], [cuneiform], yatima; *Me here.* See a note in the Additions, p. xii.

[cuneiform], sum-su [su-mu] itti-ya lištur kima yatima; *his name with me may he write like me here.*—Tig. viii. 60.

[cuneiform]. atta kima yâtima musaru sitir sum-ya akin ma kisal lumsi la-siqu akhi (palki) itti musare sitir sum-ka sukun; *thou, like me here, the lines of the writing of my name placing, and the altar cleaning, (and) victims sacrificing, with the lines of the writing of thy name do thou place.*—Esar vi. 66.

This seems all clear enough, though I am doubtful about the grammatical forms which I have translated as participles. See a parallel passage in Assur b.p. x. 105, where the word I have transliterated akin is made [cuneiform] with variant [cuneiform]. I think *yatima* is always preceded by *kima*.

IB [illegible]. See [illegible] in p. 65.

I find [illegible] in the following line:—

[illegible] ikun araku yumi-ya.—Birs ii. 25. Neb. Bab. ii. 20.

I am not sure of the reading, and the context is not clear; I would suggest "he has established the length of my days." This cannot be far from the meaning. See a note under *Araku*, in p. 51.

IBB [illegible], Yabbá.—Sen. T. ii. 66.

The well-known seaport of *Joppa*, יפו,—captured by *Sennacherib* in his third campaign, with other places, from a king *Zidqa*, the Hebrew name צדקיה.

IBL [illegible], ibili; *Camels* (?).—Sen. T. vi. 55. Arab. إبل.

Dr. Oppert reads "rams," perhaps from "rams' horns" of Josh. vi. 4, 5, but this meaning of the word is not found in the LXX or the Vulgate.

IBR [illegible], ipiri; *Excavations, earth.*

[illegible]

utir ibiri-sunu ana asri-sun; *I restored their excavations to their place.*—Neb. Br. Cyl iii. 31.

See the following line from a bilingual list:—

([illegible]) [illegible] —? II. 34 b.

The Assyrian word in this line may be read [illegible], a good Semitic form from the root [illegible], "to dig," likely to signify "excavation," and equivalent to a monogram pronounced *ibira*. We may, then, assume the value "excavations" for *ibiri*, a value perfectly suitable to the context, which represents a successful search for an inscription among the ruins of a temple. *Epiri*, the ordinary word for "ground," "mould," &c. (see p. 110), occurs twice before in this paragraph, which may be the reason why it was not used here.

IBS [illegible], ibisu; *Arid, desert.* Heb. יבש.

[illegible]

[illegible], munnadan-sunu sa ana napsat(i) apú asar ibisa illiku (du) urapplu ina tigulti (isku).—Sen. T. vi. 21.

I had given up this passage as unintelligible, but just before going to press I discovered two errors in the printed copy of the inscription,—*a* was put for *sa* in the first line, and *sadu* for *illiku* at the end. The lines are printed here correctly, and the following translation is proposed:—"Their fugitives who for life ran away, to a desert place went, (and) were pierced with arrows." This is uncertain; I should have expected *dubu*, and I am not sure that *uraptu* can be a passive. See p. 207.

Since writing the above I have found the word *ibisu* as a verb in Bavian, l. 21, but the passage is mutilated.

IGG [cuneiform], Igigi.

In p. 22, under the word *Anunaki* or *Anunnaki*, I referred to this place for any further information about the *Igigi* and *Anunnaki*; but I can do no more than set down a few extracts, which appear to show that Anu and Marduk were considered to be the rulers of these supernatural beings; I think the Igigi were also named the "great divine chiefs," [cuneiform]:—

[cuneiform]. Anu sar Igigi va Anunnaki; *Anu, king of Igigi and Anunnaki*.—Obel. 2.

[cuneiform]. Anu sar El-unsi rabbi u Anunnaki; *Anu, king of the great divine chiefs and Anunnaki*.—New Div. l. 2.

These two lines are exactly parallel; line 10 of the obelisk, now mutilated, appears to have been identical with the last.

[cuneiform] .... [cuneiform]. Marduk .... sa Igigi va [cuneiform] Anunnaki; *Merodach .... of Igigi and Anunnaki*.—E.I.H. iv. 10.

This extract compared with the first would lead to the inference that [cuneiform] was sounded like [cuneiform]; a variant in Sard. i. 10, made something in this way, [cuneiform], would show that [cuneiform] may have been pronounced *Igil*. See note in p. 115.

IGD [cuneiform].—Syl. 392.

Igidibu, which explains the monogram "and," may be read igid ibbu, "it joins phrases;" see the Chaldee עֲגַד "to join," and יָבַב "to call out;" a word from the latter root occurs once in Hebrew וַתְּיַבֵּב "she called out," Judges v. 28. In like manner *gigurit* "gathering," or "joining" [p. 179], explains the same conjunction in Syl. 461. See the Hebrew גדד in Ps. cxl. 8.

IGS [cuneiform]. Igisû, nr. Igisi, igisê, gen. *Riches*. Qy. Heb. נְכָסִים

A noun ending with a long vowel in all cases has those which require an additional syllable. See also *Duri* in p. 286.

[cuneiform], igisê [illegible]; *riches and pleasures*.—E.I.H. ii. 37.

Better than "combinations of pleasure," doubtfully suggested in p. 413.

108 mahar biltat *siriq tu igisê* kali-sina kiprati; *receiver of tributes, pouring in the riches of all countries.*—New Div. i. 7.

Compare with the above the following parallel passage from 1 R 35; both extracts are unsatisfactory, and the first is mutilated; but a collation of the two may, perhaps, make the meaning clearer. I give my version as uncertain, but it cannot be far wrong. In the transliteration I have put the doubtful syllables in italics. All the three extracts in this page are epithets of the royal promulgators of the respective inscriptions:—

mahar biltat siriq sa kali sina kiprati.

mahir biltat va igisê sa kalis kiprati; *receiver of tribute and riches from all countries.*—Sh. Ph. I. 38.

IGR Igar, c. Igara, n. igari, igarate, *pl.* *Body of a Building, Structure, mound.* Chald. [illegible]

In the translations I have used the rather unsuitable word "structure" because I do not know any single word which could express the mere body of a building as distinguished from its purpose as a palace, temple, fortress, &c.

bit-su ina igar limiti Bit-Zida namris epus; *his temple, on the mound near Bit-Zida, beautifully I made.*—E.I.H. iv. 64.

sa hekali [bit-rab] siati istabbitu bab-bab sa igara-sa; *of that palace the gates of its structure were broken down.*—E.I.H. vii. 37.

ina labare yomimu igara-sunu iqup sa igari-sunu aggur usi-sunu epti; *in old days their structure was rent, and their structures I threw down, their foundations I opened.*—Nab. Br. Cyl. iii. 29, 30.

IGR igaru-su qablatu atke ana mqul mie ahend mihirat mie ...., isid-su asursid; *its body broken up I collected, and a depth of water I obtained; facing the water .... its foundation I laid down.*—Nerig. ii. 23.

This passage relates to an old palace in ruins standing by an artificial pond.

igarate-su kima sarur pit mull uslm; *its structures like the sparkling of rising stars I embellished.*—Tig. vii. 98.

bit liben bi-lna igari-su.—15 II. 36 c.

In this extract *bit liben*, "house of brick," clearly defines one meaning of *igaru*.

—38 II. 19 b.

It seems from this that *bit igaru* would be a "wooden house."

igardte elappi.—62 II. 63 d.

Here we have the body of a ship, "the hull."

ID idi, idat, *pl.* idati, *gen. Forces.*

See p. 200 for the grammatical forms of *id*; the form *idat* was forgotten.

summa ...... marabbie l'usrbú tigulti-su (isku) la baddá ana idat biluti-a; *when ...... largely he had added his unequivocal service [or weapons] to the forces of my government, &c.*—Sarl. i. 41.

ana Sin mudammik idati-ya bit ladr-rali bit-su ina babi an-ki epus; *to the moon-god, strengthener of my hands, the house of alabaster(?), his house, in the gates of ..... I made.*—E.I.H. iv. 26.

ID

In the following quotation I think [cuneiform] should be read idâ-i, "my hands," for idâ-ya, as in binti-i, "my daughter," abi-i, "my father," and several other instances:—

[cuneiform], bubbir umman-ka dikâ killat-ka ana Babel-lil ṭi'ama idâ-i sis ma tumnis pab atta; *select thy army, strike thy tent, "to Babylon" give command, my forces strengthen, and .... O warrior thou.*—Sen. T. v. 24.

I fear this may be considered altogether too bold; ṭi'ama may be justified by [cuneiform], "command," in p. 429; I understand the meaning to be "*let the word of command be 'to Babylon.'*" I can make nothing of tumnis. The [cuneiform] of [cuneiform] is left out in the plate, but it is clear on the cylinder.

[cuneiform], idat ernai-sunu; *the walls of their cities.*—Tig. i. 81; iv. 92.

In this case and in some others I would read "walls," though I believe it to merely the same word used metaphorically—"the defences."

¶ [cuneiform], Yakin; *Father of Merodach-baladan.*

[cuneiform], Marduk-bal-adanna pal Yakin sar Kaldi; *Merodach-baladan, son of Yakin, king of Caldea.*—Botta 151, 14(2) = 122.

Compare the following, where Yakin is written phonetically:—

[cuneiform], Marduk-bal-adanna pal Yakini sar tamti; *Merodach-baladan, son of Yakin, king of the sea.*—Tig. jun. 26.

¶ [cuneiform], Bit-Yakin.—Botta 146, 10 = 22; 16[bis] 85. Neb. Yun. 32.

[cuneiform], Bit-Yakin sa kisad marrati; *Bit-Yakin, which is near the sea* [*Persian Gulf*].

[cuneiform], Bit-Yakini, in Tig. jun. 8.

¶ [cuneiform], Dur-Yakin.—Botta 151, 24(12) = 138; 152, 2 = 124.

[cuneiform], Dur-Yakin.—Botta 37, 31.

A fortified city of Merodach-baladan, captured and burned by Sargina.

ID . Idai; a City of Zamua.

eruni sa Nigdiara u Idai Nigdima aksud; *the cities of Nigdiara and Idai of Nigdima I captured.*—Obel. 51.

The construction is awkward, but justified by the notice of the same occurrence in the more recently found monolith of Shalmaneser. On the obelisk it is placed in the monarch's fourth year; on the monolith in the third:—

eruni sa Nigdima Nigdiara aktirib; *the cities of Nigdima (and) Nigdiara I occupied.*—New Div. II. 76.

IDB . Yatbari; *a country on the border of Elam.*

eli Yatbari sa itê Namma-ki ammrara galli-ya; *over Yatbari of the borders of Elam I made my servants inspectors [I made them see].*—Botta 153, 6 : 150. See Botta 16ter 78; 37, 20; 145, 8 = 20.

IDG Idiglat; *the Tigris.* See p. 128.

. —50 II. 76.

¶ . Yadaqqu.—Sen. T. i. 41. Sen. Gr. 15.

One of many tribes attacked and plundered by Sennacherib, in his first campaign, on his return from Chaldea.

IDH . Yadih.—Esar iii. 40.

A city tributary to Esar Haddon.

IDN . Yatnana; *Island of Cyprus.*

Yatnana sa malak 7 yomme ina qabli tamti ereb shamsi nishaku; *Cyprus which, a passage of seven days in the midst of the sea of the setting sun, is situated.*—Botta 153, 1 = 145.

DN [cuneiform]. Luli sar er Zidunai bulahhil-su Yunâma bêl-su ma alte kiril Abiri ana Yatnana qabal tamti innabid; *Luli, king of the city of Sidon, departed from his allegiance to his lord, and from within Abiri to Cyprus in the midst of the sea he fled.*—Sen. B. I. 18.

Written *Atnana* on the Bull Inscriptions; see p. 259.

The Assyrian name of Cyprus may possibly have been derived from a word signifying "merchandise." See אתנן in Isaiah xxiii. 18. That Cyprus is meant by Yatnana is proved by the additional bit to the inscription of *Esar Haddon*, in B.I., Vol. I, 6b. 48, where ten kings of Cyprus are mentioned with the names of the ten cities ruled by them, followed by these words in l. 11: [cuneiform], &c., "ten kings of Yatnana;" the ten cities named are those handed down to us by the Greek geographers.

IDR [cuneiform], idir; *Stoppage, entanglement.* Heb. עדר.

[cuneiform] ..... [cuneiform], pati kitar-su sa idir-su ishuru ana illiku rigusu ..... ashi ussakkis; *the nomades his followers who observed his entanglement and went to his assistance .... I utterly cut off.*—Botta 151, 22(10) = 180.

IU [cuneiform].—Syl. 685.
[cuneiform] „ 686.
[cuneiform] „ 687. *A god.*

¶ [cuneiform], iwan; *Price, or the price is.*—1 K 11. 27 b.

This word must be pronounced iwan, being followed by [cuneiform] and [cuneiform], *iwan* and *iwanna*; the Accadian column is broken in all the lines, and the equivalent for "price" is alone visible.

IUA [cuneiform]. Yahua; *Jehu.*

Name of the king of Israel who sent tribute to Shalmaneser, recorded on the second epigraph of the Nimrud Obelisk; he is named also upon an unpublished fragment of another inscription of Shalmaneser.

IUD Yahuda, *n.* -di, *g.* -dai, *adj.* *Judæa, Jew.*

muqibat sar Yahuda'a sa asar-su ruḳuqu; *expeller (?) of the king of Judæa, who his place (is) far away.*—22 BM 8.

magú Yahudi Ḥazaqiahu sar-su ... abadu; *the province of Judæa, (and) Hezekiah its king, stayed their transgressions.*—Neb. Yun. 15.

Ḥazaqiahu Yahudai sa la iknusu ana niri-ya 46 alani-su dannuti .... alme akshud; *Hezekiah the Jew, who did not submit to my yoke, forty-six his strong cities .... I approached, I captured.*—Sen. T. iii. 12.

IUḤ Yahuḥazi; *Jehoahaz.*

Yahuḥazi Yahudai; *Jehoahaz the Jew.*—Tig. jun. 61.

Occurs in a long list of chiefs of Western Asia tributary to Tiglath-pileser.

IHN Yahnagi, -gu.

VII sarrani sa Yahnagi sa Yatnana sa malak VII yumme ina qabli tamti erib shamsi; *seven kings of Yahnagi which (is) Cyprus, a voyage of seven days in the midst of the sea of the setting sun.*—Botta 153, 1 = 145. See also 16[bis] 42; 36, 24.

Dr. Oppert reads this Crete and Cyprus. I rather think the names were synonymous, and that the text itself points it out as I have translated it. Crete and Cyprus could hardly be both reached in the same number of days.

IHT Yahteri.—Sard. iii. 80.

A province lying east of the Orontes.

IZ —Syl. 474. *Timber.*

—Syl. 472.

—2 R. II. 10a. *Material for a throne.*

—2 R. II. 69. *Material for a figure.* See *Amarti*, p. 87.

—2 R. II. 18b. See *Igaru*, p. 472.

IZB izub; a *Statue*. Heb. עָצָב. Jerem. xxii. 28.

.........ki izub Ana va Dagan lizuru zakut-su; *who .... upon the statues of Ana and Dagan wrote his decrees.*—Sarg. 9.

¶ Izibia.—Botta 146, 5 = 41.

A city in Armenia, one of the fortresses of Ullusun, king of Mannai (Van).

¶ Yazbuqai.—New Div. I. 54.

A district mentioned at the close of the first column, which is broken off unfinished; it would appear from the place mentioned with it, to be somewhere near the Mediterranean, towards Cilicia perhaps, but doubtful.

IZD —Syl. 583.

May be read as *isa izdu izidu*, "who was raised in office;" this might be a definition of the monogram.

IZL Izala, Izalla.—Sard. I. 106.

Izalli.—Neb. Gr. I. 22.

These may relate to the same country, which would appear from the context of the inscription of Sardanapalus to be in the north. In Nebuchadnezzar's inscription the name occurs with several others, all unknown to me, except possibly *Hilkum*. See p. 451, where this last place is wrong printed with [cuneiform] instead of [cuneiform].

IZM Yasumḫa.—Sard. iii. 60. See *Armaḫa*, p. 353.

IZN Yaz-el.—Sen. T. v. 32.

One of the tribes which joined the confederation of the Babylonians, Chaldæans, and Susians, against Nineveh. See *Nuranu*, p. 144.

IZR Izirta, -il.—Botta 146, 3 = 41; 146, 17 = 53.

Capital city of Ullusun of Mannai (Van).

IḤ Yaḫi.

umam ṣeri adu kali-sunu ina er-ya Yaḫi lū akṣur; *beasts of the plains and hills, all of them in my city Yaḫi I collected* (?).—40 BM 16.

IḤZ iḫiṣ; *Surface.* Heb. חוץ "outside."

iḫiṣ kappu ḫuraṣu ..... babl-sa iriṭṭu; *a surface silver (and) gold .... its gates overspread.*—E.I.H. ix. 19.

I think this is better than in p. 448.

IḤL iḫilu; *Hope.* Heb. יחל.

iḫilu nisi ina sibbi gasrut-su ipla-sina; *the hope of nations; in the fulness of his power he hath founded them.*—New Div. I. 6.

This is doubtful.

IḤN Yaḫanai.—Sard. iii. 78.

A country between the Euphrates and Orontes.

IḤR Yaḫiri; *Fahir.*—Sard. ii. 22.

Name of a petty Hittite chief, king of Ḫandirabi. See p. 635, where I have inadvertently supposed Ḫandirabi to be a province of Nairi.

I'I [cuneiform]. Iyaya.—Sard. iii. 116.

A city of Gilzi.

IKN [cuneiform], Yakin.—Botta 37, 31.

[cuneiform], Yakini, *gen.*—Tig. jun. 26. See p. 474.

The father of Merodach-baladan, generally written [cuneiform]; see p. 474.

¶ [cuneiform], Yakinlû.—Assur b.p. ii. 101, 110.

Name of a king of Arvad.

IL [cuneiform], [cuneiform], ilu, ili; *a God, Gods.* Heb. אֵל

[cuneiform], ana Marduk ilu bani-ya palhis l'utakkin; *to Marduk, the god my creator, reverently I made prostration.*—Neb. Gr. i. 11. See Deut. xxxiii. 3.

[cuneiform], sarri madutu alik mahri-ya sa ilu ana sarruti izkuru(?) zikir sun; *many kings going before me, whom god to royalty hath pronounced(?) their name.*—E.I.H. vii. 14.

I follow Dr. Oppert here, though doubtfully; I do not understand *izkuru*, and I should wish, as the most natural construction, to make *sar* a genitive singular, agreeing with the king's name in the preceding clause. But on the whole I think his translation is the only one possible. Ker Porter's transcript has [cuneiform] instead of [cuneiform].

In almost every case the Accad [cuneiform], an, is used instead of *ilu*. The following extracts from bilingual slabs would show the terms to be equivalent, if it were not sufficiently obvious already:—

[cuneiform].—Syl. 751.

[cuneiform].—II. 11, 20, 27b.

The following I do not understand:—

[cuneiform].—Syl. 887.

[cuneiform].—Syl. 888.

[cuneiform].—Syl. 729.

[cuneiform].—7 II. 44d.

IL Ilati; *Godship, Divinity.*

arame palahi ilati-sunu; *I have raised the worship of their divinities.*—B.I.H. i. 36.

palahi ilati-su usakin ina lib-ya; *the reverence of his godship he hath established in my heart.*—B.I.H. ii. 7. See *Ilati-ki* in ix. 58.

Instead of this we have more commonly , Nebuc. ii. 31, or , Tig. vi. 63, or , Tig. vii. 86.

¶ Ilui; *Doorposts, Columns.* Heb. אַיִל.

is-kanali-sunu ilui abu kumina turda abu lazis-rabi va ilui abu pili rabi asurra-sun usaphira; *their conduits, columns of . . . . . stone (and) alabaster, and columns of fine large stone, I carried a wall round them.*—41 BM 36. Cf. p. 328.

abu ilui agurri.—Esar v. 16.

Here *ilui* is followed by a word which I understand to signify "brick." Mr. Talbot renders the passage "statues of the gods carved in stone." Dr. Oppert has "pierre ilu" and "agurri." They form part of the building material carried by the Hittite kings to Nineveh.

¶ Sippara.—50 II. 6a.

See the notes and extract 28 II. 26A, printed in p. 292.

¶ Ilu.—Sard. iii. 42, 45.

Name of a sanid of Laqa, a province west of the Euphrates, who was carried off by Sardanapalus to Assyria. The title of sanid appears to be one of some importance: it is given to another opponent also in Sard. ii. 78, and both were in possession of cities and soldiers. The Hebrew נָסִיךְ is translated "princes" see Josh. xiii. 21, and Ps. lxxxiii. 11. The Assyrian form, that of an active participle, would seem to imply a high priest,—one who anoints the prince and offers oblations to the gods.

ILB Ilúbi'di.—Sarg. 25.

A King of Hamath, put to death by Sargon. The name of this monarch is written in Botta 145, II—22, on the Cyprus Stone, i. 53, and in 33 B.M. 8.

ILD —7 II. 45 d.

Compare ... in this extract with ..., 7 II. 44 d, in p. 480.

¶ —20 II. 71 c.

Nabnita, "the created," Niphal of *bana*, ... the value of ... as the "offspring" or "family." I have not met with the word in the inscriptions.

¶ iladti; *Producers.* Heb. ילד

malik ili iladti bitkur magil marrap shamé va irsiti; *king of gods, producers, ruler, rolling the courses of heaven and earth.*—Sard. I. 2. Epithet of Ninib. Uncertain.

ILM ilame; *the World.* Heb. עלם—Opp.

ILN Ilani.—Sard. iii. 105.

Ilan was son of Zamua, and chief of Dagara..., a city of the mountainous country north of Assyria.

¶ Yalum.—2 Pal. 9.

A province of Assyria, joined with others and with the city of Calah under the government of *Belharran*, an officer of Pul and ...

IMD imat; *Terror, Dread.* Heb. אימה.

8 ... u ... ana ... va sibi ipnasu imat muti; *eight figures (?) of metal strong, which the wicked and the criminal repel (by) fear of death.*—Norig. I. 27.

I may repeat here the observation in 449 on the ... of prepositions.

IMD [cuneiform], muso nakiri iplahu lmat môte; *by night the dread of death came upon the rebels.*—Sarg. 20. [Lit.—Rebels, came upon, dread of death.]

[cuneiform], lmat môti aplaho şittat alai; *dread of death I brought upon the common people.*—Botta 151, 23(11) = 131.

IMM [cuneiform], yaumma.—Tig. i. 67; iii. 38; iv. 55.

See a note to pp. 180, 182, where I have with some hesitation proposed the translation "a day." I may repeat here the note printed at the foot of p. 464.

IMN [cuneiform], Yavnao; *Ionia.*—Beh. 6. No. 6, N.R. 16.

[cuneiform], Yavnai; *Ionian.*

[cuneiform], ša tûhari sa kua qabal tamti Yavnai pandanis kima nûni ibarû sa sampiha Quo va ir Şurri; *greedy of war, who like a fish in the midst of the sea of Ionia, ploughed as with a yoke of oxen, and destroyed the Que and the city of Tyre.*—Sarg. 21.

This is little better than a guess. I have supposed *pandanis* to be read *pandanis*, and have derived [cuneiform] from a root allied to the Hebrew פדן. I am not sure that *ibarû* should not be read *ibara*, as I find it in the following parallel passage. I have assumed *ibara* to be an exceptional form of *ibiru*, pleading in justification the [cuneiform], *ebiru*, "crossing over," in Sh. Ph. ii. 49. I have no doubt that we should read the word alike in both inscriptions; *ra* and *ru* ([cuneiform] and [cuneiform]) are frequently made very much alike.

[cuneiform], mušahbalpi Quo lgamti sa ir Yavnai sa qabal tamti kima nûni ibara; *spoiler of the Que, (and) of the waters which the Ionians of the midst of the sea, like fishes, traverse.*—Botta 36, 89. See pp. 100 and 184.

IMN [cuneiform], Yamani.—Botta 149, 11 = 95; 150, 5 = 101.

A usurper raised to the throne by the Hittites and expelled by Sargon.

IN [cuneiform], ina, *prep. In, into; With (by means of).*

In, into:—

[cuneiform] itti ummanate-sunu gabsâte ina er va sade aris amtahis; *with their extensive armies in city and upland I fought.*—Tig. vi. 2.

[cuneiform] sir aibi ina mati-ya lu apras; *the yoke of enemies in my country I broke.*—Tig. vi. 54.

[cuneiform], ina arki yummi; *in after days.*—1 Mich. ii. 1.

[cuneiform], ina neribi-sun pisqati sakis eram [erub, followed by ina, see p. 409]; *into their dangerous countries steadfastly I advanced.*—Gen. T. iv. 10.

¶ With, by:—

[cuneiform] ina emuq galli-ya lazzute itti 20,000 ummanate-sunu rapsati ina Tala lu amtahis; *by the ardour of my mighty servants, with twenty thousand of their extensive troops in Tala I fought.*—Tig. v. 86.

[cuneiform], ina kappi ramani-su ..... napista-su nasil; *by his own hands ..... his life he laid down.*—Botta 148, 3 = 77.

[cuneiform], sa nari-ya (mulania) ..... ina epiri [isi] ikatamu; *he who my tablets ...... with clods shall cover.*—Tig. viii. 67.

IN ina eli; *Upon; Above.*

The phonetic value of is eal, which after a preposition may optionally be put in the objective case, eali.

ina eli aktur; upon (*it*) *I wrote.*—Tig. vi. 18.

bit sa agurri ina eli-su arzip; *a house of brick upon it I built.*—Tig. vi. 19.

bilat va madatta eli sa pana utir ina eli-sunu askun; *imposts and tributes, above what before was, upon them I established.*—Tig. vi. 25.

¶ ina pan; *From before.*

sitat ummanate-sunu sa ina pan galli-ya [iskn] ipparsida niri-ya ikbatu; *the common men of their soldiers, who from before my servants fled, my yoke took.*—Tig. i. 85.

Nearly the same phrase in iii. 13, and ii. 2: but in the last case we find . Instead of *ina pan* I find more generally *ispan*, Heb. מפני, as in Sen. T. i. 22; vi. 8 (which became *ispani* in Persia; see Beh. 8, 16); or *ina pani*, Sh. Ph. ii. 44; or the Accadian , pronounced also *pan* or *ina pan*; see Sard. ii. 98, 119, and Ne. 3, B.M. 10. I suppose *ina pan* meant, word for word "through the face," i.e., "owing to the presence."

¶ *Ina* is frequently followed by *kirib* or *lib*, by which the inside of some place is usually implied. Sev Gen. xlv 6.

ina kirbi-su nuhsu l'abund; *within it abundance may it obtain.*—Norig. ii. 85.

ina kirib-su addi; *withinside it I placed.*—Tig. vii. 107.

ina libbi usesib; *within it I seated.*—Tig. vi. 21. See also Sen. T. i. 60.

¶ *Ina* (or its equivalent =), followed by , in measurement of land, is placed between the numeral and the thing measured. I think it indicates the nature of the measure used—the great or small cubit; and perhaps distinguishes the direction of the measurement, as taken in length or breadth. See examples in pp. 74, 150, 180.

IN — is very frequently substituted for in all its significations. I give here a few examples:—

, ina er Arbel; *in the city of Arbela.*—Sard. i. 69.

, ina er-su esir-su; *in his city he shut him up.*—Obel. 33. (for .)

ina kibid Assur Istar ili rabbi bili-a; *in honour of Assur (and) Istar, great deities, my lords.*—Sard. i. 70.

, uqa ina asri-su altakan; *the stele in its place I established.*—Beh. 96.

, ina gir anbar; *with a sword of steel.*—Botta 148, 5 = 77.

, ina ishat usamqit; *with arrows I slew.*—Obel. 66, 81.

> This frequently-used expression has been variously rendered; Dr. Hincks always translated it as I have done here, and he told me in a letter a short time before his death that he continued to do so. I do not know that he has anywhere given his reasons for adopting the sense of "arrows;" he mentions it in the Journal of Biblical Literature for January 1858, p. 396, and quotes Mr. Talbot's usage. I have myself translated "in armies I subdued;" see p. 340; but a collation of many passages has satisfied me that *ishu* must sometimes denote "weapons." I read *usamqit* in analogy with the Arabic root *saqata*.

, ina eli kilkhi usarkib; *upon ships I made them mount.*—Beh. 34.

, bit Ninib bili-ya ina kirib-su la addi; *the house of Ninib my lord within it I laid down.*—Sard. ii. 132.

, ina libbi altor; *on it I wrote.*—Sard. i. 69.

¶ , *ina pan*, is used in the sense of "formerly:"—

, usuma salam Ninib sutu sa ina pan la im [duku] . . . . . la ebasni; *when that image of Ninib which formerly was not . . . . . I had made.*—Sard. ii. 133.

IN More rarely, and not, I believe, before the Babylonian period, we find [cuneiform], *in*, instead of *ina*. The Babylonian form is [cuneiform].

[cuneiform], in kirbi-su sibutu l'ukasid; *within it may abundance obtain.*—Sen. Gr. iii. 48.

[cuneiform], in kupri va agurri; *with cement and brick.*—E.I.H. v. 2.

[cuneiform], in hurasi kaspi; *with gold (and) silver.*—Neb. Gr. ii. 21.

[cuneiform], in Barsipa; *in Borsippa.*—Neb. Gr. ii. 18.

¶ [cuneiform], [cuneiform], ina, *sing.* ini, *pl.* *Eye, Eyes.* Heb. [illegible], *pl.* [illegible].

[cuneiform], ina er-at nis ina-sunu asar istaru hekal-hekal itepusu; *in cities the wonder of their eyes, a place they determined, palaces they built.*—E.I.H. vii. 18.

[cuneiform], ina.—Syl. 782.

This appears with "face," "foot," "ear," &c., on a fragment of a syllabary; the equivalents are all lost.

Ina should signify a "fountain," as well as "eye," in accordance with Semitic usage; and we find the word in the more correct form, [cuneiform], on the Nimrud Obelisk, lines 69 and 72, signifying the "fountains" of the Tigris and Euphrates. But the more usual form, where "eye" is intended, is the Accadian [cuneiform], which, like the symbols of other double parts of the body, becomes [cuneiform], "eyes," by the addition of two lines. The *nis ini* of E.I.H. vii. 18, quoted above, is made by [cuneiform] in l. 35 of the same column. We have several direct evidences of the equivalence of [cuneiform] and [cuneiform], two of which follow:—

[cuneiform], *over the eye.*—30 II. 8 *b.*

[cuneiform], ini iççuri; *eyes of birds.*—40 II. 16 *e.*

This is a sort of stone, named, no doubt, from its markings; just as we say "bird's-eye maple" for a sort of wood.

IN [cuneiform], ina; *Property, Substance.* Heb. ‏און‏.

[cuneiform] pitsuti ina-same usabis; *the common men their substance I caused arise.*— Botta 145, 12-14.

¶ [cuneiform], ina; *Introductory particle.*

[cuneiform], ina Shamas va Anunitâ ana arhi sanâ u yom imbû; *now the Sun-god and Anunit to after lands and days have proclaimed.*—Nab. Br. Cyl. iii. 24.

Not u yom is doubtful on the slab.

¶ [cuneiform], yaan; *Not being.* See p. 467.

[cuneiform] . [cuneiform]—4 R. II. 11*d.* Yaasumma.

[cuneiform] . [cuneiform] 12*d.* Yaaskka.

[cuneiform] . [cuneiform] 13*d.* Yaasusu.

[cuneiform] . [cuneiform] 14*d.* Yaasu.

[cuneiform] . [cuneiform] 15*d.* Ista yaan.

According to Hebrew analogy yaasu is "I am not," yaaska "thou art not," yaasusu "he is not;" ista yaan would be "from not being;" yaasumma perhaps "not being, and;" but as I have not found in the inscriptions any forms except yaan, I cannot speak with confidence. There are many other forms on the same tablet, but the Assyrian column is nearly all broken off, and the Accadian is as yet unintelligible.

IND [cuneiform] . [cuneiform], Inadidi.—Sarg. 20.

A tribe conquered by Sargon, apparently dwelling in the south of Syria.

INH [cuneiform]. *Now, the present time.*

The meaning implied by this Accadian phrase is clearly shown by the context in the two passages where it occurs, but I have no notion of the connection between the expression and its value. I have never seen it used elsewhere.

[cuneiform], sa ulta yumui ruquti adi . . abl-su [ad] ana sarrani abi-ya rabba-sun la isparu; *who from remote days until now, his fathers to the kings my fathers their envoy had not sent.*—Botta 151, 8-110.

INH

...... ša ultu yummi ruqati adi . . ana šarrani abi-ya ...... mašrumma la lamû zikar mati-sun; *who from remote days until now,* [to] *the kings my fathers ..... had never heard the mention of their country.*— Botta 153, 2 – 146.

The insertion of ana was an oversight; the writer, no doubt, intended to say that "to their kings the name of the country (Cyprus) had never arrived."

INZ Yanzú.—Obel. 112. Botta 146, 16 – 31.

Name of a king of the Nairi who was defeated by Shalmaneser; and of another rendered tributary by Sargon.

INL Inalia. See p. 478.

INN inini.

Occurs at the close of the following line, which I cannot read:—

napḫar bile ma'dis lakaza inini.—New Div. l. 4.

INT —25 II. 22a.

IS iṣi; *Banner, Ensign, Flag.* Heb. נֵס, נָסַס.

ultu [ša] alri Šimaki rakobi danta [v. da'tá] bit-ḫallu ris(dan)ma iṣi-ya aṣkin.—Sard. ii. 53. See *Danta*, p. 260.

rakobi bit-ḫallu Zahu sa Garkamis iṣi-ya aṣkin.—Sard. iii. 60.

The phrase iṣi-ya aṣkin occurs seven times in the inscription of Sardanapalus (ii. 53, 72, 106; iii. 63, 65, 65, 60), and, so far as I have seen, nowhere else. The sentences in which they are found resemble each other so much that it is unnecessary.

IS

sary to give more than two of them. In every case but one they are preceded by chariots, and by bit-hallu (which Dr. Oppert translates "cavalry"); in that one the chariots are omitted.

Dr. Hincks proposed to translate ispu aşibu "I put up in my magazines." Dr. Oppert generally transliterated the words in italics, ispa asiti, without a translation. The first example he makes "Près de Simaki, je laissai les chars, la cavalerie les premiers..........;" the second "Je asiti ispa les chars et les cavaliers des hommes cela de Karkamis." I would propose, very doubtfully, "From near Simaki, the chariots strong(?) and battering rams(?)...... and my banners I made ready;" and "the chariots and battering rams(?) of the Zaku of Carchemish, and my banners I made ready." Whatever are the words may denote, as soon as it was done the army always proceeded on its march.

¶ iṣitu, n. iṣite, g. iṣit, cons. iṣitâte, pl. *Pile, Heap.*

ana istin iṣitu sa tilui ana istin sa qaqqadi [risdu] arşip; *to one pile of bodies, to one of heads I built.*—Sard. i. 118. See p. 210.

annute ina eli iṣite ina zaqipi azqip; *some on the top of the pile on crosses I crucified.*—Sard. i. 90. See p. 42.

babi rabbi sinâti aike ana mihrat mee iṣit-sin ina kupri va agurri usarsid; *these great gates I put together, and opposite the waters their piles in cement and brick I founded.*—E.I.H. vi. 1.

(r. [cuneiform]) pagri sunu [bari-sunu] ana iṣitâte arşip; *their bodies to piles I built.*—Sard. i. 109.

I believe *isu* and *isitu* are merely masculine and feminine forms from the same root, meaning "to lift up" anything by way of standard or flag, or trophy, or other device which might excite attention; *isu* may have been confined to military ensigns, and *isitu* rather to things piled up for show; but we have not examples enough to decide. *Ispitu* appears to have been the same as *isitu*; see p. 42.

ISN [cuneiform], isinnu; *Festivals.*

[cuneiform], ana ilati-ya rabite ina er Kalhi lû amnu-su isinnate-su ina arhi XI va arhi VI lû aakun; *for my great divinity in the city of Calah I accounted him; his festivals in the months of Sebat and Tisri I established.*—Sard. E. 134.

I take this from Dr. Oppert, except that he says "celebrated" instead of "established." I know no authority for "festivals;" as the question is of a temple of Ninib as well as of an image, I would suggest that we might read "purifications" instead of "festivals," from the Chaldee root [illegible]: the temple might require a periodical cleansing. I am uncertain whether or not the first word in the following line is the same as that under consideration. I do not understand it, and am unable to see how it is connected with the rest of the passage:—

[cuneiform], isindti-sunu damgûti abipunu rabti.—Neb. Gr. iii. 7.

ISR [cuneiform], isare; *Traditions.*

[cuneiform], ina isare sa Urub va Ilgi pal-su amur; *in the traditions of Urukh and Ilgi his son I have seen, &c.*—Nabon. i. 13.

Isare appears here as a variant of *misare*, which I connect with the Chaldee (or Rabbinical) [illegible]. I am still doubtful about [cuneiform], though inclined to think that some form of the verb "to see" is understood by it.

IEL [cuneiform], yaeli; *Wild Goats.* Heb. יְעֵלִים 1 Sam. xxiv. 2.

[cuneiform], yaeli ina qadirdte ulemmeh; *wild goats in ranges he kept.*—Brok. Obel. l. 30.

IET [cuneiform], Yaeti.—Obel. 90.

A country called Yáte on the Bull, 48 B.M. 43, where it is said to be in the neighbourhood of the city of [cuneiform].

IPL [cuneiform], Yapalla.—Tig. jun. 18.

Name of a city captured by the king, together with *Tartum.* I find no indication of the locality.

IZ [cuneiform], ipi, ipat.—Beh. 28, 58, 75, 82.

There are four passages in the Behistun inscriptions, all expressing the Persian phrase, hadâ kamnaibis asabâraibis, "he with faithful horsemen;" l. 75, the only one perfect in Babylonian, I transcribe here:—

[cuneiform], hagaru itti nisi ipi eli-ya sa sisai [or kurrai]; *he with people going out to me of horses* (*people of horses* = *horsemen*).

In l. 88 we have [cuneiform], ina sabi ipat, "with warriors going out," instead of *nisi* ipa ipi in the singular. The determinative [cuneiform] is represented by [cuneiform], as we find it also in 2 Birch. i. 16–19; ii. 10; and twice in the long lines of 3 Birch. col. iv. hieratic. The Babylonian copy proves the correctness of Sir H. Rawlinson's rendering of asabaraibis, which was objected to by Dr. Oppert, and altered to "allegers" by Spiegel (Die Altpersischen Keilinschriften, p. 107, Leipzig, 1862), who proposed to read the Persian word *Agathara* instead of *Asbara*.

IQ [cuneiform]—Syl. 510.

[cuneiform]—Syl. 511.

IR [cuneiform], *yari*.—Sen. T. vi. 49. Neb. Yun. 71.

[cuneiform], is-iki is-liyari mesir eri namri arakkis; *the columns of is-liyari with bands of shining brass I bound.*—Sen. T. vi. 49.

This is the repetition of a line printed in p. 346, with the correction of a misprint in the plate, which was discovered by inspecting a photograph of the cylinder; the correction, [cuneiform] for [cuneiform], is confirmed by the parallel passage on the Nebi Yunus cylinder, and by it I am enabled to complete the translation; the sound *mesir* is proved by the [cuneiform] of Botta 38, 35, collated with [cuneiform] in the parallel 42, 77. *Yari* may be an epithet of the tree *isti*, from a root meaning "brush," connected with the Hebrew "יער": but I rather think it a part of the word *liyari*, which follows *is-pursu* in Neb. Yun. 71. See the note in p. 346.

IRD [cuneiform], irad; *Depth.* Heb. ירד.

[cuneiform], isid-su ina irad kigalle usarsid sa rasi-su usakhir harsanis; *its foundation in a depth solidly(?) I laid down, and its head I completed thoroughly.*—R.I.H. viii. 80.

IRD [cuneiform] ...... [cuneiform], in bigalli rimim in irad erziti sapanti ...... usarsid temen-su; *with high solidity, in depth of much earth ...... I laid down its basement.*—Neb. Gr. iii. 53.

I have translated erziti by "earth," as if we had the usual ṣ, because of the generally loose orthography of the Babylonian period; but it is possible that the writer may have intended to employ a word from a root cognate with the Arabic [illegible], implying "tenacity," "toughness." I have not met with any other instance of the word so written.

¶ [cuneiform].—Syl. 393.

IRN [cuneiform], iris.

The word occurs in 3 Mich., and I think it must be a dialectical variation of the verb *irin*; the following are the passages:—

[cuneiform], imsuh ma ana pati iris-su; *he has measured, and for the future has given it.*—3 Mich. i. 18.

[cuneiform], ana yomi pati iris-su; *for future days he has given it.*—End of the closing perpendicular line of the inscription.

IRS [cuneiform], iriqsu; *their Forests.*—39 BM 22.

This is *irit-su*, usually written *[illegible]*, as in the parallel Sen. B. iv. 4. See in p. 216. Dr. Oppert derives the word from [illegible], "a forest."

IRQ [cuneiform], Yaraqi.—Sard. iii. 90.

A province lying east of the Orontes.

IRR [cuneiform], yarri; *Sea or Great River.* Heb. [illegible].

[cuneiform], ebir tihamti gallati yarri marti; *the crossing of the great sea of the western ocean.*—E.I.H. vi. 46

Doubtful. See under *Barapti*, p. 142.

IRT [cuneiform], Iritu.—Sard. ii. 69.

A city of the province of Zamua, in the north of Assyria.

¶ [cuneiform] (v. [cuneiform]), irtasu.

[cuneiform], Marduk ana bit emuki irtasu gallum ina arba umtpu-sunu epiri [lahla] kirbi-su ippah sa lusmura uparšti; *Marduk to that house having permitted the fall, the four winds he raised and the earth within it was cleared away and the foundation-stones* (?) *were seen.*—Senk. Cyl. i. 19.

I have some doubts about this, but think it conveys the general meaning.

IS [cuneiform], isi; *May I Have.*

[cuneiform], ai isi nakiri mugalliti; *may I not have enemies multiplied.*—E.I.H. x. 15. The same in Neb. Bab. ii. 31, with var. [cuneiform], mugalitu.

I subjoin a few examples of the verb is, "to have" (see Dr. Hincks's Grammar, Journ. R.A.S., 1866, pp. 493-4):—

[cuneiform], mahira la isû; *who had not an equal.*—Tig. i. 44. Esar i. 7 with [cuneiform].

[cuneiform], sa kima mul same menuta la isû; *which, like the stars of heaven, number had not.*—Sard. iii. 63.

[cuneiform], nisi-su issi sa niba la isû; *his women* [*people female*] *who number had not.*—Esar i. 24. See Sen. T. iii. 79.

[cuneiform].—Syl. 181.

ISA Isana.—New Div. ii. 48.

Name of some locality on the way from Kar-Shalmaneser (Tel-Barsippa on the Euphrates) to Arumnis.

ISB —Syl. 138.

¶ isibu, isibbu; *Who is Seated.* Heb. ישב.

(v.), isibu ma'du (v. nabdu); *who sits glorious.*—Sard. i. 21.

isibbu ma'du; *Idem.*—Tig. i. 31.

Epithet of the two kings.

ISD isid; *Foundation.* Heb. יסד.

mihrat mee isid-sin ina kupri va agurri usarsid; *opposite the water their foundation in cement and brick I laid down.*—E.I.H. vi. 1.

ina mee milli isid-sa inis; *by the waters of floods its foundation was damaged.*—E.I.H. vii. 32. See also E.I.H. vii. 61; viii. 60. Nerig. ii. 26.

isid-sa [isissa] mihirat appi ina supal mie beruti usarsid; *its foundation, opposite to the river, in a depth of clear water I laid down.*—Neb. Bab. ii. 18. See p. 113.

ISR isaru, *adv. Justly.* Heb. ישר.

raqqu la isaru ul iba' kirib-sa; *the least thing unjustly comes not within it.*—E.I.H. ix. 26. See note at foot of p. 79.

ISR [cuneiform], isru; *Rich Ornament* (?). Heb. [illegible].

[cuneiform], isru merequti-ya u sal lamassi eri namriti asdupa; *ornament polished, and figures of lamassu of painted bronze, I erected.*—Neb. Yun. 78.

Uncertain. *Merequti-ya*, which I have never seen elsewhere, may be read sipru qati-ya, "the beautiful work of my hands;" *isru* may be the nominative case singular, of which the plural is [cuneiform], israti, a word not yet determined; Dr. Hincks was inclined to read it "avenue" (see his Grammar in *Journ.* R.A.S., 1866, p. 511). *Dr. Oppert* made it "marvels" in pp. 19 and 20 of his Inscription de Nabuchodonosor sur les Merveilles de Babylone, Reims, 1866 (E.I.H. iii. 55; vii. 7); I might, perhaps, translate "an avenue, a beautiful work of my hands, and figures, &c."

¶ [cuneiform], isartu, *n.* isarti, isriti, *g. Justice.* Heb. ישר.

[cuneiform], iddina ḫaṭṭu (is-pa) isartu; *he hath given the sceptre of justice.*—38 BM 5.

[cuneiform], ḫarrana isartū tapqid-su: *the path of justice thou hast prescribed it.*—E.I.H. i. 60.

[cuneiform], ḫaṭṭu (is-sa pa) isarti usatmiḫu qata-su; *the sceptre of justice thou hast made his hand to hold.*—Nerig. i. 10.

[cuneiform], nasi ḫaṭṭi isrite; *bearing the sceptre of justice.*—Sh. Ph. i. 28. See also E.I.H. i. 45; iv. 10. Birs i. 14.

IST [cuneiform], isati; *Fire.* Heb. אש.

[cuneiform], ina isati iqalû; *in fire who shall consume.*—3 Mich. i. 34. (The last four lines are separated, on the stone, from the body of the inscription.)

This is the only example I have seen of this word phonetically written; it was often made by [cuneiform], which I suppose may be the name of a god of fire; see [cuneiform], *ina isati aqlu*, "in fire I burned;" Botta 153, 4 = 154; Sen. T. iv. 28, &c. More frequently it was rendered by the monogram [cuneiform]; see examples in p. 66; but I believe it was always pronounced isati.

IST [cuneiform], isiti; *Possession(?)*.

[cuneiform], nara eqlit [alibbi]-suna sa ultu yomme ullutí ina isiti mâti Suti ikimû; *the produce(?) of their lands which from former days (had been) in possession of the country, the Suti [Nomades] had taken.*—Botta 152, 9–135.

Uncertain. I have not seen the word elsewhere.

IT [cuneiform] — Syl. 723.
[cuneiform] „ 724.
[cuneiform] 725.
[cuneiform] „ 726.
[cuneiform] „ 727.
[cuneiform] „ 728.
[cuneiform] „ 729.

All these lines have ist for their monogram, signifying "the hand," or "troops," or "defences;" see pp. 209, 478. I think I see the meaning of some of the equivalents; the second is dikû, "the fighter;" the third maṣṣru, "the guard," and imnu, "right" hand, [Hebrew]; the fourth šumêlu, "left" hand [see p. 492]; the sixth nasû, "the lifter." I do not understand the others.

¶ [cuneiform], itâ; *Walls.* See *itati*, pp. 499, 500.

[cuneiform] (v. [cuneiform]) [cuneiform], kirar rabû tamsil Hamanû sa kala simmu made u iṣu made harrurû itâ-su esild; *plantation large, like (those of) Mount Amanus, which all with plants many and trees many is cultivated, its walls I raised.*—Esar vi. 16.

A very similar passage occurs in Sen. Gr. 58, and 42 BM 46, with *gimir* instead of *kala*, and *askup* instead of *esild*; this has helped me to the above word-for-word version, which might be more freely given in this way:—"I raised a wall around a large plantation like those of Mount Amanus, in which many plants and trees were cultivated." *Simmu* I have doubtfully rendered "plant," from the Heb. [Hebrew].

I do not know the grammatical relation of itâ and itu in the following page, but I think the root must be the same.

IT itê; *Wall, Frontier, Border.*

This word, like *put* or *pati*, is translated "the border," "the neighbourhood," "the wall," or "beyond," as the case may be; it may often be more convenient to consider it a preposition, and write "near."

adi ..... Rāsi sa itê Namma-ki sa ah nahr Vastigrar; *to ..... Ras which is near Elam on the banks of the Tigris.*—Botta 145, 6 = 18.

ana itê Mušuri sa pat Miluhha innabid; *to the borders of Egypt which is near Meroe he fled.*—Botta 150, 6 = 102.

aštak sibl la basu panû itê Babel-ki la šanaga mee rabûti kima gibis tihamati usada asalmi; *for enemies not being* [i.e. to *prevent enemies from being*] *before the walls of Babylon the unconquered (?), great waters, like the vast might of the sea, I brought near.*—E.I.H. vi. 40.

¶ Itû; *Name of some class of Persons.*

lû Naturda lû Itû va lû sinamma; *whether Naturda, or Itû, or any body whatever.*—1 Mich. ii. 6; see p. 4.

¶ Yail; see *Yâsi*, pp. 467-9.

ITD Itut; *Supporter, Upholder.* Heb. [illegible] or [illegible].

itut kun libbi Marduk; *steadfast supporter of the will of Merodach.*—Birs i. 2.

Perhaps connected with [illegible] or [illegible]; see p. 281.

ITH [cuneiform], itsʾ.—Tig. jun. 5. Botta 145, 6 – 18; 16bis 71.

One of many tribes enumerated as belonging to Assyria.

¶ [cuneiform], itsʾeme, itsʾlmt; *Lawgiver.*

See Lʾuʾum, pp. 520-1, where there are other variations of the same word.

ITM [cuneiform], Yatlma. See p. 508.

The extract from Tint col. 66, in p. 509, is only a dependent clause in a long sentence, which I did not fully understand when that page was printing; the following translation expresses the whole as literally as I can put it together:—"In like manner as I the act of writing the name of the king, the father begetting me, with the act of writing my name do perform, so do thou also, like me here, the act of writing my name......(and the image clean (and) the victim sacrifice) with the act of writing thy name perform. Assur and Istar thy prayers will hear." The gist of this misty combination is simply—"As I write my father's name with my name, thou, my son, write thy father's name with thy name, (superadding the due ceremony) and the gods will listen to thee." I use "the act of writing" instead of the awkward "writing of writing;" meaning the formation of the characters and *state* the characters formed. *Aharum*, about which I have hazarded several unsuccessful guesses, seems superfluous in the above sentence, and I have omitted it in the translation.

¶ [cuneiform], itlmmu.—Syl. 447.

ITT [cuneiform], itatu, n. itat, c. itati. *Walls.*

[cuneiform], dikta-su ina itat er Sarrapani er-su adak; *his fighting men on the walls of Sarrapan his city, I slew.*—Tig. jun. 15.

[cuneiform], itat Nimitti-Bel mihs Babel-hi ....dur sadanis epus; *the walls of Nimitti Bel, an outwork of Babel, ... the fortress, like a mountain I made.*—E.I.H. viii. 46.

[cuneiform], itti erki ana kidānu bakal rabiti .... abni; *the walls of the citadel(?) for the strengthening of the great garrison .... I built.*—Neb. Bab. ii. 15.

ITT itâti dur Babel-ki gaa tahazi-sa usaqqi; *the walls of the fortress of Babel, its defence of war, I raised.*—E.I.H. ix. 39.

anaku ina kibid Asur bili rabu bili-ya mê (ni) imna va sumali adi sa itata-ssu . . . .; *I, in honour of Asur the great lord, my lord, waters right and left of the hills of its neighbourhood . . . .*—Bavian 14.

The line breaks off here, and after two or three damaged words, apparently local names, we have usaddi ar abni, "I conveyed down in stone;" implying obviously the construction of an aqueduct, as might have been expected from the preceding lines, which narrate the digging of canals for the supply of Nineveh with good drinkable water. In this passage itata must, I think, mean "neighbourhood," and be connected with ita; the Hebrew ithon, "entrance" (keri of Ezek. xl. 15) might, perhaps, have the same root.

itata'a; *its walls.*—Botta 37, 39. See p. 398.

itâ libbi . . . . hurasi namri usalbis; *the walls of the inside . . . . with shining gold I caused cover.*—E.I.H. iii. 28.

WORDS WHICH MAY NOT BE READILY FOUND.

isit, *base;* p. 490: isid, *foundation;* p. 495.

ikun, *he hath established;* p. 470.

imat, *terror;* p. 482.

isindli, *fetters?* p. 491.

yanu, *not being;* pp. 487, 488.

K כ

Characters arranged under letter K.

, ka. Babylonian or .

, ki; more recent form .

, , ka.

, kab. Occasionally is confounded with .

or , kab; "*the left hand.*"

, kabd; "*much, weighty, honourable.*"

, kib; sometimes . In Tig. .

, kid, or sap.

, kid.

, kid.

,* kat.

, kat, or sam; "*family.*"

, kam.

,* kim; "*like, as.*"

, kum.

, kan.

, kan.

, kar; "*castle*" or "*fortress.*"

, kir.

, kir.

, kas, or ras; "*a road.*"

, kis.

, kisal; "*an altar,*" or "*sacrifice.*"

---

* I have already entered and under G; but these characters so seldom occur that their repetition will not cause much trouble.

K(a) [cuneiform], an Accadian word, is explained in the following extracts from syllabaries and bilingual slabs :—

[cuneiform] —Syl. 476.

[cuneiform] „ 477. Pi, mouth.

[cuneiform] „ 478. Ini, eye.

[cuneiform] „ 479.

[cuneiform] „ 480.

[cuneiform] „ 481.

[cuneiform]—20 II. 11 a.

This may be read aspu as ka, "irrigation," or "supply of water for drinking;" but I do not remember seeing it so used.

[cuneiform], pú; mouth.—20 II. 1 a.

The oblique form [cuneiform], pi, occurs several times in the same column as the equivalent of ka, in combinations which I am unable to translate.

Of the Accadian equivalents in these extracts I understand only pú, pi, "mouth," and ini, "eye;" but I infer from the examples which follow that ka might imply any prominent or conspicuous part of man or animal, such as the "horn," or perhaps "tusk;" also a projecting or ornamental part of a throne or altar.

¶ [cuneiform], ka; *Horn, or Tusk; Face.*

Prominent feature of man or beast, conspicuous ornament on a throne, altar, &c.

[cuneiform]
kaspa hurasa anna tikabar az-bar ka rimi ana la mani amhar-sunuti; *silver, gold, lead, copper, iron, horns of reems, without number I received them.*—Obel. 156.

[cuneiform]
yul-sunu ka-sunu itti rimi paltute ana ir-ya Asur ubla; *their skins, their horns, with reems alive, to my city Assur I carried.*—Tig. vi. 74. See Esar i. 20; R.I.H. ix. 11.

K(A) [cuneiform] kai sakiri binut tamti ambar; *horns of the narwhal(?) the produce of the sea, I received.*—43 BM 12. See pp. 113 and 272.

[cuneiform] ..... [cuneiform] kai [illegible] kai is-sai kai kussi kai kaspi ḫurasi .... ambar; *horns of altars, horns of is-sa(?) horns of thrones, horns of silver and gold .... I received.*—Sard. iii. 62.

[cuneiform] ikda sa la ida kibid ka-su; *the powerful, who hath not learned the honour of his presence(?).*—Sard. i, 4.

¶ [cuneiform], erisu; *a Bride.*

[cuneiform] erisa [ka] sapsà.—Prière de Sargon, l. 4.

The inscription containing this clause is printed at p. [illegible] of Dr. Oppert's Exp. Més., Vol. 2. The doctor's Latin version is "[illegible] blandam [illegible];" in French he writes "rends facile la [illegible]." He refers to the following extract:—

([cuneiform]) [cuneiform] . [cuneiform].—2 II. 33 c.

There is very much ingenuity displayed in rendering this very difficult inscription, but there is too much conjectural reading to justify implicit confidence.

¶ [cuneiform] , [cuneiform], *a sort of Stone.*

[cuneiform] ..... [cuneiform]. abu ka abu ḫalta va abu kagina .... lu asul; *the stones ka, ḫalta, and kagina .... I raised.*—Tig. viii. 11.

I know nothing about these stones except that they were dug up in the country of Nairi, and used in building a temple to the god Yav. The stone *Ka* is named also in Botta 152, 10=162, and in Esar vi. 6.

¶ [cuneiform] , [cuneiform] (v. [cuneiform]), *some Official Person.*

[cuneiform] (v. [cuneiform]) [cuneiform] (v. [cuneiform]) [cuneiform], ka (ku) ra (ru)-suna ina ir Kalḫi epus; *their Ka (and) Ra (or Ku and Ru) in the city of Calah I made [appointed].*—Sard. ii. 79.

The determinative shows that persons holding some office are designated here; the variant [cuneiform] is believed to signify a "servant," in the sense of minister, like our "civil servant;" of ra or ru I know nothing; I suppose ka and ra to be accusatives of ku and ru. Dr. Oppert translated "j'établis leur vice-roi à Calach."

K(A) . . . . [cuneiform], -ka; *Thee, Thy, masc.*

Used after nouns, verbs, and prepositions.

[cuneiform], bukhir ummani-ka; *choose thy army.*—Sen. T. v. 23.

[cuneiform], Assur va Istar ikribi-ka ishimmu; *Assur and Istar thy prayers will hear.*—Esar vi. 71.

[cuneiform], lu-vaida-kka; *be it known to thee.*—No. 6, N.R. 27, 28.

[cuneiform], sa eli-ka dhibu; *who to thee is favourable.*—E.I.H. i. 72.

[cuneiform], sa Ahurmazda' uta'ama ina eli-ka la imarras; *of Ormazd the law on thee shall not be harsh.*—No. 6, N.R. 34.

[cuneiform], itti-ka; *with thee.*—12 II. 46 b.

¶ [cuneiform], babu; *a Gate.*—Syl. 363.

¶ [cuneiform], kamis; *Heaped, all together, in disorder.* Arab. كم.

[cuneiform], Assur Shamas Yav va ili asib libbi-su sum-su [sa-su] zir-su ina mati l'ilquta ana ina kita sibi-su l'usasibu-su kamis; *Assur, Shamas, Yav, and the gods dwelling in it, his name (and) his race in the land may they gather up, and under his enemies make him dwell altogether.*—Sarg. 67.

K(a) [cuneiform], ana Assur-ki urd ina dibi bab rabi sa uddu sa Nineveh-ki itti ugi ar-ba sab usasib-suvati kamis; .... *to Assyria I sent, near the great gate of the sacred of Nineveh with dogs and other animals I made them dwell all together.*—Essar ii. 5.

> The beginning is lost, so that we do not know who the unhappy captives were. I have said in p. 42 all I know of ugi; for urku, "dog," see p. 541. [cuneiform] occurs nearly twenty times in a list of animals, 611, but with no explanation intelligible to me.

[cuneiform], ina pan aibi-su kamis l'usasibu-su; *from before his enemies in disorder may they place him.*—Tig. viii. 62.

> A collation of these three extracts may show the value of [cuneiform] here; a curse is implied in the text, so that we cannot read kasid, a "captor," or "conqueror," as in Sard. i. 19, 23, 69, and Essar i. 9. For the meaning of ina pan see p. 485.

K(D) [cuneiform], ki; *Earth, Place, Ground.*

[cuneiform], asru; *place.*—Syl. 161.

[cuneiform], irpita; *earth.*—Syl. 162.

[cuneiform], matu; *land, country.*—39 II. 64.

[cuneiform], ana urani sa ki-sunu (v. asar) ruhuqu ...... alik; *to cities which their place was remote ...... I went.*—Sard. ii. 42.

[cuneiform], ili masmilut-su itti .... abi-su [ad] mahruti altu kirib ki rab lipir; *the gods his guardians with the .... of his fathers of old from within the great country he joined.*—Neb. Yun. 9.

> This passage narrates the commencement of Merodach's flight with his gods across the sea, to save his life. The damaged word is unintelligible to me.

[cuneiform], matima .... ina ki itasnapiru; *whenever .... with earth shall cover (?).*—2 Mich. ii. 12.

K(i) pal Anna-bit-palusur sar Babilu-ki anaku; *son of Nabopolassar king of Babylon* (am) *I*.—Neb. Gr. I. 7.

Ki is almost always placed after names of cities, &c., when they have no determinative before them; see half-a-dozen places in Botta 16, lines 2, 3, 4, 5, 20, 22, &c.

¶ ki: *By, with; when, if.*

With:—

ina gibis ummani-a u tahazi-a gitmari ki (v. itti)-sunu amtahis; *with the power of my army and my formidable fight, with them I fought.*—Sard. ii. 103.

ikpus pisu ki Marguwai; *he made battle with the Margians.*—Beh. 69. See p. 351.

tari kali sa ki-su; *the young men all who (were) with him.*—Beh. 83.

dur mati dur umme banit ki abi-a alidi-ya ana sumu lu abbi; *that castle "the castle of the mother bearing with the father begetting me" for greatness I named.*—Hamm. ii. 28.

For the sound of *a* attributed here to see Syl. 362, printed in p. 2.

—Syl. 180.

Unless *itti* imply "with" in this extract, I do not know what it means.

¶ *Ki la*, or literally "with not," may be translated "without" or "against:"—

aibu limnu sa ki la libbi ili sarrut Babel-ki ebusu ma tahamdu rabiti qat-su; *a wicked enemy who against the will of the gods had occupied the kingdom of Babylon, and [which] his hand greatly(?) had taken.*—Botta 37, 21.

In the parallel Botta 41, 46 we have variants and for and

K(1) Marduk-baladanu ..... 12 sanati ki la libbi ili Babel-ki er Bel sakal ili ibil va iabar; *Merodach-baladan .... twelve years, against the will of the gods, Babel the city of Bel who weighs the gods, had ruled and harassed.*—Botta 151, 4(16) = 124.

I read …, *sanati*, as a phonetic complement of …, "year."

¶ When: Heb. כִּי (Gen. xlvi. 8):—

ki imuru mati sasiti; *when he saw these countries.*—No. 6, N.R. 20.

In this sense we more frequently find …, *ki*.

¶ .... ; -ki; *Thy, fem.*

lihdu ina pani-ki; *may he rejoice before thy face.*—Slab K, 162, l. 15; translated in part by Mr. Talbot.

yâti Assurbanipal hattû [pata] ilutî-ki rabiti balat yumme ruquti [bui] tab libbi-ki eim sa aliaku [dutaku] Bit-Marduk l'aliblira sêri-ya; *to me Assurbanipal, reverer of thy great divinity,* [*of Beltis,*] *life, days long, the goodness of thy heart* .....—2 Beltis 8. See *Bu*, p. 63.

I cannot read the remaining words of this inscription, which are mostly Accadian. The meaning may, possibly, be something to this effect, but it is merely a guess:—"May the goodness of thy heart grant me life, long days, and entrance to the temple of Merodach, where my feet are old."

damqutê-a l'istakan sabtu-kki; *my holy place may thy sceptre sustain.*—Inscr. du Temple de Mylitta, l. 26. Oppert's Exp. Més. p. 290.

This is addressed to the Goddess …, called Mylitta by Dr. Oppert; see a like address to Merodach in p. 212, with the only difference of gender. The *k* is doubled here, as with *ku*; see also in p. 181. *Ki*, like *ka* and *su*, would be found, no doubt, after verbs and prepositions, if the mention of females occurred more frequently in the inscriptions.

K (1) ki; *While, when.* Heb. כְּ.

ki ina Zamua usbaku-ni; *while in Zamua I was staying.*—Sard. II. 86. See also Sard. I. 58, 74.

ki ina er Kalhi usbaku-ni; *while in the city of Calah I was staying.*—Obel. 147, 158, 173.

¶ If:—

ki taqabbû umma mati annitû; *if thou shalt say that "these provinces," &c.*—No. 6, N.R. 95.

I am not quite sure of the meaning of umma (see p. 513); perhaps the translation might be "if thou shalt say thus;" but I am inclined to prefer the reading given. I cannot read the rest of the sentence.

¶ As, like:—

bilta madatti ki Assuri emid-suuti; (*as to*) *tribute, and payments, like Assyrians I placed them* [*treated them*].—Sarg. 16.

tarbasunu ki litute asbat; *their young men as hostages I took.*—Sard. II. 11. See I. 103.

22 eri halsut ki da'tâti iddin-su; *twenty-two cities as donations he gave him.*—Botta 146, 3 = 39.

ilku sarpikku ki sa Kunzinaun sarri mahri ukin eli-su; *toll-dues* (*and*) *homage, as of Gunzinan the former king, I laid upon him.*—Botta 146, 11 - 63.

ki sa anaku musarû sitir sum (*su*) sarri abi (*ad*) banî-ya .... askunu sa atta kima yatima musaru sitir sum-ya .... sukun; *in like manner as I the act of writing the name of the king, the father my generator .... do perform, also do thou, like me here, the act of writing my name .... perform.*—Esar vi. 64. See p. 499.

K(i) In the following lines, 2 Mich. i. 15, 16, *ki* denotes "as," "equivalent to." They head a list of above a dozen articles drawn up in the form of an invoice, with the value of each article stated in pieces of silver, and the total at the end. These articles were given in payment for a piece of land:—

[cuneiform]

[cuneiform]

1 rukuba adi ti'uti-sa ki 100 kaspi; *one chariot with its appurtenances, equivalent to one hundred pieces of silver.*

6 sal .... sisra ki 300 kaspi; *Six .... horses, equal to three hundred pieces of silver.*

For *pas* as a determinative instead of [cuneiform] see p. 497.

¶ By, through, according to:—

[cuneiform] ....., hattu imqut-su ma ki țalm ramani-su bilti u mandatti ....; *fear overwhelmed him, and by the will of himself [of his own accord] tribute and payment (he brought).*—Esar iii. 57.

The verb is broken off from the cylinder, together with the whole line.

[cuneiform] kaspi eqili [alibi] or alma ki pi duppáte sa almanu-su kaspi va tamkalar ana bili-sunu utir; *the money of the lands of that city, by the face of the documents of the security of it, [or as appears on the documents of its covenant] silver and copper, to their owners I restored.*—Sarg. 41.

[cuneiform] .... [cuneiform] lamaşşi sa abal sa ki pi şikal-suna irti limni [sini] utarra .... imna u sumila usasbita; *bulls and lions of stone, which by their watchful faces, terror to enemies produce, ... the right and left (sides) I caused occupy.*—Esar v. 42.

In respect of the value of [cuneiform] and [cuneiform] as "right" and "left," there is direct authority for [cuneiform] or [cuneiform] (both forms are found) in Syl. 871, where the equivalent *sumilu* is given; see p. 169. For the right hand I would

K(I) adduce the opposition of "right" and "left," as satisfactory evidence. Two extracts from the 2nd column of 39 II.—the first line with [cuneiform] and [cuneiform], the Accadian and Assyrian words for "right hand," and the second line having [cuneiform] in the Accadian, and [cuneiform] in the Assyrian column, may, perhaps, be a corroboration. I do not remember any direct proof.

¶ 1 And M....M in Botta 41, 12, apparently signifying "some....others;" but the copies are not sure, and I do not remember seeing a similar case elsewhere.

¶ [cuneiform], ke.

[cuneiform], ana Nabu daplai sa ke.—2 Pal. 1.

Dr. Oppert translates this "Au dieu Nébo, qui garde les mystères."

K(U) [cuneiform], tagalli.—Syl. 692.

[cuneiform] „ „ 693.

[cuneiform] „ „ 694.

I learn from these extracts that [cuneiform] implies "service" (root pal), and perhaps that it might be sounded sa, but I do not remember to have seen the character so pronounced. See 39 II. 64a, where sabu, "a servant," is rendered by [cuneiform]; it is quite possible that sa might have been pronounced su, as a contraction of sabu.

[cuneiform], markaqu.—31 II. 10 d.

[cuneiform], fun. „ 15 d.

[cuneiform], rati. „ 18 d.

[cuneiform], ana. „ 19 d.

These extracts appear to give the Assyrian equivalents of the postpositive Accadian [cuneiform]. In the bilingual tablets we often find the Assyrian ina rendered by the Accadian [cuneiform]; see the following:—

[cuneiform], tar-ani = maruq-qu [marut-qu]; *his child.*—9 II. 59b.

[cuneiform], tar-ani-ku = ana maruti-su; *to his child.*—9 II. 60b.

[cuneiform], tar-vas-ani = ablut-qu [ablut-qu]; *his male child.*—9 II. 63b.

[cuneiform], tar-vas-ani-ku = ana abluti-su; *to his son.*—9 II. 64b.

K(v) [cuneiform] was pronounced also dur and ur. For dur see 47 II. 18a, where [cuneiform] is glossed by [cuneiform]; and for ur see Sard. ii. [illegible] 160 and 161, in both of which we find the city of Tusha written both [cuneiform] and [cuneiform]. At the end of names [cuneiform] frequently occurs, pronounced [illegible], it is not easy to say which; it implies the case-ending and possessive pronoun; see [cuneiform] in Bro. T. I. 29 and Bro. Cyl. 7, which I should pronounce [illegible] "his [illegible]," and [cuneiform] [illegible], in Botta 151, 5–113, and 151, 15–123.

¶ Dr. Hincks was of opinion that [cuneiform] signified a servant; see the Journal of Biblical Literature, Jan. 1858, p. 393; this is confirmed by the equivalent [illegible] in 29 II. 60a, mentioned in p. 510. He also thought that it was probably a non-phonetic determinative of the names of plants. See his Grammar in Journ. R.A.S., 1866, p. 507.

¶ [cuneiform] , [cuneiform], *Dog*, Accad. Assyrian, *kalbu*. Heb. כֶּלֶב.

This Accadian compound, expressively signifying "animal-servant," is printed at the top of p. 388, from a passage in the inscription of Esar Haddon. An example of its employment as a term of contempt occurs in the following extract:—

[cuneiform]

nisi ir Pâpai nisi Lallukai kalbi [ur-ku] tarbit hekal-ya sa ana Kakmé idbubú hattie [padie] ultu asri-sunu assuha-sunuti; *the men of the city Paphos (and) Lallukun, dogs the growth of my palace, who to Kakmé had urged revolt,* [*spoken seditiously*, p. 466] *from their place I removed them.*—Botta 72, 10; 116, 1; 150, 4.

Collated from these three plates, all mutilated. Cf. Sarg. 25–29.

We have almost certain evidence of the value of [cuneiform] in the following extract from a bilingual slab containing the names of animals:—

[cuneiform] , [cuneiform], kalba.—6 II. 13 a.

[cuneiform] , [cuneiform] —39 II. 19 c.

[cuneiform] , [cuneiform] „ 20 c.

[cuneiform] , [cuneiform] „ 21 c.

I read mîraru "a whelp," the Hebrew גּוּר; in the second and third lines we have the "dog's whelp" and the "lion's whelp."

The resemblance of the Accadian word to the Greek *κύων* and the Gaelic and Welsh *cu*, is curious; more appropriate is the occurrence of *ku* as a root of the equivalents for "dog" in the Turkish *ku-pek*, the Wotiak *kuchu*, the Hungarian *ku-tya*, and in several other Turanian idioms.

K(5) (?) . (?) . —Syl. 282.

(?) . „ 108.

KA Kua.

Something appertaining to the god Merodach, if not Merodach himself; I have a note that is Merodach, but cannot find the reference.

elap Kua sariri va abni umla kakkabis samami; *the tabernacle of Bit-Kua* [*le sanctuaire mystique de Merodach*.—Opp.] *with figures and stones I have adorned like the stars of heaven.*—E.I.H. iii. 10.

See the passage from Sen. T. III. printed in p. 380, where I think "tabernacles" should be read instead of "ships."

(v.), Bit-Saggatu ...... subat bil-bit-ili Marduk Bit-Kua papaha beluti-su .... astakkan; *Bit-Saggatu .... the seat of the chief of gods(?) Merodach, (and) Bit-Kua the shrine of his power .... I established.*—Birs i. 17.

The context here shows unmistakeably that "*his power*" is Merodach's power and I think the same is implied in the first passage quoted also.

Bit-Kua papaha bil-bit-ili Marduk asnabit sassanis sallaru-usu; *Bit-Kua, the shrine of the chief of gods, Merodach, I have made conspicuous its splendour with fine linen.*—E.I.H. ii. 42.

I derive *sassanu* from שש, which in Hebrew signifies some sort of fine linen of which the holy tabernacle was made.—Exod. xxvi. 1.

Bit-Kua papaha beluti-su; *Bit-Kua the shrine of his power.*—E.I.H. iii. 24.

Merodach is certainly implied in this form of *beluti*. See p. 87.

KA [cuneiform].
bab Kam amlbis kaspi namri; *the gate Kam I covered (with) shining silver.*—E.I.H. iii. 46.

[cuneiform].—62 II. 41 c.

This bilingual extract can only mean that the tabernacle of Kam is the tabernacle of Merodach. The top of the slab is lost, but the [cuneiform], equivalent to our ditto, must have had [cuneiform] as its original expression. See pp. 349 and 357.

I have had some difficulty with the phrase [cuneiform] sometimes accompanying the name of Merodach; to the passages just quoted I may add E.I.H. iv. 3, vii. 24; Nerig. i. 13, ii. 31. In the case last mentioned [cuneiform] comes before [cuneiform], thus proving the value given. I have rendered the title by *bil bit-ili*, "the master of the house of the gods;" but as in the great Nebuchadnezzar slab we have the hieratic [cuneiform], cursive [cuneiform], instead of [cuneiform], "house," I have in the translation written simply "chief of the gods." The same group, without the addition of [cuneiform], denotes a deity considered by *Sir H.* Rawlinson to be the primitive Belus; Dr. Oppert renders it by "Bel Dagon." The name is more commonly written [cuneiform]; see Tig. i. 3; Sarg. 59; Bavian 1, &c.; but we have [cuneiform] in Neb. Gr. i. 3, and [cuneiform] in I Mich. iii. 9, and iv. 2. See p. 367 and Tig. i. 63.

KAK [cuneiform]. Kaskinda.—Obel. 122.

A city in the north, on the way to Armenia, destroyed in the twenty-fourth year of Shalmaneser.

KAM [cuneiform], kiham; *Thus.* Heb. כה

Found at the commencement of every undamaged paragraph of the Assyrian Behistun inscription. The Persian copy has no equivalent; the Scythic has *kiml*, "and," in every paragraph except the first. This has induced a belief that *kiham* should mean "again" or "and," but I think "thus" is the correct reading. The loss of the first clause in the Assyrian copy has deprived us of what would probably have decided the question.

[cuneiform], kiham ikbu-ni umma temінna sulli nuba'i la nimur; *thus they said to me that "that inscription (?) we have sought (but) we have not seen."*—Nab. Br. Cyl. ii. 55.

The word *temin* certainly denotes the foundation or platform on which a palace was built, and its root will be connected with the Arabic [illegible], explained by Golius as "planities aequaliter expressa;" but *temennu*, as certainly, it signified something smaller, for we find, in the lines preceding the above extract, that the workmen had been seeking the *temin* for three years, "to the right and to the left, before and behind," before they came to inform Nabonidus that they were unable to find it. I agree with Mr. Talbot that this was either the inscribed cylinder which was usually deposited in the basement, or an inscription on the platform itself.

KAM . . . . , Istar . . . . ana ummanat-ya • sampri ma kibsu ibsi-ma-ma umma . . . . ; *Istar . . . . . to my soldiers a vision disclosed, and thus said to them that* . . . . .—Assur b.p. vi. 23.

I do not know the sound of ; its value as a "dream" or "vision" was communicated to me by Sir H. Rawlinson. The use of masculine verbs with the feminine Istar is exceptional. The insertion of "that" before words quoted is usual in Persian; in the following passage from Sadi, *bada guft ki zahid-i yá shirá-i*, "to him he said that, monk art thou, or a perfidious art thou;" see Sir W. Jones's Grammar, p. 129; but I do not remember this in a Semitic language or in any of the older Assyrian inscriptions.

—2 R 11. 35 c.

KAN , kahan; *Agent, Advocate.* Arab. كاهن, administrator alieni negotii.

itti tamarti-su kabitti usabila adi mahri-ya rakba-su sa ana sa'al sulum-ya kahan istanappara; *with his many gifts he caused to bring to my presence his envoy [rider] who to ask peace of me as advocate came [his many gifts which he caused his envoy to bring].*—Assur b.p. iii. 24.

¶ v. v. kaisu, *subst.* kayanu, *adj.* *Firm; Strongly.* Heb. כון.

, kaina, *adv.* *Strongly.*

We have here the adverbial *a* term; see pp. 78, 88, 163, &c. I am decidedly of opinion that the final vowel in the great majority of cases, whether in verbs, nouns, or adverbs, was optional and unmeaning.

(v.) ( ) (v.) , rubâ kinu sa ana mutsur pani (v. parsi) bitkari mati-su pitqudu kaisu; *chief unwavering, who for the guidance of the heads and elders of his country is a steadfast guardian.*—Bard. i. 24.

KAN asirat Nabiû va Marduk bele-a asteni'a kainâ; *the edifices(?) of Nebo and Merodach I repaired strongly.*—Neb. Gr. iii. 6.

The first two letters are not at all clear on the cylinder.

sa . . . . damgûti Babel-ki va Barsipa-ki istesi'a kainâ; *who . . . . . the holy places of Babylon and Borsippa hath repaired strongly.*—Neb. Bab i. 10.

A parallel passage in E.I.H. i. 17 with shows that is here used phonetically, which is not unusual in the inscriptions of this date. The verb is in the indirect form, "who hath repaired."

sairium kappi sa sippe sanunu kainâ; *the . . . . . . of silver which on the buttresses was put up firmly.*—Nerig. i. 22; and see i. 31.

I imagine sairium must be some figure or other ornament.

¶ kainak; *I am Steadfast.*

This is Dr. Hincks's permansive present, first person. See his Grammar in Journ. R.A.S. 1866, p. 487.

anaku ana Marduk bili-ya kainak la batlak; *I to Merodach my lord am steadfast, not failing.*—Nerig. i. 17; see Neb. Bab. i. 20.

ana Bit-Saggatu va Bit-Zida qaqdâ kainak; *to Bit-Saggatu and Bit-Zida as ruler I am steadfast.*—Neb. Gr. iii. 4.

Qaqdâ, "as ruler," is pure guess-work, for want of anything better. The form is adverbial (see *Pallid*, p. 59), and the rest may be qaqqadu; the confusion of gutturals was usual in the lower empire.

KB [cuneiform] or [cuneiform], kap; *the Hand (the left hand).* Heb. כף.

These two characters are essentially the same, the difference being due to rapid writing; the carefully-formed [cuneiform] became [cuneiform] when the stylus was not lifted, and the horizontal line was imperfectly dashed in at the side instead of being fully drawn at the bottom.

[cuneiform] (v. [cuneiform]), Ahuzu ana kapi-ya utaqir; *Ahem to my own hand I annexed.*—Sard. iii. 71.

[cuneiform], sumilu.—Syl. 271.

See the Hebrew שְׂמֹאל, semol, "the left." The character, however, is usually employed for "the hand" simply, though where any distinction is implied, the "left hand" is understood; see p. 509. Sometimes [cuneiform], qatu, is used, but the Accadian [cuneiform], in the plural [cuneiform], is almost universal. See [cuneiform] = [cuneiform], qati-ya, "my hand," in 19 II. 47, 44,b, and also [cuneiform] id kabbi-nu = [cuneiform], sumeli-ya, "my left hand," in 19 II. 33, 56b.

[cuneiform] (v. [cuneiform]), annute kappi-suna sitti-sunu ubattik (v. ubatik); *of some their hands (and) their feet I chopped off.*—Sard. i. 117. See ii. 113.

¶ [cuneiform], kabu; *Sheep, Cattle.*

[cuneiform]—38 II. 27 *d.* *Sheep.*

[cuneiform]—38 II. 29 *d.* *Cattle.*

¶ [cuneiform], kabi; *Recesses.* Heb. [illegible]

[cuneiform], ina rie eni sa Halhal Purrat alik pulam sarruti-ya ina kabi-sina ulzid; *in the head sources of the Tigris (and) Euphrates I went, a statue of my majesty in their recesses I erected.*—Obel. 93.

Instead of ina kabi-sina ulzid, we have the following line in the parallel passage on the bulls, 16 BM 68 and 47 BM 29, where [cuneiform] takes the place of [cuneiform].

[cuneiform], ina [cuneiform] kapi sa ende ina git

KB naqabi-sa abni; *in the depressions of the mountains, in the issues of its sources, I built.*

The meaning of this is clearly that the stages were erected around about the sources of the two rivers, though it is hardly decisive as to the value of *kubi* or *naqabi*; I would connect the former with the Hebrew גב "a hollow," and the latter with נקב "to excavate."

¶ [cuneiform], [cuneiform], [cuneiform], kibu, s. kibi.

I am unable to explain this word, and can do no more than set down here a few examples of its use, as a help to further investigation.

[cuneiform] ...... [cuneiform], matima ina arqa yumi ...... kibu-sa illa-sama ina eli Bit-Ḫanbi isakkanu; *whosoever in after days ...... its* ? *shall take up, and upon Bit-Ḫanbi shall place it.*— 2 Mich. i. 22.

It looks here as if the land-mark itself, or "the name" of it were denoted.

[cuneiform], kibe tamkabar.—Sard. iii. 6.

This is like manner may denote "a mass," but of copper; it appears among other articles of copper taken as tribute, and I should rather suppose it to be some definite vessel or utensil.

[cuneiform] (v. [cuneiform]) [cuneiform], mahar Marduk sar same va irsiti abi alidi-ka epsetu-a sumgiri kibi dumqu-a; *the presence of Merodach, king of heaven and earth, the father begetting thee, my work may it bless, and continue* (?) *my welfare.*—Birs ii. 25.

[cuneiform], lisun araku yumi-ya kibu littuti; *may he grant length of my days,* (*and*) *duration to my acquisitions*(?).— Neb. Bab. ii. 28.

A similar line occurs in Birs ii. 23 with [cuneiform], *sudur*, instead of *kibi*, but I am not sure that the passages are strictly parallel. *Sudur* may be a Shaphel verb or noun, signifying "may he cause to endure" or "duration." See לְדוֹר דּוֹרִים "from generation to generation," Isa. li. 8. See pp. 41 and 478.

KB The following extracts from bilingual lists will be useful at some future time: kibi may be a verb in the first two; kibs in the others appears to be something appertaining to the human body:—

. —39 II. 7 c. Kibi-su.

. „ 8 c. Kibi-su-mun.

. —39 II. 45 a.

. „ 46 a.

. „ 47 a.

. „ 48 a.

. „ 49 a.

. „ 50 a.

¶ Kubu. . malbusu; *Clothing*.—39 II. 53 b.

. —39 II. 51 a.

. „ 52 a.

. „ 53 a.

. „ 54 a.

KBB , , kabba, n. kabbi, gen. *A Vault, Arch, Dome.* Heb. קִבָּה. Arab. قُبَّة.

(v. in ix. 14) , tahlupti ṭikabar ina kabbi va sakant pitik ari uma babi-su artatti; *coverings of copper in domes and arches, work of metal, strongly upon its gates I laid down.*—E.I.H. viii. 7.

See p. 556, for parallel passages, in which we have *kabba* for *kabbi*, with other very trifling variations. In col. vi. 18, one of the passages mentioned in that page, *kabba* has been inadvertently engraved on the slab, which I have carefully examined, but in the cursive copy the error was properly corrected.

KBB [cuneiform] Kabba.—Sard. iii. 70.

A province near the Euphrates, between Carchemish and the Orontes.

¶ Kibbâ. [cuneiform].—39 II. 55 a.

[cuneiform] " 56 a.

¶ [cuneiform], Kibaba.—Botta 147, 7 = 61.

A governor of Kharkhar, captured by Sargina.

¶ [cuneiform], is-kababi; *Shields*.—Botta 151, 9(17) = 117.

See *Is-ama* in p. 555. I am not satisfied with the meaning "*cast away*" attributed to apar there. The verb appears to have various values, some apparently contradictory.

[cuneiform].—23 II. 61 c.

[cuneiform].—23 II. 35 d.

Zarita (see zarith, "thou compassest," in Ps. cxxxix. 3), equivalent to *kababu* in the last extract, corroborates the value "shield" proposed by Dr. Oppert.

¶ [cuneiform].—Syl. 110.

¶ [cuneiform].—39 II. 59 a.

KBG [cuneiform].—36 II. 54 c. *Noble?* See p. 318.

KBD [cuneiform]. *Weight, quantity; gravity; Honour, glory.*

This monogram has all the values of the Semitic כבד, employed as a noun, or verb. I have arranged it under KBD, but most of the derivatives, phonetically written, will be found under KBT.

[cuneiform], gimri mati-su rapsati kima im habli ashup; *all his wide lands like a strong wind I swept.*—Sen. Gr. 19. Sen. T. ii. 11.

[cuneiform], ilgir-sa kabid ina Istarita; *her renown is glorious among the goddesses.*—1 Beltis 2.

[cuneiform], kabbitu.—Sard. i. 68.

[cuneiform], kabtû.—Syl. 150.

KBD [cuneiform], kabiti; *Very many.*

[cuneiform], sabit palugi nipute sa kabitti elle va saplie; *captor of exalted regions, which (are) very many, high and low.*—Tig. i. 37.

KBK [cuneiform], kibitu; see under KBT.

KBZ [cuneiform], [cuneiform], kabiṣ, u. kabiṣi; *Trampler, quasher, suppressor.* Heb. כָּבַשׁ

[cuneiform], kabiṣ aiṭuto; *the suppressor of darkness.*—Tig. v. 14.

[cuneiform], kabiṣ kimedi niši Ḥilakki Duha; *tramplers on the slaves(?) and people of Cilicia (and) on the Duha (see p. 227).*—East ii. 10.

Dr. Oppert renders kimdi by "columns," but I do not know his authority; grammatically it should be "captured."

[cuneiform], kabiṣi irṣiti [kišš] rapašti; *treading the wide earth.*—Sard. i. 3.

I do not understand the change of termination here.

¶ [cuneiform], kibiṣ; *the Tread, Trampling.*

[cuneiform], gimlut šadi namraṣute sa ana kibiṣ niši la našû; *the tops of desolate mountains, which to the tread of men were not fitted.*—Tig. iii. 26.

[cuneiform], ša . . . . . ana kibiṣ umamni u metik bûli iuakkaru-ma; *he who . . . . . to the trampling of animals or the passage of cattle shall expose it.*—Michel. 61.

See also Assur b.p. vii. 1.

KBḤ [cuneiform].—Syl. 131.

KBK [cuneiform], Kibaki.—Sard. II. 80.

A city between Comukha and a province called the "land of the goddesses." [cuneiform], with a variant [cuneiform], which I cannot read. Dr. Oppert translates it "pays des interdit."

¶ [cuneiform], Kipkipi.—Assur b.p. II. 72.

A town to which Urdamane, the king of Ethiopia, fled from Upper Egypt, on the approach of Assurbanipal with an Assyrian army.

KBN [cuneiform].—80 II. 10d.

KBṢ [cuneiform], Bit-Kappi.—Tig. jun. 80, 35.

A province included in an enumeration of places subject to Tiglath Pileser.

¶ [cuneiform], qibṣi; *Hoards, Stores, Treasures.* Heb. קבץ

[cuneiform] ...... [cuneiform], lamassi u abni ..... naṣira qibṣi musallime tallakti sarri bani-sunu; *sacred bulls and lions of stone, guarding the treasures (and) constituting the corridors of the king who formed them.*—Esar v. 44.

[cuneiform], naṣir qibṣi sarruti-ya; *guarding the treasures of my kingdom.*—Esar vi. 54.

[cuneiform], amr kipṣi cuprușu arpila iḥnud.—E.I.H. ii. 10.

I am unable to read this, and am not satisfied with the transliteration.

¶ [cuneiform], kabiṣi. See under KBZ in opposite page.

KBP [cuneiform], kappi; *Hands.* See [cuneiform], pp. 204 and 516.

In the following line kappi must denote some articles of copper:—

[cuneiform] .... [cuneiform], 3000 kappi tamkabar ..... amḥar; *three thousand* kappi *of copper ..... I received.*—Sard. ii. 132.

KBP [cuneiform] (v. [cuneiform]), kippat; *Vaults.*

[cuneiform] (v. [cuneiform]) [cuneiform] (v. [cuneiform]) [cuneiform], bil bili sa kippat shame irṣiti; *lord of the lords of the vaults of heaven and earth.*—Sard. i. 5.

[cuneiform], sa kima il-samas tallme sa kippat shame irṣiti; *who like the sun-god . . . . of the vaults of heaven and earth.*—1 Bellin 3.

KBR [cuneiform] (v. [cuneiform]), Sard. i. 28.—Sard. ii. 125; N. Div. i. 11.

Name of the grandfather of Shalmaneser. See more in p. 641.

¶ [cuneiform], [cuneiform], kupar, kupri; *Cement.* Heb. כֹּפֶר

[cuneiform], ilat kar hiriti-sa 2 kári dalti in kupar va agurri abni; *the walls of the fortification of its ditch, two long embankments, in cement and brick I built.*—E.I.H. v. 29.

[cuneiform], hirit-sa ahre sa ina kupri va agurri aqsur kibir-sa; *its ditch I dug, and with cement and brick I lined its length.*—E.I.H. iv. 61. Porter's transcript has [cuneiform]. See E.I.H. iv. 18. Nabon. i. 26, &c.

¶ [cuneiform], [cuneiform], kubar, kibir; *Size, Weight, Mass.* Arab. كبر.

[cuneiform], 4 is-timme la-erni mutahati sa 64-ta has kubar-sun hibint Hamani eli nirgalle ukin; *four columns of cedar depressed(?) which 64 . . . . . their size (or weight), in Mount Amanus upon lions I placed.*—Botta 152, 10–163; 16bis 114; 38, 65.

Doubtful; the several copies vary; we have [cuneiform] and [cuneiform] for [cuneiform]; in 16bis [cuneiform], urmahe, "lions," instead of nirgalle; in 38, 65, erni for erni.

KBR kibir-su la kupri va agurri la abnû; *its mass in cement and brick I built.*—Neb. Gr. i. 47.

See also E.I.H. v. 4; vi. 60, 62.

kubarra abnu galala ina bit Dâriyâvus sarri ipsu'.—No. 10, 1.

This is the "Window inscription" of which the Persian original has received so many different translations. See *Journ. R.A.S.*, Vol. 15, 1855, p. 153. It is agreed on all hands that the latter part of the inscription should be read "in the house of Darius the king it is made;" Castell gives "marble" as a meaning of the Chald. [illegible] and in all Semitic languages [illegible] implies "magnitude;" I would therefore suggest, as a not improbable version, "built of large blocks of marble in the house of Darius the king," alluding to the windows. This can hardly be reconciled with the Persian or Scythic copies, but there can be now no question that the proper names proposed at first are not admissible, though the Scythic transliteration renders it exceedingly probable that the first words could have no other value

---

¶ kibri, kabri; *Large, Solid.*

marati kibri sa dur dali sa kima gadû la ...... usepis; *the large cornices of the high wall which (is) like a mountain, were not neglected, (in cement and brick) I caused make them.*—Neb. Gr. i. 48.

See p. 504, where I have assigned a slightly different version. I am not sure of either.

1 ras 1½ gar 2 ammat [u] misihti dur-su ashun sa eli sadi kabri usarsida temmen-su; *one sos, one and a half gar, two cubits, the measure of its wall I established, and upon the solid rock I laid down its foundation.*—Bellin 39, 73.

The following is evidence that we may read the symbols at the beginning of this passage *kal kal kal kal kal kal kal*, whimsically put for *kabid*, "full weight" of

KBR

"measure:"—In Botta 16bis [illegible] we have [cuneiform], *imdi*, and in 38, 65 [cuneiform] repeated in several copies (16bis ..., 19, ... 35, &c.), all parallel passages, stating the weight of eight lions of stone erected at the gates of the new palace of Dur-Sargina (Khorsabad): these are obviously identical, and the first of them reads *imdi* in the usual phonetic alphabet; in the hieratic character (which is mixed here and there with the ordinary character in all Sargon's Inscriptions) any character having [cuneiform] as a component part is written [cuneiform], and additions are usually put in the middle, so that for instance [cuneiform] represents [cuneiform]; and such additions are frequently very faint on the slabs. Two extracts from the syllabary prove the meaning:—

[cuneiform] .—Syl. 140. Heb. מָלֵא, "to be full."

[cuneiform] „ 143. Heb. שָׁקַל, "to weigh."

These seven characters (with [cuneiform] instead of [cuneiform]) are repeated before the following extract:—

[cuneiform] I vas 3 qani 2 ammat nibit sum-ya [mu-ya] misihta dur-su askun ma eliniti sadi kabri usarsida temen-su; *one sos, 3 gan, two cubits, the expression of my name, the measure of its wall I established, and upon the great rock* [*or upon solid stone*] *I laid down its foundation.*—Sarg. 55.

The edifice in question in both these passages was the palace of Dur-Sargina, or Khorsabad. The measures given shew that the *gan* is half the *gar*, which Dr. Hincks, in his Astronomical paper, p. 33, estimates at three-fifths of the cubit. It would seem here to be some multiple rather of the cubit. I assume that [cuneiform], *sip*, was put instead of [cuneiform], *kab*; see pp. 372–3, where I think I ought to have read *kabru* instead of *papru*.

"The expression of my name" appears to indicate some method of enumeration by letters like that which has been in use for many centuries by the Hebrews: perhaps like the Rabbinical סִימָן at the close of each book of the Hebrew Bible, which denotes the mnemonical words chosen to represent the number of the verses, chapters, &c., in each book; as an example, at the end of Genesis ל״ד אך, equivalent to 1000 + 500 + 30 + 4 = 1534, indicates the number of verses contained in the book. I do not know how old the employment of letters for numbers may have been, but we have it in Greek monuments of great antiquity: if the Assyrians in Sargon's time were acquainted with it, this curious repetition of *lu* and *lal* may thus refer to the above "expression of my name," and may perhaps be explained.—I fear the student may tax me with trifling, but I will ask him to bear with me for half-a-dozen lines:—[illegible] is 40, so that *lu lu lu lu* make 160; לאל is 30 + 1 + 30 = 61, and *lal lal lal* would be, therefore, 183; 160 and 183 make up 343. We have now only to assume that the Assyrians, who were very lax in this matter, pronounced the king's name Zargina instead of Sargina and we get צ. ר. ג. ן = 90, 200, 3, 50, exactly equal to 343. I give this [illegible] *valeat*. There is too much assumption here to deserve much consideration, but I am seriously inclined to connect Sargon's name in some way with these seven characters.

KBR . Kipra.—Sen. T. i. 42. Sen. Gr. 15. Tig. jun. 8.

A name included in a long enumeration of tribes subject to the Assyrian monarchs.

. —40 II. 25 a.

KBRb . Kaprabi.—Sard. iii. 51.

The capital of Bit-Adini. The king crosses the Tigris to reach it. See my note in p. 99, and the remark in p. ii. of the Additions, which is incorrect. My error arose from a hasty inference that the towns which joined the Elamite king in his attack upon Babylon were Elamite.

¶ . Kapridargilâ.—Sen. B. iv. 13 - 40 BM 48.

A city near Tel-Barsip, on the left bank of the Euphrates.

KBRn . Kapranisa.—Sard. ii. 89.

A city in Syria, near Kinabi, which see in p. 487.

KBRa Kubarra; *Gobryas.*

On one of the inscriptions copied by Mr. Tasker at Nakhshi Rustam we have the following lines:—

(?) Kubarra Pidišharis ma (?) sa is .. mari sa Dariyaus sarri, in *Persian* Gubaruwa Pâtishuwarish Dârayawahush Khshâyathiyahyâ Sharastibara; *Gobryas, the Patischorian, bow-bearer of King Darius.* See Journ. R.A.S., Vol. 12. p. xix.

KBRs . Kibarnai.—Sh. Ph. iii. 52.

A province of Nairi, whose king Perassa carried tribute to Shamas Phul.

KBRt , , &c., kiprat, *pl. const.* kibrâti, *pl. abl.* *Nations, Regions.* Heb. [illegible]. Mon. . , kasid kiprat aibi; *captor of the countries of enemies.*—Tig. iv. 41.

I believe is used for *kip* by Tiglath Pileser I. only.

KBRT [cuneiform] (v. [cuneiform]), sar kullat kiprat arbata (v. arbai); *king of all the four regions.*—Obel. 16. Sard. i. 10.

[cuneiform], sar kiprat arba'; *king of the four regions.*—Sarg. 2.

The same in the Gold Tablet, line 2, with [cuneiform] instead of [cuneiform].

[cuneiform] (v. [cuneiform]), sar kissat kiprâte; *king of the aggregate of nations.*—Sard. i. 33.

[cuneiform], sa ana tip tahazi-su dannî kiprati sitanapsaqa; *who to the attack of his fierce fight the nations hath laid open.*—New Div. i. 8.

A parallel line, 17 BM 3A, has [cuneiform] instead of the monogram [cuneiform] of the preceding passage.

[cuneiform], sa kima shamsi nur ili ibarrû kiprâti; *who like the sun, the light of gods, passes over (all) countries.*—Sh. Ph. i. 12.

[cuneiform] .... [cuneiform], in kirbi-su ....., l'usbâ tiltati sa sarri kiprati; *within it ..... may the tributes (?) of the kings of nations be made to come in [or may they abound].*—Neb. Gr. iii. 51. E.I.H. x. 9. Compare Nerig. ii. 38.

¶ [cuneiform], kabruti; *Large.* Heb. כבר.

[cuneiform], kirib harsâni kabruti eqili [akib] sumraqi ina kussi arkab; *within extensive forests and rugged grounds on horseback I rode.*—Sen. T. i. 66 = Sen. Gr. 32.

See pp. 522, 523. I hesitate between *kabruti* and *gapruti*; in some cases one and in others the other may be most suitable.

KBR — 43 II. 8 a.

Kabrutâ may signify a large number or quantity, and I think we have could [coupe] in the same sense; see Sen. T. ii. 75; vi. 50.

KBS Kabsa.—Sen. T. iii. 67.

A city on the mountains above Nipur, captured with several others in the fifth campaign of Sennacherib.

¶ Kipsuna.—Tig. vi. 23. Sh. Ph. i. 46.

A city of the Comani, destroyed by Tiglath Pileser. The same name appears again with those of many other cities which had revolted from Shalmaneser, and were recovered by his son.

KBT kibit, c. kibita, c. kibitti, gen. *Honour, Glory.* Heb. כָּבֵד.

ina kibit Assur bilu rabu bil-ya itti-sunu amtahhis kapikta-sunu (sic) askun; *in honour of Assur, great lord, my lord, with them I fought, their defeat I effected.*—Obel. 53 et passim.

ana Nabu .... pal Nakimmut sa kibit-su mahrat; *to Nebo ...... son of Nukimmut, whose glory is pre-eminent.*—2 Pal. 2.

ilda sa la emid kibit ka-su [pani-su?]; *the powerful, who hath not lessened the glory of his face (or the glory of whose face hath not decreased).*—Sard. i. 4.

kibitu-kha rimiu Marduk bit epusu; (in) *thy exalted honour, O Merodach, a house I have made.*—E.I.H. x. 1.

The grammar is hardly satisfactory, but the following parallel passage will corroborate the meaning given:—

ina kibitu-ka sirti sa la unkari bit epusu; *in thy high honour, which changes not, a house I have made.*—Nerig. ii. 23.

KBT ... ina kibiti-sunu pirti; *in their high dignity.*—Botta 33, 56. See p. 111.

... sa ina kibiti-sa .... ikkisu qaqqadu Tcumman sar Numma-ki; *who in her honour .... cut off the head of Teumman, king of Elam.*—2 Bottis 2.

... kibita-sun malku bana-sun abuta l'ilik; *his glory the king who built them abundantly may he bring in.*—Botta 132, 7 = 101. See also Botta 16quater 141. (Doubtful.)

¶ ... kabtu, kabti, kabta, kabtuta; *Honourable, great; heavy; much, many.*

... sa asarida kabtu aik ili rubu Marduk; *he the elder, the honourable, the chief(?) of the gods, prince Merodach.*—B.I.H. ii. 2.

... qutur nakvuti-suna kima irkab kabti pan shame rapasti usakti; *the smoke of their burning, like a heavy cloud, the face of heaven concealed.*—Sen. T. iv. 60.

... Guggu (v. Gugu) sar Luddi .... nibit sarruti-ya kabti ina sabat(?) usapri-su; *Gyges king of Lydia ...., the mention of my great royalty in a dream [Assur] disclosed to him.*—Assur i.p. iii. 8.

I think we have here one of those dislocations mentioned in pp. 465, 410; the name of Assur follows with the conjunction "and" interposed. This interposition may, indeed, be a mere blunder, but we have it on two slabs, which have several small variations.

... kabtu ale bilati-ya emid-sunuti [emidsunuti]; *heavily the yoke of my power I placed upon them.*—Esar ii. 21.

KBT [cuneiform] nir bêlut-ya kabta eli-su ana pal ukin; *the yoke of my power heavily upon him for the future I laid.*—Tig. ii. 55.

The same in ii. 89 and iii. 85, with [cuneiform] instead of *kabta*.

[cuneiform], sallat-sunu kapta; *their spoils many.*

We have this phrase several times in the inscription of Sardanapalus (i. 82, 42; ii. 63, 64, 102, &c.). The meaning of *sallat* is not sure; it may be the plural of *sal*, "woman," or a derivative of *salal*, "plunder." Sir H. Rawlinson usually renders *sallat* by "moveables," Dr. Hincks and Mr. Talbot by "women," and Dr. Oppert sometimes by "slaves," sometimes by "prisoners." Dr. Hincks was of opinion that the Assyrians looked upon a woman as "a thing to be carried off," taking the name from *salal*, "plunder," Heb. שלל; but in the only case I remember where the word is written phonetically, [cuneiform], [*zikari u salati*, "men and women," I Mich. ii. 8] it is clearly not *sal* but *sal*. The verbal stem may then be סלל, "to praise, exalt," (סלסלה in Prov. iv. 8,) making women "things to be praised;" or more probably, judging from the single *l* in *salati*, it may be from סלא [Job xxviii. 16; Lament. iv. 2], considering them less courteously as "things to be purchased;" or worst of all from סלה, "to tread upon" [Lament. i. 15], "things to be despised."

[cuneiform], ina ..... mitmalli-ya kabtute napista-sunu asalti; *with .... my heavy maces their life I crushed out.*—Tig. vi. 67.

[cuneiform], ina simpari kabtuti hupsani-sunu uparri'; *with heavy burdens their spirits I broke.*—Sen. T. vi. 4. *See* p. 414.

The root חפן implies defence rather than aggression, both in Arabic and Hebrew; in the latter it is the "lap" or "bosom." *Hasnuti* (under *hapsanu*) and *hasanni*, both in p. 414, must come under this root, although the former was printed erroneously with *s* instead of *ṣ*; I would now translate *hasnuti*, with determinative [cuneiform], by "guardians," perhaps "the garrison," and *hapsani* by "hearts, courage, or spirits," as suggested in the note to *hasanni*.

[cuneiform] (v. [cuneiform]), kabtaku; *I am honourable.*—Sard. i. 32. See *Asaridaku*, p. 57.

¶ [cuneiform]. [cuneiform] kabitta, kabitu, kabitti; *Much, many.*

[cuneiform], sallatu kabittu ana kirib Assur-ki asalala; *plunder much to within Assyria I carried away.*—Botta 147, 12 = 72. Sen. T. i. 51.

KBT

[illegible] la niba kabittu ..... usesa; *spoil, furniture uncounted, much I took away* [*caused to go out*].—Sen. T. i. 29.

sa kala tenisti bilat-sunu [biltsunu] kabittu lamhar kirib-sa; *of the whole of men their tributes many may I receive within it.*—Neb. iii. 54. See E.I.H. x. 11; Nerig. ii. 38.

Kala cannot be considered an adjective, as it comes always before its substantive.

Ina molik tema-ya va musuh kabitti-ya pitik eri ubasim-ma unakkila nikilal-sa; *in pursuance of my command and through my many acquisitions, a mass of metal I collected and wrought it skilfully* [lit. *worked its working, or contrived its contrivance*].—Sen. B. iv. 23 = 41 BM 23.

sumhar kabitti sebe lalate kirib-sa daris l'urasa; *receipts many, abundance of tributes* (?) *in it for ever may they arrive.*—Esar vi. 46. See l. 55.

In all these forms, as observed in p. 519, the root has all the values of the Semitic *kabed*, implying anything great, morally or physically, in mass or number. The rendering will be glory, magnitude, multitude, or glorious, much, many, as the case may be. I think generally, though not always, that words commencing with *kib* imply moral greatness, and those with *kab* size or number.

¶ Bit-Kubatti.—Sen. T. i. 70; ii. 2.

Bit-Kubati.—Neb. Gr. i. 25.

I assume that these two places are the same, notwithstanding the difference of the determinatives. In the first we have a city at the foot of the Armenian mountains, north of Nineveh; the second appears in a list of places without any indication of locality.

¶ Kibetu.—2 Mich. iii. 14.

The name of one among several classes of men who are threatened with the curses of the gods in case of their being guilty of any of the offences enumerated on the tablet.

KG [cuneiform], kaqa; *Setting Sun.* I have mislaid the reference to this word.

¶ [cuneiform], kaga. See Syl. 467-481, p. 502.

I have not seen the word used in any inscription; but if it should occur, it would probably be in one of the senses suggested in p. 502.

KGD [cuneiform], qaqid; *Ruler(?)*.—Neb. Gr. iii. 4.

See the passage containing this doubtful word at the bottom of p. 516.

KGK [cuneiform], kakku; *Shield, Defence.*

[cuneiform], ana Bar-tur-bit musabbir kakku zakiri-ya bit-su in Barsipa-ki epus; *for the god Ninip-Samdan, breaker of the defence of those who rebel against me, his house in Borrippa I made.*—E.I.H. iv. 50.

[cuneiform], Il abu sa sa gapara ili iskun-su kakku-su; *the god . . . . . who is the chief(?) of the gods, hath made him his shield.*—Nerig. I. 13.

The value of kakku is assumed from a collation of the two passages, but is given as probable only; Mr. Talbot suggests that it may be some emblem of authority. The name Ninip-Samdan is from Dr. Oppert; I do not know the god of Neriglissar's inscription; the initial character is the Babylonian form of [cuneiform], "stone."

KGK [cuneiform], kikki; *Ships.*—Beh. 34.

I think kikki is the reading of the uncertain word in the following passage, printed [cuneiform]:—

[cuneiform], kaqa sa Nidintû-bel ina eli kikki ussabu sa kulu' Diglat; *the people of Nadintabelus upon ships mounted and held the Tigris.*—Beh. 34. See Kiku.

KGK Kiskku, Kiskki.—Sarg. 22. Botta 45, 10–16.

A petty king of the city of Kiskkis, in or near Phoenicia, deposed by Sargon.

¶ kakkabis; *Like Stars.* Heb. כוכב

elap Kua sariri va abna uza'in kakkabis samami; *the tabernacle of Merodach* [see *Kua*, p. 518] *with figures and stone I adorned, like the stars of heaven.*—E.I.H. iii. 12.

¶ Kikkisu.—Syl. 672.

KGM Kagmi, Kagmu.—Sarg. 25. 33 BM 6. Botta 150, 12.

A province of Armenia, near Van(?).

KGN kagina.—Tig. viii. 12.

Sort of precious stone, dug up in the mountains of Nairi. See the passage in which the word occurs, quoted under *Ka* in p. 502.

¶ Bit-kagina.

Bit-Kagina sa ir Bas ana Bil-Zirbi bili-ya essis epus; *Bit-Kagina of the city of Bas, to Bil-Zirbi my lord, substantially I made.*—Neb. Gr. ii. 48.

¶ Kaganakka.—Beh. 41.

A city of Persia, the residence of the rebel Martiya, who rose up against Darius and was put to death by the Susians.

KD kida = kibiru.—46 II. 33a.

Perhaps a "tomb," the Heb. קֶבֶר; and we have Heb. כִּיד, "destruction," in Job xxi. 20. The line preceding the above in the bilingual list exhibits the word [illegible], mitu, "death," which may afford some corroboration to the suggestion; there is very frequently some analogy in the import of the words following each other in these lists. See the lines quoted at the top of page v. in the Additions and Corrections.

KD kidû; *Vault.*—Oppert. Pers. كد.

epiri [is-mada] kidû elluti kirba-su umallû; *with earth the lofty vaults in it I filled.*—Inscr. of Mylitta, Exp. Més. 293, l. 17.

Dr. Oppert's translation is "j'ai formé les voûtes de ses niches intérieures par une terre massée."

¶ ikdi; *Strong.*

anaku kima rimi ikdi pana-suna asbat; *I, like a strong bull (?) their head I took [marched at their head].*—Sen. T. iii. 74.

See more in Additions and Corrections, p. xiv. This should have been entered in . 171.

KDB qitmati; *Gathering.* Arab. قمش.

la-pan qitmati abdi-su sa usbat eli-su edisi-su ipparsid; *from the gathering of his servants [insurrection of his subjects] who came [were made to be] upon him, alone he fled.*—Assur b.p. ix. 120.

I have doubtfully rendered edisi-su by "alone," from the analogy of the old Scottish "his lane." Or perhaps, adopting Dr. Hincks's suggestion that su might be used as a plural when the antecedent denoted "people" (see Journ. R.A.S., 1866, p. 494), the clause might be read edis pani-su ipparsid, "alone he fled before them."

KDD kididu.—Syl. 254.

¶ kadade; *Carbuncles, Gems.* Heb. כדכד.

ir sarum Istar sa naphar kadade ili va Istari basû kirib-su; *city charm of Istar, which numbers of gems of gods and goddesses are in it.*—Sen. Gr. 35.

KDL Kitlala.—New Div. II. 60, 91.

A city of Syria, near the Euphrates.

KDM [cuneiform], kitmari.—Assur b.p. i. 15, 43; ib. 47, 71, &c. &c.

I find [cuneiform] [cuneiform], *il* [illegible] *kitmari*, always following the name of the goddess Istar of Nineveh, in the long inscription of Assurbanipal. It occurs very frequently, and the phrase may be rendered "the divine [illegible] queen," from the verb *kamar*.

¶ [cuneiform], kitmosa; *Stored; Choice, fine.*—89 BM 98 = Sen. B. iv. 7. Heb. כמס.

Occurs in an extract printed in p. 488, which I have left without explanation. I have only to add that I think the preceding groups [cuneiform] should be included in the passage; the transliteration may then be [illegible] (v. [illegible]). The translation might be "Sacred-cows of alabaster and [illegible]-horn(?) whose..... are raised and their feet [illegible], whose...and form are varied, full of splendour, on their gates I erected." The epithets set down are not much better than guess-work, and little is positive beyond the fact that the sacred figures were erected somewhere about the gates.

¶ [cuneiform], kutmátí or kutammátí; *Gilded.* Heb. כתם.

[cuneiform] zimáti rimáti kúlade kutmátí sa Istar Erech belit Erech elliti ašir naru-sina ana Erech mihdá-ni; *rings of wreathed work (and) gilded vases, which Istar of Erech [Warka], the lady of Erech the lofty, restored to their place; to Erech they were presented.*—Neb. Gr. ii. 51.

The concluding bit is somewhat doubtful.

KDN [cuneiform], kirib; *Within.* See under KRB.

¶ [cuneiform], kidanú; *Protection.* Syriac ܟܕܢ. Eth. ኪዳን.

[cuneiform] 2 kári dalti..... isti kar abi ikuru usnik ma er ana kidanú usalal; *two long embankments with the fortress (which) my father had built I joined, and (to) the city for a protection I brought near.*—E.I.H. v. 32.

KDN . . . . idâti erki ana kilâti ḫalṣi rabiti . . . . abni; *walls of the erki(?) for the protection of the great castle . . . . I built.*—Neb. Bab. ii. 14.

See also E.I.H. viii. 46. Neb. Bab. ii. 7. Borig. ii. 19.

¶ . . . . , kidinni, kidinnut; *Law, Legislation.*

. . . . sakut Assur-ki [paliat] va Ḫarrani sa ultu yumme ma'duti imsussa sa kidinnut-sun (-nun-sun) batilta utir asru-sun; *the decrees of Assyria and Ḫarran, which from long days had been set aside, and their legislation interrupted, I restored (to) its place.*—Botta 144, 11 = 11.

The reading "Assyria," instead of "Baalbek" suggested by Dr. Oppert, is justified by the following extract from an unpublished syllabary, communicated to me by Mr. G. Smith: the object of naming Assyria is clear enough, whereas no motive is apparent for the insertion of Baalbek:—

. . . . (v. . . .) . . . . , kaṣir kidinnut Assur-ki batilti; *collector of the neglected laws of Assyria.*—Sarg. 5.

The verb קצר usually signifies cutting down or reducing, in all the Semitic idioms; but as it is used very commonly to express the cutting of corn and as קציר denotes "the harvest" (Ruth ii. 23), I have assumed the harvesting or gathering as the value of the verb in Assyrian. This value is probably found also in the noun kiṣir, usually translated "the mass," "the whole," &c.

. . . . , kidinnut-sa ismis askun; *its laws firmly I established.*—Bl. St. iv. 34.

. . . . , sa pahi kidinni mal-basu ḫibilta-sunu alib; *I, who were to the laws, wherever they might be, their covenants have bound.*—Botta 144, 7 and 135, 9, 10.

I understand this to mean "I have bound by law all men to the fulfilment of their duties." I have made a gross mistake in p. 441, by considering only one value of the Hebrew חבל, overlooking the more suitable meaning "pledge." I might have been led to a better reading by Dr. Oppert's paraphrase, "Il a redressé les infractions aux lois respectables que les hommes avaient commises."

KDN (v.). *Submissive.* Syriac.

, sa ultulla ana sarrani abi-ya [ad-ya] la kitnusu; *who from of old to the kings my fathers were not submissive.*—Sen. T. i. 66.

, sir sequ Nipur sadi marsi subat-sun sitkunat va la kitnusu ana niri; *upon the crests of Nipur, rugged mountains, their abode was established and they were not submissive to my yoke.*—Sen. T. iii. 70. See also Sen. Gr. 13. 21.

I have translated in p. 87 a passage which includes part of this clause; in that place I expressed doubts of my reading, which were caused by the repetition of , "bird." I have since then examined the cylinder, and find that the first is separated from the preceding word *pisit* (or *kissit*), and that looks like . This would render the passage still more unintelligible, and it may be that was a mistake, and was corrected by the scribe. I must leave this for further investigation. I consider *sitkunat* and *kitnusu* to be what Dr. Hincks termed permansive verbs.

.... , Sitirparna Eparna bil-ali dannuti sa la kitnusu ana niri simanu adi nisi-sunu .... sulula ana Assur-ki; *Sithrapharnes and Hyphernes, valiant governors of cities, who were not submissive to my yoke, them and their men ..... I carried off to Assyria.*—Esar iv. 15.

The Greek forms Sithrapharnes and Hyphernes are from Dr. Oppert; the country of these chiefs was Media, and in the Persian of the Behistun monument would probably have been written "Chitrafarna" and "Vifrana;" in the Assyrian "parna" we have exactly the form of the Scythic version.

KDP , Katpadukka; *Cappadocia.*—No. 6, N.R. 14.

KDR qitru, n. qitri, obl. *Assemblage, gathering; Union, alliance.* Ch. קטר, "to join, unite."

qitra raba iqtera itti-su gipeat-sun urah Akkad-ki isbatuni-ma ana Babel-ki tabaui; *a great gathering they gathered, with it their forces the path of Accad took, and to Babylon having come* ......—Sen. T. v. 38. See Neb. Yun. 45.

I have felt some hesitation in translating this word. Dr. Oppert writes *sahra*, probably from the Hebrew סֹחֵרָה, "a shield;" but this would hardly do for the sense of "assembling," and moreover the verb *iqtera* would not suit. I should like *kitru*, Heb. כתר, but I think this word is generally used in a hostile sense. I have, therefore, preferred *qitru*, which is found once at least in Hebrew; see Ezek. xlvi. 22, where our version reads "joined;" though I admit we have "made with chimneys" in the margin, from קטר, "smoke."

sa ummandi Ispakai Asguzai qitra la musezibi-su isaru ina kakki; *who the soldiers of Ispakai of Asguza, an army not saving him [who could not save him], scattered with arms.*—Esar ii. 30.

bili ana ummanat [rabi madi] Assur-ki emuq biluti-ya sa ana qitri-sun uddiu iktenu'u; *the chiefs to the armies of Assyria, the depth of my power, which to their troops was exhibited, were hostile.*—Assur b.p. ii. 15.

Ispabara ana turrigimilli va edir napisti ina supe va lamaqi umallu-nni va eris-anni qitra; *Ispabara, for assistance and sparing of life, with intercession and humility entreated me, and asked of me an alliance.*—Botta 151, 19—120.

Qitru occurs in the preceding line of the same inscription, which I am unable to read.

KDR [cuneiform]. assa bil-ari sa qâtâ iltu-sunu biltû asalla ma arisa-šunu qitru; *then the satraps [lords of cities] whose hands had collected, my power entreated, and asked of me an alliance.*—Esar iv. 31.

I am not quite sure of the phrase "whose hands had collected;" Dr. Oppert translates "en joignant les mains."

¶ [cuneiform]. kitru, kitre; *Homage.* Heb. [illegible] "bowed."

[cuneiform], danan Asur Nabu Marduk isme sa umbila kitre-su; *the power of Assur, Nebo, (and) Merodach he heard, and sent [caused carry] his homage.*—Botta 153, 1 = 115.

[cuneiform]. Sarludari tur Rukipti sar-sunu mahrû eli nisi Isqalluna askun sa nadan bilat kitre ibšaši-ya amid-su ma lsat abutsul; *Sarludari, the son of Rukipti their former king, over the men of Ascalon I placed, and the giving of tribute, the homage to my power, I imposed on him, and he repressed disorders.*—Sen. T. ii. 64.

The parallel passage from Sen. B. i. 21 has [cuneiform], *mandatu ibšaši-ya ukin sirus-su*, "tribute to my power I imposed on him," instead of nadan bilat kitre ibšaši-ya amid-su; a like sense is expressed in Sen. T. iii. 23 by *mandatu kitre ibšaši-ya amdidi*. The name of the king in Sen. B. i. 21 is written [cuneiform]; are the var. as for [cuneiform] in p. 149; Mr. G. Smith has shown me several instances of the same variation. Dr. Oppert writes *Sartikdatri*, Mr. Talbot *Sartapri*.

[cuneiform]..... [cuneiform], kitre mariri rasme.... asumhir-suoti; *homage of hammered images .... I made them [the gods] receive.*—Botta 152, 23 = 167.

KDR … le-alqat urrište ibbutl mahar-sun akki ma umaŝhira hišra-ya; *victims of sweet savour(?) (and) pure before them I slew, and made them receive my homage.*—Esar vi. 31.

¶ … hadaru, kadarru; *Landmark; a Coronet; Submission.*

All these forms, and others with change of the initial to *ku* and *ki*, are found in or may be inferred from the inscriptions; see also *Kabil-kudurri*, p. 516. The root in Hebrew will be כדר, implying something round. Castelli translates כדרה pila, globus, sphaera, and compares *κίδαρις*, a coronet, tiara, mitre, &c. We have thus a "landmark," which in Assyria is a stone of roundish form so far as we have them, and likewise a "coronet." I do not know how to derive the meaning "submission."

… aimmana sa illa ana ana takal eqli [alib] muta va ungah kudurri anni lamaru; *any one who shall raise, and to injury that field and to fracture this landmark shall expose.*—1 Mich. ii. 8.

Compare aimmu kibu-sa illa ana [illegible] bit Hanbi iskunu, "whoever his bulk (the landmark?) shall take up, and place on Bit-Hanbi;" 1 Mich. ii. 22. I quote this as a justification of the preceding translation, but *kibu* is doubtful; see pp. 517, 518; in the latter page I have printed *kudur kugu*, as equivalent to the "bile of a man," in 29 II. 58a; in this I may have blundered, having read … instead of …, which appears on the plate; but *kudadi* is so unlikely a form, that I am inclined to look at it as a mistake of the lithographer.

… ana mipra va kudarra umanú; *(any one who) shall take up the border (fence?), and the landmark shall change.*—1 Mich. ii. 13. The same in 2 Mich. iii. 20, with … and (erroneously) ….

… Ninib bil mipri va kudurri kudurra-su lippuh; *Ninib lord of boundaries and landmarks, his landmark may he break up (or take away).*—2 Mich. ii. 27.

KDR ..., Niśib bil kudurrati; *Niśib lord of landmarks.*—3 Mich. iv. 19.

..., Niśib-pileser tur Bel zira uppa misar-su u kudurra-su l'isśuh; *Niśib-pileser the son of Bel, the elevated, shall take up his boundary, and his landmark may he remove.*—1 Mich. iv. 4.

..., Nebo sumbilu şira upa misra va kudurra-su l'enani; *N. the lofty shall take up the border, and his landmark may he change.*—3 Mich. iv. 2.

..., sa aba nara [na-basi-a] anni mukin kudurri darati sum-su [mu-su]; *he who this tablet establishing landmark, for generations his name.*—3 Mich. ii. 40.

Printed in p. 367. The sentence is elliptical, but may be understood to imply that he who places this tablet as a landmark, to generations may his name endure. It is put over the inscription in the manner of a title, and was added at the end also, but the line has been erased, though it is still partly visible. I propose this explanation as an improvement on that in p. 367. Correct 48 to 66 in the reference there.

..., ina dubs sa Nabu-kudurri-ibni tur abul-Nabu-bil-nisi-su-mati.—3 Mich. ii. 5.

This is repeated fifteen times on the stone, but with different names, immediately after the declaration of the gift or sale of land which is recorded on these peculiar documents which I have denoted by the name of Michaux, the possessor of the first of the kind known in Europe. These names may have been those of witnesses to the sale, and ina dubs sa may be "in presence of;" or perhaps dubs may be a form of the word ..., dubba, a tablet or document (see p. 116), and we may have here the names of notaries who took legal cognizance of the sale or gift.

¶ A Coronet :—

..., kudurra ina qaqqadu-ya [ris-da] assi ma usabli ramani; *a coronet on my head I raised and retained* [*made carry*] *myself.*—Bl. St. iv. 10.

KDR *Submission* :—

kudurra emid-sunuti.—Sard. i. 73.

kudurra (v. kudurru) emid-sunuti.—Sard. ii. 47.

kudurru (v. mada) emid-sunuti.—Sard. iii. 125.

and Amuka Arastam madata kidurru [v. kudura, kidurra] sa Assur bili-ya iklá; *Amuka (and) Arastam the tribute and submission of Assur* [*due to Assur*] *my lord they withheld.*—Sard. ii. 50.

I translate "submission I imposed upon them." Dr. Oppert having found emidsu explained by kudurru on a slab which I have not seen. See his Commentary on the great Khorsabad Inscription, p. 42.

I would infer from all the foregoing detail that and as well as , at least when signifying a landmark, were identical; and I conclude that the pronunciation was kudurru (kudurra or kidurru), because kudur in the name of Nebuchadrezzar [Nabu-kudurri-usur] is written (W.A.I. vi. 65), (Senk. Cyl. i. 1), and (Senk. Br. Sh. 5, No. 4, B.L. Vol. 1).

KDRb , qitrub; *Meeting, encounter, attack.* Heb. קרב.

2 sud ar-mahi ina libbi-ya ikdi ina qitrub mitluti-ya ina siri-ya lú aduk; *two sosses* (120) *of lions with my strong heart by the attack of my mace, on my feet I killed.*—Tig. vi. 78.

(2 sud ar-mahi ina libbi-su ikdi) ina qitrub mitluti-su ina rukubi-su pattute ina siri-su ina haruti [ls-pa] ina birki [bi] iduk; (*two sosses of lions with his strong heart*) *by the attack of his mace, in his open chariot, on his feet, by his sceptre, on the knee, he killed.*—Br. Obel. i. 10.

KDRs ana Beltis bilat mati asibat bit Marduk Assurbanipal sar Assur-ki rubu paliḫ-sa sir-ahed binut kappi-sa sa ina kibiti-sa rabite ina qitrub tahazi ikkisu qaqqadu [risilu] Teumman sar Numma-ki; *to Beltis lady of countries, inhabiting Bit-Merodach, Assurbanipal, king of Assyria, prince, her worshipper, foot-slave, work of her hands, who in her great honour, in the attack of battle did cut off the head of Teumman, king of Elam.*—2 Beltis 8.

rukubi adi harrai-sina sa ina qitrub tahazi dasni rakibu-sin diku-ma va sina mumaru-sa ramana-sina ittanallaka mitharis utirra adi 2 kasbu illiku dak-suna aprus; *the chariots with their (f.) horses, which in the encounter of fierce battle their charioteers were killed, and they (f.) were abandoned, themselves (m.) they (f.) hastened (and) rapidly carried back; as far as two leagues they (m.) went, them thrown over I cut in pieces.*—Sen. T. vi. 10.

It would be impossible to express this long sentence in English literally, because masculine and feminine forms are intermingled for which we have no equivalents; I have, therefore, printed *m.* and *f.* in the above translation, the former pointing to men, the latter to chariots. I will add a periphrastic version, as clearly as I can make it, but cannot vouch for its entire accuracy:—"The chariots with their horses, whose drivers were killed in the fight, and which were abandoned, hurried off and carried away the charioteers; these proceeded two leagues [or four hours], and those who were thrown out I cut in pieces." The *sa* repeated after the possessive verbs must be taken as in the passage from Bard. II. 35, printed in p. 150; the presence of [cuneiform] shows that these are not the usual verbal conjunctions. *Dak* in 57 II. 47 a is equated to *ragadu*, the Hebrew רקד, "to curve or scatter."

* See also Sen. T. i. 23; Sen. Cr. 8.

KDRd kitradu; *Hero, valiant.* Arab. كردم, vir strenuus.

qitradu la adir dakumtu; *the hero, not sparing opponents.*—Sarg. 23. Epithet of Sargon.

KDRt katruti; *Dignity.* Arab. مكثر.

ainanu hekal [bit-rab] musub sarruti-ya markas nisi rabati subat risati va hidati asar katruti uqtanna-su ina Babilu-ki [illegible] epus; *now, a palace, the seat of my royalty, the assemblage of great men, the dwelling of supremacy and pleasure, a place of dignity I established it, in Babylon strongly I made it.*—Neb. Gr. III. 30.

KDT kitti, kitte; *Treaties, covenants.* Heb. [illegible]

sa ana napir kitte va misari-sa ... la ... la habal ... ili rabi; *which [city] for the maintenance of treaties and for governing it, a ruler unwearied (and) uncorrupted the great gods have proclaimed me.*—Sarg. 40.

I follow my predecessors in reading [illegible], assimilating the t of [illegible] to the foregoing n; but I do not quite understand the form, nor do I remember seeing it elsewhere.

napir kitti; *maintainer of treaties.*—Sen. T. i. 6.

ul la napir kitti; *he not observing the covenants.*—Botta 143, 18 = 30.

KZ Kaa. —Syl. 546.

The monogram has also the sound of *ras*; see the name of Cyrus, written in Beh. 31, and under the prostrate figure of Gomates the pretended son of Cyrus, immediately over the Persian inscription at Behistun.

KZ [illegible], kisu, kizu; *Sword-bearer.* Syr. [illegible].

[illegible], ibuśu mitûtu ana kizi ramani-šu ikbi ma umma rupiśu-nni ina kakki; *he desired death; to his own sword-bearer he said thus "pierce me with weapons."*—Assur b.p. vii. 56.

Ma appears superfluous here; for umma see p. 314.

[illegible], su kizu-su ina namṣar sibbi-šunu uptatêḫu ahai; *he (and) his sword-bearer with their crooked swords of iron they cut open each other.*—Assur b.p. vii. 58.

¶ [illegible], kisu.

Part of a gate intended to receive a statue; perhaps a niche: see Heb. [illegible], "cup."

[illegible] šarbir eri ša ina kisu babani Bit-saggatu mâtirima kaspi ša ṣippe namrum halsû; *the * of bronze which in the niches of the gates of Bit-saggatu, (and) the ornaments (?) of silver of the pediment, were created strongly.*—Nerig. i. 21.

[illegible], 8 šarbir eri .... ina kisu babani šuatu kima labiriumma mâtirim kaspi ša ṣippe kima simâti-šu risâti usziz ina kigallu; *eight * of bronze .... in the niches of those gates, as of old, (and) the ornaments of silver of the pediment, as its chief embellishments, I erected on their foundations.*—Nerig. i. 20.

These sentences, like much of the architectural detail in the inscriptions, are not very clear, and the translations must be looked upon as partly conjectural.

KZB kasbu, *s.* kasbuti, *pl.* *A certain interval of Time or Space.*

Dr. Hincks has given good reasons for stating that *kasbu* signifies "two hours." (See his Astronomical Tablet, in the Trans. of the Royal Irish Academy, 1856, Vol. 23, p. 13.) As a measure of length it may have been about eight miles, in analogy with the German *Stunde*, which means "an hour" as well as "a (German) mile." I use the word "league" when translating *kasbu* in this sense.

yummi 6-kan sa arhi Nisanni yummu va musi sitqulu 6 kasbu yummu 6 kasbu musi; *on the sixth day of the month Nisan the day and the night were balanced; six double-hours the day, six double-hours the night.*—Hincks's Astronomical Tablet, 1856.

adi 2 kasbuti illiku; *as far as two leagues they went.*—Sen. T. vi. 13. See p. 542.

Uperi sar Asmun-ki sa (malah) 30 kasbu ina gapsi tamti [nipih (v. sa sit) shamsi] kima nuni sitkunu lubbaru; *Upiri king of Asmun, who a journey of thirty leagues in the midst of the sea (of the rising of the sun) like a fish had established his abode.*—Botta 152, 12 · 144; 16[bis] 55; 37, 31.

I do not know the etymology of *lubbaru*. Dr. Oppert reads *narbasu* from רבץ "to lie down;" but I do not know that [cuneiform] ever has the power of *nar*. We might read *rubbasu*; *l* and *r* are frequently interchanged.

1½ kasbu qaqqaru ultu kirib nahr Husur mame daruti amr-sa usardâ; *one league and half of earth from within the river Husur, perennial waters in its place I caused to flow.*—Sen. Gr. 61. Sen. B. iv. 35 – 48 BM 41.

This is somewhat elliptical, but sufficiently intelligible. I would translate more freely "I caused perennial waters to flow down in the place of a league and half of earth (taken) from the river Husur."

See also in Cour iii. 27, 29, 31, 34; and Cyprus Stone, ii. 23.

Dr. Hincks derives this word from the root *kazab*, Heb. כזב "to fail," in allusion to the failure of water in the clepsydra at the end of a certain fixed time, which would in this case be two hours; but as כזב, *kazab*, though used in Isaiah lviii. 11 for the drying up of waters, really means "lying, failing, disappointing," the conjecture,

KZB though ingenious, is hardly satisfactory. Dr. Oppert, in his Commentary on the Borsippa Inscription, pp. 214–7, proposes [cuneiform], "two hours" (see [cuneiform] in p. 55, and [cuneiform], "long" (not "hours") in p. 65), but I fail to see why a division of the day should be called "two hours," when there is no evidence of the use of the primary "hour." I would rather propose the Arabic قضب, "to divide, cut off, interrupt a camel in drinking"—Golius; the meaning might be either "the division (of the day)" or the "interruption" of the flow of water in the clepsydra.

¶ [cuneiform], kuzbu; *Form, Beauty.* Heb. קֶצֶב.

The Hebrew word properly signifies "shape" or "size;" see I Kings vi. 25; vii. 37; but, like the Latin *forma*, it might include the notion of "beauty."

[cuneiform], kuzbâ, *adv. Beautifully.*

[cuneiform], bit ana Zirupanitù bilti-ya kuzbâ uza'in; *a house for Zirbanit, my lady, beautifully I adorned.*—Neb. Gr. i. 33.

[cuneiform], Bab ḫilipu Bab kuzbu va Bab Bit-zida Bit-saggatu kuurpis usmirri shamsi; *the gate of passage (?) the beautiful gate, and the gate of Bit-zida (and) Bit-saggatu, I caused make as brilliant as the sun.*—R. I. 11. ii. 51.

Doubtful, and reading uncertain; see p. 471. The third letter in *ḫilipu* is made in Bellino's fac-simile (Neb. Gr. i. 51) something in this way [cuneiform].

[cuneiform], kuzbu va alpu ḫitlupu; *form and attitude were varied.*—Sen. B. iv. 33 = 41 BM 87.

See this and another passage containing *kuzbu*, printed in Additions, p. viii. and in p. 488; I have rendered one of these passages doubtfully in p. 488, and the other in p. 521, also doubtfully; I think the translation given here is better.

¶ [cuneiform], kambitu; *Disappointing.* Heb. כזב.

[cuneiform], 140 kasbu qaqqar bizi buqattâ u aba kambiti; *a hundred and forty leagues of marshy ground, waste, and (full of) useless stones.*—Esar iii. 28. Doubtful; see another reading in p. 143.

KZG [cuneiform], Kisikki.—Botta 144, 8–9; 152, 5 = 157.

The abode of the god Lagude, associated with other ancient cities in Chaldæa to which Sargon restored the gods taken from them.

KZZ [cuneiform], [cuneiform], kiṣṣata, kiṣdata; *Thorns.* Heb. קוץ.

[cuneiform], nidurta kiṣṣata ina libbi isakkanu; (whosoever) *weeds (?) (and) thorns within it shall plant.*—1 Mich. ii. 15.

[cuneiform], kiṣṣata sikata isakkanu eqili [alibi]; (whosoever) *thorns (and) weeds shall plant in the field.*—2 Mich. ii 6.

[cuneiform], nidurta kiṣdata ina lib eqli [alib] annî isakkanu; (whosoever) *weeds (?) and thorns in the midst of this field shall plant.*—3 Mich. iii. 21.

These clauses, inserted in the legends inscribed on three blocks of hard stone serving as landmarks, express one of those acts which were to bring curses upon the doer; they are obviously formed upon the same model, as is the case with so many other Assyrian phrases, but there is usually something different, as in the present instance; I have not much doubt as to the value of *kiṣṣata*, and the other noxious plant may be expressed by "weeds," until we have something better. Some blight may be intended; see the Heb. נכו in Exod. ix. 31, 32. I am not sure that the first word in 1 Mich. should not be read nidura.

KZS [cuneiform], [cuneiform], kuṣṣu, n. kuṣṣi, obl. *Throne.* Heb. כסא.

Found only in bilingual tablets, so far as I remember. See the word repeated in the Accadian *le-gusa* in p. 817.

KZP [cuneiform], [cuneiform], [cuneiform], [cuneiform] (?), kaspu, n. kaspi, obl. *Silver.* Heb. כסף.

[cuneiform] ..... [cuneiform], kirbi-sa pitiq kaspa ..... abnanû; *within it a work of silver ..... I built.*—E.I.H. iii. 58.

I hardly know how this bit is connected; it is probably with the preceding clause, the [cuneiform] of altars. In Porter's Cylinder we have the usual [cuneiform]. See also in ix. 12, printed in pp. 448 and 479.

KZP [cuneiform], ahait(?) pasalli va kaspi pira-sun ulziz; . . . . *of sculptured work and silver upon it I erected.*—Sen. B. iv. 40 - 41 BM 35.

[cuneiform] (v. [cuneiform]), siqqat qarri kaspi va eri kirib-sun arakni (v. umalme); *connected plates of silver and bronze within them I collected* (or *brought*).—Sen. B. iv. 9 - 30 BM 28.

See p. 519, where I have read *karn* instead of *qarri*. I do not know which of the two is best.

[cuneiform], kitro zariri rasso kaspi ikki tamarta habitta ussuhir-sunuti ma uzalim mupar-sun; *homage of hammered images of pure silver, a large donation, I made them receive, and I rejoiced their hearts*(?).—Botta 16quater 127.

The parallel Botta 152. 21 - 168 has the variant [cuneiform], which is used for "silver" in almost all cases: [cuneiform] in the bilingual tablets is explained by [cuneiform]; see 2R 11. 64, 67. I think [cuneiform] may be another form of the same in the following line, which I am unable to translate:—

[cuneiform], la malala esmil kispi.—Assur b.p. vi. 110.

KZZ [cuneiform], kuṣṣi; *Decrees.* Chald. קצץ.

[cuneiform] (v. [cuneiform]) [cuneiform] (v. [cuneiform]) [cuneiform] (v. [cuneiform]) [cuneiform] (v. [cuneiform]), ili asibut er alsu nin labtat qati ya l'immahir ma pana-sun sasib kiṣṣi-sun va kun(na) pali-ya lisbû dardar (v. dardar); *the gods inhabiting this city not complete*(?) *may my hands receive, and in their presence sitting, their decrees and the stability of my years may they declare for ever.*—Botta 33, 94; 47, 101; 51, 102.

Some of this is very doubtful.

KZR [cuneiform], kuṣṣu, kuṣṣi ; *Storm, Thunder.* Arab. كبس.

[cuneiform], arḫu Ab kuṣṣu dannu ikṣulu-suma sagapsu la sirtâ illik ; (in) *the tenth month* [*Thebet*] *loud thunder came, and rain not ceasing went on.*—Neb. Yun. 42. See p. 333.

In the parallel Sen. T. iv. 75, instead of arḫu ab kuṣṣu dannu we have the following passage: [cuneiform]. See an attempt to explain it in p. 440.

[cuneiform], ina ûmmat kuṣṣi ḫalpe suripi ina ûmmat nipiḫ mul qaq-qisi sa kima eri iṭuda ; *in the days of variable storms* (*and*) *heat, in the days of the rising of the star qaq-sisi* (see p. 423), *which like bronze was dark.*—Br. Obel. l. 14.

¶ [cuneiform], kiṣṣilli ; *Royal.* Eth. ቀጸለ, qaṣalé, *crown.*

[cuneiform], asib er Kalḫi kiṣṣilli asri gal-deli ; *dwelling in the city of Calah the crowned, a place magnificent.*—Sh. Ph. i. 24.

KZR [cuneiform], kaṣir ; *a Collector, Restorer.* Heb. קצר ; see p. 535.

[cuneiform] (v. [cuneiform]) [cuneiform], kaṣir kidinnut Assur-ki baṭilta ; *restorer of the laws of Assyria* (*which had been*) *neglected.*—Botta 167, 5 ; 168, 1 ; 160, 4.

See in p. 485 the authority for rendering "Assyria" here.

¶ [cuneiform], kiṣir, kiṣri ; *Collection, Whole, Mass, Body* ; the same root.

[cuneiform], babikin-sunu lû askun kiṣir-sunu gapsa l'upisiṣa ; *their defeat I effected, their entire body I broke up.*—Tig. v. 90.

KZR [cuneiform] . . . . [cuneiform], 200 rakubi . . . . akşur ana eli kişir sarruti-ya uraddi; *two hundred chariots . . . . I collected, and into the body of my kingdom I incorporated.*—Botta 145, 24 = 35.

[cuneiform], ulituti-sunu alqâ ana Assur-ki ana kişir akşur; *their common people I brought together to Assyria, to the body I united (them).*—Assur b.p. ix. 106.

[cuneiform]. libni albin qaqqar-sa umeşi dannat-sa (dannaşu) aksud ussê-sa ina eli kişir sadi danni addi; *bricks I made (bricked), its site I prepared, its bottom I reached, (and) its foundation upon a mass of hard rock I laid.*—Tig. vii. 77.

I follow Dr. Oppert, who renders dannat-sa aksud by "je trouvai les bords," following Dr. Hincks's "reached the bottom thereof." I find the Ethiopic [Ethiopic], danana, "to stoop down," which may justify the translation.

[cuneiform]. sa ina asri namraşi uparira kişir (v. kişri) multarhi; *who in places difficult hath beaten down bodies of rebels [or a body of iniquity].*—Sard. i. 40.

See also Sard. i. 35; iii. 114.

¶ [cuneiform], [cuneiform]. Kisra.—Tig. iv. 60.

One of sixteen strong mountainous provinces about the "Upper Sea," traversed by Tiglath Pileser on his way to the Euphrates; all the names appear to be unknown; they were probably small districts.

¶ [cuneiform], [cuneiform]. Kisirta.—Sard. ii. 58.

A strong city of Basiana, under a chief named Zabinu, captured by Sardanapalus.

KHN [cuneiform], [cuneiform]—30 II. 86.

This appears to be a synonym of the River Araxes.

¶ [cuneiform], [cuneiform] ([cuneiform]). Tushan; v. [cuneiform] ([cuneiform]).—Sard. 100-1.

A strong city in the mountainous country to the north, near the Tigris. See [cuneiform]-šu, p. 511.

KI [cuneiform] (v. [cuneiform]), ka-ya; *My Face.*—43 BM 8.

The phrase [cuneiform] occurs in a passage which I do not understand; it may perhaps be read *sibir ka-ya*, "name of my presence," but the uncertainty of the context will not allow me to determine; see pp. 502-3.

KIZ [cuneiform], [cuneiform]. Kaisai.—Sard. iii. 86. 43 BM 10.

A province mentioned in both passages with Tyre and Sidon, and other places in Phoenicia.

KIM [cuneiform], kayamanu; *Statute.* Chald. קְיָם. Dan. vi. 16.

[cuneiform]. Assur-izir-pal sar sa tanita-su dandan kayamanu sa ana ḫaripte tarsu panu-su ana sitapra-an ḫatral-su isupa lib-su; *Sardanapalus the king, who his laws and his statutes hath enforced, and to the sword hath directed his face, to his conquests* (*and*) *his alliances he hath raised his heart.*—Sard. iii. 26.

See an attempt to interpret this difficult passage in p. 150; I believe the present essay to be more successful, though a word or two may be doubtful, and the construction not faultless.

¶ [cuneiform]. [cuneiform].—32 II. 25c. Arab. [illegible], *darkness.*

Kaimanu here is equated to a word which I do not know, but which may receive some light from the following extracts:—

[cuneiform] . [cuneiform] . [cuneiform].—40 II. 41c.

[cuneiform] . [cuneiform] . [cuneiform].—40 II. 42c.

[cuneiform] . [cuneiform] . [cuneiform].—40 II. 43c.

From the context of these lines it may be conjectured that *kaimanu* might signify "darkness;" in addition to [cuneiform], "dark," in the first column, it is known that [cuneiform] of the second column is a merely graphic variety of [cuneiform], "a shadow;" see p. 348. See also the gloss *ṣalam*. Ethiop. ጸለመ, *ṣalma*, "it was dark." All this should have been inserted in p. 511.

KIN [cuneiform], kayanu. See *Kaian*, p. 514; see also p. 129.

KK [cuneiform].—3 R II. 11 a.

See Journ. R.A.S., 1866, p. 503, where Dr. Hincks makes some observations on the double plural in this extract, pina and pita, "mouths;" probably "hands, faces," also; see p. 502.

¶ [cuneiform], *Be it Confirmed.*

Communicated by Sir H. Rawlinson; it is found at the end of certain documents affirming the truth of their contents. See in 3 R II. 43.5 and 44.b. See also the following extract, printed in p. 18. of Add. and Cor., but with amini instead of ammgi:—

[cuneiform]—3 R II. 62a.

Cf. the Hebrew אמן. Deut. xxvii. 15, sqq.

¶ [cuneiform], Kaki.—New Div. ii. 64.

A king of Hubushkia, plundered by Shalmaneser.

¶ [cuneiform], kiku, kaku; *Boats(?).*

The word is clearly Accadian, and the meaning given is a mere guess. I have been partly led to it by the Turkish قايق, caique, and partly by a conjecture that the word [illegible] in Neh. 34, rendered doubtfully "boats," may have been [illegible], the [cuneiform] and [cuneiform] being frequently confounded. See the passage printed in p. 481.

[cuneiform]. ili manal mati-su ina kiku-sunu ilki ana kirib elippi usarkib; *the gods, the rule of his country, in their boats he gathered* (or *in boats he collected them?*) *and in tabernacles he caused them to ride.*—Sen. T. iii. 55. See pp. 350, 387, 531.

[cuneiform]. sa nisi Bit-Yakin la-pan kakut-ya dannuti ili mati-sunu ina kiku-sunu ilka tamtil ebiru ina nibu kirib-sunu; *when the men of Bit-Yakin, before my powerful weapons, the gods of their land in their boats(?) had gathered, the sea they crossed, and settled in them.*—Neb. Yun. 92.

¶ [cuneiform]. kakkab.—2 R II. 35a.

KKA Kakia.—New Div. i. 20.

A king of Nairi, defeated by Shalmaneser in the neighbourhood of Hubushkia.

KKD (), Akkadu; see p. 173.

I give the following additional extracts:—

(v.), nisi Arrad Kaldu Arumu (v. Arumu); *the people of Arrad, Chaldæa, and Aram.*—Assur b.p. v. 32.

Sumir u Akkad u Kardunias.—Assur b.p. vi. 37.

KKM , kukum; *Linen.*

This word is also written , and sometimes with only. I have never found it except as an epithet of *lubultu* "clothing," together with another epithet *birmu*. Dr. Hincks supposed *ku* to be the determinative of plants and he rendered *ku-kum* by "flax" or "cotton," and *birmu* by "wool." See his Grammar, p. 607, Journ. R.A.S. 1866; see also *birmu*, p. 177 supra, and *ku-kum*, p. 542.

, lubulti birme va kukum; *clothing of woollen and linen.*—Botta 152, 10 = 142.

, ku-lubulti birme ku-lubulti kukumi; *clothing of woollen (and) clothing of linen.*—Sard. i. 67.

, ku-lubulti birme kukumi; *clothing of woollen (and) linen.*—Sard. iii. 55.

, lubulti birme kum; *clothing of woollen (and) linen.*—1 Pal. 10. Sard. iii. 7.

, ku-lubulti birme(?) u kum.—Esar i. 21. (Shews that is probably "wool.")

, lubulti kum birme ulabbis-suuti; *(with) clothing of linen (and) woollen I clothed them.*—Assur b.p. iv. 27.

, kulubulti birme kulubulti ku-kumi.—Sard. i. 95; see ii. 122.

KKN [cuneiform], Kûhana.—Sard. ii. 110.

A city near the Upper Tigris, "facing the hills of Matai," captured by Sardanapalus.

KKŞ [cuneiform].—Syl. 250.

Kakasiga is an irregular form; in almost every instance the Assyrian column of the syllabary has a noun in the nominative case.

KKP [cuneiform], Bit Kikupna.—E.I.H. iv. 46. Heb. כּוֹכָב kokab, "star." (See *Kakkabu*, p. 592.)

[cuneiform], ana Nin Bit-Anna bilti rahimti-ya Bit-Kikupna bit-sa ina tupqa Dur Babel-ki sukis epus; *to Nin of Bit-Anna my lady of mercy, Bit-Kikupna, her house, in an opening(?) of the wall of Babylon, conspicuously I built.*—E.I.H. iv. 56.

This goddess is rendered by Dr. Oppert "la souveraine de la maison d'Oannes."

KKS [cuneiform]; *see Kurna.*

KL [cuneiform].—Syl. 178.

[cuneiform] " 359.

[cuneiform] " 141, recently found.

I only learn from these extracts that *kal* was one of the values of [cuneiform]. See p. 197.

¶ [cuneiform], kal, kala, kali; *All.* Mon. [cuneiform].

Kal usually comes before the genitive case of its substantive, singular or plural, and may itself be considered a substantive. *Kal* and *kala* are identical. *Kali* is plural, and comes before suffix pronouns. The monogram stands for all forms.

Kal:—

[cuneiform], sa idinnu harut [is-su-pu] karri ana paqadi kal dadmi; *who hath given the sceptre of justice for presiding over all men.*—B.I.H. iv. 20. See also viii. 22.

See *Dadmi*, p. 777. Mr. G. Smith informs me that he has found on a slab dadmi equated to alāni, "cities;" the word might apply either to "men" or "cities" in most of the cases in which I have seen it used.

KL ša šarri kiprâti ša kal tenišêti bilat-sunu kabittu l'ambur kirib-ša; *from [of] kings of all countries, from [of] all mankind, their many tributes may its interior receive.*—Norig. ii. 38.

The same, word for word, in E.I.H. x. 10 and Neb.Gr. iii. 22, with *kala* for *kal*, and other trifling variations.

Kala :—

sapin Samerina kala Bit-Humria; *sweeping Samaria (and) all the house of Omri.*—Botta 36, 18 = 40, 23.

(v. ...) ša kala šimi u iṣi ḫarrum; (in) *which all plants and trees were cultivated.*—Rass vi. 15. See p. 380.

A similar passage in Sen. Gr. 36 with ..., *gimir šimi*, instead of *kala šimi*.

anaku .... šakkanakku ibšim mušim kala maḫazi-ka; *I, ... a priest constituted, restoring all thy fortresses.*—E.I.H. ix. 65. See Norig. ii. 12.

It is shown by these extracts that *kal* and *kala* are identical.

Kali :—

šarrani Martu-ki kali-šun sidis mandati tamarta-šunu kabittu adi šam ana maḫri-ya išsunû; *the kings of the western land, all of them, from various parts(?), their offering much, together with spoil, to my presence brought.*—Sen. T. ii. 55.

The eight kings are named in the inscription, and their dominions also; these are Samaria, Sidon, Arvad, Byblos, Ashdod, Bit-Ammon, Moab, and Edom. Of kings' names, that of Menahem of Samaria is the only one likely to be of any interest.

KL [cuneiform], rabi u sisi mati-ya kali-suna ina tabulte u kireti ina ipsiqta aldti kirib-su usesib; *the great men and the men of my country all of them, in service and humility, in obedience tranquil, in it I established.*—Esar vi. 34.

See also Esar i. 20; Botta 153.9—16, &c. &c. *Kali-su* in Esar v. 17 must be an error of the engraver.

The Monogram [cuneiform]:—

[cuneiform]. Assur Istar sa Nineveh-ki Ili Assur-ki kali-suna ina qarbi-sa aqri; *Assur, Istar of Nineveh, the gods of Assyria, all of them, in the midst of it I invoked.*—Esar vi. 28.

[cuneiform], sar kissat Lasanan sar kipras arbai sar kala malki; *king of the multitudes of Lasanan, king of the four regions, king of all kings.*—Tig. i. 30. See Sard. i. 10, and p. 107.

¶ [cuneiform], kalit; [cuneiform], kallat; *All.*

[cuneiform], amuqita kalit multarhi; *(who) hath subdued all rebellion (or iniquity).*—Tig. vii. 41.

In one cylinder there is a variant [cuneiform], mudaiin. In Tig. v. 66 we have [cuneiform], which would be mutarbis, "enlarging," certainly not consistent with the context; I suspect it was intended for mujirbis, "destroying," and that *bi* was an error.

[cuneiform], hartedi kalit mati; *terror of all countries.*—Obel. 77; New Div. i. 6; with [cuneiform] in 12 BM 7 and Sh. Ph. i. 28.

[cuneiform]. kullat mati-sunu ana siri-su usaknisa; *all their countries to his yoke [feet] he subdued.*—Sard. iii. 128.

[cuneiform], kullat aibi muparira; *all enemies crushing.*—Sard. i. 15.

KL ..., sar kullat kiprat arbata; *king of all the four countries.*—Obel. 16.

..., kulla Qumani ..... ina emuqi galli-ya lurata ... 20,000 ummanate-sunu rapsati ina Tala lu amdahis; *all the Comans [having made an alliance with Murur, &c.] by the ardour of my valiant servants, with twenty thousand of their vast armies, in Tala I fought.*—Tig. v. 82.

..., kullat nisi dadmi upahhir; *all the men until I assembled.*—Neb. Gr. iii. 34.

In an identical passage of the two inscriptions of Shalmaneser, *kullat nakiri-su* *'ra*, "who frightened all his enemies," we have ... on the Obelisk, l. 20, and ... in N. Div. l. 12.

I add here, not in strict alphabetical order, a few forms which appear to belong to this though I am not quite sure that they ought to be so considered:—

¶ ..., kulla; ..., kul; *All.*

..., bit-akeqate sa hekali biluti-ya garri sa ... va tabin kulla-su ... ana late ... gabiabi-su ebus; *the granary [house of grains] of the palace of my government had become too small, and the storehouse and all the buildings of it had decayed, and from its foundation to its roof I built.*—Br. Obel. ii. 8.

Doubtfully *garri* (Heb. ... "to diminish") may be a permansive verb. The absence of a suffixed pronoun at the end of a sentence is uncommon, but I think the pronoun is sometimes supplied from a preceding noun, so that instead of "from its foundation to its roof I built" we may translate "from foundation to roof I built it;" see an instance under *Kilu*, p. 543. For ... see p. 479.

..., nisi kul l'usim; *all the people I discomfited.*—Esar i. 48. Very uncertain.

KL , kilal; *the Whole.*

. suga (kupsi) hekalli-sun (su) mahda sa kilal-su la sabtat; *the substance (furniture) of his (their) palace much, the whole of which was not taken.*—44 BM 26. 45 BM 33. New Div. ii. 75. Sard. iii. 66, 75.

One translation may serve for these several extracts, which are almost identical. The last part of the clause is given with hesitation. Dr. Oppert renders it "dont la beauté est sans égale;" the property in question is in each case part of an enumeration of articles plundered.

¶ , , . kilallan, kilalin; *Wholly.*

These may be plural forms of *kilal.*

. Dul (?) ala kumina-tarda pirati abni kilallan ina saddi-sun abtuk; *lofty columns of stone* kumina-tarda *I made, (and) wholly in the mountains I fashioned them.*—40 BM 8 = Sen. B. iv. 17. See p. 481.

I read the second letter ; it is marked "doubtful" in the printed sheet, and we have a passage almost exactly parallel in 41 BM 88, which is quite clear.

.... nabar Hammurabi ..... Babilat-mis eggil [kan-ik] ..... la ahri kimdi-su kilalin ana asri-si l'utir; *the river Hammurabi ..... (and) the Babilat-mis canal ..... I dug beside it, wholly to completion I brought (it) (or to its former condition I restored it).*—Hamm. i. 23.

¶ . kalama; *All, whatever it may be.*

Ma appears here to have an indefinite force, as in *mamma*, "at any former time;" *manma*, "whoever;" *mimma*, &c. See Heb. מָה and מְאוּמָה.

. Sin-ahi-irba asariddan malki mude sipri kalama; *Sennacherib, the chief of monarchs, skilled in embellishment of every sort.*—Sen. B. iv. 20 = 41 BM 91.

KL [cuneiform] tsuri Assur-ki mudut kiml kalama; *the young men of Assyria, skilled in subjects of all kinds.*—Botta 39, 88 = 47, 95. Sarg. 64.

I have made a bold guess here: but the meaning must be something of the sort. The Syriac root [Syriac] implies intellect, prudence: and if I read the passage correctly, Sargon selected some clever youths of Assyria who knew everything, to instruct the "men of the four tongues" so often mentioned (who lived in the mountains and plains and had never paid taxes), in the ways of civilised men, and to teach them "to possess houses and to serve god and the king"—[illegible]

¶ Kalû. [cuneiform] —Syl. 285.
[cuneiform] —2 R 11. 15c.

¶ [cuneiform], kila; *Without.* From *ki*, "with," and *la*, "not."

[cuneiform], mukin tabde Marduk-baladanu sar Kaldi aibu limnu sa kila libbi ili sarrut Babel-ki epusu; *establisher of the destruction of Merodach-Baladan king of Chaldæa, an evil-minded enemy who, without the heart* [*consent*] *of the gods, had made* [*held*] *the kingdom of Babylon.*—Botta 37, 30.

This is a title taken by Sargon, in commemoration of his victory over the usurper who is mentioned in the next extract.

[cuneiform], gimir Suti sab tseri itti-ya usbalkit ma ikpuru tahaza innipru-sunu ana Sumir va Akkad-ki 12 sanate [mu-anate] kila libbi ili Babel-ki ..... ibil va ishar; *all the Suti, men of the desert, from* (*with*) *me he had alienated* [*made cross over*], *and had gathered war, and had attached himself to Sumir and Accad; for twelve years, against the will of the gods, Babylon .... he had held and harassed.*—Botta 151, 4(16) - 124.

I have taken a liberty here, in connecting the verb "attached" with "Sumir and Accad." The conjunction after *innipru* seems to forbid this, but I have more than once thought that the Assyrian enclitic *ma* might in rare cases be construed like the Latin que—"*adhæsitque illis.*"

KL . kili; *Decorations, Furniture, &c.* Heb. כלי.

. hekal adiu sipiḫu (v. ku) pusqa ša abu ka abu sumsi usepis ma usaklal kili-sa; *that palace airy (and) wide, of marble (?) and lapis lazuli I caused make, and I completed its decorations.*—Kour vi. 5.

, ana bit makunte-su la ekim-si ana bit kili la iasrah-si; *to its treasure-house he shall not carry them away, to its store-house he shall not deliver them.*—Monol. 36.

> Si must be a plural feminine here; the word refers to the columns, decorations, &c., of a palace. I think I have seen this usage elsewhere.

. la bit-kili la amiluti alpar alti usahra.—Monol. 68.

> This I do not understand; it indicates an offensive act, which is to be followed by the anger of Assur.

KLB . kulab; *Gate-posts.* Arab. كلب.

, is-dappi kulab babi-sin esmid; *of is-dappi the posts of their gates I raised.*—Botta 152, 20.

> I am not quite sure of the translation; Golius gives "lignum quo sustinetur tectum" as an equivalent for the Arabic deppi; the Chaldee and Syriac words are used for "boards" generally; the Rabbins use dappi for panels of doors. In the otherwise identical phrase from Botta 16 116, and 38, 68, the determinative is omitted. In Kour vi. 2 takes the place of dappi; see p. 16. Most probably cedar, or fir, or pine is meant, so called because it would easily divide; our own "deal," used chiefly as the name of pine or fir wood, formerly signified "divide," and we still say "deal the cards." See the Dutch deelen, German theilen.

¶ , , kulubalti; *Dresses, Cloths.* Heb. לבש.

> The word here is obviously kubalti (kubasti), and is merely a determinative. See under Kabas; see p. 553.

. kulubalti birmi kulubalti (ku)kurni attahar; *dresses woollen, dresses linen, I received.*—Sard. i. 79.

KLB . . . , kalabalta birme u kum mistakhu nipirti hekalli-su ana mahde aslula; *cloths woollen and linen, the hangings (and) valuables of his palace, abundantly I carried off.*—Esar i. 21.

. . . , labalti birme kum ana la manî ina Dimasqi ir sarruti-su ina kirib hekalli-su amhar; *dresses woollen (and) linen innumerable in Damascus, the city of his royalty, within his palace I received.*—1 Pal. 19.

. . . , labusta rabita labusta harapi diri Marduk va Zirbanitâ lu uribbi sikunti; *garments large, garments of gold and blue(?) for Merodach and Zirbanit I increased* . . . . .—38 II. 34, 35*b*.

Unsatisfactory; a few lines before we have *arba biltu ana lubu(ṣi) lu addin*, "four talents for garments (of the same gods) I gave," but the passage is damaged.

¶ . . . , Kulibarzini.—Tig. iv. 76.

One of 23 provinces of Nairi, lying in the mountainous country beyond the Upper Euphrates, which were devastated by Tiglath Pileser.

¶ . . . , kalabate, kalapate; *Harrows(?)*.

. . . , ana Lâra sadu marṣu (v. marṣi) sa ana metik rukubi ummanati la sakna [sanu] ina kalabate anbar akip; *to Lara, a rugged mountain, which for the passage of chariots and soldiers was not suited, with harrows of iron I cut (a road).*—Sard. ii. 76.

Nearly the same phrase in l. 92, with the exception of the noun. "Harrow" is a guess only, but something of the sort must be intended: the Hebrew כלוב is translated "cage" (Amos viii. 1, 2) and "basket" (Jer. v. 27); so that we have certainly something made of iron bars articulated, or linked together, which would necessarily require sharp points to cut through the hard ground.

KLD . . . , kilastan. See p. 565.

KLḤ Kalḫu, n. Kalḫi, g. Kalḫa, ac. *City of Calah.* See p. 250.

KLL Kalla; *All.* See p. 537.

¶ —4 II. 16 *d.*

We have here kikki, the name of a sort of stone in the third language of the trilingual inscriptions. The Accad reads ši [illegible], "eye of bird," and the Assyrian [illegible]. See Accad, p. 579.

¶ —4 II. 26 *a.* See also p. 358.

¶ kilili; *Crowns.* Chal. כְּלִיל.

kilili abn uknu ris-sa usalmi; (*with*) *crowns of lapis lazuli its head I completed.*—E.I.H. ix. 17.

¶ kilala, kilallan; see p. 358.

¶ qallalta; *Curse, Malediction.* Heb. קְלָלָה.

ṣiṣṣate-sunu la bane ḫiṭiti va qallalti; *their common people not doers of sin and evil-speaking.*—Sen. T. III. 6. See p. 407.

ṣiṣṣate-sunu sa ḫitta va qallalta la isu; *their common people who sin and evil-speaking had not.*—Esar II. 10.

¶ Kullar.—Obel. 50.

Kullar attapalkat [pal-at] ana Zamua sa bitani attarad; *Kullar I crossed; to Zamua which adjoins it(?) I went down.*—Obel. 50.

For the reading *attapalkat* see pp. 90, 93. For the translation "which adjoins it," given as a guess by Dr. Hincks, there is no authority; see p. 143, where I have made a guess in a note; but the passage before me, which I had not then noticed, shews that I was wrong. In line 31 we have "near Mount Aumana," which Dr. Hincks renders *Kullar*, but I do not know any authority for making *kul* one of the powers of .

KLM kilum; *Settled tarif of payment.*—R.

Sir H. Rawlinson, who has communicated to me the above value, reads it ..., "settled." I find in bilingual tablets 13, 11, 9, 10a, and 15, 11, 27–42b, but the Assyrian equivalent is mutilated in Sh. 18, and nothing more than ... in Sh. 18, in every case; once only in line 17 we have added, but the character means simply "fixed," so far as I have noticed.

¶ Kalama; see p. 858.

¶ —Syl. 370.

Kalama is explained here by "people" and "country," but it seems that the limitation was not exclusive; see pp. 448-9; I admit, however, that the translations there are not free from doubt.

¶ kalama; *All, the whole.*

ṣibip matal kalama ana ṣibarti-an muda(an)lit; *the entire destruction of the land, the whole of it, was completed.*—Assur b.p. B. viii. 7. Completed from Photog. No. 30, l. 226.

..... kaspi ḫuraṣ ... Sumir u Akkad-ki u Kardunias kalama sa sarri Numaki mahruti ..... islula; *silver (and) gold, the spoil, the wealth of Sumir and Accad and Karduniaś, the whole which the former kings of Elam had carried off.*—Assur b.p. vi. 38.

¶ (v.) kalimma rimoti-an.—Sen. T. i. 41. Sen. Gr. 20. Sen. B. i. 9.

This appears in an enumeration of animals sacrificed to Assur and other gods. Dr. Oppert translates "brebis;" Mr. Talbot reads *kali-marishati-an*, "strong bands."

¶ kullat; see p. 836.

¶ Bit-Kilamzah.—Sen. T. i. 70, 77. Sen. Gr. 18, 23. Sen. B. i. 10, 11.

A city in the mountainous country north of Assyria, captured by Sennacherib, in his second year.

KLM [illegible], bilimili.

Yav nini-rab shame va irṣiti [hi] mahri ṣabi bilimili va tamiratij-su lisnis ....—1 Mich. iv. 4.

This is part of a curse imprecated against any destroyer of the stone on which it is engraved, or doer of damage to the land defined by it; I cannot tell whether *bilimih* should be read as one word or two, or if the division should be at *pakili*, from a verb allied to the Hebrew סכך, "to protect;" *mili* may be "floods;" see p. 10. I cannot translate beyond this: "May Yav, great lord of heaven and earth, great floods of water," &c., but I give the passage for future students.

KLN [illegible] Kali-tera, Kili-tera; *Son and Grandson of the King of Commukha.*

Kili-tera pal Kali-tera sa Ṣarupin-pihuruni sar-sunu ina kirib tamhari qat-i ikstad; *K. son of K. (son) of Ṣ. their king, in the midst of the fight my hand took.*—Tig. ii. 23.

Tera will be the name of a god of the people of Comukha; see *Sadi-Tera*, in line 44.

KLP [illegible] Kalapata. See *Kalabate*, p. 561.

KLT [illegible] kilutu.—Syl. 655. *Burning.* Heb. [illegible]. See p. 162.

In addition to the evidence of the Hebrew root, we have the verb *sarap*, "to burn," frequently varying with the monogram, which, as usual with monograms, may be either noun or verb; it is pronounced *sarap*, *isrup*, &c., as the sense requires, and this is frequently indicated by the addition of a complemental syllable. The following extracts contain examples of all these usages:—

[illegible] erani ayal agur in ...ti [hur] sarup; *the cities I threw down, I destroyed, in fire I burned.*—Obel. 116. (Phonetic complement up.)

KLT [cuneiform] (v. [cuneiform]), eri sa ina kirib ḫursani danni sabtu [sunu] abbul agur ina isati asrup; *the cities, which in deep forests were situated, I threw down, I destroyed, in fires I burned.*—Sard. i. 66. (Ph. comp. sa.)

[cuneiform]. batuli-sunu batulate-sunu ana isate asrup; *their youths (and) their virgins at fires I burned.*—Sard. ii. 43. (Ph. comp. tu.)

¶ [cuneiform]. [cuneiform]. kilatan, kilattan; *All round, All about.*

The termination an seems to imply "local extension;" see shirtan, "a place of crossing;" mesitan, countries generally, but it is as yet uncertain.

[cuneiform] ([cuneiform]). lamassi eri sammite sa ablana pana u arka ina adda-sa kilatan kirib-sa ulziz; *carved figures of bronze painted, which on this side, before, and behind, on its platform all round, within it I erected.*—Esar v. 54. See p. 221.

The inscription is damaged; I have put the doubtful characters between parentheses.

[cuneiform]. babi rabi kilattan ina tamle gule Babel-bi istappila; *great gates all about, in the whole of the constructions of Babylon were contrived.*—E.I.H. v. 59.

The translation may not be quite accurate, but I think the drift of the sentence is given.

KM [cuneiform], kam, ḫam; *Some article (or weight) of Copper.*

[cuneiform] ([cuneiform]) [cuneiform] ([cuneiform]) [cuneiform], kam(i) tamkabar(i) madata-sunu amḫur; *kams of copper, their tribute, I received.*—Sard. i. 51.

This word occurs very frequently in the inscription of Sardanapalus, with and without the plural sign.

KM [cuneiform], kam, makes an ordinal number.

[cuneiform], aqa attâ-a id-duka ana nikrutu aga-anna yom 27-kan sa arḫi X piltû itipusu; *my people routed those rebels,* (on) *the twenty-seventh day of the month Thebet* [*midwinter*] *the battle they fought.*—Beh. 46.

[cuneiform], *the 7th day, the 11th day.*—E.I.H. ii. 57.

[cuneiform], *the 14th day of the 12th month.*—Beh. 15.

In the small slabs we always find [cuneiform], *kan*, for the ordinal number; see [cuneiform], *duppu 7 kan*, "document the seventh."—10 II. 94 a. For the sound *kam*, we have the name Cambyses [cuneiform].—Beh. 12. In the name of a temple of Yav called *Bit-kimmri*, in Tig. viii. 1 and 14, we find [cuneiform] as well as [cuneiform] in different copies of both lines; shewing that the character had the sound of *kim* as well as *kam*.

¶ [cuneiform], kam; *see Kakam*, p. 553.

[cuneiform] occurs in Assurb.p. viii. 43, but the line is too much damaged for translation.

¶ [cuneiform], kima; *Like, As*; equated to [cuneiform] in 19 II. 9, 10, 12 a. See p. 560.

¶ [cuneiform], kamû, kimu, kamî; *Heap, Accumulation, Getting together.* Arab. [illegible]

I have put these forms under one heading, hardly knowing what to make of them; the common root must signify "gathering" in some form or other,—"acquisitions, plunder, or stores," in the case of a noun; "to live together" when a verb; "together with" if a preposition. I am not satisfied with my translations, except in the plural forms *kamut*, *kimut*, *kamut*, where they are more trustworthy:—

Kimû, "Accumulation:"—

[cuneiform], kimû mahdû is mahḫi va alabita pirkut ashat; *an accumulation of beams, great trees, and many necessary materials I caused to be cut* [*for building a palace*].—Sen. B. iv. 31 = 12 BM 37.

KM Kamu, "To Associate:"—

[cuneiform], &c., [cuneiform], tari Sippara, &c., sa ina lanni-sunu ina kirbi-su kamû pibitte-sunu abut (v. abaddu) ma ahallim-sunuti; *the men of Sippara, &c., who in their dwellings within it* [*the city*] *had associated, their acquisitions I scattered, and I put them to shame.*—Botta 152,3 = 135. ([cuneiform] in 109,9.)

The translation is given with much doubt; Dr. Oppert's version is "Aux gens de Sippara, &c., qui habitaient au milieu de la ville pour exercer leur profession de devins, je rendis le montant de ce qu'on leur avait pris, et je les ai protégés."

Kima, "Together with:"—

[cuneiform], mansu sa irsi va la sum-su kima sum-ya lasddaru Asur u Beltis aggis [cuneiform] lalis kibû-su sa lnaba-su mah ai.

I am very doubtful of the reading of this, and I think some of it is Accadian; it is with much hesitation that I propose the following imperfect version: "Whosoever shall rise up and his name together with my name shall write, Asur and Beltis shall speedily …… and efface it in the waters." I am tempted to consider the final words as Accadian, by the explanation of Esar vi. 44. The passage is taken from a Colophon, or official attestation, in 47 II, 60 c; it follows the ordinary termination of these little notes, which were put at the end of Assurbanipal's scientific tablets.

The verb lasddaru is printed in the lithograph lsindaru, the passive voice; but Mr. G. Smith informs me that the second letter is [cuneiform]; the same error is made in the broken Colophon of Sh. 35.

Kami ishrun, "He made a Gathering:"—

[cuneiform], su adi rigi-su pabi tahazi-su ina birid nabari kima igrani kami siqut sarruti-su iskun sa iqpura usmanu-su; *he with his auxiliaries (and) his men of war, on the rivers, like a bird, gathered up the ensigns* (?) *of his royalty, and broke up his camp.*—Botta 151, 81 (3) = 120. See p. 586.

In the parallel passage 111, 8, [cuneiform], sma ispuri, takes the place of igrani kami; this may signify "like the rising of a bird." Neither version is satisfactory.

KM Plural forms:—

[cuneiform], in kamat Babilà-ki; *with the stores of Babylon.*—Neb. Gr. II. 5.

[cuneiform]. Bit-birbir . . . . . ina kamâti Babel-ki ina kupri va agurri sadanis erte; *Bit-birbir . . . . with the stores(?) of Babylon in cement and brick like a mountain I founded.*—E.I.H. iv. 11.

A pure guess. Dr. Oppert gives "aux extrémités de Babylone;" Mr. Talbot "the fish-ponds of Babylon."

[cuneiform]. sallut-suna va kamut-suna ina mahar shamsi bili ya aptur; *their spoils and their accumulations in the presence of the Sun-god I consecrated [gave up].*—Tig. v. 18.

[cuneiform]. sallut-su va kamut-su ana er-ya Asur apla-su; *his spoil and his accumulations to my city Asur I carried it.*—Tig. v. 24.

[cuneiform]. Ḥanuno sar Hazíti kamat-su [kamusya] usribu er Asur; *Khanun king of Gaza, his possessions I transferred to the city of Asur.*—Sarg. 19.

[cuneiform]. ana epis kamuti ana gab-ya itbuni ina idi pirati sa Nergal alik pani-ya [al-ya] ina ishut kussie sa Asur bila iraka itti-suna amtaḫḫis; *in order to make acquisitions [plunder] after me [to my back] when they came, by the high powers of Nergal going before me, (and) with the mighty weapons which Asur the lord furnished, with them I fought.*—New Div. l. 46.

[cuneiform].—2 R. 7 2c.

This appears to give kamu as signifying "family," but I do not remember seeing the word used in this sense.

KM [cuneiform] kima; *Like, &c.* Heb. כמו.

[cuneiform], er Hunnuṭu er dannuti-sunu kima tel abubi ashup; *the city Khunusa, their strong city, like a heap of corn I swept away.*—Tig. v. 100.

[cuneiform], kima subat usu'il; *like dust (fragments) I trod down.*—Tig. ii. 80.

[cuneiform], pagri-sunu kima mie (ai) nahri ribit er-sunu lu usardi; *their bodies like the waters of the river near their city I rolled down.*—Sh. Ph. iv. 29.

[cuneiform] (v. [cuneiform]) [cuneiform] (v. [cuneiform]), kima qinni udini iqpuri [bu] ina kirib sade dannat-sunu iskunu; *like crowded nests of birds, in the midst of mountains their strongholds they made.*—Sard. i. 50.

I think we should have here qinni with a variant kinni.

[cuneiform], kima labirimma sabirima kaspi sa qippe kima qimdli-su ristdli usziz; *(bronze figures) as of old, (and) silver ornaments of the pediments, as its chief embellishments I erected.*—Norig. i. 30, 32. See p. 544.

[cuneiform], anaku kima am ikdi pani-sunu aṣbat; *I, like a powerful bull, their head took.*—Sen. T. iii. 74. See also i. 66, 77.

Kima with its noun may frequently be looked at as an adverb, and we find the adverbial form sometimes used instead, as *sakapis* for *kima sakapi*; see the following examples:—

[cuneiform], tamti ina pagri-sunu kima napâṣi lu asrup; *the sea with their bodies as if trodden down I filled.*—New Div. ii. 78.

I think [cuneiform] should have been [cuneiform], as we find the word written in l. 67; the stone is a good deal rubbed in this part, and difficult to read.

KM [cuneiform], mie[ni] nahari-sa ina pagri [kur] qurad-su larube sahapu; *the waters of his rivers with the bodies of his soldiers were filled to crushing.*—Botta 151, 10 (22) = 130.

The phrase *qurad sahapu* or *parab kima sahapi* occurs several times in connection with rivers, mountains, lands, houses; it has been rendered "strewed like chaff," "burned like straw," "made to fall like leaves," "reddened like a slaughter-house," the object being "bodies of men slain in battle." (See Tig. iv. 11.) In Sard. ii. 114, I find "dead bodies thrown out upon the mountains;" in Sarg. 76, a dead body "flayed like the bark of a tree." These are obvious guesses, and I have made my guess unsuccessfully in p. 420. For *parab* I now propose "to overcrowd," "to press together;" the root may be inferred from the Chaldee [illegible], in Castell *superficie constipatio*, nearly the meaning of the Syriac [illegible], which will do as well, the Assyrian *s* being ambiguous in all the forms I have seen. The version will be "crowding the waters, houses, ravines of mountains, &c., with dead bodies," and "crowding the wounded into chariots." (Sen. T. vi. 70.) I have more difficulty with *sahapi*; the meanings given are—chaff, straw, dead leaves, wood, trunks of trees, a slaughter-house. The guess of p. 420, "entirely," would, I think, be admissible, but "troddens," "crushed," from a Niphal of [illegible], &c., may be more satisfactory.

See also several instances of *[illegible]* and *kima* found in pp. 570, 571. In the following line we have the adverbial form together with *kima*, an obvious tautology:—

[cuneiform], kima sal ababis sahap.—Tig. ii. 78.

In one single case I find *kima* used in the sense of "whereas," "inasmuch as:"—

[cuneiform], kima asaku bit ella aimana pira ana muanb Anû va Yav ili rabi bili-ya akbudu; *whereas I a noble house, a lofty temple, for the seat of Anu and Yav, the great gods, my lords, have accomplished . . . . .*—Tig. viii. 17.

¶ [cuneiform].—20 II. 72*c*.

[cuneiform].—23 II. 17*a*.

I have never seen [illegible] with this value, so far as I remember.

¶ [cuneiform].—37 II. 55*a*.

[cuneiform].—37 II. 49*a*. From a trilingual list of birds.

KMB [cuneiform] (v. [cuneiform]), Kambaziya; *Cambyses the Persian king.*

[cuneiform], Kambaziya mitutu ramanni-su mitil; *Cambyses death of himself he died.*—Beh. 17. See lines 12, 13.

My rendering is ungrammatical, but I believe it represents the Babylonian, which is itself, perhaps, an unskilful translation from the Persian *Kabujiya uvamarshiyush amariyata.* I fancy the Persians employed some incompetent translator, who tried to render the Persian words without accurately understanding them. I find mitutu twice in the large inscription of Assurbanipal with the value of "death." I do not know the form of mitil.

KMḪ [cuneiform], Kumaḫai.—New Div. i. 37; ii. 30.

[cuneiform]. Kumuḫâya.—Sard. iii. 96.

[cuneiform], Kumaḫai.—Tig. Jun. 46, 57.

[cuneiform], Kummuḫi.—Tig. i. 69, 75; ii. 18, 20. Sard. i. 74; ii. 87.

[cuneiform], Kummuḫi; see p. 104.

[cuneiform], Kumuḫi.—16 BM 21.

[cuneiform]. Kummuḫi.—16 BM 33.

[cuneiform], Kumaḫai.—New Div. ii. 33.

The country of Commagene, north-west of Assyria, is written in the various forms here given, and perhaps some others. I do not see that the change of determinative from [cuneiform] to [cuneiform] denotes any real difference.

KMK [cuneiform], kumiku; *Chamber, Receptacle.*—Opp.

[cuneiform]. banû kumiku sibat pateiqu; *builder of the chamber, the receptacle of garments.*—Prière de Sargon à Nisib-Sandan, l. 4. Exp. Més. p. 333.

Dr. Oppert's version is "qui a construit cet édifice pour y déposer ses armures;" but in his notes he seems to prefer "drums," or "dressing-rooms;" [illegible]

[cuneiform], banû kumeku naqbi; *builder of the nuptial chamber.*—Prière de Sargon à Nisroch, l. 4. Exp. Més. p. 336.

These versions are probable, but confessedly conjectural; we must hope for further examples of *kumiku.*

KML kumela; *Some part of a Palace(?)* [query, *entire*].

alapi kabasi sirate usepis ma imna ah kumela usasbita; *figures of lions and bulls large I caused make, and towards the right, the side of the kumela (or the entire side) I made them occupy.*—Sen. T. vi. 53.

Doubtful. I suppose kumu to be an adverb,—the Latin deorsum; see kumu, kala, &c., pp. 79, 97. *Kumela* may, perhaps, be an adjective; see the Arab. كامل. I have not seen the word elsewhere.

¶ Dur-Kumlime.—Sard. iii. 6.

City of Mesopotamia, a few days' march from Calah.

KMM ka'im, ka'mu; see pp. 102, 103.

¶ kummu, s. kummi, *gen. f. Edifice, Body of a building.*

Not used, so far as I have seen, before the Babylonian period.

.... ina resi-su kummu rabâ ana subat sarruti-ya ..... saklis epus; *in the upper part of it a large building for the seat of my royalty ..... conspicuously I made.*—E.I.H. viii. 34.

kummu illâ; *lofty edifice.*—E.I.H. vii. 38.

agurri tahlupti-sa uptattir va libitti kummi-sa isappik tilanis; *the burnt bricks of its covering were detached, and the sun-dried bricks of its body were thrown out in heaps.*—Birs ii. 4.

libitti kummi-sa va agurri tahlupti-sa abâti ekcir; *the sun-dried bricks of its body and the burnt bricks of its covering (which were) damaged, I made good.*—Birs ii. 10. See p. 144.

KMM —Syl. 89.

¶ (v.), Kummahlu.—Sen. T. ii. 19.

A city of Illipi; probably in the modern Georgia.

¶ Kammanu.—Botta 36, 23; 146, 10 = 63.

Probably Commagene, a district of Cappadocia.

¶ gummaru; *Perfect.* Chald. גמר.

an kasba va alpa hitlupa palta lald gummaru; *which as to form and position were varied, excellence and lustre perfect.*—Sen. B. iv. 23 = 41 BM 97.

Not very certain; see p. 668.

¶ —Syl. 260.

I only learn from this that the sound of the monogram was *rak*.

KMN , kumim or durmim; *Sort of Stone or Marble.*

Generally followed by *turda*, or *tarda*.

hekal abn pili ana ribat sarruti-ya sa abn ansetir abn kumim tarda va abn gabu aerpis; *a temple of fine stone, for the advancement of my royalty, of various marbles I caused make.*—Neb. Yon. 63.

abn kumim abn kumim turdu.—Kms v. 29.

In the following extract we have what is obviously the same word written *durmim* (or *tirmim*) instead of *kumim*; this renders it almost certain that the name was really *durmim*, for is never pronounced *ku*, while has frequently the sound of *dur*; see the name of *Nebuchadnezzar*, p. 561:—

la libni abn durmim tarda amadaha bili rabi Marduk abanni; *in brick (and) durmina turda, a shrine of the great lord Merodach I built.*—E.I.H. v. 15.

¶ ; see *Kinis*, p. 579.

KMS , kamṣu; *Store, Treasure.* Heb. כמס.

kamṣu izzaru mahru-sue simat yomi daruti simat baladi-ya istammu ina kirbi; *treasure they have displayed before it, the hoards of long days, the hoards of my life, they have placed within.*—E.I.H. ii. 63.

Doubtful in part; see pp. 67, 267.

¶ , kimaṣ; *Stores, Baggage.* (The same root.)

I have ventured to read *maṣ*, from its resemblance to the Scythic , *mash*; see Journ. R.A.S. 1853, pp. 80, 81. The likeness is not exact, but as near as that of to , to , and several others; and moreover the character was marked as doubtful by Westergaard, who copied the inscription, and who thought it was rather ; see Société Royale des Antiquaires du Nord, Copenhagen, 1845. The change of *s* to *ṣ* in the suffixed pronouns of the third person indicates a final sibilant or dental; in the earlier pages I have read *kilat*; see pp. 83, 162.

, ina gapli tamhari suatu ezib kimaṣ-ṣu; *in the midst of that fight he left his baggage.*—Sen. T. i. 22.

ilkai tik-su kirib kimaṣi-su ezib; ………… *in his baggage he left.*—Botta 151, 24 = 152.

Ilkai tik-su comes at the close of a long enumeration of precious articles, gold, and silver, left by Merodach-baladan among his baggage in his hasty flight from Sargon. I am afraid to translate it "the money in his possession," but I think it just possible: not coined money certainly, but small bars of precious metal, such as have been used by the Moors in Africa within our own times. I am led to this suggestion by the Hebrew verb *takan*, "to count money," in 2 Kings xii. 11, and by the Italian *contanti*, "ready money." I hope this word may occur again. I think *tik-su* may be rendered "with him."

, Dayan-assur tartanu rabu ummani rapsi ina pan (v. panat) ummani-ya kimaṣi-ya usahir aspur; *Dayan-assur the great general of the large army at the head of my army (and) my baggage I hastened, (I) sent.*—Obel. 148, 176. See also Sen. T. v. 23, 29. Obel. 157. Esar iv. 52.

KMS —50 II. 11 b.

KMR , Bil-Kamri or Hamri.—Tig. viii. l. 15.

Name of a very ancient temple of Yav, rebuilt by Tiglath Pileser.

¶ , qimra, qimrat, &c.; see pp. 180, 181.

¶ Kimaramai.—Sb. Pb. iii. 53.

This is erroneously printed in the cursive copy of the inscription instead of *Kikaramai*, which appears on the hieratic original monument. See p. 325.

KMS , kamis; see pp. 504, 505.

KMT , Kimata, Kimta; *Family*. See p. 183.

¶ , kama, kamdti, kamut, kumati; *Accumulations*. See p. 568.

¶ &c., Accadian.—1 21 l. 42–47 b.

From one of the bilingual tablets in Vol. 2, B.I., which affords us some insight into Accadian grammar. The following extracts contain the personal pronouns governed by the preposition "with," which is itti in Assyrian, and kita in Accadian. In this instance kita divides itself, and receives the pronoun within, and not before it, as other prepositions do; the reason is that ki-ta signifies place-in, and ki-mu-ta is literally place-my-in:—

, ki-ni-ta = itti-su; *with him*.—Line 42.

, ki-mun(?)-ta = itti-sunu; *with them*.—L. 43.

, ki-mu-ta = itti-ya; *with me*.—L. 44.

, ki-me-ta = itti-ni; *with us*.—L. 45.

, ki-zu-ta = itti-ka; *with thee*.—L. 46.

, ki-zunene-ta = itti-kunu; *with you*.—L. 47.

The Cornish language furnishes another case of such a division, the preposition erbyn, "against," being divided; we find er-dhebyn, "against thee;" er-y-byn, "against him," &c. The reason of the division is the same here as in Accadian.

KN , kan; *the Eighth Month.* See p. 50.

This monogram, as usual, is the initial letter of the Accadian name of the month (var. in 40 II. 8a, but wrong printed). The Assyrian name is , *Kislev*, written , *Kuṣallu*, in Tig. viii. 89, the Jewish כִּסְלֵו *Kisleu*. The Persian equivalent at Behistun is *Atriyâdiya*.

¶ , kan; *marks an Ordinal Number.* See p. 566.

, arḫ Kuṣallu yom 29-kan; *the month Kislev, day the twenty-ninth.*—Tig. viii. 89.

, sanat [ma] 22-kan Sin-aḫi-irba sar mat Assur; *the twenty-second year of Sennacherib, king of the land of Assyria.*—R.I. Vol. 1, Sh. 7, G.

¶ —Syl. 270.

¶ , kan, kenne, *sub.* *Stability, Duration, Firmness.* Heb. כן.

, bal bal Mutaggil-nabu sa Assur bilu rabu ina vatahat kun libbi-su iḫambu; *son's son of Mutaggil-nebo, whom Assur, the great lord, in the revolution (and) firmness of his heart hath approved.*—Tig. vii. 48.

, baladu daru sebo littuti kun kuṣṣi [is-gusa] va labar pale ana siriku sarka; *life enduring, abundance of tribute(?), stability of throne, to length may he prolong.*—Rich ii. 18. Very nearly the same in Birs ii. 21.

, kun[nu] pali-ya l'ikbû duriar; *the duration of my years may they proclaim for ever.*—Botta 39, 95; 31, 103; see p. 548.

KN [cuneiform] biri apre ma Shamas va Yav ibulu'inni anna kini sa kasadu temium Bit-Ulbar sir tambi sir sibri-ya kun; *pits I dug, and the Sun-god and Yav brought to me the steadfast favour of reaching the foundation-stone of Bit-Ulbar,—a state of good fortune, a state of firm hope to me.*—Neb. Br. Cyl. ii. 51.

In this statement of Nabonidus that the gods had granted him the favour of obtaining the foundation-stone (temin, see p. 510) which several preceding kings had been unable to find, there is an apparent inconsistency in the following clause, where the king seems to say that he did not find it; but several lines are half-gone, and our reading, therefore, is necessarily doubtful. I have read [cuneiform] mira, from Syl. 270, but with some hesitation.

[cuneiform]—4 II. 18 d.

We may infer from this that kun might be used in the sense of "heart," "courage."

KNU [cuneiform] kinu, kini, kinuta; *Mighty, firm, steadfast; Fixed; Appointed.* Heb. כון.

[cuneiform] (v. [cuneiform]) [cuneiform] Barsipa-ki ar narmi-su (v. naram) uppi-ama Bit-zida bit kinu ina kirbi-sa usepis; *Borsippa, his chosen city, I raised, and Bit-zida, a durable house, in it I caused make.*—E.I.H. iii. 39.

[cuneiform] ista ibna-nni Marduk ana sarruti Nabu abil-su kinu ipqidu bahulāta-su kima nabulti agarti arama bana alan-sun; *from (the time when) Marduk created me to royalty, (and) Nebo his mighty son committed (to me) his people like valued children, I have raised highly their cities.*—E.I.H. vii. 26.

KNU

ina gimir libbi-ya kinû aranu pulahti ilati-sunu; *with all my firm heart I rose up in worship of their divinities.*—E.I.H. i. 37.

ina pale-a kini ina pulahti sa Istar Agane-ki bilati-ya biri apru; *in my appointed time, in reverence of Istar of Agane, my lady, I dug pits.*—Nab. Br. Cyl. ii. 47.

In the first of the two extracts which follow *apla-kunu* denotes the great-grandson. *Apla kini* in the second shows that the grammatical concord was more carefully observed by the Assyrian writers than in the later Babylonian period:—

apla kunu sa Asur-dayan; *mighty son of Asur-dayan.*—Tig. vii. 49.

apla kini sa Nabu-pal-usur; *mighty son of Nabopolassar.*—Neb. Senk. i. 5.

ina emuqi sirate sa Asur bili-ya ina anni kenu sa Shamsi quradi ina tigulti sa ili rabi; *by the high power of Asur my lord, by the steadfast favour of the Sun, the warrior, in the service of the great gods, &c.*—Tig. iv. 44.

ina anni-kunu kinû ultu tamti elat adi tamti saplat qalli(?) attalak; *by your steadfast favour, from the upper sea to the lower sea all(?), I have gone.*—Bavian 3. Query, *kunu* here.

Shamas va Yav ibala'inni anna kini sa kamdu temiom Bit-Ulbar; *the Sun-god and Yav have afforded me the steadfast favour of finding the foundation-stone of Bit-Ulbar.*—Nab. Br. Cyl. ii. 49.

KNu [cuneiform], mûpat ammar libbi raml kinute; *she who raises the people of generous heart, (and) steadfast.*—¼ Beltis 6.

Epithet of the goddess. *Ammar* occurs frequently in the inscription of Sardanapalus after nisi, "men," meaning probably "inhabitants" (Syriac ܥܡܘܪܐ); but I give the translation as doubtful.

In the following bit *keni* appears as a substantive:—

[cuneiform], ina keni libbi-kun; *in the firmness of your hearts.*—Tig. i. 20.

¶ [cuneiform], [cuneiform], kinis; *Firmly, Durably, Steadfastly.*

[cuneiform], sa Nabu abli-su kinû naram sarruti-ya alakti illuti-su sirti kinis uptenedu; *of Nebo, his mighty son, the elevator of my royalty, the avenue of his high godship steadfastly I have maintained.*—E.I.H. i. 36.

[cuneiform], Marduk bilu [batni] rabu kinis ibnu-nni; *Merodach, the great lord, firmly hath made me.*—Birs i. 11.

The same phrase occurs in Neb. Bab. i. 16, with *ibbi-anni*, "he hath proclaimed me." See Sir H. C. Rawlinson in Journ. R.A.S. 1861, in note 4, p. 20. I would observe that in the older inscriptions, though not in those of Babylon, the *a* is often made [cuneiform], and when carelessly engraved can hardly be distinguished from [cuneiform]. This occurs several times in the Nimrud Obelisk.

[cuneiform] . . . . . [cuneiform], sa Asur . . . . . . ana sapûti mat Asur kinis ibba-su; *whom Assur . . . . to the government of the land of Assyria vigorously proclaimed him.*—Tig. vii. 48. See also line 59, and viii. 24.

[cuneiform] (v. [cuneiform]) [cuneiform], Anu va Yav kinis likhitru-ni; *Anu and Yav strongly may they encompass me.*—Tig. viii. 24.

See also Sard. i. 37. Neb. Yun. 4. 55 BM 8. Botta 138, 17 = 154.

KN [cuneiform].—New Syl. 11.

¶ [cuneiform], kani; *Tongues, or Horns.* See *Ka*, p. 502.

This word, very un-Semitically, forms a compound with salip, "drawing out." Heb. שלף.

[cuneiform] (v. [cuneiform]), ahadat salip-kani epus; *some tongue-like(?) I made.*—Sard. l. 81. See p. 22.

¶ [cuneiform], Kina.

[cuneiform]—K.I.H. ii. 54; v. 12.

This is the name of a place in Babylon, but I am unable to read or translate it.

¶ [cuneiform], Kini-hamanu.—Obel. 166. *A City of Parsua* ([cuneiform]).

Dr. Hincks believed Parsua here to be Elam; see his note to Obel. 178. We have another city, Sala-hamanu, in the same line, so that *kini* must be a distinctive prefix. According to Sir H. Rawlinson *kin* is frequently found as an initial syllable in the names of cities east of the Tigris.

¶ . . . . ., kun, kuna; *Your, Ye; masc.*

[cuneiform], sap-ya sakadi sa ina kani libbi-kun tuta-sa; [my] *glorious chief whom in the strength of your hearts ye have distinguished.*—Tig. i. 20.

The word "my" certainly seems superfluous, but we have it again, *sap-ya kun* (v. *kani*), in line 54.

[cuneiform], itti-kunu; *with you.*—12 11. 47 b. See p. 573.

[cuneiform], itasni-kunu; *he hath hated ye.*—L. 7.

[cuneiform], ina libbi-kunu; *in your hearts.*—L. 8.

[cuneiform], pani-kunu; *before you.*—L. 10.

These three extracts are from an unpublished letter written by Tar-muniya, king of Kardunias, to Assur-nazir and Nabu-dayan, kings of Assyria, communicated to me by Mr. G. Smith. The letter is much damaged, and has lost the beginning and end of every line, but I have picked out the above lines containing the word under consideration. I have found no instance of the feminine pronoun; it would probably be *kina.*

KNB Kimaba.—Sard. I. 109, 113.

A city of Kasyari.

¶ (v.), Kisiba (var. Kisipa).

ana Nisir sa Lalla Kisiba iqaba-su-ni aktirib; *at Nisir, which they call Lalla Kisiba, I arrived.*—Sard. II. 34.

Here we have the particle *ni*, which makes the indirect form of the verb (*iqabuni*), divided from the root by the governed pronoun; the construction is as *iqaba-su-ni*, "which they call it;" it occurs again at line 77 with *Lalla* or *Arubdi* (var. *Arubdi*) in Obel. 40 and in New Div. ii. 26. I do not know whether *Lalla Kisiba* be one word or two; the found in some copies would argue two places; but in *Lalla* or *Arubdi* and *Lalla Kisiba* probably the added words were only distinctive adjuncts, as in our Newcastle-on-Tyne and Newcastle-under-Lime.

¶ Kimblila.—Obel. 123.

A city of Persua. See note to *Kisi-jasunu*.

KNG Kingi-isilla-mahrai.—Sh. Ph. iii. 59.

From a long list of tributary provinces and cities of Nairi.

¶ kunuk-ku, ; a *Seal*.—40 II. 42 d.

The Accadian groups signifies a seal (see Sir Henry Rawlinson in R.A.S. 1864, pp. 202, 203), but I do not know any Semitic synonym for *kunuku*; eleven lines follow containing the word in various grammatical relations, under the forms *kunuku*, *kunuki*, *kunuka*.

kunuka-su; *his Seal*.—40 II. 43 d.

—26 II. 55 d.

¶ —39 II. 6 b.

¶ kingu sa babi.—38 II. 38 d.

Something of a gate—Qu. a night-watch; see Syr. [illegible] Q.C.

KNG ḫigal, *c.* ḫigalli, *g.* ḫigalla, *a.* *Canal; Fertility.*

This is Accadian; I have the Assyrian from Sir H. Rawlinson. I believe the word signifies an artificial canal, chiefly intended for irrigation, but that it was used also in the sense of "abundance" or "fertility," the object of such canal; it is sometimes accompanied by the phonetic complement la or li. I find some passages which neither of these meanings will satisfy.

ana Yav mumahlo ḫigala ina mada-ya Bit-nam bit-su ina Babel-ki abnû; *to Yav establishing fertility in my country, Bit-nam, his house, in Babylon I built.*—E.I.H. iv. 35.

Zaba anta ahrê Pati-ḫanik sum-su [mu-su] abbi; *the Upper Zab I dug, Pati-ḫanik its name I called.*—Sard. iii. 135.

bab ḫigali(?); *water-gate.*—Nerig. i. 20.

Name of one of the gates of Babylon; see p. 67.

nahr Libil-ḫigal palgu shamsi sîdu Babila-ki . . . . . . asta'a; *the river Libil-ḫigal, the ford of the rising-sun [the eastern ford] of Babylon . . . . . I repaired.*—Bich i. 11.

ista Imgur-Bel adi Libil-ḫigalla palgu shamsi sîdu; *from Imgur-Bel to Libil-ḫigal, the ford of the rising-sun.*—E.I.H. vii. 42.

bil ḫigalli; *lord of fertility.*—Obel. 7.

Shamas mumḫaid ir-mti-ya Yav mukin ḫigalli-ya; *the Sun-god causing me to attain my desires(?) and Yav establisher of my prosperity.*—Botta 39, 75.

I cannot read the second word satisfactorily; I have a note that Dr. Oppert translates it "dignity," but have mislaid the reference.

[illegible] ..... [cuneiform] ....., ...silâti mannati [mu-anna] ḫigalla ana alrikûh..; ...*peaceful, years abundant, to length*....—Nab. Br. Cyl. iii. 20.

The line is broken both at the beginning and end.

[cuneiform], in nuḫḫusi va ḫigalla ori simati; *with .... and a canal I irrigated them.*—Hamm. ii. 7.

[cuneiform], in nuḫḫusi va ḫigalla in maḫari-sunu etettik; ..... *I passed in their presence.*—Neb. Gr. iii. 16.

These two passages are very obscure, in the last especially I can discover no meaning whatever.

[cuneiform], nuni [ḫa] u iṣṣuri [ḫa] ḫigal apsu sa la isû; *fish and birds in streams flowing, which they had not* .....—Botta 154, 1 = 169.

Part of a long sentence, and the only bit of it that I can read. Dr. Oppert understands the whole to be an enumeration of offerings made to Assur on the completion of the great palace of Khorsabad.

[cuneiform], ḫigal rusâ bisiti sadi ḫisbi tamdi; *a splendid abundance of the produce of mines (and) clay of the* [illegible].—E.I.H. ii. 33.

This is part of an enumeration of things brought to Babylon by Nabuchadnezzar. My translation is mainly from Dr. Oppert. In some of the passages containing the word [cuneiform] I find something unsatisfactory.

KND [cuneiform]. Kundi.—Sard. i. 36.

A city of Phœnicia, classed with Sizu; their king was conquered with the king of Sidon. The name is incorrectly printed in the lithographed plate, but right in [illegible] 36.

¶ [cuneiform]. Kindâhu.—Botta 174, 4 = 64.

This city was probably on the north-west border of Media: it is mentioned with three other cities in a passage following an account of Kharkhar, and preceding another referring to the occupation of places in Media. Sargon says in the next line that he transferred the inhabitants to Assyria and gave new names to the four cities. The new name of Kindâhu was *Kar-Sin*.

KND [cuneiform]. Kandari; *Gandara.*—No. 6, N.R. 14.

A province of ancient Persia, bordering on the Indus; the Persian name was [cuneiform], *Gadara*, the n being omitted before a consonant, as in the following name, *Hidush*, "India."

¶ [cuneiform], Kindaspi.—New Div. II. 83.

Name of a king of Commagene, from whom Shalmaneser received tribute in his fourth year.

¶ [cuneiform]. Kindatamai.—Sh. Ph. III. 59.

From a long list of tributary provinces of Nairi; see *Kingi-istilis-gubrai*, p. 581.

KNZ [cuneiform], gunzi; *Rich Cloths.*

[cuneiform]

50 gamali 1000 gunzi sim mada eli madata abi-su [at-su] uraddi wa emid-su; *fifty camels, (and) one thousand rich cloths of great price, above the tribute of his father I settled, and imposed on him.*—Esar iii. 29.

The word in question may be pronounced kunzi, and may be connected with the Hebrew [Hebrew] (Ezek. xxvii. 24), which has been translated *globi aurei, cingula pensilia vel ballista aurificis*, by Fürst "bachlen, brocaded," in our version "chests;" or it may be gunzi, the Heb. [Hebrew] (Ezek. xxvii. 31), which Fürst renders "covering," "mantle;" others by "garments;" our version has "chests (of rich apparel)." In this diversity I have selected "rich cloths" as a probable meaning.

¶ [cuneiform], *the God Nergal.*—Neb. Gr. ii. 36.

Written [cuneiform] in R.I. Vol. I. Sh. 7, C.

[cuneiform]. Nergal-sar-uzur sar Babel-ki; *Neriglissar king of Babylon.*—Nerig. I. 1.

Unless we have much erroneous copying, we have evidence here and elsewhere (see pp. 68, 162, 164, 575), that with the characters [cuneiform], [cuneiform], [cuneiform], [cuneiform] and [cuneiform], there was always some confusion. When the word gabal, "battle," "middle," was intended, the character taken was either [cuneiform] or [cuneiform], but in other cases it seems that any of the forms might be used indifferently.

¶ [cuneiform]. Kunzimana.—Botta 145, 11 = 62.

A King of Kammano (Commagene in Cappadocia).

KNK Kimkhi.—Sh. Ph. iii. 1.

Kimkhai.—Sh. Ph. iii. 40.

It is probable that these names are really the same, but that one is applied to the city and the other to the people. They occur in the third campaign of Shamas-phul, which was carried on in the mountainous country on the north-east, where he destroyed the city *Kimkhi*; and afterwards informs us that the king of the *Kimkhai* brought his tribute to him.

¶ —29 II. 10 *d*.

¶ Kankanu, Kankanga; *the Accadian names of the sixth month*. See p. 50, and the correction in p. iv.

¶ kaniki; *an Authenticated Seal(?)*.

….. in-matima ina arkati yomai …. iqabú eqil [alib] ul masihi va taggil ul kaniki; *if any one in after days ….. shall say, the field is not of (due) measure and the seal is not valid.*—3 Mich. iii. 17.

The last bit is a guess, but there is some authority for it in 40 II. 42. 43 *d*, where *taggil*, "seal," is equated with *kanikiv* and *kaniku*. I suppose *taggil* would signify any stone that should be used for making an impression, and the verb *kanik* might imply that it was authentic; but I have not found the word in any other Semitic tongue. See also the following line, where *duppu*, "a document," is explained by *kaniku* or *taggil*, which must, I think, imply the authenticity of a seal:—

—29 II. 11 *d*.

KNL kanal; *Conduit, Water-course.*

This technical term, like so many of those employed in describing the architectural work and decorations of the palaces and temples of the Assyrians and Babylonians, is obscure. It is connected with water, and has sometimes the determinative ; with it seems to imply "a gutter" to carry off water. Castell gives us the Syriac [illegible] (vis, truncus, ramin), but I fear the word may have been a borrowed one. All the following versions containing it are given with much hesitation.

Is erini dalili ana sibi-sa is-kanali-sa va sulali-sa amiris; *long pines for its roofs, and its conduits, and its awnings, I adapted.*—Nerig. ii. 80.

KNL

... u hekali abu pili esto emid hanuli-su ina arni cigilti-su uasilima bil simehi Nuba.—Neb. Yoo. 77.

Any translation I can furnish seems to result in nonsense. We have first, "of that temple of fine stone I erected its bounds," followed by what may be read, allowing for some dislocation (p. 110), "I entrusted it to the uncovered ears of the God Nuba." For so reading the name of the god in the text I would refer to the following extract from a bilingual tablet containing the names of Nuba:—

—58 II. 58 a.

The first column has the word *Nis* written phonetically, the second has the ideogram *Nis*, the third has the same *Nuba* with the *simehi* of the text. I retain the name of *Nuba*, which was suggested by Sir H. C. Rawlinson as a make-shift many years ago, because no other quite satisfactory has been proposed. Dr. Oppert reads *Nisroch*.

... sakutuma(?) usumb biluti-ya emid is-kanuli-sun asdupitl (v. ilat) abo kumina turda lazir rabi va ilat abu pili rabi asurru-sun usaphira; *the sakumua(?), the seat of my power, I erected, their conduits, the aqueducts of kumina-turda and of alabaster, and columns of fine large stone I placed round about their wall.*—Sen. B. iv. 39 – 41 BM 38. See p. 50.

... rimu [va] ly-iki bab papaha sippi sigari is [ri] hanul [va] is-bab-maku .... kaspi usa'in; *the bulls (and) columns of the gate of the shrine, the gargoyles and conduits and .... with silver I adorned.*—E.I.H. iii. 49.

The variations are from Ker Porter's Cylinder. I do not know the meaning of *is-bab-maku*, which occurs in the Senkereh Cylinder also, with *sikku-su* and *sigaru-su*, as in the above extract.

KNL . . . elap sahr kanal rukubu rabuti-su elap masdahu Bimaku isinnû Suanna-ki la-kare-su marati kirbi-su umalhim; *the ship of sahr-kanal, the chariot of his greatness, the tabernacle of his glory, ... of the festivals of Suanna [Babylon], his pageant of dignity, within it I have decked.*—E.I.H. iii. 71.

The following line shews "the tabernacle of sahr kanal" of the above passage from the East India House Brick to have been a tabernacle of Nebo:—

—62 II. 62c.

¶ . . . Kanallu; *the Month Kisleu.*—Tig. viii. 89. See KSL, p. 501.

¶ . . . Kinalua, Obel. 150; Kunalua, Obel. 156; Kunulua, Sard. iii. 72, 76; 43 BM 30.

The same city is understood under this variety of spelling: it is always mentioned as the capital of Lubarna, a province in the Hittite country (Syria).

KNM . . . (v. . . .). kanmas (v. kanmáte).—Sard. ii. 75.

Some articles of copper, taken as tribute.

KNN —40 II. 22a.

—40 II. 20a.

¶ . . . kanan; *Strength, Durability.* See *Kun*, p. 576.

. . . kanani; *from the same root.*

. . . asru sûtu ana gimarti-sa ina libni kima kanani aspuk; *that place, to the whole of it, with bricks strongly I covered over.*—Tig. vii. 80.

Probable. The question is here of laying down the foundation of a temple upon a rock. The verb שפך in Hebrew is used for "pouring out water" (Deut. ix. 6) and "throwing up earth" (2 Kings xix. 32); *kima kanani* may be understood adverbially, like *kima sabap* and *kima* ..., p. 670.

KNP Kisipu.—Sard. ii. 34. See *Kisalu*, p. 581.

KNS Kisis; see p. 579.

¶ —39 II. 42 a.

¶ kansu, m. kanso, *obl.* kansuti, kansute, *pl.* *Submissive, Obedient.*

Seni sar Dayáni sa ana Asur bili-ya la kansu sallat-su [sallatsu] va kamut-su [kamatsu] ana er-ya Asur ubla-su; *of Seni king of the Dahi, who to Assur my lord was not obedient, his spoils and his accumulations to my city Assur I brought them* [it].—Tig. v. 83, and in vi. 32. See p. 395.

.... la kanse mithuris ahsudu ...., sallassu kabitta asluka ana Assur-ki; *(several Aramaean tribes) not obedient, having forcibly seized, ... plunder much I carried off to Assyria.*—Sen. Gr. 16.

The form of the final verb is anomalous: it is found in other passages, but always, I think, where the verb may be understood in the indirect form—"when I had seized," and never at the end of a complete sentence: I therefore transliterate it by ahsudu, which would be properly written ..., as in Sen T. v. 27; Botta 152, 73 = 166, and elsewhere; the more correct form would be ..., aksuda, as in Tig. iii. 83; vi. 17; viii. 14: all these are in the indirect sense. The same passage occurs in Sen. T. i. 47, but with the variant ..., *kansuti.*

.... asri kansu mudainut.—Senk. Cyl. i. 2.

Coming after the words "Nebuchadnezzar, king of Babylon," this line may signify "a place which is obedient and strong."

.... ardu kansu; *vassal obedient.*—Botta 183, 10.

This phrase is generally written with the monogram; see ...., Botta 145, 74 = 86; 117, 10 = 70; we have ...., ardi kansi, in the oblique case, Botta 151, 9 = 117.

KNS [cuneiform] yir Maniyae sar Ukki Dahae la kanse asmikut ḫarrana; *against* [*upon*] *Maniyæ, king of Ukki, a city of the Dahæ, not obedient, I took the road.*—Sen. T. iv. 3.

[cuneiform] sar mušaknis la kansute-su sa napḫar kissat danni ipilu; *King subduing those not obedient to him, who the assemblage of powerful multitudes hath ruled.*—Sard. III. 115. St. 8.

[cuneiform] (v. [cuneiform]) [cuneiform] ([cuneiform]) [cuneiform]. ana Sagi sa Gilḫi la kanisut Asur bill-ya (la) allik; *to the Sugi of Gilḫi not submissive to Assur, my lord, I went.*—Tig. iv. 6.

¶ [cuneiform], kanais; *Submissively, Obediently.*

[cuneiform]. sa ki pi assamme istanappara amma la saalma ana sari bill-ya yalḫis kanais tamarta-su kabittū umbala adi maḫri-ya; *he, according to my mouth* [*dictation*], *and word that "I have confided in the king my lord," reverently (and) obediently his gift abundant he forwarded to my presence.*—Asur b.p. x. 39.

For the use of the adverb umma, "that," followed by the words quoted, see note to Tibam, p. 514.

¶ [cuneiform]. kanâs, ac. *Obedience, Submission.*

[cuneiform]. Saravas Ammavas sa isto yummi pâte kanâs lá idá kima tul abubi asḫup; *Saravas (and) Ammavas, which from days remote submission knew not, like a heap of corn I swept.*—Tig. III. 73. See also iv. 51.

KNG —30 II. 41 a.
„ 43 a.

KNT himáti.

nisuti u pahati ardi-bil u hináti; *men and women, slaves male and female.*—1 Mich. ii. 4.

There cannot be much doubt of this version, which I take from Mr. Talbot, but all the terms are unusual. I do not remember ever to have seen *pahati* written phonetically, and very rarely *nisuti*; *hinati* is elsewhere *pinnitu*; see Tig. vi. 81; *bil* after *ardi* is probably meant to define one who serves a master, rather than one who simply owes homage, "a vassal."

KȘ kipu, n. kipá, ac. kipu, obl.

abn pili rabi kipu-su usahira; *of great fine stones its walls I carried round.*—39 BM 19.

See under *Asuru*, p. 44, where I inserted the above line, but did not then understand it.

kipá dali la kupri va agurri usahir-su; *the long walls in cement and brick I carried round it.*—Oppert's Inscr. de Mylitta, l. 13. Exp. Més. p. 283. See p. 80.

Possibly *kipi* may be a dual, "two walls," as in *kirná*, "horns," Sen. T. iii. 73; *yuti*, "hands," Esar iv. 44; *arpá*, "feet," 16 II. 81 b. See Dr. Hincks, Journ. R.A.S. 1866, p. 616.

. . . . sarbir ori sa ina kipe bab-bab Bit-Saggatu . . . la usziza sar mahri yuti . . . epúik ma . . . ina kipe bab-bab sísati kima labiri-ma . . . . . uszis; *sarbir (?) of metal which, on the wall of the gates of Bit-Saggatu . . . the former king had not erected, I . . . fashioned, and . . . on the wall of these gates as of old . . . . I erected.*—Nerig. i. 21, 30.

KṢ [cuneiform], Kûṣu, n. Kûṣi, g. *Cush, Ethiopia.*

[cuneiform], Muṣur Kûṣu sa abu (ad) banû-a ikṣudu ana [illegible] aṣbat; *Egypt (and) Cush which the father begetting me had possessed, entire I captured.*—Assur b.p. i. 112.

[cuneiform], Tarqû sar Muṣur u Kuṣi; *Tarqû king of Egypt and Cush.*—Assur b.p. i. 52. [cuneiform] in line 80.

See [cuneiform], Kûsu, among the provinces of Persia in No. 6. N.R. l. 31.

KṢL [cuneiform], kiṣalli, obl. *Embankment.* Chal. כִּסְלָא terra aggesta.—Castell.

[cuneiform] ...... [cuneiform], alamê birid sallat samti ulziz saparris usrib ina umlik aznis ina kiṣalli rabi saplanu hekal abn pili ana ribat sarruti-ya ..... epus; *them (the bulls) among the raised figures I put up, highly I placed, and arranged firmly; on the great embankment lower down, a palace of fine stone for the increase of my royalty .... I built.*—Neb. Yan. 62.

I am not sure that I have divided the clauses correctly in my translation.

¶ [cuneiform], Kiṣlivu; *Kisleu, the ninth month.*

See the list of months in p. 56. Written [cuneiform], kisallu, in Tig. vii. 89.

KṢM [cuneiform].—Syl. 385.

The same monogram in 511.384, with gloss [cuneiform], is explained by [cuneiform] in the Assyrian column.

[cuneiform].—Syl. 307.

KṢR , Kiṣiri.

The name of the place to which Sennacherib brought the contents of eighteen streams into one canal for the supply of Nineveh with water for drinking.

ultu pâṭi er Kiṣiri adi Ninevêh-ki nahr Ḫiritâ ušaḫrâ mie (ai) ennati asardâ kirib-ša Patti-Sennacherib attabi nibit-ṣa; *from the border of Kiṣir to Nineveh the canal Hiritâ I caused dig; those waters I let down in it; Patti-Sennacherib I called its name.*—Bavian 11.

See also Sen. Gr. 60; 42 BM 41 = Sen. B. iv. 34. In p. 448 I have printed *kirir ašira*, "a canal I brought," and I am still undecided which of these readings should be preferred; see also p. 463.

KṢT , kiṣiti; *Cups or Covers.* Heb. כִּסָּה or כסה.

. . . . . , kiṣiti is-erini . . . . ašlula; *cups(?) of cedar-wood . . . . I carried off.*—Sard. i. 87.

Mentioned among many articles of plunder.

¶ , Kapa.—Sh. Ph. i. 47.

One of twenty-seven cities which had revolted against Shalmaneser, but were reduced to submission by his son Shamas Phul.

¶ () , kapi; *Hollow Places, Ravines.* Heb. כף.

pagri mutlaḫṣi-šu adi aḫrub ma'dut-ši ana kapi ša šadê ittaqqata-ni taḫaza dannu ina libbi er-šu aškun; (*with*) *the bodies of his fighting men the hills I filled, his troops* [*multitudes*] *into the hollows of the hills being driven together* (*or collected*), *fierce fight in the middle of his city I made.*—New Div. ii. 78.

KP [cuneiform] (v. [cuneiform]) [cuneiform] (v. [cuneiform]), 172 ṣabî tidaki-sunu aduk ṣabî madûti ina kâpi ša sade adibuk; *one hundred and seventy-two of their fighting men I slew, many (dead?) bodies in the hollows of the mountain I left.*—Sard. ii. 47.

See also Sard. i. 65, and more under *Kâki*, p. 516.

¶ [cuneiform], kipi, *g. sing.* kipani, *pl.* *Governor.*

[cuneiform], ša Nabu-bil-sumi kipi Hararti ḫuraṣa kaspa . . . . amḫar; *from Nabu-bil-sumi, governor of Hararti (Armenia?), gold, silver, &c., I received.*—Sen. T. i. 38.

The same in Sen. Gr. 17, and Sen. B. 1. 6, with v. [cuneiform], *Hararati.*

[cuneiform], ša Tarqû . . . . itkagil ana epis ramani-su eli sarri kipâni ša kirib Muṣur upaqidu abu [ai] banû-a; *he, Tarqû, ... trusted to his own deeds against the kings, the governors, whom in Egypt the father who begat me had appointed.*—Assur b.p. i. 57. See also 77, 112.

KPB [cuneiform], Kipabarutakal.—Sb. Ph. iii. 48.

One of a long list of places tributary to the monarch.

KPD [cuneiform], kabidu; *Burdened, Loaded.* Heb. כָּבֵד.

[cuneiform], Muttalli Kummuḫai amelu patû limnu la ḫadir zikri ili kapidu sinati; *Mutallu of Commukha, a deceitful evil man, not honouring the memory of the gods, loaded with hatred.*—Botta 151, 4(16) - 112.

KPD [cuneiform], kupadinnu.

[cuneiform], 1 kupadinnu ki 6 kaspi; *one kupadinnu, equal to six pieces of silver.*—3 Mich. I. 26.

Possibly "a couple of dogs;" see ku, "dog," p. 511, and the Chaldee [illegible], a "couple" of animals. This was part of the price paid in exchange for a piece of ground; see ki, p. 509.

KPN [cuneiform], Kipina.—Sard. iii. 37, 39.

A city in Laki, on the upper course of the Euphrates.

KẒR [cuneiform], kaṣir; *Restorer.* See p. 519.

KẒT [cuneiform], kaṣuti; *Nauseous, Disgusting.* Heb. [illegible].

[cuneiform], mist-ṣa [al-ṣa] nádi kaṣuti ana ṣummê-ya la asti; *its flowing nauseous waters for my thirst I drank.*—Sen. T. iii. 80. Doubtful. See p. 1.

The parallel line in Sen. B. I. 40–1 might have cleared up the doubt here, but it is unfortunately damaged in the beginning. The only characters I can see clearly are [cuneiform] before *kaṣuti,* &c., after which the two lines coincide. I would read this first [illegible] *mist kima mie ṣeri,* "waters like water of the desert." The word lost was probably [illegible].

KaR [cuneiform], kar, s. kari, kara, pl. *Fortress, wall; Embankment, dyke; Channel.* Heb. [illegible].

I think we have always *k* notwithstanding the Heb. ק; I do not remember to have seen *q* in variants or in bilingual tablets. In the sense of "fortified towns" [cuneiform] interchanges with [cuneiform]; see *Kardunias*, p. [illegible].

[cuneiform].—13 II. 20b.

[cuneiform].—13 II. 22b.

[cuneiform].—13 II. 24b.

These extracts prove the sounds *kara* and *karu*, as well as the meaning of the Accadian words *gala*, "great," and *na*, "in," and the value of [cuneiform], "city of Nipur;" see p. [illegible].

[cuneiform].—New Syl. 128.

[cuneiform] 129.

KAR … kari ili istari asib libbi-su ele samami; *the fortresses, the gods (and) goddesses dwelling in them [it], high as the heavens.*—Black Stone ii. 6.

The mutilation of the preceding lines renders this a little uncertain.

… itat kar hiriti-sa 2 kari daliti in kupur va agurri abni sa itti kar abi ikuru esnik; *the (supporting) walls of the embankment of its ditch, (i.e.) two long defences, in cement and brick I built, and with the fortress (which) my father had built I joined.*—E.I.H. v. 27, 30.

"Its ditch" refers to the items of Imgur-Bel and Nimitti-Bel, mentioned in a clause immediately preceding. Dr. Hincks has observed that *sa* may be used for *sun* in similar cases; see *libbi-sa*, E.I.H. v. 4.

… itat erani-sunu kima kare l'esrpik; *the walls of their cities like dykes I heaped up.*—Tig. i. 89.

… kari arahti ibsu sa makat agurri aberti Buratti urakkisu sa la ushalila sittati; *embankments (for) paths he had made, and buttresses of brick along the Euphrates had constructed, and had not completed the rest.*—E.I.H. v. 5.

This is an incomplete list, all the verbs of which, as well as those for several lines before and after, are in the indirect form, influenced by a relative an eight lines higher. As we have here a fair example of the use of these indirect forms, showing how the influence of a relative [or conjunction] may be carried on for many lines together, until the direct action commences, I will give a translation of the whole passage, beginning at iv. 64:—"Imgur-Bel and Nimitti-Bel, the great walls of Babylon, which Nabopalassar, king of Babylon, my father, had made and had not completed their beauty, and whose ditch he had dug, and of two long embankments had finished their length, and embankments (for) paths had made, and buttresses of brick along the Euphrates had constructed, and had not completed the rest, and from — to —, the side of Babylon opposite the principal gate had made in brick and stone for the worship of Merodach." (now we come to verbs in the direct form,) "I, his eldest son, the chosen of his heart, Imgur-Bel and Nimitti-Bel, the great walls of Babylon, completed." Here we find no longer sentences

KAR

but ... and so on for three or four hundred lines, with two or three intervals only, such as at line 30, where we have *iti ... ...*, "with the embankment my father had constructed I joined;" and line 51, *itti sa abi ... ...*, "with what my father had made I joined." This passage is evidence of the necessity of considering these forms, which have been too frequently overlooked by translators.

kari hiritti-su ina kupri va agurri sadanis abni; *the embankment of their* [*sic*] *ditch in cement and brick mountain-like I built.*—Neb. Bab. ii. 5.

kare ... ... mee ... ana nisi Sumerim va Akkadim lu askun; *channels double*(?) *I threw up* (*dug*), *waters permanent for the men of Sumir and Accad I established.*—Hamm. i. 23.

¶ ..., garmis, *adv.* *In Ruins.*—Sen. T. i. 75. See p. 189.

The plural sign is used here phonetically, as in *Armis*, p. 594.

¶ ... begins many proper names of provinces, cities, and people; I subjoin those which I have registered, but I have no doubt that more will be found in the inscriptions:—

..., Kargamis.—Tig. v. 49.

The city Carchemish on the Euphrates, usually written .... Tiglath Pileser calls it "Carchemish of the Hittites." The modern Bir.—Hincks.

...—Obel. 76. Sard. iii. 84, 131. Kardunias.

...—Tig. Jun. 12.

...—Botta 145, 9 = 21, 16bis 61. Sen. Gr. 6.

...—Sen. T. i. 20.

...—Black St. iv. 4.

Dr. Hincks places Karduniash south of Babylon, and south of Chaldea, which he extends to the Persian Gulf.—Dublin University Mag., [illegible], p. 472.

..., Kar-Zibra.—Tig. Jun. 31.

Name of a province in the far east; see *Arapeha*, p. 66.

..., Kar-Alla.—Botta 146, 19, 20 = 55, 56.

A country subdued by Sargon, who transported the inhabitants to Hamath, the Cœle-Syria of the classical writers.

KAR ., Kar-Mubasa.—Sen. T. iv. 53.

One of thirty-four Elamite cities.

., Karumb.—Tig. jun. 7.

An Aramaean tribe, included in a large enumeration of the conquests of Tiglath-Pileser.

.—Tig. jun. 8.

Follows the preceding in the same line. I do not know how it should be read.

., Kar-Sennacherib.—Sen. T. ii. 26.

—Sen. Cr. 33.

A city so named by Sennacherib, who made it the capital of the province of Bit-Barrua (p. 124); its name had previously been Ilinza.

., Kar-Marduk.—Botta 146, 24 = 60.

Name given to the city of Kisesi by Sargon, who erected a statue of himself in it.

., Kar-Nabu.—Botta 147, 5 = 65.

New name given by Sargon to the city of , Tel-abia, on the frontier of Media.

., Kar-Shalmaneser.—Sh. Ph. ii. 9.

A city near Carchemish, captured in the first campaign of Shamas Phul.

., Kar-Yav.—Botta 147, 5 = 65.

New name given to the city of Bit-Bagaya, near Media.

., Kar-Nari.—Bavian 8.

One of the towns from which Sennacherib brought drinkable water through canals to Nineveh.

., Kar-Sin.—Botta 147, 5 = 65.

New name given by Sargon to Kindaha, near Media.

., Kar-Assur.—Tig. jun. 11.

A city built by Tiglath Pileser "on the mound of Hihiri, which they call Humut." See pp. 402, 432. There is no direct mention of the locality, but the preceding names relate to Aramaeans, and the following to the cities of Babylonia.

., Kar-Istar.—Botta 147, 5 = 65.

New name given by Sargon to Anzaria, near Media.

., Karsa.—No. 6, N.R. 10.

This province was written , Karkâ, in Persian, and , Karka, in Scythian. Locality uncertain. See Sir H. Rawlinson in his Persian Vocabulary, Journ. R.A.S. Vol. 11, p. 98.

KaR Kar-Ṣibutai.—Sh. Ph. iii. 5.

A city of [illegible] (or [illegible]), from which the king received a tribute of horses; see p. [illegible].

¶ Kar-Sargina.—Botta 147, 5, 6 = 65, 66.

New name given by Sargon to the city of Kharkhar, which he rebuilt and fortified, as a check to Media; he also erected a statue of himself in it, establishing at the same time the worship of Assur there.

KiR — Syl. 387.

„ 388.

„ 389.

I have not seen this monogram used for any other sound than *kir*.

„ 390.

„ 481.

„ 544.

„ 98.

var. —Sard. ii. 105.

KuR —New Syl. 117.

„ 118.

Guided by these recently-discovered fragments we may now safely restore the following lines from the Old Syllabary:—

—Syl. 518.

„ 519.

„ 520.

„ 521.

„ 522.

„ 523.

KuR , qaru; (whom) *he hath Proclaimed.* Heb. קָרָא.

, sarri maduti alik maḫri-ya sa ilu ana sarruti er qaru zikir-sun ina er-er sa ini-sunu asar istânu; *the great kings my predecessors [going before me], whom the god to the royalty of the city hath proclaimed their renown, in cities, the delight of their eyes, a place have established.*—R.I.H. vii. 15.

Qaru is a permansive verb, third pers. sing. in the relative form, with k instead of q, as usual in the inscriptions of Nebuchadnezzar; it should have been ranged among the verbs, but is placed here for the convenience of students.

KRA .—4 R II. 62c.

KRB , , , , , kirib, c. kirba, a. kirbi, obl. kirbu, nc. *The Inside, Interior.* Heb. קרב.

This word is a substantive, but it is used more frequently as a preposition, signifying "in," and is now and then preceded by *ina*; with *ana* the meaning is "in," or "into," and with *ultu* "from within." We find in a few cases *kirbu, kirbi*. See also *qerbu*, pp. 129, 131.

Kirib as preposition:—

, bilat-sunu [bilatsunu] kabitti l'amḫar kirib-sa; *their tributes abundant may it receive within it.*—Neb. Gr. iii. 53. E.I.H. x. 12.

.... , papaḫa Nabiū sa kirib Bit-Saggatu .... ḫuraṣi usalbis; *the shrine of Nebo which is in Bit-Saggatu .... with gold I caused cover.*—Neb. Gr. i. 35.

, lamasa asira sa musallime imma u musa kirib-sun l'istabru; *a sacred figure, a guard for protection by day and night, in them may they maintain.*—Botta 138, 16; 12, 108. Oppert 100.

KRB dur-su va subat-su aamur-su ana kirib tamti addi; *its castle and its seat I overthrew, and cast into the sea.*—Esar. i. 19.

urhi la pitusi tudi pasqati sa lapan suli marsuti ullanû-a kirib-sun mamman la illiku sarrani pani mahruti; *paths not opened, swamps extensive, which, before the rugged mountains beyond me, within them never had gone the former ancient kings.*—Hen. Tig. iv. 5.

Instead of the crude *kirib* we find not unfrequently the word inflected:—

Nabiû va Nanâ in hidâti va risâti subat tub libbi kerba-su usesib; *Nebo and Nana, in joy and supremacy,* (on) *a seat good to the heart* (*to their wishes?*), *in it I made them sit.*—Neb. Gr. ii. 25. See also iii. 22.

kirba-sa; *in it.*—Nerig. ii. 40.

kirba-sun; *in them.*—E.I.H. vi. 47.

Ina kirib, kirbi, within:—

epis la paras ilati-suna rabiti ina kirib-su addi; *a statue not false of their great godships in its interior I put.*—Tig. vii. 107.

kisal Ninib bili-a ina kirib-su uparri(hi); *an altar to Ninib, my lord, in it I consecrated.*—Sard. ii. 135.

I am not decided about the verb which I have rendered "consecrated;" I do not understand the termination *i* in a perfect verb, and have assumed without authority a word [illegible], in p. 448, in order to get rid of such a form; though I admit that we have [illegible] as a variant in l. [illegible] of this column. It seems certain that we have two roots [illegible] and [illegible] of the same value; see [illegible] in Sard. ii. 87, [illegible] in the parallel passage, New Sard. i. 36, and [illegible] in [illegible] iv. 74 and iii. 29.

KRB . ina kirbi-sa sibatu l'ukrud; *within it repose may it approach.*—Nerig. ii 35.

The same passage in E.I.H. v. 6 with var. *sibati*; also in Neb. Gr. iii. 45 with the addition of ina *Babila-ki*, and var. . In the eight-line brick, Sh. 52, No. 8, the passage is written in this way:—

. ina kiribi-sa ina Babila-ki sibati laksa.

Laksa is clearly a mistake; *Babila* and *kiribi* are doubtful, but I find *kiribi* again in l. 8.

. libûa ina kirbi-sa ana daerati salmat; *may salmat(?) come within it for ever.*—E.I.H. x. 17. See p. 168.

Ana kirib, to:—

. sin labbi sal labbi ana kirib Nineveh-ki er biluti-ya arki-ya usebila; *sons and daughters to Nineveh the city of my power after me he sent.*—Sen. T. iii. 39.

Dr. Oppert and Mr. Talbot both translate "male and female slaves" here: I have some doubt on the matter, and will carefully consider it under L B.

. sisi adi marsiti-suna liti kurral la mina sallata kabitta ana kirib Assur-ki usala; *the people and their children, with horses innumerable, plunder much, to Assyria I carried off.*—Botta 147, 18 = 73.

Ultu kirib, from within:—

. ultu kirib tamti amas-su ma akkisa qaqqad-su [qaqqassu]; *from within the sea I reached him, and cut off his head.*—Esar i. 17. Uncertain.

. sallat-sunu (sallaqunu) alpi-sunu lu-sini-sunu ulta (ta) kirib sade usrida; *their women, their cattle, their sheep, from within the mountains I brought down.*—Obel. 137.

KRB *Kirib, kirbu, kiribu, kirbi*, the inside:—

kirib-su kima libbi abinui; *its inside to my desire(?) I built.*—Tig. vii. 97.

I have no confidence in this version, and I am much inclined to suspect an error in the original inscription. We find *ina libbi* as often as *ina kirbi* for "the inside," and in the hurry of writing such a mistake is not unlikely. Sir H. Rawlinson translated "outside the temple I fashioned (everything with the same care) as inside." This must have been the sense intended, but not expressed. Dr. Hincks's version was "I made the interior of it as well as itself." Mr. Talbot ". . . . I built and I finished within it." All the translators have felt the difficulty.

Bit-Shamas sa kirib Senkoreh sa istu yomani ruqûti innû tilanis kiribu-su kaana lamphu; *the temple of the Sun which (is) in Senkoreh, which from days remote had lain in heaps, (and) its interior like rubbish was piled up.*—Senk. Cyl. 1. 15.

We have *kiribu* here for the usual *kirbi*.

epir kirbi-su lqsub sa lussura nparidi; *the earth of the interior was removed, and were seen the foundations.*—Sen. Cyl. 1. 21.

simat palati-ya isimmu ina kirbi; *a monument(?) of my life they placed in the interior.*—E.I.H. ii. 63. See p. 98.

¶ kiribtu; *Alliance, Union.* [The same root.]

ana yâsi va zirriti-ya kiribtu dabita l'ikrubu-ni; *to my people and my seed good alliance may they grant me.* [Literally "union may they unite to me."]—Tig. viii. 25. See p. 467.

The Hebrew root commonly signifies "approach" rather than "union," or "inclusion," which is the Assyrian value; but this value is not unknown in Hebrew; we have it in Gen. xxiv. 3, Abraham is dwelling *be-qirbo* "among" the people;—in xlv 6 the famine is *be-qereb* "in" the land.

KRB [illegible] kirubu, kirubo : *Earth*.

It may be expedient to collate here two passages narrating the same proceeding, one from the Nebi Yunus Inscription, the other from Taylor's Cylinder; they will be found to explain each other:—

[illegible]—Neb. Yus. 60, 61.

[illegible]—Sen. T. vi. 35.

Neb. Yus. Kima akutti-tama kirubû mâda ultu kirib nualli
Sen. T. Kirubû ma'da ultu kirib nualli va tamirti er kima akutti-tama

la aslata çira-ma usraddi maççar hekali mahriti esib ma ina kirib
la aslata ina eli l'usraddi maççar hekali mahriti esib ma ina

kirubo sa ultu naalli asbata tûbi umalli
maççar naalli sa ultu vabli nahr asbata tûbi umalli

I think it will appear from this collation that *kirubu* must signify "earth," being used as a variant of *çaççar*. The original value was probably the "inside," as in the preceding *kirb*; the inside of a mound, or of the bed of a river; "something to fill up with." I feel sure that instead of the impossible *ina kirib kirubo sa ultu naalli* we should have *ina kirubo sa ultu kirib naalli*, "with the earth which from the inside I had raised;" see pp. 603 and 610. I would then translate the Nebi Yunus passage in this way—"Much earth (which) from the inside I raised, I took (and) spread (?) over the site of the former palace I left, and with the earth which I had raised from the inside I took (and) the mound I filled up."

The words from Sen. T., which I have transliterated by *kima akutti-tama*, are erroneously printed in the plate *kirib kutti-mama*; see pp. 80 and 146, where I have collated a similar clause from Lay. v. 1, printed [illegible]. In this clause likewise there is a misprint, the word engraved on the cylinder being [illegible], as I learn from Mr. [illegible], who has kindly examined the passage at the British Museum. The same word, printed correctly at last in Nak. Yun. 60, appears at the head of the sentence quoted, but it is more immediately connected with the preceding bit, making with it *kirbi sira ana sihurti-su appar kima* adwri anus, "that palace the whole of it, I overthrew, *kima* (?) I crushed, and," &c. Now as the two passages tell the same tale, and were probably taken from the same original account, they ought to explain each other, and this they do, so far as to the general import, but they leave some difficulties, which I cannot unravel; *kima* before the verb *adwri* can hardly be an error, appearing as it does in three inscriptions, but I do not remember to have seen such a construction elsewhere. The following is a version of the Nan. T. passage, given word for word, but having one word transposed as in the Neb. Yun. passage, and the unexplained words in italics:—"Much earth (which) from inside I raised, as *sumirti* or *kima* I crushed and took, (and) over I spread; the site of the former palace I left, and with the earth which from the bed of the river I had raised, I took and the mound I filled up."

[illegible] .... [illegible]
[illegible]
[illegible]

sar .... sa ana asumb namo nadati va pite kirebe saqap sippāti lakunu uzun-su; *king* ..... *who to the introduction of flowing streams and* ..... *plantation of trees hath given his attention* [*applied his ears*].—Botta 37, 38.

I do not know the meaning of *pite kirebe*; the orthography of *saqap* is doubtful, but we have a similar phrase in Mon. 75, with the ordinary [illegible]; see p. 397.

¶ [illegible], karbal; *Clothe, Cover.* Heb. כַּרְבֵּל.

[illegible]
[illegible], Gimirri karbal qati-sunu [sul] rappah; *the Scyths covering their hands with* ..... —No. 6, N.R. 13.

Rather doubtful. The Persian has *Saka Tigrakhauda*, which was rendered by Westergaard "Scythian archers," by Rawlinson "Tonsuphori," meaning the same. The Babylonian appears to signify "Scyths covering their hands with *rappah*," a word which I cannot explain. The Scythic does little more than transliterate the Persian, writing *Sakka appa tikrakauda*, "the Scyths who were Tigrakauda," with the pluralizing *p*. See *Gimirri*, in pp. 192–3. The Cimmerians [Κιμμέριοι] have, on account of their name, been looked at as Celts, and especially Welshmen (Cymry, pronounced Kymry); but I am inclined to think *cymro* to be merely *cyn-bro*, "the first country." The Welsh dictionaries give no *cyn-bro*, with this meaning; cf. Pembroke = *pen-bro*, "land's end;" and *bragae Galli agrum dicunt*, quoted by Zeuss from an old scholium on Juvenal; see Gram. Celt. p. 575. I have noticed under the same heading the reading *Nammiri* for *Gimirri*, as occurring twice in the Behistun Inscription. Although printed *Gimirri*, the alteration was sanctioned by Sir H. Rawlinson, who had originally so copied the word from the rock, but had subsequently changed it on the authority of Westergaard and Tasker's copies of the Nakhsh-i Rustam Inscription. See Journ. R.A.S., Vol. 15, p. 220.

KRB [cuneiform], kigalla, kigalla; *Solidity; Solid; a Solid Foundation.*

[cuneiform], in kigallá rísti ina irad erriti ragmati ina kupri va agurri usarsid temen-sa; *with great solidity, at a depth of much tenacity, in cement and brick I laid down its foundation.*—Neb. Gr. iii. 32. See p. 493.

I have had some doubts about *erriti*, thinking that it was merely an irregular spelling, and that *erṣiti* was intended; but considering that *erer* would hardly be used in the sense of "ground," that [illegible] is rendered by "robur" in Zeph. ii. 14, and that Golius makes the Arabic [illegible] "firmus fuit, radicibus in solum firmiter defixis," I have decided upon the translation adopted.

[cuneiform], ṣalami..... ina kigalli ramani-sunu sakis ussuzum; *images on their own solid base conspicuously were put up.*—Sen. Bit. iv. 15 = 40 BM 1.

[cuneiform], ussi-sa ina irad kigalla usarsid; *its foundation in a solid depth I laid down.*—E.I.H. viii. 60. Nearly the same in Vol. 1, Sh. 52, No. 6, l. 4.

[cuneiform], kigalli sa tiamme tamkaluv sa alam-sunu sunnapalli siru-sun ulusid; *the bases of the bronze figures(?) whose forms were admirable, upon it I placed.*—Neb. Yun 63. (A mere guess.)

[cuneiform], asirtum kaspi sa sippe kisu ṣimdti-sa rimdti usziz ina kigallá .... sisati sa kirib Bit-Zida; *ornaments of silver of the pediment as its chief device I erected on firm bases .... which (are) in Bit-Zida.*—Norig. i. 30. See p. 515. Doubtful.

KRD [cuneiform].—43 II. 1a.
[cuneiform] „ 2a.
[cuneiform] „ 3a.

KRḤ [cuneiform] (v. [cuneiform]). kirḫu; *Citadel.* Syr. [Syriac], cella.

[cuneiform] (v. [cuneiform]) [cuneiform] (v. [cuneiform], [cuneiform]) [cuneiform] (v. [cuneiform]) [cuneiform], er marṣi dannis 2 durani labi kirḫa-su kima uban (v. ṣuṣi) sade sakis; *a city strong very; two fortresses on opposite sides of its citadel, like tops of mountains (were) situated.*—Sard. ii. 105 = New Sard. ii. 93.

KRL [cuneiform]. katalli; *Party-walls.* Heb. כֹּתֶל.

[cuneiform], hekal [bit-rab] katalli-sa sa sutmur karasi paqâdi kurrai ṣanaki sintakam sarpiss sarrani aliket maḫri abi-ya tûbo-sa ul ipsi sabat-sa ṣuḫḫurat; *the palace (and) its dividing walls, for the custody of chariots, studs of horses, harness(?) (and) furniture, the preceding kings my ancestors made; its body was not, its site was small.*—Sen. T. vi. 28 = Neb. Yun. 55.

KRM [cuneiform].—New Syl. 125. See p. 195.

KRN [cuneiform]. kiria; *Heaped, Piled.*—Tig. ii. 22; iii. 54; iv. 10.

Perhaps akiria, "I piled;" a is implied in [cuneiform], the a is expressed in iii. 54. See Verbs.

¶ [cuneiform]. Kirini.—Tig. iv. 60.

One of an enumeration of twenty-three provinces of Nairi.

¶ [cuneiform]. Karnela.—Sard. iii. 90.

A city near the upper course of the Euphrates.

KRN

karanâ, kurunnû, kurunnu; *Horned Cattle.* Heb. קרן.

These forms occur in Neb. Gr. in three several passages, all of like general import: I have already printed them partially in pp. 97 and 133, without understanding anything more than that a statement is made of birds and fishes supplied for a lake, and I think cattle also for an adjoining park. I now give the three passages without any further attempt at explanation:—

Nûnâ iççura sammma ṭillâ çimat appari diçpâ ḫisibti dabi dumuk-su
Nûnû iççurû usumma bilâ ... mat apparîâ daspâ çirara kurunnû
Usumma bulâ nûnû iççurû ... mat appari tibih çirara labbi ...

amnû kurunnû daspâ sikar çatû karanâ ellu karanâ.—Neb. Gr. i. 61.
sikar çatû karanâ ellâ diçpa ḫisibti dabû bul-su amnû.—Neb. Gr. ii. 32.
kurunâ milli-sû.—Neb. Gr. iii. 13.

. . . . . kurunnu likira çarra-sun nisukai gulâ eli-sunu [mahḫu-sunu] umkis;
. . . . . *horned beasts* . . . . *upon them I placed.*—Esar vi. 38.

I have printed this already in p. 83, under *likira*, which I have doubtfully rendered "camel," from a word translated "dromedaries" in Isaiah lx. 6, and Jerem. ii. 23. I also remember that çiri, "necks," occurs twice in the epigraphs of the Black Obelisk of Shalmaneser, meaning the "humps" of camels. I would, therefore, very doubtfully suggest for the missing bit of my translation "dromedaries whose humps (or necks) are placed high;" but several letters are damaged, and the words which I think I can read hardly afford any meaning suited to the context.

kurunnu dar(çi) luru biblat sadi elli risit mati kisitti qati-ya sa ana milki sarruti-ya uççibu; *horned cattle* . . . . *the midst of the lofty mountains, high places of the countries, acquisitions of my hands which for the glory of my royalty are enduring.*—Botta 154, 8 = 170.

Doubtful. This passage and the one which follows it in the inscriptions are by no means clear on the monuments, and have not yet been successfully read.

—2 R. 11, 38c.
—Syl. 173.

¶ [cuneiform], Kirri.—Obel. 139.

Name of the brother of a king of the Qusi (Gusi? p. 159), appointed by Shalmaneser to the government of Tarsi, one of the cities belonging to his brother.

KRB [cuneiform], karri.

I have found sikat (or pikhat) karri in the three following passages, meaning something ornamental (made of silver or copper) and useful (associated with columns, beams, &c.). I cannot translate karri in this combination; one of the values of pikat, "roofs, coverings," is suggested under sippat in p. 819:—

[cuneiform], hekal ana subat sarruti-a ana multa'it bilutti-a sa darite ina libbi addi upim umarrih pikat karri tamkhatur alme-si; *a palace for the seat of my royalty, for the fulness of my power, which [for future] generations in the interior I had prepared for, I placed [built], I consecrated; a roof of .... of copper I added to it.*—Monol. 13.

The use of si as in alme-si is exceptional, but it occurs twice more in this inscription, lines 35 and 36; see also Neb. Yun. 66 and Sen. T. vi. 77.

[cuneiform], la-iki la-gapuri pikat karri sa sakan kirib-sa la inasi la er sane hekal sanite la imkan; *the columns, the beams, the roofs .... which are placed in it he shall not take away; in a second city a second palace he shall not place.*—Mon. 10.

[cuneiform], pulab tardai sa kirib barakhkhati etipsu umahla yummis umammir pikhkat karri kaspi va eri kirib-sun usallim; *the fountains, whose jets I made play in the ponds, shone like the day; a covering ..... of silver and bronze in them I completed.*—39 BM 95 = Sen. B. iv. 8.

I think this reading and rendering better than what is printed in p. 319, but there is still some uncertainty remaining.

KRS ... sa ina tarzi sarri abi-ya ana karri nisirti suqere ina pilani sadi Amanana ukkinni pani-su; *(building materials) which in the time of the kings my fathers for protected fortresses appropriated(?), in the parts of Mount Amanus were laid up before it.*—40 BM 43 Sen. B. iv. 18. Uncertain.

This passage should rather have been put in p. 583; it is part of an amplified narration of the building of a magnificent palace in Nineveh. A shorter account will be found in the last column of Taylor's Cylinder, of which translations have been printed by Dr. Oppert and Mr. Talbot. Two slightly-differing copies exist of the amplified account; both are unfortunately damaged, and the one published in 1850 by the British Museum, Bb. 38-42, is incorrectly printed, as might have been expected at that early date; the other is not yet printed.

¶ Durrigalzu.—Nab. Brok. Cyl. ii. 32. R.I. Vol. 1, Pl. 4, No. xiv. l. 4; ii. 1; iii. 2.

One of the early kings of Assyria. Dr. Oppert reads the name Kourigalzou.

¶ Dur-Durrigalzi.—Tig. jun. 8.

Occurs in a very long enumeration of the acquisitions of Tiglath Pileser.

¶ —49 II. 59c.

KRS Karus: *Cyrus, king of Persia.*

la imaqqanu sa la Barziya anaku pal-su sa Karus; *may they not suppose(?) that I am not Bardes, his son of Cyrus.*—Beh. 21.

The first words are very uncertain; the others are perfectly clear. The redundant possessive pronoun is not uncommon in genuine Assyrian; see ir sarruti-su sa *Arrame*, "his capital city of Arramu;" New Div. ii. 48.

anaku Barziya tur Karus; *I am Bardes, son of Cyrus.*—Detached Inscr. No. 1, l. 3.

KRS ..., karas; *an Edict*. Chald. כְּרַז.

..., usus ul ibsi ma ul ustabil karas-su; *the ear was not given and his edict was not issued.*—Sen. Gr. 41.

Assurbanipal .... sa Shams u Yav uzni rapastu usarsu-su ma usuzzi ustabila karas-su deppa harat isitar isuk ipru; *Assurbanipal, king, &c., who the Sun-god and Yav wide ears have granted him [made him powerful], and (who) hath set up and issued his edict, an engraved document hath written, compiled, and promulgated.*—Colophon in 43 II.

See Mr. Talbot's Glossary, No. 209, which has furnished me with this illustration. I consider *harat* (or *harit*) to be allied to the Hebrew חֶרֶט, a tool for engraving; the same word signifies in Hebrew a "bag" or "pocket;" see 2 Kings v. 23; it would be curious to find the mention of a "pocket edition;" the slab is a small one. The word which I have transliterated *usuzzi* can only be so read by supposing an error in the first character; the second, which I have never seen in any other inscription, is shown to be pronounced as in S. I. 334.

I give two extracts more which I cannot translate, or even read with any confidence:—

..., sa gab ma ipsari riti sarru gabdala karas ulkidti.—Sb. Ph. l. 22.

..., slabu la umbbu karas-sun.—Assur b.p. in. 53.

¶ ..., kiris; *Support*. Heb. כִּרְסֵא.

..., hari aspi hurasi kiris ibbi sa sidi sana ambar; *eighty bracelets of gold, (and) the ivory supports of their feet I received.*—Sen. T. vi. 3. See pp. 367, 438.

Doubtful; Dr. Oppert writes *les sceaux en ivoire*.

KRS

In the following passage *kiris* would seem to be some kind of metal; Mr. Talbot reads *kiris* "gold" in his notes on Sen. T. vi. 8 (Journ. R.A.S., Vol. 19, p. 161), unless there be some typographical error, which I suspect from the omission of the preceding word *hurasu*, "gold?"—

[cuneiform] ir-iki is-erni is-surman bisli mesir kiris va eri ussikis ma uratte babi-sun; *posts of pine and smooth bar (with) bands of kiris and bronze I bound, and fastened (or strengthened) their gates.*—38 BM 24 Sen. B. iv. 3.

[cuneiform] usú kirib-sa asnil kiris sulhai sabi iqgi milli [adan] kisi lum libbi aramir.—42 BM 44 = Sen. B. iv. 30.

[cuneiform] iqqari same kiris sulhu qinnu iqnum ma sab iqgi milli [adan] kisi atappiru.—42 BM 47 = Sen. B. iv. 33.

I can only refer here to p. 316, where I have already said all I know about the two preceding extracts.

¶ [cuneiform], karasi; *Chariots.*

[cuneiform], ina sir Nipur karasi unsekin; *in the neighbourhood [at the foot?] of Nipur the chariots I placed.*—Sen. T. iii. 71. See also iv. 8.

[cuneiform], ana entasur karasi; *for the custody of chariots, &c.*—Sen. T. vi. 28 = Neb. Yon. 33. See p. 608.

[cuneiform] .... [cuneiform], gipis ummani-ya ul upahhir ma ul aqgura karasi ...... ana Asdodi allik; *the power of my soldiers I did not restrain, I did not get together the chariots; to Ashdod I went.*—Botta 150, 9 = 98.

KRS [illegible], karassie.

[illegible]. elappi galal adibbú babalati-sunu usselbú lamusunu karassie ina danani u ramqi marsis ubilunu-mma umabita bald-sin; *ships large made ready their people, they rested innumerable as in chariots, with strength and rapidity laboriously they advanced and seized their gates.*—3R BM 12. Uncertain.

¶ [illegible], karesi; *Tables, Seats.* Arab. كراسي.

[illegible], karesi daliti la nobi astapak-su; *long tables [seats], not to be told, I accumulated them [it].*—Neb. Gr. iii. 25.

KRT [illegible], [illegible], kiriti, kireti, *old Humility.* Heb. כרע.

[illegible], kali-sunu ina tabulte u kireti ina kuiqte sildti kirib-su ussib; *all of them in service and humility, in obedience quiet, in it I established.*—Esar vi. 34. See p. 556.

[illegible] (v. [illegible]) [illegible] (v. [illegible]), itti pabati (bil-ucm, p. 85) mati-ya akli mpiri rald autried 11 yomml tamarta-sunu kabitta amhar ina kirili unsulb-sunuti ma ustakun(na) nigutu; *with the chiefs of my land, the able, the precious, the*

KBT *princes, the officers; fourteen days their offering much I received, in humility I seated them, I established ordinances.*—Botta 10, 29.

This passage is compiled from Sheets 8, 9, 10, 15, 21, which are all mutilated in part, and all incorrectly engraved; but they supply each others' deficiencies. I suppose the fourteen days to apply to the acceptance of offerings from vanquished kings, who are stated in the preceding lines to have made their submission. Some of the epithets are uncertain, but the drift of the passage is hardly doubtful.

¶ [cuneiform], [cuneiform], Kirtiara, Kirteara.—Sard. II. 40, 39.

Name of a petty king of Larbusa (l. 40) and Bara (l. 39), two cities evidently appertaining to the same part of the country, which appears to be in or near Susiana.

KaS [cuneiform] . [cuneiform] . [cuneiform].—Syl. 684.

It has been suggested with great probability that the difference between [cuneiform] and [cuneiform] is graphic only; [cuneiform] as the sign is frequently written in this way [cuneiform], and when doubled, the characters very nearly resemble [cuneiform], which is a frequent form of kas. See p. 42.

[cuneiform] . [cuneiform] . [cuneiform].—Syl. 391.

This monogram may possibly denote "enemy," or "hostility," but I have never seen it used.

[cuneiform] . [cuneiform] . [cuneiform].—Syl. 548.

The Assyrian word is lost, but the meaning must be "two;" this is supposed to be corroborated by the Turanian analogies of *kit*, *kät*, *kat*, and *iki* of Magyar, Ostiak, Wotiak, and Turkish; it is shown also by the following passage from the Behistun Inscription:—

[cuneiform], ina malti II sikrut iphuruna-mma illiku' ana tarşi Umisşi; *in the second time the rebels formed*, and *went to the meeting of Vomisa.*—Beh. 55.

I should have supposed *masti* to be "the second" in this passage, in which the Persian text has *patiy duvitiyam*; but in l. 63 we have *masti* with a different monogram, where the Persian text reads *patiy tritiyam*.

[cuneiform] . [cuneiform], Harrane.—38 II. 22b.

Proves that the monogram was pronounced *harran*; see p. 451, where further extracts, numbered 23 to 26, show that *harran* denoted *urha*, "path;" *derega*, "road;" and *mutaga*, "passage."

KAS [cuneiform], ina 2-i harran-ya ana Babel-ki sa ana kasadi summura-su bitmadis allik; in my second road, to Babylon, on whose capture I had rejoiced, eagerly I went.—Bavian 43. Uncertain. See p. 409.

[cuneiform], li' kali malki sa eli Harran anrapala-su itrusu; the victor [swallower] of all kings; who over the city of Harran his power(?) hath strengthened.—Botta 175, 4.

We have [cuneiform] and [cuneiform] in the parallel passages 178, 7, and 167, 2, still further proving the phonetic value of [cuneiform]. The same phrase occurs in Barg 4, and the last clause in Botta 14, 11; 66, 6; and elsewhere in the inscriptions of Sargon: it is a sort of title of that monarch. I have no clue to the meaning of anrapala.

KIS [cuneiform], City of Kis.

[cuneiform], sa Marduk-pal-adanna sarri Kardunias adi ummanat Numma-ki risi-su ina tamirti Kis-ki astakan abikta-su [sisi-su]; of Merodach-baladan, the king of Karduniias, together with the warriors of Elam his auxiliaries, in the neighbourhood of Kis I settled his defeat.—Sen. T. I. 21 = Sen. B. i. 4. Sen. Gr. 6 omits risi-su.

¶ [cuneiform]—40 II. 6 a.

From a list of Gods and of the cities in which they had seats.

¶ [cuneiform].—Syl. 383.

¶ [cuneiform], kisi.—42 BM 45 and 47 = Sen. B. iv. 37 and 38.

May be the name of some bird, but very uncertain; see p. 316.

KuS ([cuneiform]) [cuneiform] . [cuneiform].—18 II. 48 b.

The monogram is shown here to have been pronounced *kus*; and it is explained by [cuneiform], *nuhu*, "to rest," "to be tranquil," the Hebrew נוח. This is corroborated by [illegible] 6, 7, 8, where we have [cuneiform], *munahhu*, "repose," Heb. מנוחה, and [cuneiform], *anuhu*, "I rest," Heb. אנוח. See Sard. l. 44 (printed in p. 348), where the monarch says that at the commencement of his reign the Sun-god threw his beneficent shade ([cuneiform]) upon him.

¶ [cuneiform] . [cuneiform] . [cuneiform].—New Syl. 86.

[cuneiform] . [cuneiform] . [cuneiform].—Syl. 420.

¶ [cuneiform], Kûs; *Cush*.—No. 6, N.R. l. 31. See p. 501.

KSB [cuneiform], kasap; *Price, Money*. Heb. כסף.

[cuneiform]

kasap eqili [alild] eri aôsa ki pi duppâte sa sinnane-sa kaspa va sîparu ana bili-suna utir ma ana riggati la rusi sa kasap eqli la pibû eqli mihir eqli ahir pana-suna addin-sunuti; *the price of the lands of that city, according to the face of the tablets of its guarantee [title-deeds], silver and copper, to the owners of them I returned, and in solid bullion [weights not broken]; who the price of the land not wished for, land before (or) land behind instead of them, I gave them.*—Sard. 41 and 42.

See Journ. R.A.S. 1864, p. 195, where Sir H. Rawlinson remarks "I am not sure "whether the words 'silver and copper' refer to the weight of metal given to the "proprietors for their lands, or to the material of the tablets on which the title-"deeds were written...... Probably, however, the latter is the true application; "as I have never in one single instance found copper given as a representative of "value, although gold, silver, and iron are mentioned in almost every transaction "of sale or barter."

¶ [cuneiform] . [cuneiform] . [cuneiform].—Syl. 190.

¶ [cuneiform], Kasbu. See p. 513.

KSD [cuneiform], [cuneiform], [cuneiform], [cuneiform], kasadu, kasadi, kasad; *Approach; Acquisition.* Arab. كَشَدَ.

The root KSD implies nearness, and may be rendered "approach," "reach," "attain," "take possession," "capture." Arabic dictionaries give us kasada, "gain;" kasida, "a relation;" kashada, "qui affinitatem contrahit." The Assyrian forms are—

Kasad; capture, acquisition, taking possession, arrival, &c.
Kasid (*active participle*); the acquirer, or conqueror.
Kisud (*passive ditto*); the captured, a captive.
Kisad; neighbourhood, presence; near.
Kisid; the thing acquired, an acquisition.

The monogram [cuneiform] is used for the root KSD both in nouns and verbs; see [cuneiform], var. [cuneiform], aksud, "I captured," Sard. ii. 87; [cuneiform], v. [cuneiform], aktasad, the same, Sard. ii. 87; [cuneiform], v. [cuneiform], kisitti, "acquisition," Bu. 14.

¶ *Kasad, kasadu, &c.*; Arrival, Attainment, Capture:—

[cuneiform], sar Numma-ki kasad erani-su isme ma imqut-su [imqussu] hattu; *the king of Elam (of) the capture of his cities heard, and fear struck him.*—Neb. Yun. 39.

In the parallel Gen. T. iv. 68 and 70 we have [cuneiform] for [cuneiform], Elamai for Numma-ki, and [cuneiform] for kasad. See both passages in page 410, and observe the very singular dislocation of words in the Gen. T. inscription.

[cuneiform], ana kasad Musri Assur bilu umahra-ni ma birti Elamuni ..... lu asbat Musri ana pihati-su aksud; *to the capture of Musur Assur the lord urged me, and through the mountains of Elamuni ...... I took (my way); Musur to its entirety I captured.*—Tig. v. 67.

See a similar construction in iii. 5), at the bottom of p. 128. I think *birti asbat* in such sentences implies a passage through mountains.

[cuneiform], ana kasad mati satina astakan pani-ya; *to the acquisition of these countries I set my face, (or I put before me).*—Botta 146, 1-10.

KSD [cuneiform] (v. [cuneiform]) [cuneiform] (v. [cuneiform]) [cuneiform], ili rabi ina tub libbi va kasad irnite tabis l'itsurru-su; *may the great gods in goodness of heart and acquisition of triumphs preserve him.*—Tig. viii. 62.

[cuneiform], Shamas va Yav ibalu'inni anna kini sa kasadu temlana Bit-Ulbar; *the Sun-god and Yav brought to me the high favour of attaining the written tablet of Bit-Ulbar.*—Neb. Br. Cyl. ii. 50. See note on *temin*, p. 513.

[cuneiform], ana kasadi ana Madai; *on my reaching to Media.*—Beh. 57.

Kasadi is *kasad-i*, "my reaching." See ummani, "my army," qati, "my hand," in Dr. Hincks's Grammar, Journ. R.A.S. 1866, pp. 518-9.

[cuneiform] .... [cuneiform], anaku ana Asur, &c., ana kasadi nibi danni asshar-sunuti ma supe-a arrad(?) isma; *I to Asur, &c., on the arrival of the powerful enemies, prayed to them, and my prayers .... they heard.*—Sen. T. v. 52.

The verb sadar usually signifies to "levy a tribute," but in this case, as in some others, the meaning is "to pray" or "invoke;" there may have been some connection implied between an urgent prayer and a forcible levy. The same root signifies "pouring out libations;" see mashkara and mushkir in 7 l, ix. A, l. 8. I cannot find a value for arrad (or likvar); it occurs again in l. 2 and l. 75, where it is equally unintelligible to me; I do not remember it elsewhere.

[cuneiform], ana la kasadi ina mati-su; *for my not arriving* [*that I might not arrive*] *in his country.*—Tig. ii. 45.

Kasadu appears as a nominative in the inscriptions of Babylon:—

[cuneiform], kuu kussi [is-guza] labari pale sumkutu sakiri kasadu mada sibi ana siriktu surkû; *stability of throne, long years, slaughter of rebels, capture much of enemies, to length lengthen.*—Birs ii. 22.

KSD *Kasid (act. particip.)*; Acquirer, Conqueror:—

kasid kiprat aibi; *acquirer of the places of enemies.*—Tig. iv. 41.

kasid mati aibi; *acquirer of the countries of enemies.*—Tig. vii. 42.

kasid er Zidunni sa ina gapli tamti; *the acquirer of the city of Sidon which (is) in the midst of the sea.*—Esar i. 9.

kasid ulta [ta] tamti anta u tamti kita sa Nairi u tamti rabite sa dime Shamsi adi mati Ḫamani; *acquirer from the upper sea and lower sea of Nairi, and the great sea of the setting sun, to mount Amanus.*—12 BM 14.

See a similar sentence extending to six lines, beginning l. 6, *kasid sa ... sapiḫ Shamsi*, "from the highway of the rising sun," and ending at l. 11, with *adi tamti rabiti sa sapiḫ Shamsi*, "to the great sea of the setting sun;" with a dozen names of countries and one or two little descriptive words intervening.

Kisudi (pass. particip.); Captives:—

kabis kisudi nisi Ḫilakki Duha asibut ḫursani sa dibi Tabal; *treading on captives, the men of Cilicia and Duha inhabiting the forests which (are) facing Tabal.*—Esar ii. 10. See pp. 287 and 520.

Kisad, kisadi; Near; Neighbourhood:—

Ilamû-a ina Halule sa kisad Tiggar mishunu sidirta pan maski-ya pulte ina sanʼale ishatl-aun; *before me in Halul which near the Tigris is situated, ranks before my lines they occupied, and shot forth their arrows.*—Sen. T. v. 43.

Not quite certain: see pp. 121 and 314. See Botta [illegible] 10–77; 10[illegible], 42.

KSD [cuneiform]. ista Al-ibur-sabû sulo Babel-ki adi kimdu nahr Utkiprat-ki; *from Aibur-sabû without Babylon to the neighbourhood of the Euphrates.*—Norig. II. 17.

I take sulo, "without," from Dr. Oppert's Grammar, 2nd edit., p. 95; but see sulat-sulo-su, Sen. Gr. 40, printed in p. 4.

[cuneiform]. la ahri kimdi-su; *I dug near it.*—Hamm. I. 23. See p. 558.

[cuneiform]. qaqqadi [risdu] Sandusarri va Abdimilkutti ina kimdi nisi rabi-sun alib; *the heads of Sanduarr and Abdimilkut in the presence [nearness] of their great men I suspended.*—Esar I. 51.

I follow Dr. Oppert in translating alib "I suspended," but I do not know the root of the verb.

[cuneiform]. kimdate-sunu nashhiq adis ukrata supnate-sunu uparri' gabis kima milli [alib] gapsi sa zagabtû qimmai va mussi-sunu asrdâ; *their country without I laid waste completely; (their) fields and their lives I destroyed within; like a great torrent of rain (their) valuables and their treasure I swept down.*—Sen. T. v. 76.

In the above passage I have supposed kimdate to be a plural of kimd, and to signify the country in the neighbourhood. Mussi I read "treasure," not coin, but gold and silver, from מכס; but the whole passage is somewhat uncertain. See former attempts in pp. 172, 180, 556.

Kisid, kisitti, kisiti(?); Acquisitions, Spoils:—

[cuneiform]. nisi [sa] kisitti qati-ya (sa-ya) sa matl sa apliu-sina-si sa .... alpû ina libbi usasbit; *the people, the acquisitions of my hands, of the countries which I had captured of (many countries here named), I collected, (and) within I settled them [made them occupy].*—Bt. 15.

KSD [cuneiform] (v. [cuneiform]) [cuneiform], kisitti qâti-ya; *the acquisitions of my hands.*—Tig. vii. 8.

[cuneiform], 1 nambhar tamkabar 1 sirmak tamkabar sa kisitti va madatte sa Kummuhi ana Assur bili-ya akis; *one namkhar of copper and one sirmak of copper, of the spoils and tribute of Comukha, to Assur my lord I dedicated.*—Tig. ii. 59.

[cuneiform], ina kisitti sakiri mallûti sa ina tukulti ili rabi bili-ya iksuda qata-ya isid nakbani sa Assur-ki u Akkad-ki usepis; *of the accumulated(?) spoils from rebels which, in the service of the great gods, my lords, my hands had taken, the foundation of fortresses of Assyria and Accad I caused make.*—Esar iv. 48.

[cuneiform], ar znatu ana issuti asbat nisi mati kisitti kap-pi-ya [sa-ya] ina libbi usesib; *that city again I occupied, the men of the countries, the acquisitions of my hands, within it I seated.*—Botta 142, 2 · 62.

Dr. Oppert translates here and elsewhere (l. 65) the city I "rebuilt," but it was only a re-occupation. *Zabat*, I think, can only imply "taking."

In the following line we have the passive form sakisitti in the same sense;—

[cuneiform] (v. [cuneiform]) [cuneiform], 25 ilani sa mati sinati sakisitti (v. sakisitti) qati-ya; *twenty-five gods of those countries, the acquisitions of my hands.*—Tig. iv. 88.

[cuneiform] ([cuneiform]) [cuneiform], sume kisitti arani-sa Kudur-nahunda sis Elamé; *heard of the capture of his cities Kudur-nakhunda, the man of Elam.*—Sen. T. iv. 60.

Here *kisitti* implies the "capture" instead of the "thing captured." I do not remember finding this elsewhere except in the doubtful case of [cuneiform] in the next extract. I enclose the irregular one in parenthesis, because I do not see it in the photograph.

KSD [cuneiform], kisitta and kappi and mulli and aba lazir rabû alik; (to) the *acquisition of silver-mines, salt-mines, alabaster quarries, I went.*—Obel. 105.

Dr. Hincks was inclined to read the first word *mata*, "mines;" but the *mat* would in this case hardly be repeated; perhaps, however, the repeated *mat* may have been a non-phonetic determinative, and *kisitta* should be the thing captured, which tells against my interpretation. The omission of a preposition before an objective noun I have never seen elsewhere connected with the verb *halak*.

[cuneiform], asmgir tamkabar epus kisitti mati sa ina ili-ya bili-ya aksudu er suatu ana la sabata va dar-su la rasapi ina eli altur; *a tablet of copper I made, the spoil of the countries which, through my god my lord, I took; "that city not to be occupied, and its wall not to be built," upon it I wrote.*—Tig. vi. 16.

I have translated *ili-ya* "my god," instead of "Assur," "Ya," and "Jah," of the earlier translators. In this I follow Dr. Oppert's more recent version.

[cuneiform], ina palahsi iskui Assur kasidati . . . . .—Assur b.p. viii. 50. Doubtful.

¶ [cuneiform].—Syl. 250.

[cuneiform].—23 II. 3e.

The right-hand column must have had *kussu*, "throne," in this last extract.

KSI [cuneiform], Kasiyara.—Tig. i. 70.

[cuneiform], Kasiyari.—Brok. Obel. i. 17.

A hilly country on the road to Comukha. See [illegible], p. [illegible]

KSK [cuneiform], Kaski.—Sarg. 15.

[cuneiform], Kaskayal.—Tig. ii. 100.

I have put these two forms together, but I am now inclined to think the places are not the same; the former word occurs in an enumeration of all the provinces subject to Sargon, but it is inserted in that part of the enumeration which includes Armenia; Dr. Oppert renders it Colchis. The word in the inscription of Tiglath Pileser is expressly mentioned as designating a people of Syria (of the Hittites).

KSK [cuneiform], Kis-si.—Sen. T. i. 22, 38. Sen. Gr. 6, 13. Tig. jun. 11.

A town near which Sennacherib defeated Merodach-Baladan in his first campaign; it is mentioned in Sen. T. and Tig. jun. with Babylon, Borsippa, Warka, Nipur, Cutha, and Sippara; Dr. Oppert calls it *Kis*, Mr. Talbot *Kush*. The following extracts are from a list of strong places in Babylonia; the left hand column is uncertain in the second extract:—

[cuneiform] —50 II. 12a.

[cuneiform] —50 II. 34a.

¶ [cuneiform] —45 II. 52c. Kishanû.

KSL [cuneiform], kiṣal, c. kiṣallu, n. kiṣalli, g. kiṣalla, ac. *Altar, Mound.* Chal. כִּסְלָא.

The Chaldee word is rendered by Castell "tumulus, agger;" but kiṣalla appears sometimes with a meaning which I cannot determine. The monograms [cuneiform] and [cuneiform] are used in the sense of "altar."

[cuneiform], kiṣalli.—Syl. 363.

[cuneiform], kiṣalla „ 459.

[cuneiform], kiṣallî [ni] l'ipusu la-aiqu l'iqqi ana asri-suno l'utir; *may he raise altars, sacrifice a victim, (and) set (them) up again in their places.*—Tig. viii. 57.

This is exactly Sir H. Rawlinson's translation; see also l. 48, where there is a similar passage, but in the first person.

[cuneiform], kiṣal l'ibbus la-aiqu l'ikki ana asri-su l'utir; *the altar may he cleanse, a victim may he sacrifice, to its place may he restore.*—Sen. T. vi. 69.

Dr. Oppert has recently translated kiṣal "bas-relief."

[cuneiform] ([cuneiform]) .... [cuneiform] (v. [cuneiform]), kiṣal tabbat is-erini (-su) ...... aslula; *handsome altars(?) of cedar-wood .... I carried away.*—Sarl. i. 87.

KSL [cuneiform], ina yumme su kigal bit Istar bilat-ya ina pi lishi siqit bani parsu urabbi ana kisirti Beltis kigal suatu pan (si) usabir-si akka (v. akki); *in that day the altar of the House of Istar, my lady, in the entrance of the quiet chamber of retirement(?) I enlarged, to the possessions of Beltis that altar in her presence I dedicated.*—2 Beltis 6, 7. Doubtful.

[cuneiform] .... [cuneiform], ina kigalli rabi saplanu hekal abnu pili ana rabut sarruti-ya ..... usepis; *on the large mound below, a palace of fine stone for the greatness of my royalty .... I caused build.*—Neb. Yun. 62.

[cuneiform], kigalla-su marab urabbi; *its mound greatly I enlarged.*—Esar vi. 17. "Terrasse-routes."—Talb.

I do not see what *kigal* and *babui* mean in the following passages, which are connected with the custody and management of horses:—

[cuneiform] kigalla sa babuû marab usrabbi; (*for the care and custody of horses, &c.*) *the* kigalla sa babuû *greatly I enlarged.*—Sen. T. vi. 60 = Neb. Yun. 67.

Dr. Oppert renders this "j'ai agrandi la grande cour de la porte, au moyen;" Mr. Talbot has "I greatly extended the defences(?) of the great gate of Nineveh;" but I believe *babui* to be one word.

[cuneiform], sa hekalli adu tulé-su al ibsi sa rabburat subat-su ana rukis kurral al tagdula babuû kigallu labaris yummi; *of that palace its body was not* (i.e. *the body of the building no longer existed*), *and small was its site; for the establishment of horses, large was not the* babuû kigallu *of the old days.*—Neb. Yun. 58.

KSM [cuneiform], kisml. See p. 627.

KSN [cuneiform], Ḥarani.—Tig. vi. 71.

[cuneiform], Ḥarran.—Botta 172, 7.

[cuneiform].—38 II. 22b.

See note on Ḥarran, p. 456; but Ḥarran must imply something more important, if we may judge from passages which occur so frequently in the inscriptions of Sargon relative to the laws of Assyria and Ḥarran; see the note on *Kidinni*, in p. 584, and collate the passages in Sarg. 6; Botta 36, 9; 16, 10; 144, 10=16, &c.

KSS [cuneiform], Kisesu, Kisesi.—Botta 16, 16; 146, 23-39.

Name of a city to which Sargon gave the name of Kar-Marduk, and where he erected a statue of himself. It is named among places in Armenia. See p. 597, where that name is inadvertently printed *Kiesi*.

KSP [cuneiform], kispâte; *Some Material of War.*

[cuneiform]. epis kispâte mitpanate va uqi simtakre umata tahazi nazzadi kurral.—Sen. T. vi. 56.

I have inserted this already in pp. 149 and 389, but without any translation; it is part of a longer passage mentioning the erection of a large barrack or store-house, for containing and exercising horses, chariots, &c. We might read it "to make *kispâte mitpanate* and to put up furniture, wealth of war, *yokes* of horses, &c." I had read *kisasâte*, but seeing *mitpanate* in Dr. Oppert's transcript I have examined the cylinder, and found [cuneiform] instead of [cuneiform], as published. I do not understand either of these words.

KSR [cuneiform]. Kasar; *a King.*—43 II. 48c.

The resemblance of Kasar and Kaisar is curious. I hardly venture to suggest any connexion, but the word might have been borrowed from the Greeks; the name was recorded historically five centuries B.C., and was no doubt known much earlier.

¶ [cuneiform], kiṣurri; *Tracts of Land.* Arab. كسر.

[cuneiform]. Kammanu ana siḥirti-sa umaššit ma, urappis ki-surri (mati suatu); *Kammanu in its entirety I caused take, and extended the lands (of that country).*—Botta 146, 10-32.

I am not sure that the words in parenthesis should be included.

KSS . Suti sabi seri ina tuqulti umuqit kisurri-sunu ummati sa ina dilih mat ibbilu umdigila pani-sun; *the Nomades, men of the desert, to servitude I subdued, their waste lands which in the troubles of the country were spoiled, I gave up to them.*—Botta 152, 4 = 156. Uncertain.

KSS , kasu; *a Servant, or Worshipper.*

, kasu ili rabi; *servant of the great gods.*—Bard. I. 11, 21; iii. 127. St. 1.

Epithet of Sardanapalus; I have not seen the word elsewhere, and I do not know any Semitic analogy, but the meaning cannot be far wrong.

¶ , kasû; *Gathering, Accumulation.*

, mili kasâ mê rabuti kima gibis tihamti usalmi'a; *by a flood, a gathering of waters great like the depth of the sea, I secured it.*—Neb. Gr. ii. 12.

¶ , , , .
kissû, kissati, *g.* kissata, *a.* *People, Nation; Supremacy.* Chal. כנש.

The following extracts from the syllabary will, I think, justify a translator in reading *kissû* and *kissati* "people" or "nation." It is true that the Hebrew root is כנס, but the Chaldee has כנש:—

. . .—Syl. 650.

. . .—Syl. 378. See p. 288.

, ina lite kissu-ya va sibbiluti l'irtadu-su; *by tributes(?) my nation and my power may they extend.*—Monol. 50.

I am inclined to think the word should have been written *kassi*, and have translated accordingly. More than one value may be attributed to *lite*, which I shall consider more carefully in its place.

K88 [cuneiform], simat bilati-su ana kissati va zirruti-su ana mezzuz Bit-ḫarris mat satra ana daris lippata; *the preponderance of his power to his people and his lineage, for the exaltation of Bit-ḫarris of the land of the east, for ever may it be proclaimed.*—Tig. i. 25. See pp. 137, 283, 453.

[cuneiform], sa kissuta va tamma ana malki-ya isrukuni misir mati-sunu rabbum ikbiuni galli-sunu [ishu] danuti abub tahazi qati-ya l'umalluhu; *(the gods) who legions and laws to my dominions have furnished, an extended border of their countries have declared, (and) their mighty servants, loving war, to my hands they have entrusted.*—Tig. i. 47.

Some words are doubtful here.

[cuneiform], hekal kisuto-ya subat sarruti-ya sa er Kalḫi la iandi; *the palace of my supremacy, the seat of my royalty, which in Calah, he shall not surrender.*—Monol. 27.

[cuneiform], ina yumme suma ina pi ili rabi sarruti bilmti kissuti usâ; *at that time, by the mouth of the great gods, to royalty, to power, to supremacy I rose.*—Sard. i. 31.

[cuneiform], tanatu kisuti-ya sutarte va ilkakat qurdi-ya sa mati Nairi etappasu ina libbi satur [sar]; *the laws(?) of my surpassing nation and the accounts (qy. pictures) of my conquests of the lands of Nairi (which) I had effected, upon it I wrote.*—Sard. ii. 6.

KSS [cuneiform] (v. [cuneiform]) [cuneiform] (v. [cuneiform]), litas (v. lite) kiśsati ina libbi alțur (v. sar); *the records of my nation upon it I wrote.*—Sard. II. 91.

¶ [cuneiform], [cuneiform], [cuneiform], kissat, kissati; *Multitudes, Legions; Many, All.*

Kissat appears to be a plural of *kissu*; it would, therefore, imply "gatherings." Dr. Oppert usually translates "legions," with which no fault can be found; I often use "many," or "all," as more convenient, though not so literal.

[cuneiform], mutteœur kissat ili; *ruler of all gods.*—Tig. I. 1. Epithet of Assur.

[cuneiform] ([cuneiform]) [cuneiform], sar kissat Lasanan; *king of the multitudes of Lasanan.*—Tig. I. 30. One cylinder has [cuneiform] only.

[cuneiform] (v. [cuneiform]). sa napḥar kissat nisi ibilu; *who many legions of men is ruling.*—Sard. I. 36.

Napḥar implies nearly the same as *kissat*; etymologically it would be "gathered," the Niphal form.

In Babylonian *kissat* is written in all letters:—

[cuneiform], paqid kissat same va irșiti; *administrator of the whole of heaven and earth.*—Birs I. 13.

In the following extract I think the verb *takipu* is allied to *tipu*, "governor." (See p. 553.)

[cuneiform] ..... [cuneiform], atta ..... sarruti kissat nisi takipu-ani; *thou ... to the rule of many men hast appointed me.*—E.I.H. I. 64.

[cuneiform] as an independent phrase would be read *sar kissat*, "king of legions;" see Sarg. 2, where there is a variant [cuneiform]. In the titles of kings this phrase is of frequent occurrence, and it is not unfrequently made by [cuneiform]; compare the following lines:—

[cuneiform].—1 Pal. 1; 3 Pal. 2.

[cuneiform].—Sarg. 2.

The reading and translation in both cases will be as follows:—

Sarru rabbu, sarru dannu sar kissati sar Assur-ki; *king great, king powerful, king of legions, king of Assyria.*

KSS ..., ultu ris sarruti-ya adi maat [mu] 3-kan eqli kistit; *from the beginning of my reign to my third year I collected the whole.*—Botta 152, 13 = 141.

KST ... —23 [l]. 46 *c*.

¶ ..., kisti; *Concealment.* Heb. [Hebrew word, illegible] "to hide."

..., ana eqab napsati-sun (si-mu) innaptû ihlupu kirib kisti; *for saving their lives they fled, they passed into concealment.*

This is taken from a battle-scene in the British Museum, published by Dr. Hincks, at p. 35 of his Polyphony, Dublin, 1863. Dr. Hincks reads qisti, "thorns." Heb. [Hebrew word, illegible].

¶ ..., Kustaspi, *g.*—Tig. jun. 57.

A chief of Comukha who paid tribute to Tiglath Pileser.

KT ..., kiti, kita; *the Earth; the Country, Land.*

Kiti is Accadian, and it is usually, I think, pronounced *irsiti* by students of Assyrian. Perhaps we should say that ... is *irsi* ([Hebrew word, illegible] Heb.), and *ti* the phonetic complement (see Syl. 162, printed in p. 505). *Kita* may be considered an adverb meaning "below," and it is frequently used in contrast with *ana*, "upper;" in Accadian "earth-in" and "heaven-in."

..., ditar *sh*ame [an-e] va irsiti [kiti]; *ruler of heaven and earth.*—Obel. 6.

..., kabisi kiti rapasti; *subduer of the broad earth.*—Sard. i, 5.

..., Teuspâ Gimirai sab manda sa asar-sa ruhuqu ina kiti Hubusqa adi gimir ummani-su ura(s)sibu ina kakki; *Teuspâ the Cimmerian, an exiled warrior, whose place was afar in the land of Hubusqa, with all his soldiers, I pierced with arrows.*—Esar ii. 6.

KT [cuneiform], sa ina sarri abi-ya [ad-ya] sin la ikbusu hit mati-sun; *who, among the kings my fathers none had ever subjected their country.*—Esar iv. 12.

[cuneiform], sa ina tarqi sarri abi-ya kiti Assur-ki la ippalkitunu-ma la ikbusu qaqqar-sa; (*Medians*) *who in the face of the kings my fathers the land of Assyria had not crossed, and had not subjected its territory.*—Esar iv. 23.

¶ [cuneiform], ana; [cuneiform], kita; *Above, Below*:—

[cuneiform], kasid ultu [ta] tamti anta u tamti kita sa Nairi u tamti rabite sa dimu shamsi adi sad Hamani Hatte ana paigimri-sa; *conquering from the upper sea and lower sea of Nairi and the great sea of the setting sun, to Mount Amanus (and) Syria [Hittites], the whole of it.*—1 BM 15.

[cuneiform], ina 24 pali-ya Zaba anta(u) etebir; *in my twenty-fourth year the lower Zab I crossed.*—Obel. 111.

I do not understand the insertion of [cuneiform] here.

[cuneiform] ..... [cuneiform], sa sa ..... sikrut Assur anta u kita istanana; *the king who ..... the enemies of Assur above and below hath fought.*—Sard. iii. 120.

We have *elit u saplit* ([cuneiform]) in a similar phrase, l. 77, with variants *kita* and *kite*.

[cuneiform] ..... [cuneiform], 3 sa buda anta im-sutu ..... 3 sa buda kita im-martu; *three sass long above on the east, ... three sass long below on the west.*—I Mich. i. 7; also lines 9 and 11. See p. 74.

KT *Ina kita* may be considered a preposition, and translated "under:"—

[illegible], ina kita abbi-su Ursalia-su kamis; *under his carcase may they make him remain altogether.*—Sarg. 67.

See — [illegible], ina kita-ya, "in submission to me," in Assur b.p. x. 14.

[illegible]—Syl. 366.

See p. 138. The no doubt fortuitous resemblance of [illegible] is curious; see also the Persian گیتی, *gíti.*

¶ [illegible]. Kati.—Obel. 128, 132, 159, and New Div. i. 52.

Name of a petty chief of the Qui (see p. 130), dethroned by Shalmaneser.

¶ [illegible], kuti; *Service, Acandina.*

This word appears to be formed from *ku*, "a servant," like *kisi* from *ki*. See p. 510, and pp. 339, 340, 341, where I have treated of this word and its Assyrian equivalents at some length.

When I printed these pages I had not fully considered the value of [illegible] as "a weapon" rather than "a servant." In many cases I find a difficulty in knowing which of the two senses is intended; the distinction is certainly not shown by the presence or absence of [illegible], as may be seen by the first example copied in p. 340. I give here a couple of sentences where there can be no doubt of the value of *kuti* as "weapons:"—

[illegible], rapiba-nni ina kakui; *kill me with weapons.*—Assur b.p. vii. 57. See p. 344.

[illegible], Urpá sa Urardi ina pulahti-su rabiti ina kakke ramani-su usbit napista's; *Ursa of Armenia, in his great fear, with his own weapon, took away his (own) life.*—Sarg. 27.

¶ [illegible]. Kuta-ki; *the City of Cutha, near Babylon.*—Obel. 82.

In the parallel passages on the Bulls (15 BM 27 and 42 BM 15) this city is written [illegible], *Tiggabir.* [illegible], which has been read *Tiggabbal*, is doubtless the same place, though I am not aware of any direct proof of it.

KTA [cuneiform].—Tig. jun. 40.

[cuneiform].—17 BM 1. Qy. [cuneiform] omitted by error.

[cuneiform].—Synchr. Hist. ii. 14.

The name of the Tiglath-Pileser whom I distinguish by Tig. jun. See in p. 541, where I have inadvertently omitted [cuneiform] in the name as written in Tig. jun. 40. The omission in 17 BM 1, if there be an omission as I suppose, may have been a typographical error.

KTG [cuneiform] . [cuneiform].—23 II. 45 c.

KTU [cuneiform], kitas.—Obel. 111.

I have entered this under *kis* in p. 629. I am inclined to think it an error, having always found *kis* in similar names

---

KTL [cuneiform] . [cuneiform].—40 II. 57 c.

KTM [cuneiform], katim; *Concealed.* Arab. كَتَمَ.

[cuneiform] [cuneiform] [cuneiform], epir siri-sunu kima im-kab kabite ua dunni eriyati pan shame rapsuti katim; *the dust of their feet like a heavy cloud of .... the face of the broad heaven concealed.*—Sen. T. v. 47.

See p. 158, where I have printed very doubtfully dunni eriyati, "many flocks;" Dr. Oppert, in the preface to his Grammar, p. xxi. proposes zunni eriyati, "abundant showers;" if we might read zunni, which I can hardly admit, I would translate "*flowing showers,*" from the Chal. [illegible] "to move," "to flow."

¶ [cuneiform] . [cuneiform].—23 II. 46 b.

KTR [cuneiform], qitas; *Party, Company; Auxiliaries.* See p. 527.

[cuneiform] [cuneiform] [cuneiform] [cuneiform], Suto kitar-su ua kitir-su iabara sa illiku rispat-su (risputu) adi Marsmanai aalis asakkip; *the nomades, his party, who his embarrassment observed, and went (as) his helpers, together with the Marsmani, utterly I cut off.*—Botta 151, 22 = 130.

KTR kitirri; *a Cornice, Capital.* Heb. כֹּתֶר.

sitir sumi-ya ina kitirri epitâti-su askun; *the writing of my name on its additional capitals I placed.*—Birs ii. 13.

I have translated ebati "damaged" in p. 144, on a very unsatisfactory etymology; I now propose "additional," from the Chaldee אוּסְפָא, which is given by Castell as something added to a building. As the repair of a temple is in question, this may be the preferable version.

¶ Kudurri. See p. 539.

KTT kaititi; *Fragments.* Heb. כתת.

usesir mupa-sa kirib kaititi asurrakki-sa usphuru gi elasis abni sadi danni itti kupri akşi ana eqil [alib] alta admo mule-sunu usalbi'a utir; *I restrained the course of it* [*a canal*] *within its scattered bed* [*fragments tangled below*]; *the bottom raising by strong mountain stones, with cement I covered, and earth from the waters I took up, and its flowing I restored.*—Sen. Gr. 30.

Not quite perfect, but the passage certainly implies the cleaning out of an old canal mentioned in a previous passage, by damming it and dredging up the earth from the bottom. My failures in p. 48 and in the note page v. arose chiefly from finding in Bellino , which I supposed to be some unknown river; a collation with the parallel 83-7-18 15 recently showed me that the second letter was , awkwardly disguised in the printed copy for want of the proper type; the unknown river at once became , the "cement" (p. 60) with which the stone dam was consolidated.

GROUPS WHICH I CANNOT ARRANGE ALPHABETICALLY.

7 II. 66 d.

" 46 d.

" 47 d.

40 II. 56 a.

" 60 c.

" 61 a.

WORDS WHICH MAY NOT BE READILY FOUND.

ADDITIONS AND CORRECTIONS.

Page 517, line 16. Revd. iii. "6" read "66."
" 519, last line but one. Revd. i. "65" read "55."
" 520, line 8. For "[illegible]" read "[illegible]."
" 534, last line but two. For "127" read "122."

Add to page 551, line 8, , Kagar: Accad. To say.

The only Assyrian passage in which I have found this Accadian verb is on the Bull, 17 B M 8; where it occurs with the Assyrian phonetic complement [illegible]; the parallel Tig. jun. 10 has sa ... iqabbu-ni-ai, "which ... they call it." This is printed in p. 462, and a note on the word is printed at the foot of p. 462, where I have erroneously supposed that [illegible] might have been an error of copy.

L ל

Characters arranged under letter L.

[cuneiform], la.

[cuneiform], li; or [cuneiform], [cuneiform], [cuneiform], [cuneiform].

[cuneiform], lu; or [cuneiform].

[cuneiform], mal; or [cuneiform].

[cuneiform], lil; or [cuneiform], [cuneiform], [cuneiform]. Bab. [cuneiform].

[cuneiform], mis; or [cuneiform].

[cuneiform], lā, lam; or [cuneiform], [cuneiform].

[cuneiform], lu, lum; later form [cuneiform].

[cuneiform], lab, lib; sometimes mir and pak.

[cuneiform], lib; or [cuneiform].

[cuneiform], lad.

[cuneiform], lal.

[cuneiform], lik.

[cuneiform], lul; sometimes confounded with [cuneiform], and even [cuneiform].

[cuneiform], lis; or [cuneiform].

[cuneiform], lisan, "*tongue.*"

[cuneiform], alpi, "*cattle.*"

[cuneiform], [cuneiform], libnat, "*brick.*"

L(A) la, ul; *Not.* Heb. לא, אל.

La, with verbs:—

sa ista yume pite kandsu lā idû; *who from days gone submission have not known.*—Tig. iii. 75.

sa ...... ab-i banû-a ipuss-ma la usaklilu sipir-sun; *which .... my father my generator made*, and *did not complete their beauty.*—E.I.H. iv. 71.

La, with adjectives:—

ana Kummukhi lā magiri .... lu allik; *to Comukha not obedient .... I went.*—Tig. i. 89

Subari sappute lā magiri amkhuts; *the Subari, predatory (and) disobedient, I subdued.*—Tig. ii. 87.

Ana la, usually implies something not to be done:—

erani ana la mani akhud; *cities not to be counted I captured.*—Obel. 87.

This very frequent expression is found with all varieties of spelling: see mani, Tig. v. 7; mani, Sard. ii. 116; mini, Tig. v. 63; minuti, Sen. T. ii. 17; manuti, Neb. Yun. 60; *kasaru* without *ana*,* in BM 18.

ana la kasad-i ina mati-su; *for my not arriving at his country* [*in order that I might not get to his country*].—Tig. ii. 45.

er sasu ana lā sabate va dur-su lā rasapi; *that city not to be occupied, and its wall not to be built.*—Tig. vi. 17.

* In the parallel Sen. B iii. 77 there is full space for ana; I think I see traces of the word, but the slab is defective.

L(a) [illegible], nisi Babel-ki ana la sibaza-su lua kuppi [la-gam] usesibu-su; *the men of Babylon, that he might not besiege it, on the throne seated him.*—Sen. T. v. 17.

I take the word "besiege" from the Heb. סבב, which is not unfrequently used in a hostile sense, but I have not met with the Assyrian verb elsewhere. Moreover the root should be שבת to judge from *sabata* and *sumpi* in the preceding extract; the version is consequently doubtful.

Ina la, with a noun, "*for want of*:"—

[illegible] ...... [illegible], tamerata-su sa ina la mami magabta suluku sa ta taki ettati va nisi sa mie [ni] siqi la idd .... saqé; *its vicinity which with want of water dry had become, and whose takettati(?) and people water for drinking knew not of, ... I gave to drink.*—Bavian 6. See p. 454.

I change [illegible] to [illegible] without hesitation; *sululu* I read as a *fem. plur.* permansive; *basu* in the causative form equally has the meaning of "becoming," or simply "being."

[illegible] ul; *Not*:—

[illegible], er mata ul akasud; *that city I did not capture.*—Tig. v. 28.

[illegible], malki gabrai ul ibsi; *kings my equals were not.*—Botta 145, 1-12.

[illegible] (v. [illegible]) [illegible] (v. [illegible]), bit sâtu ippul ul epus 1 susi sanâte [mute] usses-su ul in(a)ndu; *that house fell, he did not (re)build it, one soss [sixty] of years its foundation was not laid down.*—Tig. vii. 66.

La or *la* is used with all words; *ul*, I think with verbs only. Once, and there only in the Persian epoch, I find *ul* with nouns and pronouns:—

[illegible], ul anaku ul sir-ya ina dinâtû asigga; *neither I nor my family from the laws have turned away.*—Beh. 104.

L(A) The Accadian [cuneiform], an, is sometimes used instead of la:—

[cuneiform] (v. [cuneiform]) [cuneiform], ša lan tabani an (lá) la šanana tibnu; (to) whom in war not any second [rival] has been made.—Sard. i. 1.

This is a curious bit, though the meaning seems clear. I suppose tibnu to be a permansive passive from [illegible], "to make," and šanana may be "a second man," though I do not remember to have seen la "a man" (Heb. [illegible]) nor šanana "second;" [illegible] is common enough in that sense.

[cuneiform], ša nin-šu la išû; who his equal had not.—New Div. i. 10.

In the parallel 1 R 37 we have la instead of an, and [cuneiform] occurs as a variant of [cuneiform] in St. 31.

[cuneiform] —New Syl. 30.

L(B) [cuneiform], li (for limiti); Vicinity, or Dependency.

[cuneiform], 820 ali tsiri ša li(miti)-šunu alme akšud; eight hundred and twenty small towns of their vicinity, I approached, I captured.—Sen. Gr. 12.

See limeti in the parallel Sen. T. i. 55, where we have, however, only 420 towns, [cuneiform]. Similar abbreviations are found in p. 553, [cuneiform] gali, p. 210 [cuneiform], &c. &c.

¶ Li is sometimes made by [cuneiform], but rarely; compare [cuneiform] Neb. Bab. ii. 21, and [cuneiform] E.I.H. v. 16, the same passage; and see [cuneiform], gali, in Tig. iv. 2. The proper secondary power of [cuneiform] is lim (8).

[cuneiform] —New Syl. 79.

L(U) [cuneiform], [cuneiform], lu; Prefix denoting Past Time.

[cuneiform], lu umail; I trod down.—Tig. ii. 20.

[cuneiform], lu allik; I went.—Tig. ii. 69.

[cuneiform], lu asti; I drank.—Sen. T. iii. 80.

[cuneiform], lú ebir; I crossed.—Tig. v. 58.

[cuneiform] ([cuneiform]) [cuneiform], lu (or lú) adpuk; I poured out.—Tig. vi. 104.

I do not see the positive value of lu in these cases; the past tense very frequently occurs without such additions, and in two copies of the same inscription we find lu written where one omits it; possibly the past time may have been more emphatically marked by the addition.

L(U) *Lu* in the Babylonian period appears, in a very few cases, before substantives; I hardly know what value to attribute to this particle, which seems superfluous in these cases. I have only recorded the following instances.—

Nabiûkudurriuçur lu sar zaninu l'iuakin ina pi-ka; *Nebuchadnezzar the king, the architect, may he be established by thy countenance.*—Birs ii. 30.

anaku lu sar maito ..... lu sakkanaku; *I, the king constituted ..... the high priest.*—E.I.H. ix. 60, 62.

lu-valda-kka gab saib lu nisu Parças; *it shall be known to thee, man, dweller, Persian man.*—No. 6, N.R., l. 28.

¶ *Lu* must be "either," "whether," "or," in the following extracts:—

..... ina matima ..... ina ahi tari lu-ri-u ..... lu nuturda lu itu va lu aiuqama .... eqil [alib] anatu lu ana el amarsku lu ana sigu naqqu lu ana ramani-su lusakkanu; *if hereafter .... among the brothers (or) sons of my family .... whether impotent or able, or any one, ... that field either to a god shall give, or to damage shall expose, or upon himself shall settle.*—1 Mich. ii. 5, 6, 10, 11.

Similar passages occur in 2 Michaux, with a still more numerous repetition of *lu* (not *lu*): see i. 31, 37, 33; ii. 3, 4, 5; we have *lu* seven times in 3 Mich. iii. 9–14. occurs also in 1 Mich. ii. 12. The value is quite clear in all these examples, and the word would seem to be often required; but I have not met with it in any other document.

¶ . lu; *Sheep, or Goats.*

Probably pronounced *lu* where the meaning is "sheep."

alpi plol(?) madatu-su amhar; *cattle, sheep, his tribute, I received.*—Obel. 135.

L(r)

1 alpu 10 lu-arili 10 kurani 20 kalimmu riecte-su ana ilani Assur-ki bili-ya akin hal ria; *one bull, ten rams, ten goats, twenty* kalimmu riecte-su, *to the gods of Assyria, my lords, I dedicated;—all the flock.*—Sen. T. i. 60.

The parallel passage in Sen. B. i. 9 omits after , and reads instead of . Another parallel passage in Sen. Or. 79 omits , gives twenty goats, and reads *before* , which is, doubtless, correct. I have followed Dr. Oppert in translating "rams" and "goats." For the twenty "kalimmu rieste" Dr. Oppert translates "brebis comme holocaustes d'oblation;" Mr. Talbot reads bull-..., and translates "strong-heads." Sen. B. i. 9 omits at the end.

without addition probably denotes all sorts of sheep, and perhaps goats likewise. I believe , *lu-rial*, are "sheep" specially, and , *lu-arili*, "rams" or "goats." , *lu-niqu*, "a sacrifice," may imply a sheep as the victim. Dr. Hincks thought *lu* to be "a determinative prefix to words signifying sorts of sacrifices;" see his Alphabet, p. 65.

pini (lu) dumuti lu-niqut ibbiti lu akki: *sheep fat, victims white, I sacrificed.*—Bavian 32.

pahade pini (lu)(?) mahaid libbi-sunu ana bibhat libbi-ya itti (lu)-niqati-ya ellute (...) ana Asur bili-ya lu aitaqi: *flocks(?) of sheep, the produce of their bellies, to the desire of my heart, with my elevated sacrifices (as appointed), to Asur my lord I offered up.*—Tig. vii. 15.

Pahade I have doubtfully rendered "flocks" from the Arabic فخذ, which signifies "divide into families."

sallat-sunu [sallagunu] kapte kima murat lu-sini asluk; *their spoils (or women) many, like the young of sheep I carried off.*—Sard. i. 52.

sallat-sunu alpi-sunu lu-sini-sunu ta kirib sade usrida; *their women, their cattle, their sheep, from among the hills I brought down.*—Obel. 137.

L(U) [cuneiform], lul maddi lamassi sa abon pili pisa ina er Tasliate ipsaqu ana malsap babi-sin; *mountain goats (and) bulls of fine cut stone in the city Tasliat they fashioned for a decoration [cover over] of their gates.*—38 B M 9.

¶ [cuneiform], a monogram, for נשא, "to take," and עבר, "to pass through."

[cuneiform] ([cuneiform]) [cuneiform] (v. [cuneiform]), ana samb napsati-suna [si-suno] ana gab-ya ulloni [sddani] niri-ya imbutu; *for the saving of their lives after me [to my back] coming up, my yoke they took.*—Sard. i. 81.

With the phonetic complement [cuneiform], at, the meaning is *admit;* in the following passage we have this with the fully-written word in a variant reading:—

[cuneiform] (v. [cuneiform]), er Tuskha ana issuto asbat; *the city of Tuskha again I occupied.*—Sard. ii. 3.

When [cuneiform] is followed by the phonetic complement [cuneiform], iq, it represents the verb [cuneiform], etiq.

[cuneiform] (v. [cuneiform]) [cuneiform], sade marsute sa ana metik rukubi u ummani la simkan [suna] etetik ana Numme alik; *rugged hills, which for the passage of chariots and soldiers had not been made fit, I passed through, (and) to Numme I went.*—Sard. i. 46.

¶ [cuneiform], Accadian. *A Tablet, or Inscription.*

This value is shown in the following extract from the Syllabary; the left side shows also that G was one of the sounds of the character:—

[cuneiform], dibba.—Syl. 542.

The following bits are fragmentary, like all the Semitic part of the Behistun monument. The first bit is the translation of the Persian col. iv, par. 11:—

[cuneiform], ki dibbi annut lapisina; *if these inscriptions thou shalt conceal.*—Beh. 102.

I suppose a verb pasan, metathesis of Heb. צפן.

L(v) . . . , sitta hi dibbi sa asmku epusu u habitta . . . ; *then, if the inscriptions which I have made and the many . . . .*—Beh. 101. From Par. 10.

The following is nearly Dr. Oppert's restoration, E.M. p. 257; the version is much the same as that which I proposed in my Scythic paper, read before the Royal Asiatic Society, July 6, 1852—"Let him not think (for that reason) that they are lies." Journ. R.A.S., Vol. 15, p. 179:—

Ibbus ul igabbi umma parsâtâ situ; *(those things which) are done, let him not say that lies they (are).*—Beh. 100. From Par. 8.

It might, perhaps, be better to consider simply as having a secondary power of *dib.*

, eleppu; *Ship.*—Syl. 280.

This was inadvertently omitted from p. 687.

(A)L —Syl. 358.

(D)L —Syl. 359.

¶ , li; *Above.* Heb. עַל.

, basha sá eli sa lua yumme pani usrbi sir mesihti hekali mahriti uraddi; *that estimate (?) above what (it was) in former days I enlarged, over the measure of the former palace I extended.*—Sen. Gr. 56.

I have never seen this form elsewhere; the preposition usually employed is , or the equivalent , which appears in the parallel passage in BM 17. *Basha* is a desperate guess; I have never seen the word elsewhere.

(U)L ul; *Not.* See under *Lu*, p. 636.

(B)L , ellu, illu; *Exalted, Noble; Valuable.* Heb. עִלָּה.

Used most commonly as a determinative of precious metals; as "gold;" , "silver." See *hurasu*, "gold," p. 445, and *kaspu*, "silver," pp. 447-8. As a phonetic letter it is pronounced *ilu* or *ellu*.]

, nabnitu illutu sa Tiglath-Pileser; *the illustrious offspring of Tiglath-Pileser.*—Obel. 19.

See p. 541. We have a line exactly parallel in 11 BM 12, with the second word phonetically written , *illuti*.

LAL [cuneiform], Laila.—Esar iii. 10.

Name of a king of Yadih, tributary to Esar Haddon.

LB [cuneiform], dibbi; *Tablet.* See *Lu*, Accadian, p. 640.

¶ [cuneiform], lab, labbu; *Heart; Son, Daughter.*

[cuneiform], itruku labbu-su kima iççuri edis ipparsid; *his heart became soft, like a bird away he fled.*—Sen. T. iii. 48.

[cuneiform]. ina gabli tamti ruqis issu sa labba-sun itruku; *in the midst of the sea far away they heard, and their heart was softened [fainted].*—Botta 153, 6 = 148.

[cuneiform]. ana Babel-ki mahazi Bel saqil ili ina elis labbi nummur panl hadis erub [erum, because of u following]; *to Babylon the fortress of Bel, the weigher of the gods, in exultation of heart (and) radiance of face joyfully I proceeded.*—Botta 152, 8 = 140.

See ina uggum *labbi-ya*, "in the vengeance of my heart," Sen. T. v. 67; Botta 151, 5 = 118.

[cuneiform]. ikbud labba-sun ana epis taqunta [lz-lal]; *their heart hardened to make resistance.*—Sen. T. v. 7.

The lithographer has written [cuneiform] for [cuneiform]. See p. 843 for the value of this Accadian group.

[cuneiform]. sakris ana il-rabbi epusu iplah labba-sun; *rebelliously towards the god " they acted, their heart feared.*—Sen. T. ii. 73.

I do not know what god is meant. Dr. Oppert translates the first clause "ils avaient agi en se révoltant contre le droit."

[cuneiform]. libba'a ul ihyaq; *its interior he did not investigate.*—Sen. Gr. 40. Sen. T. v. 23.

I think this would be a better version than that printed in p. 4, but I am not sure that [cuneiform] is ever used in the sense of "interior." See the following word [cuneiform], sa.

LB [cuneiform], ina yumme suma adi-al labbut ili rabi sa Asur u Samas gardi-suna semys ana sâte; *in that day I elevated the hearts of the great gods, of Asur and the Sun-god their triumphs I exalted for future times.*—New Div. l. 49.

¶ [cuneiform], labbis; *In Heart, Courageously.*

[cuneiform], supp-a usrat ismû illiku riguti labbis asnatib; *my prayers * * they heard, they came in help, in heart I was protected.*—Sen. T. v. 84.

Labbis is made [cuneiform] in the plate, but the photograph shows [cuneiform] distinctly. We have *labbis* *asmagir* with [cuneiform] in Botta 146, 4 = 60. See p. 718. I cannot find any meaning for *usrat* (or *labrat*), which occurs also in lines 8 and 73; I do not remember the word anywhere else.

¶ By a natural transition *lab* is used for a *son* or *daughter*, and it is then generally accompanied by the determinative of *male* or *female*:—

[cuneiform], zis-labbi sal-labbi siparti ummani mala basû muttabilut bekali su sanya-tima sallatis aman; *sons and daughters, the body of soldiers, all that there were, the defenders of his palace, I brought out, and accounted as spoil.*—Sen. T. l. 80.

See also Sen. T. iii. 59. I do not understand the [cuneiform] after *bekali*; it may possibly signify "sixty," meaning the number of soldiers brought out, but its position is unusual; I have, as a guess, translated it as if it had been inadvertently put for *sa*. In both these passages Dr. Oppert and Mr. Talbot translate "male and female slaves" where I have read "sons and daughters." But we have [cuneiform] and [cuneiform], *lab-labbi* and *lab-libbi*, lines 21 and 22 of 3 Pul (35 l. of B.I.), in a genealogy, where the meaning seems placed beyond doubt, however inaccurately the degree of paternity may be expressed. We have also the Scythic analogy of the Behistun Inscription, where [cuneiform] certainly signifies "a son." See also the following extract from a bilingual slab:—

[cuneiform], bis binû = lab labbu.—2 II. 62c.

LB &c., lib, c. libbi, g. libba, n. *Heart; Interior.*

In the sense of "heart," "courage," &c., and appear to be synonymous, and might be pronounced in the same way. I think *lib* is found more frequently than *lab* in the monuments of Babylon, and that the Assyrians preferred *lab*. The following extract proves the identity of the words:—

lib = labbu.—26 II. 51 c.

Heart:—

Nabiû va Nanâ in hidâti va risâti sulat tab libbi kerba-su usrib; *Nebo and Nana in joy and gladness (on) a seat of goodness of heart in it I seated.*—Neb. Gr. ii. 25. [irregularly put for .]

lib-su taqunta upla; *his courage [heart] opposition carried away.*—New Div. ii. 71.

In Sard. i. 61

ana ebis Bit-Saggatu nasa-sal libb-i; *to the building of Bit-Saggatu my heart raised me (or he raised my heart).*—E.I.H. iii. 19.

palahti ilati-su usakin ina libbi-ya ana sadada sirla-su usaiha-sal libba; *the worship of his divinity he has placed in my heart, to bear his tabernacle(?) he has made firm my heart.*—E.I.H. ii. 9, 10.

kima anaku ..... libbi ilati-sunu rabiti ušiba; *whereas I ...... the hearts of their great godships gladdened.*—Tig. viii. 33. See p. 570.

LB

ina šumuma libbi niši-šu mukind; *in steadfastness of heart his people do ye maintain.*—Nab. Br. Cyl. i. 12; iii. 38.

I derive doubtfully ------ from ----, "to establish," Heb. כון.

palaḫti ilûti-ka rabitû libbu'a šukin; *in reverence of thy great divinity his heart do thou maintain.*—Nab. ii. 26.

kima libbi ebišuni; *according to my heart I built.*—Tig. vii. 98. See p. 602 and note.

2 šuši ur-maḫi ina libbi-šu iqdi; *two sosses* [120] *of lions by his courage fell.*—Brok. Obel. l. 3.

I was inclined to translate this "in it he cut down" (see the Heb. גדע); but the following passage, which differs in the last words only, has been my guide to a correct version:—2 *šuš ur-maḫi ina libbi-ya iqdi*, "two sosses of lions by my courage fell."—Tig. vi. 77.

ina gimir libbi-ya; *with all my heart.*—E.I.H. i. 37.

aibu limnu ša ina la libbi ili šarrut Babel-ki ebušu; *an enemy wicked, who against the will* [*heart*] *of the gods, the kingdom of Babylonia held* [*made*].—Botta 41, 42.

Inside, Interior:—

...... šuddi marṣute va nirbite namrašâte ša ina maḫra šarri-ya umuna libbi-šunu la idû ..... etetiq; *mountains difficult and wilds rugged, which formerly our kings their interior had never known* ..... *I crossed.*—Tig. iv. 55.

See p. 464 and note at the bottom.

itmam libbâ ina kaspi ḫurași; *he completed the inside with silver (and) gold.*—Neb. Bab. i. 23.

LB

The following phrases may be referred to this meaning:—

[cuneiform] pali nabali libbi-su; *his children, the offspring of his body.*—Tig. ii. 29, 47.

[cuneiform], ana Lallar eli salam sarruti-ya ina libbi usmid; *to Lallar I went up, a statue of my majesty within it I erected.*—Obel. 81.

See also Tig. vi. 91 and Sen. T. i. 82.

[cuneiform], ina 2 yomme mithuşu ina libbi askun; *for two days the fight in it I made.*—Sard. iii. 19.

[cuneiform], ina libbi-su la niqui ellute ana Yav bili-ya lu aitaqi (v. aitaqqi); *in it* [*in its inside*] *noble victims to Yav my lord I sacrificed.*—Tig. viii. 9.

[cuneiform], 27000 + 200 + 60 + 90 nisi asib lib-sa aslula; *twenty-seven thousand two hundred and ninety people dwelling in it* [*inhabiting its interior*] *I carried off.*—Botta 145, 12 = 24.

[cuneiform], ili asib lib-sun ki ladia upahhir; *the gods inhabiting their interior every one* [*to one*] *I collected.*—Botta 151, 10 = 126.

¶ [cuneiform], lib.—Syl. 552.

Shows one of the sounds of [cuneiform]. I do not see the value of *parum.*

¶ [cuneiform], Libe.—Sard. i. 46.

A city occupied by Sardanapalus in his first campaign. It is mentioned as a principal city of Zamua; this is not Elam, as I once thought from the similarity of names, but a mountainous country probably on the borders of Armenia.

¶ [cuneiform], dibbi, *or* dippi. See p. 648. See also *duppu*, p. 216.

LB ( ) , labi; *Facing each other.* Arab. لَبَّ.

, ana er Tela akhrib er dannu dannis 3 durani labi; *to the city Tela I approached, a city very powerful, (with) three castles facing each other.*—Sard. i. 114.

This phrase occurs again, with other names and numerals, twice in the same inscription, ii. 99 and 105; in the former of these there is nothing worth notice; the latter I subjoin as evidence of the value of , marsi:—

(v.) (v.), er marsi dannis 3 durani labi.—Sard. ii. 105.

The Arabic dictionaries explain labbu "ex adverso respexit domus domum."

¶ , , alap, g. alpi, pl. *Cattle.* Heb. אֲלָפִים. Mon. .

occurs in epigraph 2 of the Nimrud Obelisk, among the articles comprising the tribute [gifts] of Musri. Dr. Hincks, in his Translation printed in the Dublin University Magazine for October, 1853, suggested that *Musri* implied the Kurdish country. He translated alap "an elephant," but in his last work he read it "an ox;" see Gram. p. 418. Except in this case I have not found the word written phonetically on any monument. In every other instance, so far as I remember, we have the monogram, or rather Accadian word, . Direct evidence of this value will be found in 16 II. 29d, in a bilingual passage, where the Assyrian , pan alpi, "before the oxen," is rendered in the Accadian.

¶ . , Humba; *Name of an Elamite God.*

See p. 459, and read for there.

LBB . . , ilbia, labbu.—Syl. 287.

¶ , la nabi; *Unnumbered.*—Neb. Gr. iii. 13, 26.

See pp. 69 and 465.

¶ , Labbanat.—Tig. Jun. 8.

See this printed in p. 199, and add from the same line the following name, which was inadvertently omitted:—

. .

LBB , rabbaṣu; a *Resting Place.* Heb. רבץ.

..... Uperi sar Asmun-ki sa' ..... ina qabli tamti nipiḫ shamsi kima nûni sitkunu rabbaṣu danan Assur Nabu Marduk ismo; *Uperi, king of Asmun, who .... in the midst of the sea of the rising sun like a fish had established a resting place, the power of Assur, Nebo, and Marduk had heard.*—Botta 152, 14 = 146.

See also Botta 164 bis 37; 67, 84; 41, 69.

¶ , labbâti.

I have no clue to the meaning of this word.

, saddukki la labbâti tuklati-sun aklum.—Bot. 152, 13 = 157.

This appears in Dr. Oppert's Inscription (*Journ. Asiat.* 1863), translated "statuis (quae) non erant conformia cultibus eorum sacrificavi." The passage is mutilated in Botta's Inscriptions in the copies I have examined. I have not found anywhere; but in 164, 7, I find , *isqu-sun.* I cannot suggest any translation. See *isqi* in p. 878.

, murrabi parqiti la labbâti maḫar-sun akhi.—Botta 154, 3 = 173.

Dr. Oppert has not translated this. I have said all I could about it in page [illegible].

, matti ba la naparkâ erib-su (?) labbâti biltat malki kiprat arba' imdanaḫḫaru kirib-su; *countries unsubdued * * * tribute of kings of the four regions they received within it.*—Sen. Cr. 89.

I think the first part of this line is not quite accurately copied.

.—Syl. 148.

LBD lib tamnu pirn.—Tig. i. 86. See p. 289.

¶ libit, c. libittu, &c. *Work, Brick-work.* See *libn*, p. 651.

(v.) (v.) (v.) libit gati-ya damgiti hadis naplis; *the work of my hands, the holy places, bountifully do thou bless.*—Senk. Cyl. ii. 16.

libit gati-ya ana damikti hadis naplis; *the work of my hands to good fortune bountifully do thou bless.*—Neb. Bab. ii. 24.

libit gati-ya enqura hadis naplis; *the work of my hand favourably (and) bountifully do thou bless.*—Brick printed by Oppert, E.M. p. 270.

> *Enqura*, the shaphel of *qura*, is exactly analogous to the הַקְרֵה of Gen. xxiv. 12, in our version "send good speed." As the root of *libit* is *libn*, the Heb. לבן, signifying "a brick," and as the works in question are always buildings, I have ventured to translate *damgiti* "holy places;" but I believe the import of all these passages was exactly the same. See pp. 192, 243, 244.

ana il-liban bil same libitte va il-gimgim rabi tur ra Bel le-niqut akhi; *to the god Liban, lord of foundations of brick-work, and the great Gimgim, son of Bel, a victim I sacrificed.*—Sarg. 50.

zunni va ridu unaqqá libitsa-su agurri tahlupti-su uptattir ua libitti kummi-su kamplk tilanis; *the rain and the wet had broken up its brick-work, the burnt-brick of its casing had split, and the crude brick of its body was heaped in heaps.*—Birs ii. 3, 4.

LBD [cuneiform], Lebda.—Sh. Ph. i. 49.

One of twenty-seven places which had revolted from Shalmaneser, and were recovered by his son Shamas Phul. See *Ada*, p. 19.

¶ [cuneiform], labuttû; *a Class of Persons.*

[cuneiform], lû labuttû lû akhu lû kibatu sa Bit-Ada; *whether* labuttu, *or* akhu, *or* kibatu *of Bit-Ada.*—3 Mich. iii. 18.

See *Kummu*, p. 414, and *Kibatu*, p. 433.

LBT [cuneiform], Labtaru, Labtari.—Sard. ii. 13, 88, 102; iii. 110.

A son of Tubusu, king of Nirdun; written [cuneiform] in ii. 102, iii. 110. See p. 251.

LBI [cuneiform]. Albaya.—Tig. iv. 80.

One of twenty-three provinces of Nairi, devastated by Tiglath-Pileser.

LBK ([cuneiform]) [cuneiform].—48 II. 30*e*. Chal. לבך, "hold fast."

LBL [cuneiform], Libil-higal.

Name of a river or stream in Babylon. See p. 582.

¶ The following terms are used in genealogies, signifying descendants, but with small pretension to accuracy; after going up to his grandfather a king might write himself down as son's son, without thinking further enumeration necessary:—

[cuneiform], lib-libbi; *fourth descent.*—Tig. vii. 55. Sard. i. 30.

[cuneiform], lib-pal-pal; *third descent.*—3 Pul. 19.

[cuneiform], lab-labbi; *fourth descent.*—3 Pul. 21.

[cuneiform], lab-libbi; *fifth descent.*—3 Pul. 22.

See also the following:—

[cuneiform].—24 II. 54*a*.

[cuneiform].—20 II. 62*e*.

LBL [cuneiform], Ilingas.—Sen. T. ii. 23. Sen. Cy. 23.

Capital city of the province of Bit-Barra, in Illipi (Albania of the Greeks); it was captured by Sennacherib, and called by him Kar-Sennacherib (p. 587).

¶ [cuneiform], [cuneiform], labalal; *Dress.*

I think I have said all I know of this word in pp. 560-1. It is found also in Sard. i. 86; Tig. jun. 63; Botta 152, 10 = 148; Assur b.p. ii. 76, &c. &c.

[cuneiform], libbiamal; *Garments.* See p. 249.

LBN

[cuneiform].—Syl. 146.

¶ [cuneiform], libn; *Brick.* Heb. לבן.

[cuneiform], usalbina libnat-su [libnassu]; *I caused make bricks for it* [*make its bricks*].—Sarg. 10.

In the parallel passage Botta 37, 48, we have [cuneiform], ibita.

[cuneiform], usi-su addi ana ubla libnat-su [libnassu]; *its foundation I laid down, and placed its bricks.*—Botta 38, 52.

[cuneiform], libni albin; *I made bricks.*—Tig. viii. 75.

[cuneiform], ilbina libni mada; *they made bricks much.*—Rass v. 3.

See also E.I.H. v. 19; viii. 60, 67. Senk. Cyl. ii. 6.

[cuneiform], alabun libni epis ir va bit; *I made bricks to build city and house.*—Sarg. 10.

Usalbina libnat-su and *alabun libni* are precisely analogous to the *nilbenah lebenim* and *libnu hal-lebenim* of Gen. xi. 3, and Exod. v. 7.

[cuneiform] (v. [cuneiform]) [cuneiform], asra sitn ana qibarti-su ina libni kima kannal arpuk; *that place, to the whole of it, with bricks strongly I covered.*—Tig. vii. 80. See p. 187.

In all cases *libn* implies "crude brick," in contrast with *agurri*; see p. 16.

I have not found the theme written phonetically, unless it be *libit*, printed in page 649, which appears rather to be "brick-work" than "brick." Dr. Hincks thought it would be *libin*, with a feminine theme *libint*, implied in *libnassu*. I have doubtfully written *libn* in singular and *libni* in plural, with another plural *libnat*; and am inclined to consider *libit*, *libitta*, &c., to be what Dr. Hincks called "a collective singular, used for a plural." (See Journ. R.A.S. 1866, p. 169.)

LBN *the God of Bricks.*

...... ana ili-šu bil uššu libitte .... la-niqa akki; *lord of foundations of brick-work .... a victim I sacrificed.*—Sarg. 50. See p. 649.

¶ *the monogram of the Third Month, Sivan.* See p. 50.

ina arhi III yum 22-kan lime Dagan-bilkur; *in the month Sivan, day twenty-second, in limu [eponym] of Dagan-bilkur.*—Bard. iii. 1. See also ii. 51.

arhu ši ilu libnat nabû šum-šu [nu-su]; *the month of the God of Bricks they call its name.*—Sarg. 46.

I do not quite understand this line, in connection with the context; perhaps the month was so named because the third month (*May*) was favourable for brick-making, after the frost of winter had mellowed the clay. We have a passage something of the same import in Botta 37, 47. Dr. Oppert considered that indicated also the Babylonian *foot-measure*, being the length of a brick. See E.M. Vol. 2, p. 269.

¶ is used for brick in some Babylonian inscriptions, as in Neb. Gr. i. 31, iii. 38, and elsewhere; possibly the additional characters may denote an Accadian epithet. See p. 60.

—37 II. 5a.

—37 II. 10c.

I do not understand these extracts; if be column, as I have thought, labnu, "brick," is intelligible; but see pp. 131 and 166. The import of the second line I cannot guess at.

¶ A few forms in LBN which former translators have considered as one word, I would divide, reading them la bani, or la bani, "doing nothing," or "idler"—

rukubi ina la bani lu ezib; *the chariots in idleness I placed.*—Tig. iii. 45.

This seems probable; the king tells us he had reached a country where mountains rose up like sharp metal spikes, and the chariots had to be left behind. Former translators have placed them "in waggons," "in the plain," "on the low ground," "dans la plaine argileuse," &c. But I propose my reading with some hesitation.

LBN [cuneiform] Bit-karsi(?) ina la bana la akšur; *Bit-karsi unoccupied I shut up.*—Sard. II. 134.

Doubtful; Dr. Oppert reads *labena* "brick." His translation is "*Je dégradai les briques pour bâtir ce palais.*" [cuneiform] was certainly a palace or temple, but the reading of the name is uncertain.

¶ ([cuneiform]) [cuneiform], Labnanû; *Lebanon.*

[cuneiform] is erini-ya sa ista sadi Labnanû is-tir illiti ublâ ana zululu . . . . ušašhe; *my cypresses which from mount Lebanon, royal Babel-wood, I brought, for awnings I planed smooth.*—E.I.H. iii. 22.

I am doubtful about "Babel-wood" (see page [illegible]), and would refer to [cuneiform] in page [illegible]; I believe the monograms are the same, however pronounced, and the meaning may be "work-shops" or "stores."

Lebanon is frequently written [cuneiform]; see p. [illegible].

[cuneiform] erinû dalûti ultu Labnanû dišti ana zululi-sa lû ublâ; *cypresses tall from Lebanon the grassy for its awnings I brought.*—Neb. Gr. iii. 36.

LBR [cuneiform] labiru, *adj. m.* labirtu, *fem.* *Old.*

[cuneiform] labar, labaru; *Length (of Time).*

[cuneiform] labaris; *Decaying.*

[cuneiform] labirimma; *of Old Time.*

[cuneiform] labirutu; *Length of Time.*

[cuneiform] labireti; *Wide Places(?).*

In all these forms, except perhaps the last, the root appears to be "old age," meaning either "decay" or simply "long life." I have sometimes thought that "length" is the fundamental idea, but always "length of time." I do not know any other Semitic root connected with this.

LBR Labiru, *Old*:—

, dur-su labiru ansukir . . . . . dur bil alim (tu) usse-su adi gabiabi-su arsip; *its old castle I threw down . . . . . a new castle from its foundation to its roof I built.*—Sard. ii. 3.

, tal labiru lû anakir adi eli mie (ni) le usabil; *the old mound I threw down, to the top of the water I brought (it)*, [*i.e. to the level of the water*].—Sard. ii. 132; iii. 136.

, ana Bit-anna lamassu-su damiktu utir temin-ma Bit-anna labiri ahit apre ma eli temina-su labiri ukin uses-sa; *to the temple of Anna its holy image I restored, the old basement of Bit-anna I reached, I disclosed, and upon its old basement I placed its foundation.*—Neb. Gr. ii. 56, 58.

See this and a similar passage in p. 29 with the note. See also Nebuc. i. 51, and Nerig. ii. 5.

(v.), temin-su labiri ahit apre (v. abbe); *its old basement I reached, I laid bare* [*v. proclaimed*].—Senh. Cyl. ii. 2.

Labar, *Length*:—

(v.) (v.) (v.) (v.); Asur mulabbir (v. musalbir) pali sarri episi-su nasir ummani-su dar-sa Ninib makis temen adumi (v. ar-su, ali-su) ana labar yumi ruqûti salbû-su; *Asur lengthening*

LBR *the years of the king its builder, protector of its army (and) its wall, Ninib placing the foundation of its city, to the length of remote days may they extend it.*—Sarg. 61.

The variants are from Botta 22, 15, and 39, 22. I translate ... "may they extend it" because there is no other verb, but I do not remember any other similar instance.

[cuneiform] (v. [cuneiform]) [cuneiform] (v. [cuneiform]) [cuneiform] (v. [cuneiform]), balat yoomal ruqûti kunnu kussi labar palo-a l'isankin mâta-kka; *life to remote days, firmness of throne, length to my years may thy sceptre establish.*—Senk. Cyl. ii. 20.

See also Mich ii. 21; Birs ii. 21.

[cuneiform], ina labaru yomma igara-sona igrub; *by length of days their structure was damaged [split].*—Neb. Br. Cyl. iii. 30.

Labaris, *Decaying*:—

[cuneiform], (ana) labaris yomme ina milî [adan] kissate timmen-sa la enisu; *by length of days, by gathered floods its basement was not decayed.*—Sen. Gr. 53 = 39 BM 18.

Ana is omitted in Sen. Gr. 53, and is probably printed by error in Sh. 39. See p. 19 for the explanation of [cuneiform].

[cuneiform] (v. [cuneiform]) [cuneiform] (v. [cuneiform]) [cuneiform], labaris yoomal timmen-sa enis; *through length of days its platform was decayed.*—Sen. T. vi. 39. Neb. Yun. 56.

[cuneiform] (v. [cuneiform]). ina anni ziggurat suatû labaris illik; *in this (time) that tower to decay had gone.*—Nabon. i. 20.

Mr. Talbot renders ina anni "under me," "in my time;" probably right; see anni, "me," after verbs, and annium, "mine," Sard. i. 30; I have taken the demonstrative pronoun as the most simple notion; but the forms are undoubtedly allied.

The meaning involved in labaris, "old age," "length of days," and "decay," is clear enough, but difficult to express in the adverbial form, which we have before us. I am driven to paraphrase, instead of the word-for-word rendering which as a rule I aim at.

LBR **Labirimma**, *Of Old Time*:—

[illegible] mulak mie-su kima labirimma ana itê Bit-Saggatu usteswir; *the course of its water, as of old time, to the walls of Bit-Saggatu I directed.*—Nerig. ii. 4.

[illegible] kima libirimma elnis abni-su; *as of old time strongly I built it.*—Bira, additional bit.

I have translated *elnis* "strongly," and in some cases by "from the foundation." Mr. Talbot makes it "anew," corroborated by the following extracts from a bilingual slab relating to ships:—

[illegible] elnutu.—46 II. 11*b*.

[illegible] labirtu.—46 II. 12*b*.

In the first of these lines we have *elnutu* equated to [illegible], "new" (p. [illegible]); in the second *labirtu*, "old," equated to [illegible], "dead" (p. 14[illegible]), which in the case of a ship must signify "old" or "worn-out." In 33 II. 51*b* we have "Nebo passing to a new house," [illegible], and see a note on [illegible] in p. 93. I may repeat here the observation already made in p. [illegible] on the character [illegible], that its resemblance to [illegible] has not unfrequently caused a confusion between the two. Further examples of *kima labirimma* occur in p. 544 and Neben. i. 25.

Labirutu, *Length of Days*:—

[illegible] sa ipsit qati-su va nadan zibi-su ali ili rabi ithibu ana abbuta va labiruta illiku; *(he) who the work of his hand and gift of his zibi(?) to the great gods hath attributed(?) and in abundance and length of days hath walked.*—Tig. vii. 54.

Ithibu may be *ithu*; for *zibi* see pp. [illegible]; *nadan zibi* occurs in Assur b.p. iv. 48, but the passage is incomplete.

Labirati, *Squares or Streets(?)*:—

[illegible] sa Nineveh-ki er bilúti-ya subat-sa usrabbi ribati-sa ustakan [sana] labirati va suqdul ustamdi; *of Nineveh my capital city its site I enlarged, its dimensions I determined, the squares(?) and market-places I extended.*—Sen. Gr. 68.

LBR Labarna, Liburna.—Sarg. iii. 71, 81, 134. St. 17. Obel. 140.

A chief of the Patinai (or Patinians), put to death by his people. Dr. Hincks placed these people on the Orontes.

¶ ; see *Lamaşi.*

LBS —Syl. 387.

¶ ma'dis-dannis.—47 II. 54b.

Ma'dis, "greatly," and dannis, "strongly," are often used, but I do not remember

---

¶ —51 II. 1a and 5a, and see under *Babilat*, p. 71.

¶ labsati, labasta; *Clothing.*—38 II. 34, 48. Heb. לבש.

Generally written *lubulti, lubulta.* See pp. 658, 660-1.

LG —Syl. 760.

We only learn from this that *lik* is one of the sounds of

¶ —Syl. 379.

¶ etetiq; *I Passed;* var. —Sard. i. 48.

See the values of as a verbal monogram, p. 640.

LGB —Syl. 542. *Hap.*

,, 544. *Kir.*

,, 545. *Rim.*

,, 546. *Lagabu.*

I have found with the value of *gil* (implied under *kir*), *hap*, and *rim*; but do not remember *lagab.*

LGD —Syl. 356.

LGD [cuneiform], Lagudu.—Botta 114, 9-9; 152, 5-157. Cyp. i. 16.

Name of a deity, especially worshipped at Warka.

LGL [cuneiform], Lagalaga.—Sard. ii. 29.

A city of the province of Zamua, plundered by Sardanapalus.

LGM [cuneiform], Lagamaru.—Assur b.p. iv. 77.

In a list of the gods of Elam. See לָעֹמֶר in the name of Chedorlaomer, Gen. xiv. 1, 9.

LGŞ [cuneiform], Lakṣal.—Sh. Ph. iii. 53.

A province of Nairi, tributary to Shamas Phul.

LD [cuneiform].—Syl. 590.

We have here a proof that lat is one of the values of [cuneiform]. The syllabaries afford positive evidence of the values of sat and mat also, besides kur, with probability of at least two more. See [cuneiform], bullut, p. 356; [cuneiform], pimlat(?), p. 189.

¶ [cuneiform].—Syl. 386.

The monogram of the tenth month is certainly [cuneiform], but I do not know how it is connected with [cuneiform].

¶ [cuneiform], lidu; a Son; equated to [cuneiform] in 30 II. 47, 53.

See also [cuneiform], lidanu, in i. 424. These are clearly from ילד, but I have not seen the words used in any inscription.

LDB [cuneiform], latbasu; *Covered; Painted(?)*. Heb. לבש.

[cuneiform], ina dappi šu-erni sakirie latbasu usatrisa yalsi-sa; *with smooth planks of pine-wood skilfully covered [painted?] I adjusted its awning.*—Neb. Yun. 34. Not quite certain.

See more in p. 546 from Sen. B. iv. 25, 29-41 BM 89, 84.

¶ [cuneiform]

This is erroneously lithographed in Sen. T. v. 84 instead of [cuneiform] "in heart." See p. 642.

LDD [cuneiform], Luddi; *Lydia.*

[cuneiform] Gu(g)gu sar Luddi nagú sibirti bahba aere rûqa; *Gyges, king of Lydia, a province in the vicinity of the sea, a place remote.*—Assur b.p. iii. 6.

¶ [cuneiform], limaddu [liuddu]; *Were Skilled.* Heb. לָמַד.

[cuneiform], kisata qurudi-ya sa mithuz tahâz limaddu lu alqi; *bands of my warriors, who (in) fight and destruction were skilled, I collected.*—Tig. ii. 67.

¶ [cuneiform], ittallakuna-mma; *They Went.*—Neb. Yun. 20.

See Smith, Assurbanipal, pp. 107, 209: the meaning seems clear, but the initial *G* as a phonetic complement is unprecedented, and some letters in l. 77 are doubtful.

LDK [cuneiform], ladku; *Acknowledged.* See Verbs.

[cuneiform], ladku sar sarri [v. sarrani]; *the acknowledged, the king of kings.*—Tig. ii. 30. Sard. i. 21.

LDN [cuneiform], Lidini; *a City of Cyprus.*—Fragment of Esar Haddon, l. 13 in Sb. 41, Vol. I, R.I.

¶ [cuneiform].

[cuneiform], harbasu tahazi-ya kima lidan suhar-sun ishup kumrate-sun usassiru; *the fierceness of my fight, like * *, overwhelmed their whole body(?), their defences they abandoned.*—Sen. T. vi. 16.

In Sen. T. iii. 47 we have *harbasu tahazi-ya*, which must have some such meaning as that given here. *Suhar* is very doubtful; see some unsuccessful guesses in pp. 320, 637; I have here supposed that סחר may have been the root; see Tig. vi. 12, where *siharti* means "entire," as in very many passages. The final letter of *ishup*, "overwhelmed," is made [cuneiform] in the plate, but it is [cuneiform] in the photograph; the spelling is not quite correct, but we have the same form in Obel. 84. I have nothing to propose for [cuneiform].

LDT [cuneiform], lidute; *Fearless.*

[cuneiform], sarrani likdute lidase altu git Samsi adi erib Samsi ana sipri-a usaknisa; *kings mighty (and) fearless, from the rising sun to the setting sun, to my feet I have subdued.*—Sard. III. 131.

We have a parallel passage in III. 14 with [cuneiform] (*la kaitsu,* "fearless") instead of *lidute*; I have no other evidence of the value I attribute to *lidute*. Possibly [cuneiform] may have been copied by mistake instead of [cuneiform].

[cuneiform].—2 II. 65*c*.

[cuneiform] " " 66*c*.

[cuneiform] " " 67*c*.

The value is clearly "family" or "offspring." Heb. [Hebrew] this is further shown by the equivalent *sulsite* in line 71; see p. 482.

¶ [cuneiform], lattatu, littuti, *pl.* *Tributes.*

[cuneiform]. lattatu lībūa da'rda'r ana yumme ruqute libana kirib-sa; *may tributes come perpetually, to days remote may they remain within it.*—Neb. Yun. 93.

[cuneiform]. sebe lattute (v. 10) kirib-sa daris l'arme ua l'usbá lalá-sa; *may plenty (and) tributes in it for ever arise, and may its fullness abound.*—Esar vi. 48.

[cuneiform], sebe littuti kussi [sugam] va labar palie ana sirikti surka; *plenty, tributes, stability of throne and length of life to length may they prolong.*—Rich II. 17.

See also Birs II 20; Neb. Bab ii, 2[?]

LDT [cuneiform] bit epusu .... ina kirbi-su (v. su) sibuta (v. ti) l'ukund l'unbá littuti; *a house I have made, within it may plenty arrive, may tributes abound.*—E.I.H. x. 8 = Neb. Gr. iii, 50.

See also Merig. S. 88, and Brick l. 7 in Pl. 53, No. 4, Vol. I, B.I.

[cuneiform] ... littútu mahar Marduk sar same va irsiti abi alidi-ka epsitá-a sumgiri; *may a series of tributes, (and) the presence of Marduk the king of heaven and earth, the father who generated thee, my work favour.*—Birs ii. 25.

Littutu has been translated "revenues," "tributes," "good luck," &c.; either would seem to be applicable. It is a feminine plural agreeing with *l'ikud* and *l'ubá*. Castell gives us Chal. לִיתָא, *opulens, fortuna*, which would imply "good luck."

LH [cuneiform], [cuneiform], [cuneiform], [cuneiform]. lih, c. liha, m. lihi, obl. lihat, f. *Violent, Vehement; Consuming.* Qy. Heb. לָהַט, לָהַב.

[cuneiform], lih kali malki sa eli Harrana el-va palu-su itruyu; *(king) consuming all kings; who over the city of Harran ..... hath held rule.*—Botta 167, 8.

Bulikhi and *Harran* are connected in the introductory lines of several of Sargina's inscriptions; *Bulikhi* occurs two lines earlier in the text before us. This must imply something more general than would be inferred from the mere mention of a couple of cities; we know that *Bulikhi* stands for Assyria (see p. [illegible]), and may hope to find some such explanatory note respecting *Harran*. See p. [illegible].

[cuneiform], lih tamhari sa ina gabi tamdi Yamnai sandanis kima nûni ibarû; *(king) vehement in fight, who amidst the sea of Ionia swiftly(?) like a fish, crossed over.*—Sard. 21.

I have very doubtfully rendered *sandanis* by "swiftly," looking to the Arabic صنديد; Dr. Oppert translates "dans des vaisseaux."

LH [illegible] (v. [illegible]) [illegible], anaku sar tiba qapli saly ari u ḫarmel; *I, king, vehement in war, destroyer of cities and forests.*—Sard. i. 34; iii. 130.

[illegible], sulsur la libi la ḫabal; *ruling not violently nor oppressively.*—Sarg. 40.

See p. 443, where I have rendered the words differently; I had not then considered Sir H. Rawlinson's translation in Journ. R.A.S. 1864, p. 200. There are still some difficulties in the way of a correct version, as observed by Sir H. Rawlinson, and I am unable to translate literally; but I think the following paraphrase will represent the meaning. I begin in the 40th line, after sumi-ya, "my name," and make the following relative pronoun so agree with the primitive understood in the possessive ya:—"(I) whom the great gods have named for the guardianship of the land(?), and its government, ruling not violently, not oppressively."

[illegible], libat Anunaki; *Consumer of Anunaki.*—1 Beltis 3.

Epithet of Beltis. See p. 72.

LHL [illegible] (v. [illegible]), Lahlahi.—N. Dir. i. 30, 31.

The city of Ahuni the son of Adini; the name is omitted on the Black Obelisk of Nimrud.

LHR [illegible], la-ari; *Barren.* Heb. אָרָה "to gather fruit," &c. Ethiop. ዐረረ arara, "to reap."

[illegible], edis ipparsu ana la-ari; *away they fled (to) barren places.*—Sen. T. i. 18.

[illegible] (v. [illegible]), tudat la-ari pasqati sa amr-sina hadluddu rabis etettiqa (v. qa); *marasure barren (and) devious, whose place [which their place] was solitary, greatly I passed over.*—Botta 145, 3 = 15. Sarg. 11. See pp. 142 and 463.

I hardly know which of the translations proposed may be thought most trustworthy; on the whole, considering that rabis, "greatly," usually precedes the verb which it qualifies (see Tig. i. 57; Obel. 52), I prefer the version above given, taking "greatly" in the sense of "proudly" or "vigorously."

LHT [cuneiform]. Likhai.—Botta 17, 10; 19bis 95; 145, 7 = 10.

Name of a tribe plundered by Sennacherib, together with several others, among which are the Syrian names Aram, Hauran, Hagaran, and Nabat; Sen. T. i. 44. Sargon places them on the rivers Surappi and Ukni, near the Persian Gulf; see p. 185. The name is written Likhau and Likhdu in Sen. T. i. 44, and Tig. jun. 7. In Botta 16bis 71 it is made [cuneiform], which must surely be an error of the copyist.

LZ [cuneiform], Laz.—Tig. jun. 12. 17 BM 16. Neb. Gr. ii. 37.

A goddess, wife of *Nergal*. Rawlinson and Oppert thought it might be *Nergal himself* (B.M. Vol. 2, p. 371); Hincks proposed *Nibhaz*.

¶ [cuneiform]. Alzi.—Tig. i. 64; ii. 90. Obel. 42.

A province in the country lying near the sources of the Tigris and Euphrates. It was held by the Moschi, and was tributary to Tiglath-Pileser.

LZB [cuneiform].—Assur b.p. i. 34.

Probably Assyrian; it occurs in the following line, which is unintelligible to me:—

[cuneiform]

LZZ [cuneiform]. lazza; *Noxious*. Syr. [Syriac]

[cuneiform]. Gula ..... çimma lazza ina zumri-su lishkun; *the goddess Gula .... noxious vapour on his frame may she bring.*— 1 Mich. iv. 6.

This is one of the maledictions invoked upon any one who may damage the land which is the subject of the inscription, or injure the document itself. So far as I can read the unusual hieratic forms of the other similar inscriptions which I have called 2 Mich. and 3 Mich. we have almost identical lines on them also, the principal difference being that the verb [cuneiform], *lishshi*, "may she cause to be" is put in 2 Mich. ii. 39 instead of *lishkun*, and that *lishkun* is written [cuneiform] in 3 Mich. iv. 16. I am not sure of the word *zumri* in them. Dr. Oppert reads it *azza* and *lishik*, and translates "qu'elle répande dans son corps un poison non tarissable."—Gramm. 2nd edit., p. 115.

LZM [cuneiform].—Botta 151, 8(81) = 117.

I cannot read this word, but think it may be Assyrian. Dr. Oppert translates it "lacquer."

LḪ [cuneiform].—Syl. 549.

[cuneiform] „ 550.

Generally pronounced *lah*, more rarely *lih*. *Sukkal* is written here with *s*, in Birs ii. 10 with *ṣ*, and by *Sir H. Rawlinson* with *s*. The [cuneiform] in the Assyrian column is ambiguous. See *Zukkalu* in pp. 312-3, where I have said all I know about the word.

¶ [cuneiform].—23 II. 1 c.

In a bilingual list relating to buildings; probably a bar or *rafter*; see [Hebrew], a plank, in Ezekiel xxvii. 5, and [Hebrew], a bar, Exod. xxvi. 26.

¶ [cuneiform]. liṭi; *Hostages*. See p. 665.

¶ [cuneiform]. Laḫi.—Tig. iv. 10.

A province of Ṣugi, in a mountainous country east of the Tigris, laid waste by Tiglath-Pileser.

LḪA [cuneiform]. Laḫmata.—Tig. jun. 5.

One of a long enumeration of tribes subdued by Tiglath-Pileser up to his seventeenth year.

LḪL [cuneiform]. ilḫalate.—Sarg. 29.

Printed as a variant of *ikdulate*; I think it must be an error.

LḪR [cuneiform]. Laḫira, *n.* Laḫiri, *g.* Laḫira, *ac.*

A city in the neighbourhood of Babylonia: it was captured by Shalmaneser in his eighth year (15 BM 24), and was engaged in the rebellion of Saggab (Sen. T. v. 26). See also Sen. T. v. 10; Bellino 27, 29; Tig. jun. 13.

LḪS [cuneiform]. Iḫis.—Tig. iv. 58.

One of sixteen strong cities in the mountainous country north of Assyria, traversed by Tiglath-Pileser on his way to Nairi.

LḪT [cuneiform]. laḫiti; *Trouble*. Qy. Heb. [Hebrew].

[cuneiform]. ana ḫulti va laḫiti l'iriaddu-su; *to sickness and trouble may they reduce him.*—3 Mich. ii. 37.

¶ [cuneiform]. Laḫuti.—Sard. iii. 82, 83.

A province near the Orontes, sacked by Sardanapalus.

LT [cuneiform] liṭi, liṭa(t)ṭe; *Hostages.*

[cuneiform] liṭi-suna aṣbat billat va madatta eli sa panu ettir ina eli-suna askun; *their hostages I took, tributes and donatives, above what before was, upon them I imposed.*—Tig. vi. 30.

We have here very curiously [cuneiform] for [cuneiform]. I had thought that the plural sign was only displaced, but the sense requires sum, and we have it in a phrase exactly parallel, i. 47.

[cuneiform] ṣabit liṭi sakin lite eli kull-sina mati; *taking hostages (and) imposing laws upon all their countries.*—Sard. i. 17; iii. 117. St. 3.

In this as in the preceding extract the distinction of liṭi and liti is strongly marked, and the repetition can hardly allow a doubt of its reality.

[cuneiform] ki liṭuto ḫad ina libbi-suna tila ul ezib; *as hostages one among them alive I did not leave.*—Sard. i. 108.

[cuneiform] ṭuri ṣabuit libbi-su va kimti-su ana liṭutte aṣbat; *the youths, offspring of himself and his family, for hostages I took.*—Tig. ii. 48.

Nearly the same in Tig. v. 19.

[cuneiform] liṭi-su aṣbat; *his hostages I took.*—Obel. 184.

The same phrase with [cuneiform] in Sard. iii. 69, and [cuneiform] in iii. 77.

[cuneiform] ṭuri (v. ṣiṣi)-suna ki liṭuto aṣbat; *their youths as hostages I took.*—Sard. ii. 11.

These examples seem to prove that liṭi implies "hostages," and liti "laws;" liṭi signifies persons taken, and liti something imposed. For the relatively few cases in which liṭi are imposed (askun or sakin) we may understand "I imposed the delivery of hostages." See Tig. ii. 85; v. 88, &c. For liti see under LT.

LṬT [cuneiform], alṭuti; *Dark Deeds; Darkness.* Heb. עֲלָטָה.

[cuneiform], sapina gimir alṭuti; *the sweeper-away of all dark deeds.*—Tig. ii. 88.

[cuneiform], kabis alṭute; *trampler on dark deeds.*—Tig. v. 64.

[cuneiform], musaknis gimir alṭute; *subduing all darkness.*—Tig. vii. 44.

LIR [cuneiform], liyari. See [cuneiform], p. 346, and [cuneiform], p. 482.

LK [cuneiform], ilku; *Toll, Duty.* Chal. הֲלָךְ.

[cuneiform], ilku sumikhu ki sa Gunzinanu sar mahri ukin eli-su; [*payments of*] *toll* (*and*) *submission, as of Gunzinanu the former king, I imposed upon him.*—Botta 148, 11 – 83.

LKB [cuneiform], Lakabri.—Sen. T. v. 32.

One of the tribes engaged in the rebellion of Suzub; see *Lakiru*, p. 664.

LKK [cuneiform] (v. [cuneiform]). alkakát, ilkakat; *Narration, Tradition.*

[cuneiform], alkakat gurdi-ya mamma sa ina mati etepusu ina garbi-su asṭur; *a narration of my victories whatever that in the countries I had accomplished, upon it I wrote.*—Obel. 71.

[cuneiform] (v. [cuneiform]) [cuneiform] (v. [cuneiform]) [cuneiform], alkakat (v. ilkakat) gurdi-ya (u) ipsit umluti-ya ina kirib-su alṭur; *a narration of my victories and of my triumphant deeds, upon it I wrote.*—New Div. i. 50; ii. 60.

LKŠ [cuneiform] (v. [cuneiform]) [cuneiform] (v. [cuneiform]) [cuneiform]. Ilhakat gardi-ya (v. -a) sa mati Nairi etappasu ina libbi asṭur [sar] ina er Tuska azqup; *a narration of my victories, which (in) the countries of Nairi I had gained [done], upon it I wrote, (and) in the city of Tuska I put up.*—Sard. ii. 6.

[cuneiform]. mu-dā ena-ga sa ana alkakāt ili rabi basā uzund-su; *the renowned, the glorious, who to the traditions of the great gods his ears are [ready].*—Birs i. 4. Epithet of Nebuchadnezzar.

Mu-dā ena-ga are Accadian; *mudā*, "renowned," from *mu*, "name:" see Lenormant, p. 74: for *ena-ga*, "glorious," see p. 156. I have seen *ilkakat* rendered "glory," I think by Dr. Oppert; this is not improbable, as we might say "the glory of my victories," and "the glories of the gods." I prefer "narration," though I do not know of any analogous Semitic root. Fürst suggests a connection between the Hebrew [Hebrew] and the Sanscrit [Sanskrit], *lih*; a hardy philologer, aware of the connection between *q* and *p* (*quod*—*pod*, *mag* = *trag*), and inclined to a rough bit of etymologic manipulation, might add [Sanskrit], *lipi*, and a Prakrit *dipi* from Kapurdigiri—the old Persian *dipi* of Behistun; all leading round to the Assyrian *duppi*, "records." See Journ. R.A.S., Vol. 15, p. 197.

LKṢ [cuneiform]. Lakiṣu; *Inscription of Sennacherib.*

Published in Layard's "Discoveries in Nineveh and Babylon," London, 1853, p. 152. Probably the Lachish of 2 Kings xviii. 14.

LL [cuneiform]. lal; *various values.*—

[cuneiform], malû; *full.*—Syl. 140.

I believe [cuneiform] ([cuneiform]), *lala*, "fullness," "abundance," is explained by this extract from the Syllabary; see p. [illegible].

[cuneiform], maṭû.—Syl. 141.

We have [cuneiform] equivalent to *maṭû*, "fall," "slip," in [illegible] (Heb. [Hebrew]), and to [cuneiform], *ṣuru*, "sick," in [illegible] (Heb. [Hebrew]), both implying "weakness," "deficiency."

[cuneiform], sapaku; *to pour out.*—Syl. 142.

See a note near the foot of p. [illegible], explanatory of [cuneiform].

LL [cuneiform], saqalu; *to weigh.*—Syl. 143.

As an example of this value of [cuneiform] we give the following:—

[cuneiform], ana Babel-li mahazi Bel saqal ili .... hadis aruh [erum from following m]; *to Babylon the fortress of Bel (who is) weigher of the gods, ... gladly I passed.*—Botta 152, 8 - 140. See p. 409.

This might lead to the inference that [cuneiform] was the Arcad equivalent of [cuneiform]. In 11 II. 1-26 there are eight Arcad verbal forms of [cuneiform] with the corresponding Assyrian forms of the verb saqal, in which we find *k*, *g*, and *q* used indiscriminately. See also the following lines:—

[cuneiform].—13 II. 44*b*.

The Assyrian I read *kaspa isqul*, "he weighs silver." I do not know the Accadian form.

[cuneiform] eqil; *slothful.*—27 II. 41*b*. Heb. עצל.

[cuneiform].—27 II. 42*b*.

The Assyrian ina-ezziti may be "the two hands idle," ina being the dual form; it is curious that we have an unusual dual adjective in Eccl. x. 18, [illegible], "two (hands) idle," in our version "much slothfulness" [in pigritiis in the Vulgate]. This might indicate that [cuneiform] was an intensive form of [cuneiform]. A comparison of [cuneiform], from line 43, qati u sivi eqalani, "hands and feet idle," with the above extract in line 42, showing eqali and eqalani in direct sequence, confounding e and a, exhibits the carelessness of the scribe; and a still more striking instance may be seen in 11 II. 1-8 above cited; in a grammatical tablet more accuracy might have been expected.

[cuneiform], maaqu; *a chain.*—48 II. 7*b*.

[cuneiform].—24 II. 55*a*.

[cuneiform].—62 II. 44*b*.

I would read this abbaru sa mardi, which might signify "crossing of the sea," if Dr. Hincks' reading could be correct (see p. 37); but I have not found any example of the word, unless this be one.

[cuneiform] is used as a verbal monogram for *aslur* in the following passage:—

[cuneiform] (v. [cuneiform]) [cuneiform] (v. [cuneiform]) [cuneiform].

With some doubt about the first words, I render this ina issu ushalli (v. lu) ruda sarruti-ya ashar-sunuti (v. kal-sunuti), "in maintaining the domination of my royalty I separated them."

[cuneiform], targi; *opposite, facing.*

I have received the above extract out of an unpublished fragment from Mr. G. Smith. I do not remember seeing [cuneiform] used with this value.

LL [cuneiform], supalulu.—Syl. 144.

Supalulu, with some variation of spelling, appears to mean "threatening," or some other infliction. It is, perhaps, from the shaphel form of galal, "to curve." [cuneiform] is used phonetically in [cuneiform], the river Lalla.

¶ [cuneiform], lil.

[cuneiform].—Syl. 202. New Syl. 149.

Lil was translated "quiver" by Dr. Hincks; see his Astron. Tables, 1856, p. 30. He translated the verb [cuneiform], *alila*, "to put to rest (applied to arrows put up in their quiver)," and supposed [cuneiform], *lala*, to mean "repositories." See p. 678. I have usually rendered the verb "I conveyed (in boats)." See the Verbs.

¶ [cuneiform] ([cuneiform]), [cuneiform], lala, n. lale, obl. *Fulness, Abundance.* See [cuneiform].—Syl. 140.

[cuneiform], l'usbâ lalâ-sa.—Esar vi. 45.

[cuneiform], lala-sa l'usbiâ.—Neb. Gr. iii. 47.

[cuneiform], lala-sa l'usba.—Birch, Pl. 32, l. 6, Vol. I.

[cuneiform], lalâ-sa l'usbi.—E.I.H. x. 5.

[cuneiform], lalâ-sa l'usba.—Nerig. ii. 34.

The translation in all these is "may its fulness increase," meaning the fulness of a house or palace, which is, I think, usually a feminine noun, though the sa in Neriglissar shows that the rule was not without exception.

[cuneiform], lale balatu l'usbi; *in abundance may (my) life increase.*—Neb. Brok. Cyl. i. 26; ii. 24.

Both passages are mutilated, but they complete each other. As Nabonidus is speaking of himself, we may safely supply the pronoun.

[cuneiform], lale mat l'isbi; *in abundance may the land increase.*—Nabon. ii. 31.

[cuneiform], palta lalâ kummuru *excellence and fulness were united.*—Sen. B. iv. 24 = 41 BM 28. See p. 498.

[cuneiform], lalâ usamlila; *abundantly I caused fill it.*—Neb. Yun. 64.

I have made an adverb of *lalâ* from the examples of *basa, bala, pulfâ*, &c.; see pp. 78, 88, 89.

LL ⸺ Lala, Lalla.—Sard. ii. 34, 77.

See in p. 581. I do not know whether one or two cities were called by these names; both appear to have been in the province of *Zamua*, in the high lands north or north-east of Assyria.

¶ Lule.—Sen. T. ii. 35. Sen. B. i. 18. Neb. Yun. 13.

King of Sidon, who fled before the arms of Sennacherib, and escaped to Cyprus; Josephus calls him Elulæus, king of Tyre; see Antiq. ix. ch. 14.

¶ lule, obl. *Twisted or Wreathed Ornamental Work.* Heb. לול.

ultu hekal gapli es sa Nineveh-ki ana ribat sarrati-ya usaklilu ana tabrati kissat nisi lule umalla-si; *after that the palace amid the city of Nineveh for the greatness of my royalty I had completed, for the admiration of multitudes of men with wreathed work I filled it.*—Sen. T. vi. 27.

(v.), sal lamassi abu-lamir-rabi ka sapi sa illuru nasâ kitmusa sitta-sun palsu kasbu bitlupu lule malû lus bab-sin ulziz (v. ulziz); *sacred cows of alabaster and reems' horn, whose illuru(?) are raised (and) fine their feet, size (and) form varied, with wreathed work everywhere in their gates I erected.*—39 BM 26 = Sen. B. iv. 7.

See pp. 469 and 556. I am still doubtful of several words in this passage.

bit sâtu ana tabrâti usepis ana sâ daggalu kis(sat) nisi lule usmallû; *that house for admiration I caused build, and as a standard for multitudes of men, with wreathed work I caused fill.*—R.I.II. ix. 35.

LL … tabi rabi sināti ana taprâti kis(sat) nisi lale umallû; those great gates, for the admiration of multitudes of men, with twisted work I caused fill.—E.I.H. vi. 21.

---

aLL …, …, alla, alla; *Afterwards, Then.*

…, alla sa anaku aduku ana Gumâtû; *after that I had killed Gumata.*—Beh. 19.

Alla ought to have been a very useful word, but it occurs only in this passage; and unless the word *alla* arranged with it, which is likewise a word only found in one passage, be really allied to *alla*, the latter was probably invented by the Persians. *Ana* is superfluous, and in such constructions is found only in the Persian period.

…, babulate-ya gapsûte aiko ma alla ussikka assapi; *my many people I gathered, and then submission I enforced* (*I caused to accept*).—Sarg. 46.

---

iLL …, illa; *Upon.*

…, musahhid Kar-alla sa pâri Assurlik bil-er-ussu illa risa usima; (*I*) *the devastator of Kar-Alla, who the tiara of Assurlik their city-ruler upon* (*my*) *head have placed.*—Sarg. 33.

Compare Botta 16, 16, and see …, ii, to p. 641).

¶ …, …, …, …, illu, *n.* illi, *obl.* illa, *ac.* illuta, *pl.* *Lofty, Exalted, Noble, Royal.* Mong. …, …, …, illu, illuti, illuta. Heb. [illegible].

In a very few cases we find *illat*; this may be due to a change of gender; I am not sufficiently acquainted with this part of the grammar to speak with confidence.

…, ina bab illa adi Istar-sakipat-tebisa; *from the high gate to Istar-sakipat-tebisa.*—E.I.H. v. 46.

I transcribe the name of the place from Dr. Oppert's Inscription de Nabuchodonosor sur les Merveilles de Babylone. Reims. 1866.

ıLL iş-gumri iş-erni pirati tarbit Hamanû šadi illi unatrim eli-šun; *beams of tall cypresses, the growth of Amanus the lofty mount, I adjusted over them [the palaces].*—Sen. T. vi. 46. See p. 200.

damgûtû-a l'iśmkun šibţu-kha ina pi-ka illu ša la nakari; *my holy places may thy sceptre establish by thy lofty countenance, which is not hostile.*—Neb. Bab. ii. 27.

(?), eli temini-ša labiri ipri illati amkuk ša ahiz libnat-su [libnassu]; *upon its old platform the heaped-up earth I cleared away, and I placed its bricks.*—Senk. Cyl. ii. 5. See *ipri*, p. 118.

The last letter is doubtful: it is printed …

—24 11. 46a.

ša bîtu an-ki ina agurri abni šamat illiti ulla reša-ša; *of the Bit-an-ki in brick (and) noble lapis lazuli I raised its head.*—E.I.H. iii. 16.

This temple is called in l. 18 one of the "mansions [*šuvvi*] of Babylon." In l. 67 we have … (?) … instead of *ša bîtu an-ki*, followed by the same words as in the above passage, and the temple is called one of the "mansions of Borsippa."

ištu šadi Labnanû iş-Babel illiti ubla; *from Mount Lebanon noble Babel-wood I brought.*—E.I.H. iii. 23. See pp. 393, 659.

—30 II. 186.

See p. 724. I have supposed that under might signify the "farther sea," but on comparing the above examples I think we might say "the great sea."

oLL [cuneiform] (v. [cuneiform]) [cuneiform], nabnita illatu sa Tigulti-Bar; *the noble offspring of Tiglath-Pileser.*—Obel. 39 = 12 BM 12. See p. 341.

The following pair of parallel passages will prove the value of [cuneiform]:—

[cuneiform].—Botta 16[illegible] 130.

[cuneiform], ina pi-sa illi lissakin; *by his lofty countenance may it be established.*—Oppert's Botta 189, compiled from 100, 7; 132, 15, &c.

[cuneiform].—Botta 16[illegible] 133.

[cuneiform], ina nummur bun(n)i-sa illati kinis lippalis; *by the might of his lofty statues steadily be it favoured.*—Oppert's Botta 187, compiled from 100, 6; 132, 16, &c.

[cuneiform] is much used as a determinative of precious metals—as [cuneiform], "gold;" [cuneiform], "silver." See p. 641.

---

uLL [cuneiform], ullu, ulli, ullati, &c. *Further, former, remote; That, those.*

This word is given in Dr. Oppert's Grammar as the remote demonstrative pronoun, fully declined, and I have little doubt that such was its original value; see my long note to p. 411, and compare the Latin *ultra* and the antiquated *olle*; but I have rarely found it used in any form other than *ullati*, and with the adjectival value of "remote" in time or place. I arrange *ullani* and *ullu-ullu* under the same heading.

[cuneiform] ..... [cuneiform], garri sar ana la suhhuri nari [abu-nabani-a] sarpis ma sa ahi ulle ina mihirti lamzu 62 ina 1 ammat .... sumuh rabat-su [rubassu]; *the royal street not to be small, edicts I caused make; and what of that side in front was strong, sixty-two* * *cubits ...., I measured its width.*—R.I. Vol. 1, Sb. 7, l. 20.

The grammatical construction of this passage is not quite clear, but the meaning must almost certainly be "I issued orders that the royal street (King Street) should not be narrow; and I measured a width of 62 cubits from the farther side of the road, where it was consolidated." See p. xvi of Additions and Corrections, where I have supposed that the form [cuneiform] was only employed where two dimensions were given; the passage quoted above proves that my conjecture was wrong.

ULL ucre eqlil [alibi]-suna sa ulta yomme ulluti ina taldi mati Suti ekimû; *the tillage of their fields, which from former days, by holding the lands, the Suti (desert-men) had possessed . . . . .*—Botta 138, 3 = 135.

I cannot complete this sentence, and I am not sure that the proposed version is correct.

sa ulta yomme ulluti la illiku sar panî mahri-ya; *(a province) which from former days (in days of yore) not had entered a preceding king before me.*—East iii. 33.

panama ulta yomati ulluti adi pale Nabu-pal-uçur sar Babel-ki; *at any former date, from days of old to the years of Nebopalassar, king of the Babylonians.*—E.I.H. vii. 9.

For the meaning attributed to *panama* see the note under *kalama*, in p. 558.

kima sa yommi ulluti ullâ resi-sa; *as of old days I raised its head.*—Birs, additional bit, l. 3.

mata sa Imnarra tabbanâ ullôta gabbi ina imni Ahuramazda' nitebus; *those (works) which are seen excellent, those all by the power of Ormazd we have done.*—No. 15, D, l. 15.

¶ ullmai; *Further.*

Gimirri sa ahi ullual sa nahar marrati; *the Saca of the further side of the river.*—No. 6, N.R., l. 17. See p. 182-3.

ULL We have ullani repeatedly combined with ul in a tedious ungrammatical passage from an inscription of Xerxes:—

Madai u mati maniti sa lisanu mati sa mati u mata sa aḫami ugâ sa mahr marrata u aḫullani alli sa mahr marrata sa aḫami ugâ sa gaggar yummamita u aḫullani alli sa gaggar yummamita; *the Medes and the other countries and other tongues of the lands and people(?) of this hither side of the sea, and of that further side of the sea; (also) of this hither side of the desert land, and of that further side of the desert land.*—H, 9 and 11.

This is from a copy by Westergaard, printed in the Transactions of the Soc. R. des Antiq. du Nord, Copenhagen, 1845. It is marked H, but it has no relation to the No. 3, H, of the trilingual inscriptions, nor has any Persian copy of it been found. It is only twenty-four lines in length, but the whole of the above extract occurs again from line 15 to 20. I have not seen elsewhere the mati u mati which I have doubtfully rendered "lands and people."

¶ ulta-ulla; *From Old Time.*

temimma dara dura'a pili sa ulta-ulla itti sitir baramma larat-sa larit; *a tomb durable its duration for the future, which from old time with writing of the graver its engraving was engraved.*—Sen. Gr. 30.

See p. 376. I have still some doubts. See Talbot's Glossary, No. 272.

sara makla ..... sa ulta-ulla sarrani alikut mahri abi-ya [ad-ya] sibaut-a bilute Assur-ki ebusu; *a well-built place ..... which from days of yore the kings going before, my fathers before me, had made the government-(house) of Assyria.*—Sen. Gr. 36.

LL

sa ulta-ulla sarrani abi-ya palam-sun tamsil basti-sun ana emud kirib bit-mati ibus; *(of) which from old time the kings my fathers their images, as their likenesses(?) for erecting in their palaces [territorial houses], had made.*—Sen. B. iv. 16 = 40BM14.

The word which I have doubtfully rendered by "likenesses" might perhaps be translated rather "family records" or "representatives of the family." See p. 189.

ana mat nisi Bisi va mat nisi Yasubi-gallai sa ulta-ulla ana sarrani abi-ya la kitnusu lu allik; *to the land of the Bisi and land of the Yasubi-gallai, who from of old, to the kings my fathers were not submissive, I went.*—Sen. T. i. 65.

---

sa anaku ebusu u sa abû-a ibusu ulla-suma Ahuramazda' l'issur; *what I have done, and what my father has done, that (whatever it was) may Ormazd defend.*—No. 15, D, l. 20. See note on me, p. 358.

The letter marked with a star is engraved [cuneiform sign] in Westergaard's plate, but it is obviously an error of the engraver.

LLB Illibai, Illibi.—Botta 145, 6 = 16; 74, 6.

Illipai, Illipi.—Sarg. 14, 2. Botta 147, 10 - 70.

Ullaba.—18BM35, 28; a mutilated tablet of Tig. jun.

Sir H. Rawlinson places this country about Azerbaijan, Dr. Oppert considers it the Albania of Strabo, and Dr. Hincks supposed it to be the province of Luristan. All these localities point to that part of the country of Daghestan, now belonging to Russia, where it joins the Caspian Sea

LLB . Alhabral.—Botta 146, 13 = 55.

Allibria.—3 Pul. 6.

A province of Syria apparently, the inhabitants of which were removed to Hamath by Sargon. The , of Sard. iii. 109, is read by Dr. Oppert *Allabtir* (*Allabria?*), but this appears to have been a city in or near Armenia; I should rather be inclined to read the name *Allabria*.

LLG , lalligu; *a Bowl*. Heb. גלל.

, lalligu tarçâti tamkahar; *strong bowls of copper.*—12 BM 38 = Sen. Bil. iv. 31.

This is somewhat uncertain: see p. 234.

¶ lalagina.—Neb. Gr. ii. 36.

I have rendered this "large sheep" in p. 183, supposing *lala* to be an Accad. plural of ; see p. 658. The passage in Neb. Gr., as *gina* 8 *lala gine*, may perhaps have signified the fixed number of eight sheep every day.

¶ , lilikku; *Liberty of Going*. Heb. הלך.

, ul lilikku askun-su ma samazir-su; *I did not grant him the liberty of going, but I caused him to be kept separate.*—Assurb.p. viii. 30.

This may signify either that the prisoner was not allowed to depart, but was retained in custody; or else that he was not allowed to be seen, but was kept in solitary confinement; samazir may be the shaphel form of nazar, "to guard," or of nazar, "to separate."

¶ . . Alligi, *g*.

. . . . . , sum [su] sa Alligi Asbilakanu . . . . . abbi; *the name of Alligu I called Asbilakanu.*—New Div. ll. 35. See *Aligu*, p. 32.

¶ . . .—Syl. 117.

¶ , hurazu; *Gold*. See p. 448.

See 2011, where in l. 634, is explained by in line 67.

. . .—Syl. 111.

LLD illad; *Family.* Also implied in illatsu. Heb. ילד.

sú Marduk-pal-adanna sa ina halak garri-ya mahre halikta-su [pisi-su] askunu sa upazzira illad-su rigim iskoti-ya dannuti va tip tahazi-ya izri etur; *he, Merodach-baladan, (who, in the course of my first expedition his defeat I had effected, and had broken up his family,) the throwing of my powerful weapons and the shock of my fierce fight avoided.*—Sen. T. iii. 53.

damú-su tari nabnit libbi-su illad-su [illatsu] 3 sosi ruqqi eri 5 nirmak tamkabar itti ili-sunu hurasi va kaspi dumeq nimsmatri-sunu usá; *his wives, his sons the offspring of his body, his family, three soses [180] cakes of metal, five nirmaks of copper, with their gods silver and gold, the choice of their valuables(?) I took away.*—Tig. ii. 39.

¶ *Fastened, bound, fitted; Trained (to the Yoke).*

biltat madatú kurrai simdat ip-niri eli-su askun; *taxes, (and) tribute of horses fitted to the yoke, upon him I imposed.*—Obel. 170. See also line 183.

rakubi kurrai simdat ip-niri-su hallupai sabi hallupai kurrai sali sabi bekalati-su maltat-su kapta asial; *his chariots (and) horses fitted to the yoke, covers (armour?) for horses, women (and) men of his palaces, largely I carried off.*—Sard. iii. 32. See also ii. 121.

LLD In the following passage is omitted, but implied in the which follows:—

ummani-su rukubi-su çimdaqu aṣuḫa ana ir-ya Assur upla; *his soldiers, his chariots fitted to the yoke, I removed, to my city Assur I carried.*—Sard. iii. 45. See also Sard. i. 86.

In New Inscr. i. 18, 22, 48, is put instead of *çimdat* (ç-mid); see examples in p. 532. In the following extract *çimdat* is written phonetically:—

rukubi-ya çimdat niri ana emuq mati-ya eli sa pana utir usarkip; *my chariots fitted to the yoke, for the benefit of my country, above what before was, I caused build.*—Tig. vii. 28.

From the equivalent *çamqu*, in 48 II. 7 b (see p. 654), I should have expected *çamqut*, "chained," instead of *çimdat*; it is true the sibilant is not the same, but such differences are not rare. The example, however, of Tig. vii. 28, appears decisive. Buxtorf gives us a Rabbinical צמד, "submovit." I do not know whence derived; the meaning would suit in the case of horses.

¶ —Syl. 146.

¶ , kaspu; *Silver.*

See 48 II., where in l. 664 is explained by in l. 676. See also *kaspu* in p. 547-8, and *kasap* in p. 615.

LLU —Syl. 146.

LLZ —Syl. 302.

LLK , alaku; *a March.*

alaku basia ina kirib Ninua illika-ma unnuk; *a circuitous march into Nineveh he marched and repeated (returned?).*—Assur b.p. i. 62.

Printed in p. 431 with inaccurate translation.

LLK ..., iṣ-allakani; *Name of a Tree.*

..., iṣ-erinu iṣ-liškarinu iṣ-allakani ista mati sa apilu-sinati .... lu alqa; *cypresses [and other trees named] from the countries which I took possession of them .... I collected.*—Tig. vii. 18.

LLL ..., Lalla.—Obel. 109.

Name of a chief of Milide, a province beyond the Upper Euphrates, near the country of the Tubali.

¶ ..., Lalli.—New Div. ii. 83.

Name of a king of Lakandai on the Euphrates, who paid tribute to Shalmaneser.

¶ ..., Lallâ.—Sard. ii. 62.

... (v. ...), nahar Lallâ etebir; *the river Lallâ I crossed.*—Sard. ii. 62.

A river near the province of Zamua, north of Assyria; between the city of Zamri and the high lands of Elal(?).

¶ ..., lilla: see *lil*, p. 669.

¶ ..., Lulla.—Sard. ii. 34, 77.

See under *lulu*, in p. 678, and under *Kinabu*, in p. 561.

¶ ..., Lallukan.—Botta 146, 21 – 57.

... ., nisê .... Lallukan ultu asri-sunu amar-sunuti ina lib Dimasqi Hatti usesib-sunuti; *the people .... of Lallukan from their place I separated them, and in Damascus of Syria [Hittites] I settled them.*—Botta 146, 21 – 57.

I believe that the name lithographed in Sarg. 29, which looks as if intended for Latakai, is really Lalukai, and probably the same place with this; I have not found any indication of its locality.

¶ ..., allalli; *Very Powerful.*

..., allalli ili; *most powerful of the gods.*—Sh. Pal. i. 8. Epithet of Ninib. Doubtful. See *alilu*, p. 33.

LLL . Lallume.

Lallume rapsati ina kirib tamhari ina kakki lu amqit; *the broad lands of Lallume in the midst of battle with weapons I subdued.*—St. 6. Sard. iii. 110.

. *Lalume*, is mentioned in Black Obel. apparently in connection with the lands of Nairi; and *Lalumi*, in an unpublished fragment of Tiglath-Pileser I. No doubt all these forms express the same province; the following extract relates to cities which are probably situated in or near Lallume.

(). 150 eri sa er Larbuqal er Dur-Lalumni er Buniqal er Baral aksud; *one hundred and fifty cities of Larbuqa, Dur-Laluma, Buniqa, Bara I took.*—Sard. ii. 44.

This is expressed in a very unusual way, but I suppose the places called cities must be districts. *Buniqal* has a variant *Bunniqal*. I believe that both passages relate to places in the north of Assyria.

¶ . Lallar.—Obel. 31.

A province to which Shalmaneser went up from Mount Amanus, and where he erected an image of himself.

¶ . lallan.

() , ina resi (lu) arkati ina ziliki lallan mihrit 4 (v. 8) sari 8 babi rabi apti; *in the heads (or) extreme parts, in ..... facing the four [v. eight] winds I opened eight great gates.*—Botta 39, 74 = Sarg. 56.

In the passage immediately following it is explained that two gates were opened at each of the cardinal points of a palace. I think *resi arkati* signify projecting porticoes, literally "heads coming after." *Ziliki lallan* I cannot guess at; they are perhaps Accad technical terms. The variants given are from the inscription which I designate by Sarg. Dr. Oppert's version is "En longueur et en largeur, aux angles de la circonvallation, vers les 8 directions, j'ai percé 8 grandes portes."

¶ . —22 II. 18c.

LLM , lalmu, Accadian; *King, Ruler.*

, lalimu iraa; *mighty ruler.*—Neb. Yun. v. 38 BM 2.

Explained by , sar, "a king:" see 31 II. 41 c, cited in Talbot's Glossary, No. 208. The following is from a List of Animals:—

 . .—8 II. 6b.

¶ . , lalmû.—40 II. 40b.

¶ , , illamû, *prep. Before (in time or place).*

, illamû-a Ispabára sar-sun ari-su dannuti bit-nisirti-su uvassir su, ana ruketi innabid; *before me Ispabára their king his strong cities (and) his guard-houses quitted, and to distant (places) fled.*—Sen. T. ii. 9.

(v.) , sa 350-ina malki labiruti sa illamû-a bilut Assur-ki ebus(u) sa Bisapparu babbat Bel sinuusu ina libbi-sunu asar-su ul usanni; *of three hundred and fifty ancient kings who before me held the government of Assyria and ruled the people of Bel, any one among them his place had not touched.*—Botta 37, 41. See , p. 38.

, illamû-a ina Halule sa kisad Yaediggar miskanu sidirta yan barki-ya sabtu sa sam'la isketi-sun; *before me, in Halul, which is near the Tigris, placing their ranks, the front of my lines they occupied, and sent forth their arrows.*—Sen. T. v. 47.

See p. 619, and a note in p. 311

LLM Ilamû-a ṣidru miskanu ma'lu kakkî-sun; *before me their ranks placing, they sent forth their weapons.*—Sen. T. ii. 77.

¶ lilmaku.

This word occurs three times in the large slab of Nebuchadnezzar. Oppert transcribes it zakmuku, and apparently considers it connected with some feudal ceremony. As my translations are merely guess-work, I subjoin those of Dr. Oppert likewise:—

ina lilmaku ris satti.—E.I.H. ii. 56.

Dans les zakmuku du commencement de l'année.—Oppert.

elap mauluku lilmaku isinnû Suanaki; *the tabernacle, the shrine lilmaku, the festival of Suanna-ki [Babylon].*—E.I.H. iv. 1.

Le sanctuaire qui fait la gloire des zakmuku dans les fêtes de Suannaki (Babylone).—Oppert.

ina isinû lilmaku tabe ili bil bit ili Marduk irubu ana kirbi Suanna-ki; *during the festival lilmaku take of the lord of the house of the gods, Merodach, they passed to the inside of Suanna-ki.*—E.I.H. vii. 23.

Pendant la fête zakmuku tale du maître des dieux, Mérodach, ils sont entrés dans Suannaki (Babylone).—Oppert.

LLN illan, elan; *Beyond.*

ultu [ta] ebirtan Zaba-kita adi Tel-bari sa illan mat (v. er) Zabâ; *from the crossing of the lower Zab to Tel-bari which is beyond the country (v. city) of Zab.*—Sard. ii. 130; iii. 123. St. 10.

The above sentence is found in three places, with a few variant readings, all very easily reconciled, the only real variation being that the Zab is made a city in one instance and a province in the others. I have observed before (p. 397) that the river Zab gave a name to a province as well as to a city; and, in fact, the determinatives of province and city are not unfrequently confounded. See pp. 379, 381, 408, 452, &c. In the following lines all the variants of the phrase "beyond Zab" are collected:—

Ilan Zabi.—Sard. ii. 130.

—Sard. iii. 123.

—St. 10.

(v.) —Var. of St. 10.

¶ ullanû: *Before, Preceding.*

ullanû-a kirib-sun mamman la illiku sarrani pani mahruti; *before me into them never went the kings preceding former.*—Sen. T. iv. 5. See Sen. Gr. 38.

ullanû-a ina pali me mahre ina Sumir va Akkad-ki itpara idi hali sini sab libbi Sunanu; *before me, in the time of the former king, in Sumir and Accad, broke out evil bands, men inhabiting Sunanu [Babylon]**.—Bl. St. i. 9.

The lines which follow this are broken and unintelligible, and some uncertainty results in the above translation.

LLS lilṣu; see under *liliṣ*, p. 678.

¶ illaṣu; see under *ilaṣ*, p. 678.

¶ Ullusunu, Ulsunu.—Botta 73, 5; 93, 6. 146, 2, 4, 8, 14 – 38, 40, 44, 50.

A king of Minni (Van), deposed by his brother Aza, but restored to his throne by Sargon.

LLE lal-e; see 13 ll. 30, 318 in p. 687.

¶ —Syl. 148.

* From a line which I printed in p. 419, implying that Imgur-Bel was the wall of Sunanu, I ought to have seen that Sunanu was a name of Babylon, but I misunderstood the legend entirely. I have recently seen, from Mr. Talbot's remarks on the Birch Stone, that he suspected the identification four years ago.

LLP . illipi, -pai; see *Illibi*, p. 676.

LLR . —20 II. 4a.

¶ . —New Syl. 80.

¶ illarum; see pp. 408, 534.

LLS . Lalandal.—New Div. II. 83.

A city on the Euphrates, mentioned with several others tributary to Shalmanezer.

¶ . . —Syl. 115.

LLT lilati.

. —35 II. 25 a.

. —32 II. 18 a.

. " 19 a.

I do not know if anything can be made out of this; pilar pasum should imply "the circuit of the day," or twenty-four hours. I should have expected lilati to be the night, from Semitic analogies; see לילה; but I have not seen the word used in any inscription.

LM . . —Syl. 559.

¶ (), lam (*for* la); *Not.* Doubtful.

() (v.) (v.), ina 2 yumme la Shamas napahi kima Yav u rihsi eli-sunu azgum; *on two days before the Sunrise(?), like Yav the inundator upon them I rushed.*—Sard. II. 100 = New Sard. II. 94.

I would suggest doubtfully that lam might be read la, and that la shamas napahi might signify "not yet sunrise." I put the rihsi from the recently-found Monolith of Sardanapalus, not yet published: this explains the enigmatical of the documents printed.

LM —Syl. 114.

—26 II. 43*a*.

This is double authority for rendering *kwd* "a tablet," but I do not remember seeing the word so used.

¶ lime, *n.* lime, *abl.* limmu, *n.* limme, *abl.* *Date, Year.*

This word is used in dating Assyrian documents: it was usually followed by a name which, like those of the Roman Consuls, indicated the year intended. There has been some discussion on the supposed rank of the persons whose name was used, and it was at first thought that he must have been a high priest; but in the absence of evidence the word eponyme has been of late adopted; in a considerable number of dated slabs that I have seen, where I have found any indication of the position of the bearer of the name, he has been some governor of a city,—the , *saknu*, "ruler," or , *bil-...*, "edile;"(?) three such cases will be found among the passages quoted below. I believe that *lime* signified simply "family;" see the following extract from a bilingual list:—

—29 II. 74*c*. See *kimtu*, p. 183.

The following dates are from published documents:—

, arhi Kuzallu yeumi 20-kan lima Ina-iliya-allik rabbi kali; *in the month Kisleu, day 20th, lime of Ina-iliya-allik rabbi kali* (chef des essayeurs, Oppert).—Tig. viii. 89.

ina arhi Soqitar(?) yeumi 20-kan lima Bel-Simeani Bil-... ir Gargamis; *in the month Soqitar(?), day 20th, lime of Bil-Simeani* (B.C. 691?) *Edile of the city of Carchemish.*—Sen. T. vi. 74.

The following, as well as several like passages, marks the date of an event in the inscription of Sardanapalus:—

ina lime Assur-idin (B.C. 885?).

In some cases we have , "mine," and , *ramman*, "my own year," or , "the same:"—

, ina lime annium; *in my lime.*—Sard. i. 89.

, ina lime ramma-a; *in the lime of my own year.*—Sard. i. 90.

, ina lime .... sun; *in the same lime.*—Sard. i. 101.

This character is made by mistake in the printed inscription.

LM The following passages afford examples of [illegible]:—

[illegible], ina limmu Dayan-Asur ultu [ta] Nineveh-ki attusir; *in the time of Dayan-Asur* (B.C. 856) *from Nineveh I departed.*—Obel. 45.

It is singular that the eponyme is put here instead of the number of Shalmaneser's regnal year, which is found in every other case on the inscription; this gave rise to some misunderstanding before the discovery of the Canon in which Dayan-Asur appears as the fourth name among Shalmaneser's eponyms. On the bulls containing what we may call a different edition of the same inscription we have regularly [illegible], ina 4 palia, "in my fourth year," in that part where, notwithstanding much mutilation, enough remains to show that the same events are narrated as under the eponyme of Dayan-Asur on the obelisk.

[illegible], ina arhi ..... limmu Musiziel (?) bil-sem ar Lahiri; *in the month of .... in the time of Musiziel edile of the city of Lahiru.*—End of prisms of Esar Haddon.

The name *Musiziel* is from Dr. Oppert; Mr. Talbot reads *Mazarel*. I do not generally understand the phonetic rendering of the eponymes.

[illegible]. limmu Nabu-lih sakan (?) ar Irbaal; *the time of Nebulih, ruler of the city of Arbela.*—Sen. Cy. 1.

For the sound of *lih* attributed to [illegible] see note in p. 602.

LMD [illegible]. See under LMT, p. 692.

¶ [illegible], la-mada; *Greatly, Entirely.* Heb. מאד.

La appears to give emphasis here, and perhaps we may find such a value in *la ar* and *la sim*, in p. 6[illegible].

[illegible]. arki parpitû ina mati la-mada imida; *then lies in the countries greatly abounded.*—Beh. 14.

[illegible]. nisu sa upparragi la-mada mal-su; *the man who is a liar (do thou) entirely spoil him.*—Beh. 97.

¶ [illegible], limuttu; see under *limnu*, p. 690.

LMM Lamassu, Lamaççu; *Sacred Images of Bulls; Guardian Spirits.*

lamaççu.—Syl. 173.

sedu.—Syl. 174.

Under the heading of these extracts from the Syllabary, explaining twice (intended surely for and), first by the Assyrian *lamassu* and then by *sedu*, I take the opportunity of entering the phrase , which so often occurs in inscriptions relating to the embellishment of palaces and temples. This phrase is generally understood to imply the sacred figures of lions and bulls with human faces which are erected in the doorways or along the walls of these edifices, where they were supposed to afford protection from enemies and evil-doers generally, as well as from evil spirits; they were, in fact, themselves considered to be guardian spirits, or at least to ensure the presence of such spirits. See Sir H. C. Rawlinson's note in Journ. R.A.S. 1864, p. 260. Dr. Oppert considered to be the bulls and the lions; in transliterating I usually put *sedu* for the former and *lamaççu* for the latter, because I find representing in 17 II. 4 a, and equivalent to in 18 II. 44 a; in like manner in Esar vi. 53 we have as a variant reading of ; I have not found any departure from this practice except in Syl. 174, above quoted. In 10 II. 44 a *sedi* occurs as the equivalent of , which is explained by , *sabitu*, in 48 II. 43 a (see page 283). In one single instance I have found , which I understand to be sacred serpents.

sedi lamaççi çirute sarpis ana imna u sumela usaçbita; *bulls (and) lions large I caused make, and on the right, the complete (?) side I made (them) occupy.*—Sen. T. vi. 52. Cf. Neb. Yun. 74. See p. 572.

sedi u lamaççi sa abni sa ki pi sikuli-sunu irti limni utarru naçiru qibsi musallimu tallakti sarri bani-sunu imna u sumela usaçbita; *lions and bulls of stone, which, by their watchful faces, fear to enemies carry, guard the treasures, (and) constitute the avenues of the king who made them, the right and left I made occupy.*—Esar v. 41.

For the value of the monograms which I render "right" and "left," see pp. 309–10 and 510.

LMM (v.), sedi damqi lamassi damqi nasir qibsi sarruti-ya; *sacred bulls propitious, sacred lions propitious, guarding the treasures of my royalty.*—Esar vi. 58.

> I do not understand , which occurs here as a variant of , *damqi*; it is very clear on the lithographed plate.

.... (v.) (v.), sal lamassi abna-bair-rabi ka amsi .... ina babi-sin ulzis (v. ulzid); *sacred cows of ivory (and) oxens' horn .... in their gates I erected.*—Sen. B. iv. 6 = 39 BM 25. See pp. 534 and 670.

, ana Bit-Anna lamassa sa damiqti utir; *to Bit-Anna the sacred image of good fortune I restored.*—Neb. Gr. ii. 55.

> I do not know whether this version or the one given in p. 518 is the best; the construction is elliptical, and the phrase might be completed "the image which (is the pledge) of good fortune."

¶ , lumlum.

...... (v.) , sa .... musatira ipasitu ana sum-su [su-su] isatara va lumlum [v. ...] limna ...; *he who* .... *the writing shall efface and his own name shall write, and the* * *shall wrongfully appropriate* [*or cut off*].—Tig. viii. 70.

> I can suggest no probable meaning for this word or its variant; the translators of 1857 made avowedly doubtful guesses—"who shall divide the sculptures," "who shall cut away the emblems." Dr. Hincks had singularly misconceived the construction of the whole sentence, and rendered the passage "where some enemy shall speedily deface it." Dr. Oppert left it blank, but in 1865 translated "s'y appropria les faits remarquables dans ce récit," which is, I think, the meaning, though hardly a translation; and moreover it ignores the evil intent. Dr. Hincks saw that must be read *limna* because it begins a new line, and thence brought in the word "enemy;" I have rendered it as an adverb; see p 92.

¶ ( ) .—3 II. 234.

LMN Lamaman.—Sard. i. 76, 81.

Name of the father of Ahiyababa, king of (Sura on the Euphrates), who was put to death by Sardanapalus at Nineveh (i. 80). The same name occurs in Tig. jun. 65. Dr. Hincks was of opinion that the word signified "nobody;" that "son of Lamaman" was a delicate way of indicating a man of low origin.

LMN Limnu, limnû, *subst.* *Wrong-doers, wicked men.* Limnûtu, limnu, limnati, *adj.* *Evil, bad; Sore, diseased.*

sa limnu la bana panû lidti dur Babel-ki gun tahazi-su umaqqi; *that the evil-doers may not make head, the defences of the wall of Babylon, its shield of war, I have raised.*—E.I.H. ix. 38.

The construction is somewhat irregular, but we have in E.I.H. vi. 29, a very similar sentence with and sabil, instead of sa limnu. The idiomatic phrase "make head" is exactly represented by bana panû, which occurs in both passages.

assû masarati Bit-Saggata dunnunû limnû va saggi-su ana Babilû-ki la şanagê sa manama sar mahri la ipusu in kamat Babilû-ki dur dali bukar Shams adde Babilû-ki usashir; *for the stronghold of Bit-Saggata fortifying (against) wicked men and robbers of it, to Babylon the unshackled, what never a former king had done in the kamat(?) of Babylon, the long wall the ford of the rising sun of Babylon, I carried round.*—Neb. Gr. ii. 8.

This is a good deal involved, but the following translation, not quite so closely rendering word for word, may make it more intelligible:—"In order to fortify the stronghold of Bit-Saggata against its violators and robbers, for (the benefit of) Babylon the unshackled, I carried the Eastern Ford of Babylon around the lofty wall, which no former king had ever done in the kamat(?) of Babylon." I do not understand kamat, see p. 588. For the last clause of this sentence compare E.I.H. vi. 29; both passages are printed together in p. 160, and the erroneous trans-

LMN

lation given there may be corrected from the above. This extract contains seven or eight instances of the addition of *u* final, so common in the Babylonian inscriptions. In two of these cases, *pasrypu* and *makrim*, separate characters are added, involving the *u*. The similar forms, *hubin* and *hubina*, occur in p. 460. I have already, in p. 611, expressed an opinion of the nunnating character of these terminal vowels. See further in p. 652.

[cuneiform], sa limnû va aibi lanun lunt mûti; *which (upon) evil-doers and enemies pour down fear of death.*—Norig. l. 27.

A better translation than that in p. 467.

Adjectives:—

[cuneiform] .... [cuneiform], sir gimir ummanâti sakiri limnuti ...... alal; *upon the whole of the soldiers, malignant rebels, ... I rushed.*—Sen. T. v. 61.

See pp. 266 and 577, where I have erroneously read *abuti* instead of *limnuti*; I fear I may have done so in other cases.

[cuneiform] ...... [cuneiform] .... [cuneiform], mutima lan arqa yasami ...... eqlî [alibbi] annuti ...... ana idi limnuti iramza; *whosoever in after days ...... these fields ...... to evil hands shall deliver up.*—2 Mich. ll. 1.

I am not sure of the root or form of *iramza*, but am inclined to derive it from *ramu*, "to put up;" it occurs again in 1 Mich. ll. 9.

[cuneiform], pan limnuti; *bad heads.*—17 II. 31 *a.*

[cuneiform], ina limuttû [limuntu?]; *bad eye.*—17 II. 31 *a.*

[cuneiform], pû limnu; *sore mouth.*—17 II. 32 *a.*

[cuneiform], lisan limuttû; *sore tongue.*—17 II. 32 *a.*

These are all printed with their Accadian equivalents in p. 619.

¶ [cuneiform], Lamena.

[cuneiform], ana Lamena allik alai iškurru ana sarqu issabtu; *to Lamena I went, the people were alarmed, a rugged mountain they took [occupied].*—Obel. 133.

Lamena appears to have been in Mount Amanus. Except the name, the same phrase occurs in Bard. l. 44; ll. 35, 60.

LMN [cuneiform], la mene or lammenu; Unnumbered.

[cuneiform], habalati-sa umaniše lammenu; their people they rated innumerable.—38 BM 19.

Uncertain; compare another translation in p. 612, and see p. 685.

¶ [cuneiform]. Ulmania.—Sard. i. 55. New Div. i. 16.

A variant reading in Sard. makes this a city. I think it is in the northern high lands of Assyria.

LMṢ [cuneiform]. lamaṣa, lamaṣṣa. See pp. 568, 569.

LMT [cuneiform], limet, c. limetu, n. limeti, obl. *Neighbourhood.* Heb. למת.

[cuneiform]. ana istin ipša sa tibni ana istin sa qaqqadi [ris-du] arṣip ina ipduni ina limet er-sunu qaqqadi-sunu ina libbi u'il; *to one pile of bodies, to one of heads, I built; on high-places in the neighbourhood of their city their heads in the midst I piled up.*—Sard. i. 118.

I believe I have done right in translating [cuneiform] "to one pile:" [cuneiform] is not preceded by [cuneiform] in l. 17 of Behistun. See p. 319.

[cuneiform], Dabigu er birtu sa Hatti adi erani sa limetu-sa akšud; *Dabigu, the frontier town of Syria [Hittites] with the towns of its neighbourhood I captured.*—Obel. 33. See also l. 193.

I follow Dr. Hincks's version, but with some doubt; I have hitherto considered Birtu as a proper name. See p. 175.

[cuneiform], sipik ipri [ind] ana limeti-sa ana elian ašpuk; *a heap of earth in its neighbourhood to a height I heaped.*—Brok. Obel. ii. 13. See p. 119.

LMT Sometimes limet may be understood as a preposition, and rendered by "near:"—

[cuneiform], ana pataas Madai limet Kar-Sargina ulasuina amarta; *for the subjection of Media near Kar-Sargina I fortified a bulwark* [*made a strong fortress*].—Botta 117, 6 . 66.

[cuneiform], ana Sin mu madda damiqti-ya bit ti Anna bit-su ina igar limiti Bit-Zida ummaris ebus; *to the god Sin, who supports the fulness of my dignity, the shrine of Anna his temple, on the mound near Bit-Zida beautifully I made.*—E.I.H. iv. 64. See p. 320.

In one case I have found *li* instead of *limiti*; see p. 637.

LN [cuneiform], ilan; *Beyond.*—Sard. iii. 123. See p. 684.

¶ [cuneiform], lanû. Doubtful.

[cuneiform], ana mada napisti nisi Babilû-ki lanû; *for invigorating the lives of the people of Babylon I did it(?).*—Neb. Gr. ii. 15.

Mr. Talbot reads [cuneiform] adnan, but I have not seen any authority for such a reading. The character in Bellino's place is more like [cuneiform] than his usual [cuneiform]; but I have not seen it elsewhere. The Arabic [illegible] may authorise "invigorating," but the whole is uncertain.

¶ [cuneiform], Ilimma. See p. 651.

LNN [cuneiform], lanai; *Dwellings.* Heb. לון.

[cuneiform], &c., [cuneiform], tari Sippara-ki, &c., sa ina lanai-sunu ina qarbi-sa kamû; *the young men of Sippara, &c., who in their dwellings within it were associated.*—Botta 132, 3 = 133. See more in p. 567, and read [cuneiform] instead of [cuneiform] in the first line there.

LNQ [cuneiform], lu-niqu; *a Victim, a Sacrifice.* Syr. ܢܩܐ immolavit, libavit.

The Hebrew נקד, "pastor," may possibly be connected with this. *Lu* may be the "sheep" or "goats" of p. 630, so that *lu-niqu* would be the sacrificial sheep or goat; in one copy at least of Tig. vii. 15, *lu* is omitted. For the second *niqu* see the following:—

[cuneiform].—Syl. 157.

[cuneiform]. Ina libbi-su lu-niqut ellute ana Yav bill-ya lu aliq(q)i; *within it victims to Yav, my lord, I sacrificed.*—Tig. viii. 9. See also viii. 48, 57; Sarg. 50; Sen. T. vi. 69.

In almost every instance the verb *naqu* is used with *lu-niqu*, but I find *epus*, "I made," in Obel. 82, 15 BM 87, and 46 BM 15, all nearly parallel passages.

[cuneiform]. ana mahazi rabi alik lu-niquti ina Babel-ki Barsip-ki Kuto-ki epus; *to the great fortresses I went, sacrifices in Babylon, Borsippa, (and) Cutha I made.*—Obel. 82. See p. 630.

In the following case we have [cuneiform], which must, I think, be in this single case read *zabi*, from a root *zabe* connected with the Hebrew זבח:—

[cuneiform], lu-niquti ana ilani-ya lu zabi; *victims to my gods I sacrificed.*—Sard. iii. 89.

[cuneiform], lu-niquti ana ili-ya akki; *victims to my gods I sacrificed.*—New Div. i. 20.

See p. 93, where [cuneiform], and even [cuneiform] alone, are shown to be put for *akki*. Compare the two following parallel passages:—

[cuneiform].—Sard. iii. 135.

[cuneiform].—Monol. 10. Pulugi (kull) karasi (sukut riarie) ana Assur bill-a u bitkuri mati-a aqi; *a choice (of all sorts) of animals (white heads?) to Assur my lord and the chiefs of my country I sacrificed.*

For [cuneiform], *kali*, added in the Monolith, see 16 II. 316, and 26 II. 120. In both cases it is shown to be equivalent to [cuneiform].

LṢ , ilṣâti; *Gratification, Favours.* Heb. עלץ.

bil rabi eli sa yomme pani ušašnia ma urakkiṣa ilṣâti; *the great chiefs above what was in former days I empowered, and I conferred favours* (on *them*).—Assur b.p. i. 120.

LṢP . , laṣbati.—Assur b.p. vi. 116.

, rabi kitsmi (?) munrit laṣbati 3-ḳaṣi 4-turḳalli pab-ikṣami (?) rizi ...... alpi u ṣeni elini ma'du ustula ana Assur-ki; *chief bowmen* [p. 311], *assistants*, laṣbati, *men of* 3-ḳaṣi, *drivers of four-wheeled chariots* [pp. 136, 118], *common bowmen, herdsmen,* ...... *cattle and sheep,* (*with*) *conductors many, I carried off to Assyria.*—Assur b.p. vi. 116.

Some of this is very doubtful.

LP , dibbi; *Tablet.* See *in*, p. 640. See also *duppu*, p. 215.

¶ , alpi; *Cattle.* See , p. 647.

See . , 2911. 234, incorrectly printed 2911. in p. 618.

LPD , libit; *Brick-work.*—Senk. Cyl. ii. 16. See p. 649.

LPN , . , lapan, lapani, *prep. From, before. Adv. Previously.* Heb. לִפְנֵי.

, lapan ḥatti va sibriti ana Numma-ki innabid; *from fear and destruction to Elam he fled.*—Sen. T. v. 34.

I have rendered *sibriti* by "destruction," as a shaphel form of *bara* (see Heb. ברא in Josh. xvii. 15, and Ezek. xxiii. 47). We have the same word on the Michaux Stone, col. iv. line 17, where it expresses one of the curses invoked upon any person who should damage the inscribed tablet

LPN …… *nisi* …… *sa lapan iskuti-ya ipparsidu ultu kirib sadi userida-sunu la er Hardispi er Bit-Kubatti usasib; the people …… who from my power had fled, from within the mountains I brought down, and in the towns of Hardispi (and) Bit-Kubatti I settled.*—Sen. T. i. 82.

I agree with Mr. Talbot in considering [illegible] an irregular form of [illegible].

nisi Bit-Yagin sa lapan iskuti-ya dannuti kima barirne ikruru ili [illegible]-sun ina kiku-sun itku; the men of Bit-Yagin, who from before my strong power like a garment broke away, the gods their guardians in their boats they collected.—Sen. T. iv. 32.

There are some doubtful points here:—For *barirne* see pp. 122, 123. [illegible] occurs too rarely to be quite sure, [illegible] in Obel. 175 was doubtfully translated "celebrated" by Dr. Hincks, and after him by Dr. Oppert (see p. 105, where I hazarded a conjecture, which I would now recal). [illegible] analogies point to "rush," "drive," "leap," "run."

I rendered [illegible] in p. 503 as in the above passage, but in p. [illegible] I divided the word, making it [illegible], "the rule of the country." I cannot say which of the two readings is preferable. I have found the word or words only three times, and always in the same context.

tadi pasquti sa lapan mati marsuti ullanu-a kirib-sun [illegible] la illiku sarrani pani mahruti; morasses wide (and) countries difficult, which previously beyond me within them never former kings had gone.—Sen. T. iv. 6.

I gave a somewhat forced version of this passage in p. [illegible], but I now see that if *sa lapan* ("which previously") be put after, instead of before, [illegible], the whole becomes quite clear. See similar cases of transposition in pp. [illegible], 416, and 419.

asbatu lapan duri rabi sukpi.—Botta 151, 7(19) ‑ 137.

Dr. Oppert, with much hesitation, proposed to render this "[illegible] les travaux devant le grand mur." I would suggest "he had broken up like [illegible] before the great wall." See [illegible] in [illegible] II. 2, p. 648.

LPN The following extracts are from Persian inscriptions, which always read *lapani* instead of *lapan*:—

[cuneiform], arki uqu gabbi lapani Kambuziya ittikru'; *then the people all from Cambyses revolted.*—Beh. 16.

[cuneiform]. Ahurmazda' Liṣṣur-anni lapani mimma biši; *may Ormazd guard me from whatsoever evil.*—No. 6, N.R. 33.

[cuneiform]. uqu mâdu lapani-šu iptaral; *the people greatly from him kept away.*—Beh. 20.

The verb is very doubtful. I can only propose it as a clumsy Persian attempt to represent the reflected form of the verb *paṭu*, to "set aside;" see [cuneiform], "he puts aside," in Sard. i. 6. Possibly the [cuneiform] of No. 6, N.R. 23 may have been a similar attempt to denote the "separating" of Darius to be king over the land.

[cuneiform]. *ša lapani-ya attâ-a*, is all that remains of a sentence at Behistun of which the Persian equivalent in lines 23, 24 is "yathâšâm hachâma athahya, awathâ akunavyatâ," *as to them by me it was said, thus it was done.* I propose to take l. 16 of the Nakhsh-i-Rustam Inscription as its representation (see Sir H. Rawlinson's Analysis of the Babylonian Inscription of Behistun, p. lxxi.), which is in the Persian "*tyašâm athahya* ava akunavatâ," *what to them I said, that they have done* (l. 17), where *lapani* is represented by [cuneiform]:—

[cuneiform], ša lapani-ya attâ-a iggabba-aššunu ana epeš-šu ibbašu'; *what from me myself was said to them, the doing is they did.*

I follow the restoration of Sir Henry Rawlinson (Analysis, p. xxviii.); ana is frequently used to denote the narrative tense in the Achaemenian Inscriptions; see Beh. 16, 20, 42.

Lapan is certainly connected with לִפְנֵי but it is not the same; *pan* represents פָּנִים "face," and both denote the preposition "before," taking suffixed pronouns when required, as לְפָנָיו and *lapani-ya*. But they are not identical; *lapan* means "from," which *lipnei* does not without the addition of מִן (see Jonah i. 3 and 2 Kings v. 27), nor is it ever used adverbially. Moreover the Assyrian *la* is never, like לְ, a prepositional prefix.

LPT [illegible] —48 II. 41c.

[illegible] „ 47c.

The gloss in l. 41 proves the sound of [illegible]: the Accadian in l. 48 denotes a "bad eye," and the Assyrian defines the malady to be a turning of the eye (Heb. [illegible]) probably a "squint."

LZ [illegible], alzu; *Attitude(?)*.

I have found this word once only, employed in Sam. B. iv. 29–11 RM 29, to denote some quality of certain figures used in decorating a palace; they are mentioned as "diversified in form and attitude;" the only Semitic word analogous is the Hebrew [illegible], usually rendered "rejoice." The value "attitude" is selected as probable, independently of any etymology, and perhaps it may be considered as comporting with and influenced by joyous feelings. See in p. 698.

LZN [illegible], lu-ṣini, lu-ṣeni; *Sheep*. Heb. [illegible].

[illegible] alpi lu-ṣini biltat va madata bal ambar; *cattle, sheep, taxes, tribute, he brought (and) I received.*—Tig. II. 52.

[illegible] sakulātu-sunu ikṣur usalid maraāt-sunu kima marat lu-ṣeni imnu; *droves of them he confined (and) caused to bring forth; their young like the young of sheep he accounted.*—Brok. Obel. l. 22. See more in pp. 638–40.

LQ [illegible].

These three words appear, from the fragments of three lines of the Syllabary, Sam. 165, 166, and 167, to be of the same value; but this is suggested as probable only.

¶ [illegible]. Laqe.—Sard. i. 94; ii. 128; iii. 38, 121. Sa. 8, 16.

[illegible] and [illegible]. Laqai.—Sard. iii. 27, 30, 34, 38, 43.

These names appear to refer to the same places, although mentioned sometimes in connection with the Lebanon and the Mediterranean, and sometimes with the narrows (ḥinṣi) of the Euphrates. We have also [illegible] in 1. II. 44, among places in Syria.

LQA Luqia.—Sard. ii. 89. Probably the Lycus, the Upper Zab.

I proposed this identification in p. 77, but absurdly added "in Cilicia." As the monarch was coming from the country of Gilhi, which I suppose to be Kurdistan (p. 177), the Upper Zab is at least admissible. In 16 BM 21 we have a city ... *Luqi*, in a miscellaneous enumeration of places.

LQD liqat; *Gatherer, fem.*

samat ikribi liqat nisi ili; *hearer of prayers, gatherer of the people of god.*—1 Beltis 7.

See Syl. 4..., which gives ... *li*, as the reading of ....

LR Lára.—Sard. ii. 60, 76.

A very mountainous province, bordering on Zamua in the north of *Assyria*.

¶ la ari. [See *la'ari* in p. 4..2.]

I have registered the phrase ... *ina sari la ari*, meaning, I think, a place unfavourable or objectionable, but have lost the reference. The following lines from bilingual slabs may be useful in finding the value of the phrase wherever it may be found:—

— 38 II. 7 *d*.

— 48 II. 43 *d*.

—48 II. 44 *d*.

¶ —39 II. 50 *b*.

LRB Larbaga, -gai.—Sard. ii. 89, 44.

A city which I have sometimes been inclined to place near Elam, sometimes farther north. I think that on the whole the evidence tends to point to the country of Nairi.

LRD la-ardi; *Rams or Goats.*—Bra. T. i. 60.

See p. 4... In Esar vi. 47, we have ..., in some copies ..., in an enumeration of animals maintained in the grounds of the palace which the king had built in Nineveh. These were probably kept for the purposes of war, as they are named with soldiers, as well as arms and other warlike implements. See pp ...-9.

LRK , likku. See p. 677.

LRS , , Larsâ-ki; *Larissa.*

, Bit-Utra sa Larsâ-ki ana Shamas va Ai bili-a esis epus; *Bit-Utra of Larissa for the Sun and Moon-gods, my lords, firmly I built.*—Neb. Gr. ii. 47.

Larsa in Cyp. i. 35; generally ; see pp. 677 and 676. The modern name is *Senkereh.* *Utra* means the "rising sun;" see pp. 69 and 188.

LSN , , , lisan, a. lisanu, a. lisanâta, *pl. ac.* *Language, Tongue.* Chal. לשן. Monog. .

.... ( ) ( ) , Bit-appâti .... sa ina lisan marta-(ki) Bit-hilanni (v. -hini) ianappa-su usepisa; *Bit-appâti .... which in the language of the west country Bit-hilani they hold it up (call it), I caused build.*—Botta 132, 17 ~ 161 = Botta 16bis 106. See pp. 115, 424.

The same sentence is written with the monogram in Botta 88, 69, and with in 93, 17.

, sar mati sa naphar lisanâta gabbi; *king of countries who (have) a number of languages all.*—No. 5, O, 16.

No. 6, N.E. 5, the same with .

, mati matâti sa lisan mâtitâ; *other countries and another language.*—H, lines 7 and 16. See p. 675, and observe the ungrammatical sa.

, lisan lemuttâ; *a sore tongue.*—17 II. 32 b.

, babbat arba' lisani *the people of the four languages.*—Sarg. 62.

LSN

This monogram was used with the addition of to denote the ancient and now unknown province of Sumir, written phonetically , and , which was joined with the better known Accad (see p. 179) to form a united kingdom. The title of Kings of Sumir and Accad was assumed as well by the monarchs of Babylon before the establishment of Nineveh as the capital of this empire, and after its destruction in the seventh century, as by the allied or dependent Babylonian provinces during the supremacy of Assyria. Hammurabi, in the earliest Semitic inscription we have, tells us that the gods had given the people of Sumir and Accad into his power, and that he dug a canal and executed other works for them. During the first centuries of Assyrian rule I do not remember seeing any mention of Sumir, but after the close of the upper dynasty in the eighth century, B.C., we have the title assumed by Tiglath-Pileser II. Then Sargon (Botta 151, 15—153) mentions it in speaking of the Babylonian usurper Merodach-baladan; and when Sennacherib afterwards expels the usurper, he replaces him in Babylon by his son Esar-Haddon, conferring upon him the title (col. iii. 65), which the latter subsequently assumes in his own inscriptions, as the Babylonian monarchs also occasionally did after the fall of Nineveh. The king whom I have called Pal, and who has received so many different names, speaks of his ancestor Tiglath Bar [B.C. 890], the father of Sardanapalus, as bearing the title (3 Pal 30), but no inscriptions of this prince have reached us. Like the Salic Land of French writers, nothing but the name of Sumir is left; but it was probably in Southern Chaldea. Of the various ways of writing the name of the United Kingdom I have registered only the following:—

Nisi Sumeri va Akkadi.—Hamm. i. 20, 28; ii. 1.

—3 Pal 30. Botta 151, 15(3) = 153. 17 BM 1.

—Sen. T. iii. 65; iv. 38.

—Black Stone i. 4.

Mada Sumer va Akkadi.—Neb. Gr ii. 16.

¶ —Lasanan.

Scholars are not agreed on the meaning of this group. Sir H. Rawlinson writes "Lashanan;" Dr. Oppert "nations" or "people;" Mr. Talbot proposes to divide it la sanan, and to translate it "not having a second" or "unrivalled." There is something ungrammatical about the form of the word as an adjective, but I adopt this as the most probable value.

( ) ( ) , sar kis(sat) la sanan; *king of the legions unrivalled.*—Tig. i. 29.

, idlu gardu tamih harri [li-pa] la sanan; *the warrior, the conqueror, holding a sceptre unequalled.*—Tig. vi. 56.

LSN [cuneiform], sar Istar(?) ulta-su'me malkut la sanan umallû qatu-su; *king (whom) Istar(?) hath favoured him, and kings unrivalled have filled his hands.*—1 Pal, l. 2; 3 Pal, l. 5.

For the omission of the relative see pp. 773 and 777. I am not sure of the goddess Istar; the likeness of [cuneiform] to [cuneiform] might suggest Beltis. See p. 771 for the value of [cuneiform].

[cuneiform], sar la sanan; *king unparalleled.*—Sard. i. 10.

LT [cuneiform] ([cuneiform]) [cuneiform], [cuneiform], lit, litut; *Edicts, laws, orders, decrees; Records, narratives, memorials.*

This word, in the absence of any Semitic analogy, has had a large variety of meanings given to it. I see it translated prodigies, marvels, glory, justice, power, recital, list, and even totally different meanings are given to an identical passage occurring twice in the same document. I have thought it best to give an unusually large number of examples, from which it will appear that *liti* has only two values, "laws" and "records," with slight modifications.

Laws and Edicts:—

[cuneiform] (v. [cuneiform]) [cuneiform] ([cuneiform]) [cuneiform] (v. [cuneiform]) [cuneiform], salam basmal-ya epus liti va dan(n)uti ina libbi altur ina Ṣuri asnis; *an image of my person I made, decrees and edicts upon it I wrote, in Ṣur I put (it) up.*—Sard. iii. 23.

The passage which follows this is marked by Dr. Oppert as a quotation. I have given a somewhat doubtful version of it in p. 651. I would now alter the phrase in that page beginning "who his laws," &c., to "whose decrees and statutes are firm, and who to the sword," &c. Correct also the blunder of the head-line, where I have rendered dupnuun by "statute" instead of "standing."

[cuneiform], sa la kansuti-ya usaknisu ana niri-ya ina liti u danuti usaisu-inni ser aibi-ya; *(the gods) who those disobedient to me subjected to my yoke, (and) by laws and edicts raised me above my enemies.*—Assur b.p. x. 31.

[cuneiform] (v. [cuneiform]), lita va dannuti eli Laqe altakan; *laws and edicts over Laqe I established.*—Sard. i. 93.

LT [cuneiform]. liti u daeani eli Suhi askun; *laws and edicts over Suhi I established.*—Sard. iii. 23.

[cuneiform] (v. [cuneiform]), zalam sarruti-a sarbá epus lita va tanati [ina lib] astar [v. altar] ina gapli bekali-su umais nari-a epus tanati iruti-a ina lib sar [altar] ina bab-rab-su askun; *an image of my royalty enlarged I made, edicts and decrees (upon it) I wrote, in the midst of the palace I put it up; my tablets I made, my irresistible decrees [or decrees of my throne, see pp. 374 and 384-5] on it I wrote, in the great gate I fixed it.*—Sard. i. 98.

Observe here the transference of the pronouns; bekali-su umais and ina bab-rab-su askun, instead of bekali umais-su and ina babi rabi askun-su.

Decrees or Ordinances of the gods:—

[cuneiform], zalam sarruti-ya epus sa liti Asur bili-ya [belui] eli-su astur ina Isirti er sarruti-su ulmid ahralik; *a figure of my royalty I made and the ordinances of Asur my lord upon it I wrote; in Isirti the city of his royalty [capital city] I erected (it) for after times.*—Botta 146, 17 - 53.

Dr. Oppert reads the last word ahratas, but I think "after times" is the more probable translation. See p. 458.

[cuneiform], &c., [cuneiform], ultu Asur, &c., eli sakiri-ya ina liti usasisu-ni sa amrú ana libbi-ya; *after that Asur, (and other gods) over my rebels [those who rebelled against me] by (their) decrees had raised me, and I had carried out what (was) in my heart [out of the spoils of these rebels I built fortresses in Assyria, &c.]*—Esar iv. 40.

LT [cuneiform] ..... [cuneiform], ina Ili u damnal sa Ili rabi bili-ya sa galli-ya umtha sa aruppita uagap gari-ya .... mitharis abil; *by the decrees and ordinances of the great gods my lords, who have attached my servants to me, and have effected the slaughter of my enemies,* [*these countries*] *I have firmly held.*—Botta 145, 4 · 16.

The blank which I have left in this passage is filled up in the original by an enumeration of the possessions and acquisitions of the monarch, taking up nearly six long lines.

Collected Laws and Ordinances :—

[cuneiform]. ṣalam bunnal-ya epus tanatil Asur bil rabu bili-ya u litil kasmati-ya ina kirib-su altur ina eli tamti usaziz; *the figure of my person I made, the decrees of Asur, the lord (and) prince, my lord, and my collected laws, on it I wrote, (and) on the (shore of the) sea* [*of Nairi*] *I erected.*—New Div. I. 27.

See similar passages in New Div. ii. 44 and 56, with tanati instead of tanatil.

[cuneiform]. (ṣalam [cuneiform] ya sarbá epus tanati Asur bili rabu bili-ya u) litil kasmati-ya ina Nahri etappas ina kirib-su altur); [*a figure of my person enlarged I made, the decrees of Asur, the great lord, my lord, and*] *my collected laws, which in Nairi I had made, upon it I wrote.*—New Div. ii. 63.

[cuneiform], sar sa ...... barmul kali-suna iplu sa bilat-suna imhuru sabit litl sakin lite ali kali-suna maal; *the king who .... all their territories hath possessed and their tributes received, taking hostages (and) establishing ordinances over all these countries.*—Sard. i. 17 · iii. 117. St. 5.

The distinction between lit and litl is well marked in this passage.

LT [cuneiform] (v. [cuneiform]) [cuneiform] (v. [cuneiform]). (palam bunnani-a epas) litat (v. lite) kasanti ina libbi sar (v. altar); (an image of my person I made), collected laws upon (it) I wrote.—Sard. ii. 91.

Records, or perhaps Lists:—

[cuneiform], abu nara naspis na lita kisitti qat-i [sa] sa eli-sun astakkanu sira-sun usastir ma ina garbi er ulsiid; a tablet I caused make, and a record of the acquisitions of my hands, which upon them I had effected, upon it I caused write, and within the city I erected.—Sen. T. ii. 5.

[cuneiform] .... [cuneiform], litat gardi-ya .... ina nari-ya va timmeni-ya altar; the records of my victories .... on my tablets and my platforms I wrote.—Tig. viii. 39.

¶ [cuneiform] —2 II. 57c. Family?

¶ [cuneiform], gabsa; Surface. Heb. גב Ezek. xliii. 13.

[cuneiform] ...... [cuneiform]. hekal gabri na ina [duk-a] ana munab bilati-ya kirba-sa abni ..... tiblati epiri (isi) danu-sun [kinu] addi na gabsa-sun ukinna gusuri la erui [erini] rabi eli-sun usatrim; a palace unrivalled [rivals not it had] for the seat of my power in it [Khursabad] I built, ... layers of earth firmly(?) I laid down, and their surface I levelled [settled]; beams of cedar large upon them I arranged.—Botta 153, 16 .. 160.

Sense of this is uncertain. See 2411. 44a, p. 678, for the reading gabsa, which I had not seen when I wrote the note in p. 252. Buxtorf quotes Kimchi for the value "surface."

LT , Lita-Assur.—New Dir. ii. 34.

A new name given to the city of Nappigi by Shalmaneser, who changed the names of three other cities at the same time. The only one of them whose place is known to me is Tel-Barsip on the Euphrates. See p. 173.

¶ .—23 II. 7c. Heb. [illegible], to erect.

From a Semitic list of words relating to buildings.

¶ , alti, *Wife.*

, dam, is equated to *alti* in 14 II. 40a. See p. 238, l. 16, where I have read [illegible] as the Assyrian equivalent of the Accad dam without authority. Erase , &c., in l. 17.

¶ , , altu, *prep. From; adv. When,* or *After that.*

Sometimes written , [illegible]; and not uncommonly we have the Accadian , ta.

, alsi .... altu kirib sadi [illegible] ina er Hardispi er Bit-Kubatti usarib; *the people .... from within the hills I brought down, and in the cities of Hardispi and Bit-Kubatti I established.*—Sen. T. ii. 1.

, altu yom rukuti lassamû [illegible] la sutesuru mase mie-su; *from remote days were neglected and not kept right the issues of its waters* [*the issues were neglected and not kept right*].—Birs i. 31.

, altû kirib tamti abar-su; *from the midst of the sea I passed him.*—Esar i. 17.

In p. 801 I have read the verb [illegible] "I reached him," which may, perhaps, be the best rendering.

Ultu....adi; From.....to:—

, altû sit shamsi adi erib shamsi ittallaku [illegible] mahira la isû; (*who*) *from the rising sun to the setting sun had marched, and an opponent had not.*—Esar i. 7.

LT *When, or After that:—*

[cuneiform], alte bekal gapli ev sa Nineveh-ki ana ribat sarruti-ya usaklilu ana tapridi kissat nisi lubo usallu-si; *after that the palace within the city of Nineveh for the greatness of my royalty I had completed, for the admiration of all men with wreathed work I filled it.*—Sen. T. vi. 23.

See also under *lki*, in p. 703, from Esar iv. 48.

Into and To:—

[cuneiform] istu yum pite; *from days of yore.*—Tig. iii. 74.

[cuneiform] istu usui-su adi gablubi-su; *from its foundation to its roof.*—Tig. vi. 99.

[cuneiform], istu ebirtan nahar Zabi supali; *from the crossing of the Lower Zab.*—Tig. vi. 40.

[cuneiform] ta (v. istu) Numme attusir; *from Numme I departed.*—Sard. i. 51.

[cuneiform] ta kirib sade usrida; *from the mountain I brought down.*—Sard. i. 60.

[cuneiform] ulte-ulla; see p. 673.

LTB [cuneiform], Latiba.—New Div. i. 49.

A city west of the Euphrates, on the way to Carchemish.

LTM [cuneiform], Iltemarin.—Sen. T. iv. 64.

Name of an Elamite city, captured and burnt by Sennacherib.

¶ [cuneiform], iltanu; *the North.*

[cuneiform].—30 II. 8 d.

LTM ..., la tûri; *Without Delay, Straightforward.*

Arantu la tûri akšud; *the Orontes without loss of time I reached.*—New Div. ii. 101.

This is just possible; see lâ in p. 6.. The phrase is insulated, so that there is nothing to guide us one way or another. The Hebrew ... will certainly admit of the meaning given. See Deut. i. 23.

WORDS WHICH MAY NOT BE READILY FOUND.

ADDITIONS AND CORRECTIONS.

PAGE

619, l. 2. For ... read ....

636, l. 12. Read "iamtâ."

657* ..., libtat; *Works, Quarries.*

mallat asnati abne pili pisp ina libtat el-nin-mira ina irsit er Balalai ussalid; *female figures of fine solid stone from the quarries of El-nin-Satra, in the land of the city Balada I caused produce.*—Sen. B. iv. 10 40BM12.

I have supposed *libtat* to be a plural of *libit* (p. 643), and to denote "quarries," but with hesitation. The passage refers to statues for adorning a palace at Nineveh.

657* ..., Ilgi; *Son of Urukh(?), one of the earliest Chaldean kings.*

Brick from Warka and Niffer, in R.I., Vol. I, Nos. 3-10. Also Nabon. Cyl. i. 18, 17, 27.

682* ...—2 II. 86.

I read *lulim-lulim.* Shows that the Accadian *lulim* was adopted by the Assyrians.

www.ingramcontent.com/pod-product-compliance
Lightning Source LLC
Chambersburg PA
CBHW032045220426
43664CB00008B/874
* 9 7 8 3 7 4 1 1 7 3 2 8 8 *